THE
CAMBRIDGE EDITION OF
THE LETTERS AND WORKS OF
D. H. LAWRENCE

THE WORKS OF D. H. LAWRENCE

ST. MAWR
AND OTHER STORIES

D. H. LAWRENCE

EDITED BY
BRIAN FINNEY

CAMBRIDGE UNIVERSITY PRESS

CAMBRIDGE

LONDON   NEW YORK   NEW ROCHELLE
MELBOURNE   SYDNEY

Published by the Press Syndicate of the University of Cambridge
The Pitt Building, Trumpington Street, Cambridge CB2 1RP
32 East 57th Street, New York, NY 10022, USA
296 Beaconsfield Parade, Middle Park, Melbourne 3206, Australia

Printed in Great Britain by the University Press, Cambridge

Library of Congress catalogue card number: 82–14584

British Library Cataloguing in Publication Data
Lawrence, D. H.
St. Mawr and other stories. – (The Works of
D. H. Lawrence)
I. Title II. Finney, Brian
823'.912[F] PR6023.A93
ISBN 0 521 22265 6 hard covers
ISBN 0 521 29425 8 paperback

CONTENTS

GENERAL EDITORS' PREFACE

D. H. Lawrence is one of the great writers of the twentieth century – yet the texts of his writings, whether published during his lifetime or since, are, for the most part, textually corrupt. The extent of the corruption is remarkable; it can derive from every stage of composition and publication. We know from study of his MSS that Lawrence was a careful writer, though not rigidly consistent in matters of minor convention. We know also that he revised at every possible stage. Yet he rarely if ever compared one stage with the previous one, and overlooked the errors of typists or copyists. He was forced to accept, as most authors are, the often stringent house-styling of his printers, which overrode his punctuation and even his sentence-structure and paragraphing. He sometimes overlooked plausible printing errors. More important, as a professional author living by his pen, he had to accept, with more or less good will, stringent editing by a publisher's reader in his early days, and at all times the results of his publishers' timidity. So the fear of Grundyish disapproval, or actual legal action, led to bowdlerisation or censorship from the very beginning of his career. Threats of libel suits produced other changes. Sometimes a publisher made more changes than he admitted to Lawrence. On a number of occasions in dealing with American and British publishers Lawrence produced texts for both which were not identical. Then there were extraordinary lapses like the occasion when a compositor turned over two pages of MS at once, and the result happened to make sense. This whole story can be reconstructed from the introductions to the volumes in this edition; cumulatively they will form a history of Lawrence's writing career.

The Cambridge edition aims to provide texts which are as close as can now be determined to those he would have wished to see printed. They have been established by a rigorous collation of extant manuscripts and typescripts, proofs and early printed versions; they restore the words, sentences, even whole pages omitted or falsified by editors or compositors; they are freed from printing-house conventions which were imposed on Lawrence's style; and interference on the part of frightened publishers has been eliminated. Far from doing violence to the texts Lawrence would have wished to see published, editorial intervention is essential to recover them. Though we have to accept that some cannot now be recovered in their entirety because early states have not survived, we must be glad that so much evidence remains. Paradoxical as it may seem, the outcome of this recension will be texts which differ, often radically and certainly frequently, from those seen by the author himself.

Editors have adopted the principle that the most authoritative form of the text is to be followed, even if this leads sometimes to a 'spoken' or a 'manuscript' rather than a 'printed' style. We have not wanted to strip off one house-styling in order to impose another. Editorial discretion has been allowed in order to regularise Lawrence's sometimes wayward spelling and punctuation in accordance with his most frequent practice in a particular text. A detailed record of these and other decisions on textual matters, together with the evidence on which they are based, will be found in the textual apparatus or an occasional explanatory note. These give significant deleted readings in manuscripts, typescripts and proofs; and printed variants in forms of the text published in Lawrence's lifetime. We do not record posthumous corruptions, except where first publication was posthumous.

In each volume, the editor's introduction relates the contents to Lawrence's life and to his other writings; it gives the history of composition of the text in some detail, for its intrinsic interest, and because this history is essential to the statement of editorial principles followed. It provides an account of publication and reception which will be found to contain a good deal of hitherto unknown information. Where appropriate, appendixes make available extended draft manuscript readings of significance, or important material, sometimes unpublished, associated with a particular work.

Though Lawrence is a twentieth-century writer and in many respects remains our contemporary, the idiom of his day is not invariably intelligible now, especially to the many readers who are not native speakers of British English. His use of dialect is another difficulty, and further barriers to full understanding are created by now obscure literary, historical, political or other references and allusions. On these occasions explanatory notes are supplied by the editor; it is assumed that the reader has access to a good general dictionary and that the editor need not gloss words or expressions that may be found in it. Where Lawrence's letters are quoted in editorial matter, the reader should assume that his manuscript is alone the source of eccentricities of phrase or spelling. An edition of the letters is still in course of publication: for this reason only the date and recipient of a letter will be given if it has not so far been printed in the Cambridge edition.

ACKNOWLEDGEMENTS

First and foremost I would like to thank Mr George Lazarus who made available for my use the corrected typescript of St. Mawr in his private collection. His helpfulness and hospitality to numerous Lawrence scholars such as myself have been a great encouragement.

I would also like to thank the following libraries for their generosity in making available their materials: the manuscript and notes of 'The Wilful Woman' and the typescript of 'The Flying-Fish', Bancroft Library, University of California at Berkeley; University of Illinois at Urbana-Champaign; Stirling Library, University of London; the typescript of 'The Overtone', University of New Mexico; and the manuscripts of 'The Overtone' and 'The Princess' and the typescript of 'The Flying-Fish', Humanities Research Center, University of Texas at Austin. Grateful acknowledgement is made to the Martin Secker estate for permission to quote from unpublished letters and to the University of Illinois Library at Urbana-Champaign for access to them.

I am also indebted to the following individuals for help and advice in preparing this volume: Carl Baron, Michael Black, James T. Boulton, L. D. Clark, Irene M. Moran of Bancroft Library, Andrew Robertson, Keith Sagar, Warren Roberts and Lindeth Vasey.

May 1982   B.H.F.

CHRONOLOGY

11 September 1885	Born in Eastwood, Nottinghamshire
September 1898–July 1901	Pupil at Nottingham High School
1902–1908	Pupil teacher; student at University College, Nottingham
7 December 1907	First publication: 'A Prelude', in *Nottinghamshire Guardian*
October 1908	Appointed as teacher at Davidson Road School, Croydon
November 1909	Publishes five poems in *English Review*
3 December 1910	Engagement to Louie Burrows; broken off on 4 February 1912
9 December 1910	Death of his mother, Lydia Lawrence
19 January 1911	*The White Peacock* published in New York (20 January in London)
19 November 1911	Ill with pneumonia; resigns his teaching post on 28 February 1912
March 1912	Meets Frieda Weekley; they elope to Germany on 3 May
23 May 1912	*The Trespasser*
September 1912–March 1913	At Gargnano, Lago di Garda, Italy
February 1913	*Love Poems and Others*
29 May 1913	*Sons and Lovers*
June–August 1913	In England
August 1913–June 1914	In Germany, Switzerland and Italy
July 1914–December 1915	In London, Buckinghamshire and Sussex
13 July 1914	Marries Frieda Weekley in London
26 November 1914	*The Prussian Officer*
30 September 1915	*The Rainbow*; suppressed by court order on 13 November
June 1916	*Twilight in Italy*
July 1916	*Amores*
15 October 1917	After twenty-one months' residence in Cornwall, ordered to leave by military authorities
October 1917–November 1919	In London, Berkshire and Derbyshire
December 1917	*Look! We Have Come Through!*
October 1918	*New Poems*
November 1919–February 1922	To Italy, then Capri and Sicily
20 November 1919	*Bay*
November 1920	Private publication of *Women in Love* (New York), *The Lost Girl*

10 May 1921	*Psychoanalysis and the Unconscious* (New York)
12 December 1921	*Sea and Sardinia* (New York)
March–August 1922	In Ceylon and Australia
14 April 1922	*Aaron's Rod* (New York)
September 1922–March 1923	In New Mexico
11 September 1922	Arrives in Taos and meets Mabel Dodge Luhan
19–20 September 1922	Begins opening of a novel based on the life of Mabel Dodge Luhan with her co-operation ('The Wilful Woman'), abandoned at Frieda's insistence
23 October 1922	*Fantasia of the Unconscious* (New York)
24 October 1922	*England, My England* (New York)
March 1923	*The Ladybird, The Fox, The Captain's Doll*
March–November 1923	In Mexico and USA
27 August 1923	*Studies in Classic American Literature* (New York)
September 1923	*Kangaroo*
9 October 1923	*Birds, Beasts and Flowers* (New York)
21 November–*c.* 12 December 1923	Travels from Mexico City to London via Vera Cruz and Havana (a journey later used for 'The Flying-Fish')
December 1923–March 1924	In England, France and Germany
17–20 December 1923	Suggests collaboration with Catherine Carswell on a novel the theme of which he subsequently adapted for 'The Princess'
3–5 January 1924	Visits Frederick Carter in Shropshire, the setting of which he subsequently used for *St. Mawr*
March 1924–September 1925	In New Mexico and Mexico
c. April 1924	Probably writes 'The Overtone'
5 May 1924	Moves to Kiowa Ranch, the setting of which he subsequently used for *St. Mawr*
c. early June 1924	Probably writes first version of *St. Mawr*
mid June 1924	Writes 'The Woman Who Rode Away'
later June–13 September 1924	Writes second, longer version of *St. Mawr*
7 July–30 September 1924	Dorothy Brett types *St. Mawr*
30 August 1924	Goes on trip to the Rockies which he subsequently used for the setting of 'The Princess'
August 1924	*The Boy in the Bush* (with Mollie Skinner)
10 September 1924	Death of his father, John Arthur Lawrence
30 September 1924	Sends the MS and Brett's typescript of *St. Mawr* to Curtis Brown, New York, and the carbon copy typescript to Curtis Brown, London

late September–8 October 1924	Writes 'The Princess'
11 October 1924	Brett completes the typescript of 'The Princess' by the day they leave Kiowa Ranch
9 November 1924–23 February 1925	Stays in Oaxaca, the setting for the opening of 'The Flying-Fish', where he contracts malaria
c. 11–19 March 1925	Probably dictates opening of his unfinished story, 'The Flying-Fish', most likely writing the remainder of the fragment by 25 March
23 March 1925	Returns proofs of *St. Mawr* to Secker while ill from malaria and tuberculosis in Mexico City
25 March 1925	Leaves Mexico City for Kiowa Ranch, New Mexico, arriving 5 April
March, April, May 1925	'The Princess' first published serially in the *Calendar of Modern Letters*
14 May 1925	*St. Mawr Together with The Princess* published by Martin Secker
5 June 1925	*St. Mawr* published separately by Alfred Knopf
September 1925–June 1928	In England and, mainly, in Italy
7 December 1925	*Reflections on the Death of a Porcupine* (Philadelphia)
January 1926	*The Plumed Serpent*
June 1927	*Mornings in Mexico*
24 May 1928	*The Woman Who Rode Away and Other Stories*
June 1928–March 1930	In Switzerland and, principally, in France
July 1928	*Lady Chatterley's Lover* privately published (Florence)
September 1928	*Collected Poems*
July 1929	Exhibition of paintings in London raided by police. *Pansies* (manuscript earlier seized in the mail)
September 1929	*The Escaped Cock* (Paris)
2 March 1930	Dies at Vence, Alpes Maritimes, France
January 1933	*The Lovely Lady* (containing 'The Overtone') published by Martin Secker, and by the Viking Press in February
October 1936	*Phoenix* (containing 'The Flying-Fish') published by the Viking Press, and by Heinemann in November

January 1947   *The Portable D. H. Lawrence* (containing
                                the first appearance of 'The Princess' in
                                America) published by the Viking Press

1971   *The Princess and Other Stories* (containing
                                the first publication of 'The Wilful
                                Woman') published by Penguin Books,
                                Harmondsworth, England

CUE-TITLES

A. Manuscript locations

Lazarus	Mr George Lazarus
UCB	University of California at Berkeley
UIll	University of Illinois at Urbana-Champaign
UT	University of Texas at Austin

B. Printed books

Brett — Hon. Dorothy E. Brett. *Lawrence and Brett: A Friendship*. Philadelphia: J. B. Lippincott, 1933.

Carswell — Catherine Carswell. *The Savage Pilgrimage: A Narrative of D. H. Lawrence*. Chatto and Windus, 1932; reprinted by Cambridge University Press, 1981.

DHL Review — James C. Cowan, ed. *The D. H. Lawrence Review*. Fayetteville, Arkansas: University of Arkansas, 1968– .

Luhan — Mabel Dodge Luhan. *Lorenzo in Taos*. New York: Alfred A. Knopf, 1932.

Nehls — Edward Nehls, ed. *D. H. Lawrence: A Composite Biography*. 3 volumes. Madison: University of Wisconsin Press, 1957–9.

Tedlock, *Lawrence MSS* — E. W. Tedlock. *The Frieda Lawrence Collection of D. H. Lawrence Manuscripts: A Descriptive Bibliography*. Albuquerque: University of New Mexico, 1948.

INTRODUCTION

INTRODUCTION

The short fiction and Lawrence's American sojourn

The short fiction collected in this volume was written between 1922 and 1925 when D. H. Lawrence lived in the USA and Mexico.[1] The pieces are of greatly varying length: 'The Overtone', a short story; *St. Mawr*, a short novel; 'The Princess', a long short story; 'The Wilful Woman', a fragment of a novel (titled by Keith Sagar); and 'The Flying-Fish', a short story fragment.[2] With the exception of 'The Overtone', these stories make use of American settings and reflect the impact that the new landscape and its peoples had on Lawrence's outlook and writing during this period. Equally, in all these stories except 'The Overtone' modern men and women, whether from the Old World or the New, are brought into stark contrast with the impersonal, ageless landscape of the American continent and its inhabitants. Even 'The Overtone', with its English setting, mirrors the animistic vision which Lawrence discerned in the American Indians and which he embodied in the figure of Pan, who also appears in *St. Mawr*.

Almost a year before his arrival in the USA, Lawrence had been invited to come to Taos, New Mexico in November 1921 by an American admirer of his work, Mabel Dodge Luhan. Born in 1879 the only child of a rich banker, Charles Ganson, she had been married first to Carl Evans, who was killed in an accident, and by whom she had a son, John; next to Edwin Dodge, whom she divorced after ten years; and then to Maurice Sterne, a painter. A patroness of the arts who had recently established her own art colony at Taos, she was currently living with an American Indian called Antonio Luhan (whom she later married) after the break-up of her third marriage. Lawrence made definite plans to go to Taos, but then hesitated; he left Europe for America via Ceylon and Australia, so that he did not reach Taos until September 1922.

[1] The dating of 'The Overtone' is necessarily conjectural; see pp. xxi–xxiii below.
[2] In keeping with the Cambridge edition policy of adhering to the contents and order of the collections of DHL's short fiction published in his lifetime, and adding the uncollected and unfinished pieces, this volume derives from *St. Mawr Together with The Princess* (Martin Secker, 1925). One other story 'The Woman Who Rode Away' belongs with this group because of date of composition and setting, but it was collected in *The Woman Who Rode Away and Other Stories* (Secker, 1928), which forms the basis of another short fiction volume.

The first fictional piece that he wrote after his arrival was 'The Wilful Woman', the opening segment of a novel based on Mabel Luhan's life, which he had agreed to undertake in collaboration with her. For both the Lawrences she proved too forceful a woman to work with or live near. The novel was quickly abandoned and in early December the Lawrences moved out of 'Mabeltown', as he dubbed her colony in Taos, to stay at Del Monte Ranch some miles away in the Rocky Mountains. There they remained until mid-March 1923. During this first period of his stay in the United States Lawrence wrote several articles about his experience of life in America,[3] rewrote *Studies in Classic American Literature* and added a number of poems to *Birds, Beasts and Flowers* which he prepared for publication.

Restless again by the spring of 1923, Lawrence left New Mexico with Frieda for Mexico City and Chapala, Mexico where he settled for over two months while he wrote 'Quetzalcoatl', the first version of *The Plumed Serpent*. Then in July they left for New York from where Frieda sailed for England to see her children after a serious disagreement with Lawrence, while he, unwilling to return to Europe, went back to Mexico via Los Angeles. Between September and November he revised Mollie Skinner's novel as *The Boy in the Bush*. Finally in late November he capitulated to Frieda's pressure to return and took the boat from Vera Cruz back to England.

His stay in Europe between December 1923 and March 1924 was a dismal failure. By late March he was back in Taos with Frieda and the Hon. Dorothy Brett ('Brett' as she was known to her friends), the daughter of the second Viscount Esher. Born in 1883, she had been a student at the Slade School of Art in London and was an artist; she was the only one, among the several friends who had been invited, to accept Lawrence's invitation to join him in starting a new life together in New Mexico. With her bobbed hair, trousers and ear-trumpet she was destined to provide the model for numerous characters in Lawrence's subsequent writing. By 4 April he had written three stories, 'Jimmy and the Desperate Woman', 'The Last Laugh' and 'The Border Line', in which, he confessed to his agent, Curtis Brown, he had worked off some of the depression into which his visit to Europe had thrown him.[4] In the same letter he continued, 'I want to go on doing stories – I hope cheerful ones now – for a while.'[5]

[3] E.g. 'Indians and an Englishman'; 'Taos'; 'Certain Americans and an Englishman'; 'Model Americans', a review of Stuart Sherman's *Americans*; and 'Au Revoir, USA'.
[4] These stories were published in *The Woman Who Rode Away and Other Stories*. Lawrence's reaction against the Old World is evident in 'London Letter' (see p. xxii below) and 'Letter from Germany', which were also written at this time.
[5] Letter to Curtis Brown, 4 April 1924.

On 5 May the Lawrences moved up to the ranch on Lobo Mountain (subsequently renamed Kiowa Ranch) that Mabel had given to Frieda (in exchange for the manuscript of *Sons and Lovers*). At once he was plunged into major repair work on the ranch cabins which occupied him full-time for the next month. After his return to the USA he wrote several articles, including 'Pan in America': its similarity to 'The Overtone' (a story using the same Pan motif) suggests that the story was written at around this time. When building work was virtually complete in early June, Lawrence turned his attention to writing three long short stories in succession: 'The Woman Who Rode Away', *St. Mawr* (really a short novel) and 'The Princess'.

On 11 October 1924, three days after 'The Princess' was finished, the Lawrences left the ranch for Oaxaca, Mexico, where they wintered from 9 November to 25 February 1925. By the end of January Lawrence had finished re-writing 'Quetzalcoatl', besides writing several articles that were to be included in *Mornings in Mexico*. Then in early February he caught influenza and malaria from which he almost died. After his arrival in Mexico City later that month the doctor diagnosed tuberculosis and advised him to return to the ranch rather than risk crossing the Atlantic. It was during his period of recuperation that Lawrence wrote 'The Flying-Fish', which remained unfinished.

In late March 1925 he returned to Kiowa Ranch where he remained until September. During this final phase of his American sojourn he wrote his biblically-based play, *David*; revised 'Quetzalcoatl' as *The Plumed Serpent*; and wrote numerous articles, many collected in *Reflections on the Death of a Porcupine*. Finally, in September 1925, he left America. Although he continued to think of the ranch as a permanent home, he never returned.

'The Wilful Woman'

On 11 September 1922 the Lawrences reached Taos where they were lent an adobe house by Mabel Luhan. She had been anxious for Lawrence to write an American novel. She records that on the evening of 18 September Lawrence asked her to collaborate with him on such a book. In her highly-coloured memoir of him she states:

He said he wanted to write an American novel that would express the life, the spirit, of America and he wanted to write it around me – my life from the time I left New York to come out to New Mexico; my life, from civilization to the bright, strange world of Taos; my renunciation of the rich old world of art and artists, for the pristine valley and the upland Indian lakes.[6]

[6] Luhan 52.

The following morning Lawrence visited Mabel Luhan in her home to begin the collaborative work. When it became apparent that the project entailed morning visits, however innocent on Lawrence's part, passing through Mabel's bedroom to the sun-roof where she was dressed in nothing but a housecoat, a jealous Frieda soon intervened. Frieda later recalled: 'I did not want this. I had always regarded Lawrence's genius as given to me. I felt deeply responsible for what he wrote. And there was a fight between us, Mabel and myself: I think it was a fair fight.'[7]

Fair or not, she had her way. On 21 September, the day after Frieda's intervention, Mabel made one further attempt to revive the project on Frieda's terms: 'I did try it once in her house. I went over there in the morning, and he and I sat in a cold room with the doors open, and Frieda stamped round, sweeping noisily, and singing with a loud defiance. I don't think that anything vital passed between Lawrence and me.'[8]

On the next day, the 22nd, Mabel had to go away, and Lawrence subsequently sent her a note informing her: 'I have done your "train" episode and brought you to Lamy at 3 in the morning.'[9] In fact the surviving opening fragment of this novel breaks off with her waiting at Wagon Mound at 8 p.m. for the arrival of the train three hours later that would take her on to Lamy.[10] Lawrence's note also asked Mabel for notes on the following episodes in her life:

1. The meeting with Maurice [Sterne].
2. John [Evans], M[aurice]. and you in Santa Fe
3. How you felt as you drove to Taos
4. What you *wanted* here before you came
5. First days at Taos.
6. First sight of Pueblo
7. First words with Tony [Luhan]
8. Steps in developing intimacy with Tony
9. Expulsion of M.
10. Fight with Tony's wife.
11. Moving in to your house

A further page of jottings seemingly written down by Lawrence during one of his meetings with her has been found.[11]

[7] Frieda Lawrence, "*Not I, But the Wind...*" (Santa Fe, 1934), p. 152.
[8] Luhan 64–5.
[9] Letter to Mabel Dodge Luhan, *c.* 6 October 1922.
[10] Tedlock (*Lawrence MSS* 51) speculates that an additional mauscript has been lost, but the final deleted passage (see textual apparatus 203:9) corresponds with Lawrence's note.
[11] The jottings on a one-page autograph manuscript located at UCB, are the following:
        ash in the room
    you can say what you like we've got to get our
            force with a man

In the event Mabel's attempt to write about her past life for Lawrence's benefit came to nothing: 'I was not a *writer*', she explained. 'I was accustomed to the personal equation.'[12] So the novel died a natural death. The untitled seven-page fragment of autograph manuscript that has survived offers a glimpse of one of Lawrence's first attempts to write about America after his arrival there.[13] It was first published in 1971 in the Penguin edition of *The Princess and Other Stories*, edited by Keith Sagar; he invented the title, 'The Wilful Woman'. (Lawrence repeatedly accused Mabel Luhan of exercising too much will-power of the kind shown by the heroine of this extract.)[14] That title is retained here to avoid further confusion in identifying this fragment which is printed in Appendix I.

'The Overtone'

While there is no external evidence for dating 'The Overtone', internal evidence makes it likely that it was written in the spring of 1924, most

---

she saw overlying body in light—
Mabel dreamed Maurice's face & an Indian face
coming through with steady glow
leaves all round—
transport & fear—anticipation—transfer

---

travelling
hotel—8.30—⟨big men⟩ men—Their guilt sense
suspicion

---

broken-hearted
Tony—smell of wood—Maurice hectic, waiting
to be nice, making it—dignity romance—
Maurice & John over telephone—Where are you—Sarah's
—Who is Sarah? (both at it)
Use M. as thing—having expected to be made better—get
force from a man (relieve head)

Pointed brackets indicate a deletion. The first deleted word after 'hotel—8.30— ' may at one time have read 'bag', and the first word in the sixth line from the end may read 'Lamy' (instead of 'Tony').

Written upside down on the sheet to the right of the section beginning 'she saw overlying' is the following:

In that hour of dusk between
vespers and nones
When no good woman

[12] Luhan 66.
[13] Located at UCB.
[14] E.g. letters to Mabel Luhan of 17 October 1923 and 9 January 1924.

probably between 4 April and 5 May 1924. Nevertheless, the dating of this story must remain conjectural.

The internal evidence concerns Lawrence's use of the Great God Pan in 'The Overtone' as a counterforce to Christ and modern civilisation. Pan first appeared in Lawrence's earliest novel, *The White Peacock*, and continued to feature sporadically throughout his career, reappearing in his final work, *Apocalypse.*[15] But for a short period in his life Pan became a major motif in his prose writing. In her study of the myth of Pan in modern times, Patricia Merivale claims that there is what she terms a 'Pan cluster' which 'is made up of images from virtually every work Lawrence wrote between 1924 and 1926'.[16] Lawrence's unhappy stay in Europe during the winter of 1923–4 re-kindled his interest in Pan as an antidote to a civilisation suffering from the ill-effects of an ascetic Christian ethos. The 'London Letter' that he wrote to Willard Johnson on 9 January 1924 opens this phase by lamenting that 'When Jesus was born, the spirits wailed round the Mediterranean: Pan is dead.'[17] He goes on to evoke Pan's modern metamorphosis as the centaur or horse in the American Southwest where the spirit of Pan still lives on. One can discern here the germ of the idea for *St. Mawr* which he was to write in the summer of 1924. His further association in the letter of the Pan-like horse with American Indians anticipates his essay 'Pan in America' written between May and June 1924:[18] there Pan is shown to survive in the Indian tribes which live in such intimate relationship with the natural world.

The three stories that Lawrence wrote between January and April 1924 all hinge on a conflict between Pan or one of his present-day adherents on the one hand and cerebral, life-denying anti-heroes on the other. One of the three, 'The Last Laugh', introduces Pan in person; he lures the anti-hero into uncharacteristic sexual promiscuity (one of Pan's attributes), desecrates a Christian church in a snowstorm, and finally punishes those characters who deny the Pan-like qualities in themselves. The fiction of this period is infused with references to the Pan legend. *The Plumed Serpent* identifies Cipriano with 'The everlasting Pan' (chapter xx). In *St. Mawr* the spirit of Pan first resides in St. Mawr himself and more dimly in Lewis, the groom; later it is transferred to its more potent manifestation in the New Mexican landscape. The minor character Cartwright, by contrast, is portrayed as a 'fallen Pan'.[19]

'The Overtone' shows a clear affinity to this 'Pan cluster'. Renshaw, the

[15] *Apocalypse and the writings on Revelation*, ed. Mara Kalnins (Cambridge, 1980).
[16] *Pan the Goat-God* (Cambridge, Mass., 1969), p. 194.
[17] 'Dear Old Horse, A London Letter', *Laughing Horse* (May 1924), [p. 4].
[18] Letter to Mabel Luhan, ?12 May 1924.
[19] See below 67:10–14.

husband, like Cartwright, is a fallen Pan: 'Pan was dead in his own long, loose Dane's body.'[20] His wife is identified by Renshaw with Christ at whose birth Pan died. She anticipates heroines like Dollie Urquhart in 'The Princess' whose sexual frigidity destroys the Pan-spirit in their men. The third character in 'The Overtone', Elsa Laskell, means to reconcile in herself the Renshaws' conflicting loyalties. One of Pan's nymphs, she is determined to seek out a true faun of Pan's as her mate, while giving the Christ-ethos its due.

There is no mention of this story by name in Lawrence's correspondence, nor was it published during his lifetime, nor has the kind of paper used for the twelve pages of autograph manuscript[21] been found elsewhere among his letters or other writings. The manuscript shows that he subsequently revised the original version in different ink, rewriting between the lines two major paragraphs and several shorter passages, and adding in smaller writing on the last page an additional ending;[22] in it Elsa Laskell's monologue is slightly extended, after which the narrative reverts to a more naturalistic conclusion. Since the story ends at the foot of a page where Lawrence had begun and then crossed out a new sentence, we cannot know whether he intended to continue it, or whether, as seems more likely, he simply decided to bring the story to its present end. The only evidence for dating the revision occurs where the introduction of Renshaw's 'inner sun' thematically anticipates 'The Flying-Fish' and 'Sun', both written in 1925.[23]

The only surviving typescript is a twenty-one-page carbon copy with corrections in an unknown hand.[24] It was apparently transcribed from the manuscript after Lawrence's death for the first published appearance of the story in *The Lovely Lady*, which Martin Secker, his principal British publisher since 1921, brought out in London in January, and Viking Press, New York, in February 1933. Textual collation reveals a number of identical discrepancies between the typescript and both first editions,[25] leading to the conclusion that one publisher used the proofs supplied by the other. All the evidence points to its having been Secker's proofs which were sent on to Viking. In the first place Secker was responsible for compiling *The Lovely Lady*. Secondly his edition appeared a month earlier than Viking's. Thirdly certain differences between typescript and first editions involve the capitalising of references to Christ, an alteration more likely to have been made by Secker in England.[26] Comparison of the autograph manuscript and typescript with

[20] See below 13:16.
[21] Located at UT.
[22] See note on 7:35 and pp. 16:38ff.
[23] See 11:6–13.
[24] Located at University of New Mexico.
[25] E.g. 5:8, 6:5, 9:1 etc.
[26] E.g. 15:21, 24, 26, etc; cf. *St. Mawr* 42:28, 29, 43:5, 16.

the first editions also shows that two lines of dialogue were omitted by Secker and Viking (9:24–7), whether deliberately because it was thought that they were too sexually explicit or inadvertently it is impossible to say. The autograph manuscript is the only authoritative text since it represents the final state in which Lawrence left the story.

St. Mawr

On about 5 June 1924 Lawrence informed Mabel Luhan: 'I began to write a story.' On 18 June he wrote to Miss Nancy Pearn, of the London office of his agent Curtis Brown, who specialised in placing work with periodicals. After discussing 'those three difficult stories' he had written earlier in the year, he continued: 'I shall send you soon a couple more – one is finished, one is being done again.'[27] The two most likely candidates are 'The Woman Who Rode Away' and *St. Mawr*, one of which he began about 5 June and one of which he was rewriting on 18 June.

Although the order in which these two stories were begun cannot be determined, it is known that Lawrence wrote two versions of *St. Mawr*. Powell's 1937 descriptive catalogue of Lawrence manuscripts records two autograph manuscript versions of *St. Mawr*, one 129 pages long, complete and as published, the other being 41 pages (numbered 17–58) of an earlier version.[28] Both were destroyed in the fire which burnt down Aldous Huxley's house in 1961.[29] As for 'The Woman Who Rode Away', Powell and Tedlock list only one autograph manuscript, now unlocated,[30] and we know from Mabel Luhan's memoir that she was shown it on 23 June 1924.[31] Only two weeks later on 7 July, Lawrence was able to send to his agents in London and New York the two typescripts of this story which had been produced for him by Dorothy Brett.[32] The available evidence, therefore, suggests that the story that was finished by 18 June was 'The Woman Who Rode Away' and the one 'being done again' was *St. Mawr*.

Whether or not it was the story he began by 5 June, the first version of *St. Mawr* was probably finished during the first half of June, i.e. it was being *rewritten* by the 18th. Brett began to type *St. Mawr* almost immediately after

---

27   The letter is addressed to 'Miss Pearse'; for the 'difficult' stories, see p. xviii above.
28   Lawrence Clark Powell, editor, *The Manuscripts of D. H. Lawrence: A Descriptive Catalogue* (Los Angeles, 1937), p. 12, item 14A.
29   Sybille Bedford, *Aldous Huxley: A Biography* (1974), ii. 274.
30   Powell, *Manuscripts of D. H. Lawrence*, p. 13, item 15; Tedlock, *Lawrence MSS* 53–4.
31   Luhan 237–8; the date of the visit is fixed by a letter to Thomas Seltzer of 23 June 1924.
32   Letter to Curtis Brown, 7 July 1924.

finishing 'The Woman Who Rode Away' by 7 July;[33] she must have been typing the *second* version from Lawrence's manuscript because Powell's description suggests that Lawrence revised an autograph manuscript, not a typescript. Thus the second version was begun before 18 June and was well advanced by 7 July.

Lawrence appears to have revised the original first sixteen pages of manuscript and then rewritten the next section anew (what had been pp. 17–58 in the original manuscript). What we cannot know is whether the first version stopped at p. 58 (and was therefore a *short* story), or, alternatively, if Lawrence reverted to writing on the original manuscript with p. 59. If the latter were true, and Powell's brief description is unhelpful in this respect – then the length of the first version will never be determined.[34] It is possible, since Lawrence coupled the two stories in his letter to Nancy Pearn of 18 June, that they were both long; this would indeed have helped to make them both '*very* difficult to place'. On 23 July, he referred to *St. Mawr* in a letter to Martin Secker as his 'second long-short story', indicating that he was still thinking of it as similar in length to 'The Woman Who Rode Away'. On 30 July he informed Miss Pearn that he was 'just winding up *St. Mawr*, a story which has turned into a novelette nearly as long as *The Captain's Doll*'.

On the other hand, judging from its position in her narrative, Brett's description of the point which Lawrence had reached in rewriting the story also belongs to the end of July: 'You are full of your new story, of Mrs Witt...You read out the scene of the tea-party, of the tart Mrs Witt, the scandalized Dean and his wife, and the determined Lou.'[35] This may suggest that Lawrence thought that he was 'winding up' the story having reached the equivalent of page 100 of the typescript, which eventually ran to 181 pages. If so, at this time he did not envisage continuing the story by following Lou Carrington and Mrs Witt to America. He still conceived of *St. Mawr* as a satire on English society, epitomised in the rural life in Shropshire (where he had spent three days from 3–5 January 1924 with Frederick Carter in Pontesbury) and the urban social whirl of London. According to Harry Moore, Lawrence based Cartwright on Carter and several other minor characters on people he met at Pontesbury.[36]

---

[33] Brett 123; cf. Luhan 244, and letter to Curtis Brown, 7 July 1924.

[34] See the introduction to *The Trespasser*, ed. Elizabeth Mansfield (Cambridge, 1982): DHL on several occasions incorporated manuscript pages from the first version into the second when his revision was not extensive.

[35] Brett 137. Since Brett gives no dates in her memoir and writes in brief, unconnected episodes, it is often difficult to pinpoint the time accurately.

[36] Harry T. Moore, *The Priest of Love: A Life of D. H. Lawrence* (New York, 1974), pp. 348,

Lawrence was ill at the beginning of August, which explains why he was still writing to Secker on 8 August: 'I've nearly got to the end of my second "novelette –" – a corker.' In fact he was to take another month to finish it. This delay may have been the result of the combination of his poor health, his twelve-day trip to the Snake Dance (13–25 August) and, possibly, his decision to add the long American coda, a decision perhaps not taken until after the Snake Dance trip. One can only speculate whether this trip induced Lawrence to extend the story and shift its setting to the American Southwest, where, as he wrote to Middleton Murry on his return, 'This animistic religion is the only live one[,] ours is a corpse of a religion' (30 August 1924). This sentiment equally underlies Lou's decision at the end of *St. Mawr* to keep herself for the wild spirit of the New Mexican landscape. Finally, in answer to an enquiry from Secker about the state of his 'novelette', he replied on 13 September: 'Yes, the novelette *St. Mawr* is finished and Brett is typing it out. It's good – a bit bitter – takes place in England, then moves to this ranch – some beautiful creation of this locale and landscape here. But thank God I don't have to write it again. It took it out of me.'

Dorothy Brett took much of the rest of September to complete the typing which was done probably in sections as it was written. It was far from a professional job. When he was just over half-way through the second version, Brett reports Lawrence complaining: '"Why, oh why can't you spell the same way I do, when it is in front of your nose!"' 'Why not, indeed?' Brett continues. 'I never knew and I never did spell the same way you did.'[37] The surviving ribbon copy typescript of *St. Mawr* shows the care with which Lawrence corrected it. It is 181 pages long,[38] and contains over 180 single-word substitutions, the alteration or addition of about 55 short phrases and the interlinear rewriting of 8 passages, involving some 50 lines of typescript.

On 30 September Lawrence recorded in his diary: 'Sent to Barmby (Curtis Brown) – *St. Mawr*: also MSS. of the same...Sent the copy of *St. Mawr* to Curtis Brown, London.'[39] To both Curtis Brown and Martin Secker he suggested publishing *St. Mawr* with 'The Woman Who Rode

391; cf. Nehls, ii. 316, 318, 514–15. Moore also stated Lou Carrington was modelled on Jan Juta's fiancée, Elizabeth Humes, a southern American girl DHL had probably met in Capri, 1919–20, and Mrs Witt partly on Miss Humes's mother and partly on Mabel Luhan.
[37] Brett 138.
[38] The typescript is in the collection of Mr George Lazarus. The pages are numbered 1–178; Brett made five errors in typing the page numbers, necessitating the addition of 'A' to four pages (38A, 125A, 128A, 138A) and one amalgamation ('19 and 20').
[39] Tedlock, *Lawrence MSS* 98. A. W. Barmby was the manager of the New York office of Curtis Brown.

Away' and 'The Princess' (which he had begun to write by the end of the month). Simultaneously he offered as an alternative title 'Two Ladies and a Horse', an option not taken up.[40] Lawrence was not exact in his terminology when referring to manuscripts and typescripts. So it is not possible to identify 'the copy' in his diary entry above with the carbon *copy* of the typescript. Indeed, the similarities in the revisions in the ribbon copy typescript and Secker's text suggest that the former was used by the English printer.[41] (Lawrence characteristically made different revisions in typescript copies, refining whichever copy was corrected later; so the missing carbon copy typescript may have had some different readings.)

On first reading *St. Mawr* Martin Secker wrote back to Curtis Brown: 'I now quite agree with you that it would be a pity to include any other material which would otherwise be available for another collection of stories in the future, and I will therefore produce this as a full-length novel.'[42] On learning of Secker's response Lawrence readily agreed to the separate publication of *St. Mawr*.[43] Then on 8 December Secker wrote to Curtis Brown that, on second thoughts, he wanted to make the volume consistent in size and style with his other Lawrence publications, and could hardly charge seven shillings and sixpence for a book only 160 pages long: 'I feel strongly that the best way to treat *St. Mawr* is to make it the first story of a collection of three, or possibly of only two, if the length of this latter is fairly substantial.'[44] 'Secker is good at changing his mind!' Lawrence commented on 10 January 1925. In the same letter he informed Curtis Brown that he had authorised Barmby to let Knopf, and not Seltzer, publish *St. Mawr* on its own.[45] But by 29 January it was Lawrence who was changing his mind: 'Barmby sent the Knopf agreement for *St Mawr*', he informed Curtis Brown. 'I too would rather this story were published by itself, although it is short.' But by then the die was cast. Knopf went ahead with

[40] Letters to Curtis Brown, 30 September 1924 and Secker, 2 October 1924. Nor apparently did Secker like the titles suggested by DHL in his letter of 17 November to Curtis Brown.

[41] The typescript has a note on the first page ('Corrected typescript of') in the hand of Laurence Pollinger, who worked for Curtis Brown, London, indicating that it was the copy sent to London. It also has a few pencil markings throughout probably made by the printer.

[42] 24 October 1924, UIll.

[43] Letters to Curtis Brown, 6 and 17 November 1924.

[44] Martin Secker, *Letters from a Publisher: Martin Secker to D. H. Lawrence and Others 1911–1929* (1970), p. 34.

[45] Although Thomas Seltzer had been DHL's American publisher since 1920, he was teetering on the verge of bankruptcy; so DHL was looking for a more secure publisher and turned to Alfred Knopf.

his volume of *St. Mawr* as a separate publication, while Secker prepared to publish *St. Mawr Together with The Princess.*

Early in February while in Oaxaca Lawrence caught influenza and malaria, which brought on an attack of tuberculosis after his arrival in Mexico City later that month. During the illness he received duplicate sets of proofs for *St. Mawr* from Secker.[46] Although Secker intended Lawrence to return one set of corrected proofs to him and the other to Knopf, in the event it appears that Lawrence returned corrected proofs only to Secker on 23 March just before leaving for the USA.[47] It further seems likely that Knopf sent Lawrence final proofs of his own edition,[48] since Lawrence wrote to Blanche Knopf after his return to Kiowa Ranch the following month (18 April 1925): 'I didn't correct the St. Mawr proofs very well – felt too sick. Am better. – But there were only typographical errors, a clerk can find them. I didn't know you wanted a revised set of *Secker* proofs.' This suggests that the Knopf corrected proofs were not entirely trustworthy; neither set of proofs has been located.

The similarity of wording and punctuation in the Knopf and Secker texts leads to the conclusion that one was set from the proofs of the other. It appears likely that it was Knopf who set his proofs from Secker's uncorrected proofs. Knopf attempted several times to delay the publication date, while Secker sent his proofs to Lawrence in late February.[49] The inference from Lawrence's letter of mid-April to Blanche Knopf quoted above is that proofs of Knopf's own edition were subsequently sent to Lawrence. That Knopf set from uncorrected Secker proofs is further substantiated by the examples of Lawrence's punctuation which appear in Knopf's text but which were probably deleted at a late stage from the Secker text.[50] Knopf must have wanted the duplicate corrected Secker proofs as an easy, quick method of obtaining corrections for his own setting, but when Lawrence failed to forward them, Knopf must have decided to send a set of his own proofs to Lawrence. Thus the Knopf edition includes some revisions not made in

---

[46] Letter from Secker to Alfred Knopf, 29 January 1925, UIll.

[47] Letter to Secker, 20–3 March 1925.

[48] See note to 59:29 below.

[49] For Knopf's attempts to delay, see letters from Secker to Knopf, 29 January 1925 and to Curtis Brown, 4 February 1925, UIll. On Secker's proofs, see letter from Secker to Knopf, 6 March 1925, UIll: 'About ten days ago I posted to [DHL] sets of proofs of "St. Mawr".'

[50] E.g. see entries in textual apparatus for 54:11, 55:39, 56:10. Secker removed most of DHL's dashes that followed final punctuation, but some of them must have been included in his first proofs because Knopf incorporated them into his edition. Secker probably deleted several of the remaining dashes during proof revision. It is unlikely that Knopf would reintroduce these dashes exactly where DHL had had them, or that Knopf would have incorporated only a few of DHL's dashes if he had been setting independently from DHL's typescript (or checking against it). It is also unlikely that DHL added dashes in proof.

Secker's proofs, although, because Lawrence was still unwell, these are few. On 28 April Secker informed Knopf that he would send him three advance copies 'directly we receive stock'.[51] It is possible that these would have reached Knopf in time to affect his printing.

A week before publication Secker received an order from W. H. Smith and Son for 200 copies of *St. Mawr* 'provided that certain words are deleted from page 65'. These words made up the short sentence: 'Even our late King Edward.' This sentence follows the Dean's derogatory remarks about 'goaty old satyrs' whom he finds 'somewhat vulgar'. Secker complied with the request and 200 copies were altered.[52] *St. Mawr Together with The Princess* was published by Martin Secker on 14 May 1925. *St. Mawr* was published on its own by Alfred A. Knopf on 5 June 1925.

A comparison of the English and American editions of *St. Mawr* with the corrected ribbon copy typescript shows that both English and American compositors made numerous silent alterations to Lawrence's spelling and punctuation which have been perpetuated in subsequent editions. Further specifically American house-styling is evident in Knopf's edition. The only authoritative text for *St. Mawr* is therefore the corrected typescript, which is used as the base-text in this edition. But where this differs from the English and American first editions in more than punctuation and where they are in agreement with each other, it has normally been assumed that Lawrence himself incorporated the change in the proofs he returned to Secker.

'The Princess'

During Lawrence's brief visit to London in the winter of 1923–4 he stayed at 110 Heath Street with Catherine Carswell and her husband. She has recalled how he was confined to bed there with a cold between 17 and 20 December 1923.[53] On being reproached by Lawrence for her current failure to write anything, Catherine Carswell told him of a novel she had in mind:

The theme had been suggested to me by reading of some savages who took a baby girl, and that they might rear her into a goddess for themselves, brought her up on a covered river boat, tending her in all respects, but never letting her mix with her kind, and leading her to believe that she was herself no mortal, but a goddess.[54]

A short while after this conversation Lawrence called her back to his sickroom and produced a written outline of such a novel, going on to suggest

---

[51] Letter from Secker to Knopf, UIll.
[52] Letter from Secker to Messrs W. H. Smith and Son, 8 May 1925, UIll. See 64:40 below.
[53] Carswell 199–200; cf. letters to Mabel Luhan, 17 December 1923 and Secker, 20 December 1923.   [54] Carswell 201.

that they might collaborate on it. Mrs Carswell soon gave up the attempt at writing the beginning, but she retained and subsequently printed Lawrence's outline, which bears an obvious resemblance to 'The Princess':

A woman of about thirty-five, beautiful, a little overwrought, goes into a shipping office in Glasgow to ask about a ship to Canada. She gives her name Olivia Maclure. The clerk asks her if she is not going to accept the Maclure invitation to the feast in the ancestral castle. She laughs – but the days of loneliness in the Glasgow hotel before the ship can sail are too much for her, and she sets off for the Maclure island.

The Maclure, who claims to be chief of the clan and has bought the ancestral castle on his native isle, is a man about forty-five, rather small, dark-eyed, full of energy, but has been a good deal knocked about. He has spent ten years in the U.S.A. and twenty years in the silver mines of Mexico, is somewhat grizzled, has a scar on the right temple which tilts up his right eye a little. Chief characteristic his quick, alert brown eyes which seem to sense danger, and the tense energy in his slightly work-twisted body. He has lived entirely apart from civilized women, merely frequented an occasional Indian woman in the hills. Is a bit cranky about his chieftainship.

Olivia arrives a day too soon for the festival, at the patched-up castle. Maclure, in a shapeless worksuit, is running round attending to his house and preparations. He looks like a Cornish miner, always goes at a run, sees everything, has a certain almost womanly quickness of perception, and frequently takes a whisky. He eyes Olivia with the quick Mexican suspicion. She, so distraught, is hardly embarrassed at all. Something weighs on her so much, she doesn't realize she is a day too soon, and when she realizes, she doesn't care.

As soon as he has sensed her, he is cordial, generous, but watchful: always on the watch for danger. Soon he is fascinated by her. She, made indifferent to everything by an inward distress, talks to him charmingly, but vaguely: doesn't realize him. He, a man of forty-five, falls for the first time insanely in love. But she is always only half conscious of him.

She spends the night in the mended castle – he most scrupulously sleeps in the cottage below. The next day, she is mistress of the absurd feast. And at evening he begs her not to go away. His frantic, slightly absurd passion penetrates her consciousness. She consents to stay.

After two days of anguished fear lest she should go away, he proposes to her. She looks at him very strangely – he is just strange to her. But she consents. Something in her is always remote, far off – the weight of some previous distress. He feels the distance, but cannot understand. After being in an agony of love with her for six months, he comes home to find her dead, leaving a little baby girl.

Then it seems to him the mother was not mortal. She was a mysterious woman from the faery, and the child, he secretly believes, is one of the Tuatha De Danaan. This idea he gradually inculcates into the people round him, and into the child herself. It steals over them all gradually, almost unawares.

The girl accepts from the start a difference between herself and the rest of people. She does not feel quite mortal. Men are only men to her: she is of another race, the

Tuatha De Danaan. She doesn't talk about it: nobody talks about it. But there it is, tacit, accepted.

Her father hires a poor scholar to be her tutor, and she has an ordinary education. But she has no real friends. There is no one of her race. Sometimes she goes to Glasgow, to Edinburgh, to London with her father. The world interests her, but she doesn't belong to it. She is a little afraid of it. It is not of her race. When she is seventeen her father is suddenly killed, and she is alone, save for her tutor. She has an income of about three hundred a year. She decides to go to London. The war has broken out – she becomes a nurse. She nurses men, and knows their wounds and their necessities. But she tends them as if they were lambs or other delicate and lovable animals. Their blood is not her blood, their needs are not the needs of her race.

Men fall in love with her, and that is terrible to her. She is waiting for one of her own race. Her tutor supports her in the myth. Wait, he says, wait for the Tuatha De Danaan to send you your mate. You can't mate with a man. Wait till you see a demon between his brows.

At last she saw him in the street. She knew him at once, knew the demon between his brows. And she was afraid. For the first time in her life, she was afraid of her own nature, the mystery of herself. Because it seemed to her that her race, the Tuatha, had come back to destroy the race of men. She had come back to destroy the race of men. She was terrified of her own destiny. She wanted never again to see the man with the demon between his brows.

So for a long time she did not see him again. And then her fear that she would never see him any more was deeper than anything else. Whatever she wanted, she wanted her own destiny with him, let happen what might.[55]

The outline ends at this point, but Lawrence did tell Catherine Carswell that it couldn't have a happy ending.[56]

Evidently the idea remained in Lawrence's head throughout the next nine months, during which he returned to New Mexico with Frieda and Dorothy Brett. It is quite possible that Lawrence had at least partly modelled the heroine of this outline on Brett whom he was seeing frequently during December 1923. Catherine Carswell first identified Brett as the sitter for the Princess of the published story.[57] Brett herself has given an account of a one-day expedition which she made about 30 August 1924 to the Lobo peaks of the Rocky Mountains with Lawrence, Rachel Hawk and other riders from the Hawks' dude ranch.[58] Mr and Mrs A. D. Hawk owned Del Monte Ranch, Questa, where the Lawrences stayed during the winter of 1922–3 and it is likely that their son William and his wife Rachel provided the models for the Wilkiesons in 'The Princess'. In her account of the one-day excursion

[55] Ibid. 202–4.   [56] Ibid. 201.
[57] Moore, *Priest of Love*, p. 393.
[58] Brett 149–52; cf. letter to Margaret King, 31 August 1924.

Brett recalls how they reached a plateau from which could be seen far below in the valley 'a tiny green lake, blue green and dark: Columbine Lake, round which the drama of your story "The Princess" is written'.[59] She also records meeting three Indian huntsmen that day who, like the two who appear in the story, deny having shot any game despite suspicious-looking bulks in their saddle bags.

A letter written to Martin Secker on 13 September 1924, informing him that *St. Mawr* was finished and that Brett was typing it, makes no mention of 'The Princess' when suggesting that *St. Mawr* might be published together with 'The Woman Who Rode Away'. The first mention of this story comes in a letter to Curtis Brown on 30 September. In both this letter and one Lawrence wrote to Secker on 2 October he suggests publishing 'The Princess', a 'story I am doing', together with 'The Woman Who Rode Away' and *St. Mawr*: 'They are all sad. After all, they're true to what is.'[60] On 8 October he recorded in his diary that he had finished 'The Princess',[61] and the same day he informed Curtis Brown that on the weekend of the 11th he would be sending him the typescript which was being produced, presumably by Dorothy Brett.

Knopf, Lawrence's new American publisher, chose to publish *St. Mawr* on its own, while Martin Secker preferred to publish *St. Mawr* together with 'The Princess'. On 4 February 1925 Secker learned that Curtis Brown had sold the magazine rights of 'The Princess' to the *Calendar of Modern Letters*, a new critical journal edited by Edgell Rickword and Douglas Garman. Secker readily agreed to postpone publication of *St. Mawr Together with The Princess* until mid-May so that the story could appear in the March, April and May numbers of the *Calendar*.[62] Instead of sending Secker Lawrence's corrected typescript or a copy of it (as Secker twice requested[63]), in early March Curtis Brown sent him the *Calendar*'s proofs of 'The Princess' which had been set up from the corrected typescript.[64]

On receiving the proofs of *St. Mawr* on 23 March Lawrence noted the absence of any proofs of 'The Princess'.[65] It is highly unlikely that he was sent any by the *Calendar*: on 6 April 1925 Lawrence wrote to Edward McDonald to say that he hadn't seen 'The Princess' but would ask for relevant copies of the *Calendar*, which he did in a letter to Curtis Brown

[59] Brett 151.
[60] Letter to Catherine Carswell, 8 October 1924.
[61] Tedlock, *Lawrence MSS* 99.
[62] Letter from Secker to Curtis Brown, 4 February 1925, UIll.
[63] Ibid., and letter from Secker to Curtis Brown, 28 February 1925, UIll.
[64] Letter from Secker to Curtis Brown, 3 March 1925, UIll.
[65] Letter to Secker, 20–3 March 1925.

on the same day. This suggests that the *Calendar* proofs were probably not corrected by Lawrence. On the other hand Lawrence did correct Secker's proofs, which Secker received back from him by about 10 April.[66] As Lawrence was still recuperating from his illness at this time they probably received the same scant attention that he gave to the *St. Mawr* proofs the previous month.

'The Princess' fared less successfully in America. On 17 April 1925 Lawrence informed Miss Pearn that it was 'still wandering this side'. On 23 June he replied to a cablegram from his agent indicating that although he had thought of writing a third story in addition to 'The Princess' and 'The Woman Who Rode Away' to make up a volume for American publication, he would leave it to Curtis Brown to decide instead whether to allow Edward O'Brien to publish 'The Princess' in his forthcoming anthology, *The Best British Short Stories of 1925*. However Secker objected to the republication of the story in England so soon after his own book;[67] so 'Jimmy and the Desperate Woman' appeared in O'Brien's anthology instead. 'The Princess' remained unpublished in America until Diana Trilling included it in her selection, *The Portable D. H. Lawrence*, in 1947. The text she used was Martin Secker's 1934 compilation of *The Tales of D. H. Lawrence* which derived its text from Secker's original version of 1925, *St. Mawr Together with The Princess*.

The 51-page autograph manuscript of 'The Princess', which Lawrence wrote between late September and 8 October 1924 survives.[68] It is a remarkably clean manuscript with few erasures, corrections or interlinear revisions. Both typescripts are missing. The *Calendar* and Secker versions differ from one another on only a few occasions and always in minor ways: all are consistent with printers' house-styling or transcription errors or Lawrence's corrections to Secker's proofs, although there is no evidence on the basis of which one can distinguish between these possible causes. Where differences do occur between the published texts, Secker's, which was corrected by Lawrence, must normally have the greater authority. Other differences from the manuscript which occur in both published versions may be presumed to derive from Lawrence's corrections to the typescript, or from unnoticed errors of transcription made either by the typist or by the *Calendar*'s compositor. On four occasions one line, and on one occasion three lines of the text in the autograph manuscript appear to have been omitted

---

[66] Letter from Secker to Curtis Brown, 15 April 1925, UIll.
[67] Letter from Secker to Curtis Brown, 9 July 1925, UIll.
[68] Located at UT; cf. Tedlock, *Lawrence MSS* 54–5.

in error either by the typist or by the compositor.[69] No subsequent printing
of the story has any textual authority. The base-text for this edition is the
autograph manuscript. It has been emended only when the English first
edition and the *Calendar* text are identical in introducing substantive
changes. The manuscript is the authority for accidentals.

'The Flying-Fish'

On 11 March 1925 Lawrence learnt from the doctor, whom Frieda called
in to see him in his hotel bedroom in Mexico City, that he was suffering
from tuberculosis. Predicting that Lawrence would live for only a year or
two more at the most, the doctor advised against their planned sea-crossing
to England. 'Take him to the ranch,' he told Frieda; 'it's his only chance.'[70]
About the same time Frieda, full of hope, informed Dorothy Brett: 'The
doctor says in a year Lawr's lungs should be quite cured, but he must not
write...'[71] It seems likely that Lawrence began dictating to Frieda the
opening of his unfinished narrative, 'The Flying-Fish', between 11 and 19
March, immediately after Frieda had been given instructions by the doctor
that Lawrence 'musn't paint or anything'.[72] However on 19 March, after
a hiatus of eight days in his correspondence, Lawrence took up his pen again.
It is possible that simultaneously he took over from Frieda the actual writing
of 'The Flying-Fish'.

The autograph manuscript of 'The Flying-Fish' has been described by
both Powell and Tedlock, although it has since disappeared: the first nine
pages were in Frieda's handwriting, 'Lawrence having dictated them to her
when he was too ill to write', Powell explains on Frieda's authority.[73] But
from the last line on page nine until he breaks off on the fortieth page of
the manuscript, the writing was Lawrence's own, including occasional
extensive interlinear revision.[74] Tedlock also transcribes an entry in one of
Lawrence's notebooks of the time headed 'SUGGESTIONS FOR STORIES'
beside which Lawrence has added 'never carried out!' The first title is 'THE
FLYING FISH': unlike the other entries, this has no plot-summary, perhaps
because he was already at work on it when this entry was made. The next
suggested title is 'THE WEATHER-VANE': in its plot-summary Gethin Day
of Daybrook (the hero of 'The Flying-Fish') marries a local girl whose
excessive will-power eventually causes her own death by lightning.[75]

---

[69] See 168:5–6; 178:40–179:1; 188:20–2; 194:29–30, and 36–7 below.
[70] Frieda Lawrence, "*Not I, But the Wind...*", p. 167; cf. letter to Curtis Brown, 11 March
     1925.
[71] Letter from Frieda Lawrence to Brett, University of Cincinnati collection, no date.
[72] Ibid.   [73] Powell, *Manuscripts of D. H. Lawrence*, p. 17.
[74] Tedlock, *Lawrence MSS* 55.   [75] Ibid. 56–7.

This notebook entry offers contemporary evidence that Lawrence thought of 'The Flying-Fish' as a story, not a novel as his American friends the Brewsters later suggested. According to their account, over three years later in July 1928 Lawrence announced to them that he was going to read to them 'an unfinished novel he had started on the way back from Mexico when he was very ill, and written down by Frieda from his dictation. It was called "The Flying Fish".'[76] Urged at various times subsequently to finish it, his reply, according to Achsah Brewster, was 'I've an intuition I shall not finish that novel. It was written so near the borderline of death, that I never have been able to carry it through, in the cold light of day.'[77] These quotations make it seem likely that Lawrence wrote the rest of this incomplete story before leaving Mexico City for Taos on 25 March 1925.

The first part of section 1 ('Departure from Mexico') drew on Lawrence's recent experience of taking the train back north from Oaxaca while still recovering from an attack of malaria. He also drew on his earlier journey from Mexico City to Plymouth, England (including his overnight stop in Havana) between 21 November and 12 December 1923 for the remaining parts of the unfinished story.[78] As Edward McDonald has suggested, the entire piece is highly autobiographical:

Gethin Day's experiences were Lawrence's experiences: that desperate illness in Mexico, that sickening revulsion from the sinister and savage tropics, that nostalgic longing for his native land, that journey towards home by land and water, with its matchless descriptions of earth, sea, sky and the living things which inhabit them. Here is...the story of what Lawrence himself once saw, felt, suffered, and, almost miraculously, lived through.[79]

On 13 August 1929 Lawrence was still telling the Brewsters: '*The Flying Fish* remains where it was.' The previous year he had indicated to them how the story might have ended: 'The last part will be regenerate man, a real life in this Garden of Eden.'[80] However, one has to bear in mind the date at which Lawrence reputedly said this. In July 1928 he was deeply involved in revising part 1 and re-writing part 2 of *The Escaped Cock*, a novella which is wholly about 'regenerate man'. It is difficult to see the Gethin Day of 'The Weather-Vane', a man who voluntarily yokes himself to a woman whose malignant will-power makes him ill, as the embodiment of Lawrence's ideal, 'regenerate man'. It is far more likely that he was offering the Brewsters a

[76] Earl Brewster and Achsah Brewster, *D. H. Lawrence: Reminiscences and Correspondence* (1934), p. 288.   [77] Ibid.   [78] Cf. Carswell 196.
[79] Edward D. McDonald, ed., *Phoenix: The Posthumous Papers of D. H. Lawrence* (1936), p. xxvii.
[80] Brewster, *Reminiscences and Correspondence*, p. 288.

retrospectively imposed ending to a story which he had decided to leave unfinished at the time.

'The Flying-Fish' remained unpublished and almost certainly untyped until Edward McDonald needed typed copies to include the story in *Phoenix: The Posthumous Papers of D. H. Lawrence* in 1936. The American edition appeared in October and the English edition in November of that year. Both texts were printed from the American setting.[81] The surviving ribbon copy and carbon copy typescripts of this fragment were probably prepared for McDonald's use in editing *Phoenix*.[82] There is no evidence that either typescript was corrected against the original autograph manuscript. It would seem that the carbon copy typescript was used to set up the type, since some, though not all, of the words italicised in *Phoenix* are underlined in ink and 'ital' written above them on this copy. These corrections with their instructions for the printer appear to represent unauthorised additions by an editor or printer intent on eliminating inconsistencies in the punctuation of the original manuscript. All of them could have been made without reference to the autograph manuscript. This process of normalisation was taken a stage further in the published text (probably at proof stage) which incorporated yet more italicisation of foreign words, other 'improvements' in punctuation and corrections to Lawrence's sums concerning the number of passengers on board. Under the circumstances one should treat with suspicion Tedlock's claim that 'the text published in *Phoenix* follows that of the manuscript except for a division indicated by spacing [on page 797], not in the manuscript.'[83] In the absence of the autograph manuscript it is safest to assume that the uncorrected ribbon copy typescript (despite a few obvious transcription errors which it shares with the carbon copy) is closest to Lawrence's unfinished and uncorrected text: this is used as the base-text for this edition. As it remains incomplete, 'The Flying-Fish' has been placed in Appendix II.

---

[81] Letter from Marshall Best of Viking Press to Edward Garnett, 15 July 1936, UT: 'They [Heinemann] are using our plates…'.

[82] The ribbon copy, 34 pp., is located at UCB, and the carbon, 34 pp., at UT.

[83] Tedlock, *Lawrence MSS* 56. See 224:8 below.

Reception

St. Mawr

By 5 June 1925, the date on which Knopf published the American edition of *St. Mawr*, it seems likely that Lawrence had received copies of both British and American editions.[84] Shortly after, Martin Secker sent him the first of the English reviews. On 18 June he wrote back to Secker: 'I never thanked you for the copy of *St Mawr* which came safely. I hope it does well. The *Times Supplement* review was quite good.'

The review in the *Times Literary Supplement* turned out to be the only favourable notice in the British press that summer. The book was reviewed unfavourably in at least eight British periodicals, besides three other equivocal reviews. By 13 August Lawrence had read enough press notices to realise that *St. Mawr* was destined to receive a generally hostile reception in England, and he wrote to Secker: '*St. Mawr* a bit disappointing. The Bloomsbury highbrows hated it. Glad they did.' In fact Raymond Mortimer was the only critic among the book's reviewers who could be identified with Bloomsbury.[85] However, it seems that Lawrence took him to be representative of the forces antagonistic to his work.

Indeed the generally adverse reception of *St. Mawr* reflects the usual response of the English literary establishment to Lawrence's work at this time. Most of the reviewers charged him with subordinating his art to a philosophy towards which they were antagonistic. Gerald Bullett set the tone in the first review of the book to be published, in the *Saturday Review* on 23 May 1925: 'Not content with story-telling he is now very definitely a man with a message. He is bending all his intelligence to the task of persuading us that intelligence is a mistake' (p. 556). One after another, the reviewers accused Lawrence of anti-intellectualism. A. N. M[onkhouse] sarcastically titled his notice in the *Manchester Guardian* 'The Horse as Hero', while Louis J. McQuilland expostulated in *G. K.'s Weekly* that Lawrence 'must be forsaking all humanity in making the hero of his latest published work, "St. Mawr", a stallion'.[86] Edwin Muir, in the *Nation and Athenaeum*, articulated the substance of this widely held charge with greater clarity than most: 'his philosophy is obscure – he has never yet formulated it clearly; and his intuitions, so profound once, seem to have become falsified'. In particular he argued that Lawrence manipulated his characters to suit his

---

[84] See letter to Idella Purnell Stone, 5 June 1925.
[85] *Vogue* (London), Early July 1925, p. 39.
[86] 29 May 1925, p. 7, and 30 May 1925, p. 237, respectively.

ideological purposes, by making 'his women talk as only he himself writes in the more didactic pages of his books', and by treating Rico as a villain rather than a fool, so tacitly admitting him as an equal. Lawrence's artistic failure, Muir claimed, extends to his technique: 'St Mawr...is formless; the development loose and arbitrary, the ending insignificant, showing a weakening of power.'[87]

Of the equivocal reviews the most percipient was Ida Wylie's notice in the *Queen*. She recognised that for Lawrence 'the body is...a symbol, the outward expression of a great mystery'. She continued: 'In "St. Mawr" for instance...the splendid stallion which is the central figure is not merely an animal. It is the representative of freedom – of the power and beauty of life.' Nevertheless, she concluded, the story 'is interesting, but it is not great'.[88] The anonymous reviewer of the *Times Literary Supplement* was equally perceptive and less grudging in his praise: '[*St. Mawr*] is not only rich with irony and poetry, but it succeeds, perhaps more completely than Mr Lawrence has yet done, in expressing, those ultimate perceptions of his through a group of living symbols.' This reviewer also paid tribute to the power with which Lawrence evokes the presence of the New Mexican landscape in the closing section of *St. Mawr*: 'Whether he is painting the wonder of the vast landscape, or the squalor bristling in the mountain glory, or the mingled enmity and beauty, it calls up his astonishing magic of phrase.'[89] A belated review in Middleton Murry's *Adelphi* in November 1925 (p. 456) grudgingly acknowledged the power of the story, especially in the American finale, to overcome its earlier didactic tendencies.

The American publication of *St. Mawr* met with a more favourable reception. Perhaps this was partly because, being published on its own, it was treated less as a long story than as a short novel. At least five reviewers gave their qualified approval to the book – in the *New York Herald Tribune Books*, *New York Times Book Review*, *Independent*, *World* and *Saturday Review of Literature*. The *Chicago Daily Tribune* gave *St. Mawr* a mixed review,[90] while only the *New Republic* and the *Dial* published adverse notices, the latter too late to affect initial sales.

Lawrence read and liked Stuart Sherman's review of *St. Mawr* in *New*

[87] 30 May 1925, pp. 270–1. Other unfavourable reviews were *Observer*, 24 May 1925, p. 4; *Calendar of Modern Letters*, June 1925 by H. C. Harwood, p. 328; *New Statesman*, 20 June 1925 by P. C. Kennedy, pp. 285–6; and *Empire Review* by John Sydenham, July 1925, pp. 83–4.

[88] 29 July 1925, p. 22. Other equivocal reviews were *Vogue* (London) and *London Mercury*, June 1925 by Milton Waldman, p. 210.

[89] 28 May 1925, p. 365.

[90] 27 June 1925, p. 9.

York Herald Tribune Books. On 11 July 1925 he wrote to Sherman: 'I like to know what you say, because you do care about the deeper implication in a novel.' Sherman, together with the reviewer of the *New York Times*, set the high standard for subsequent American reviews. In particular, Sherman stressed the non-naturalistic convention in which Lawrence was writing: 'The novel is not a contribution to contemporary "realism", and should not be so approached. It is a piece of symbolism.'[91] Both reviewers also placed *St. Mawr* firmly in the comic tradition. As the *New York Times* review expressed it, despite Lawrence's 'profound and thoughtful questioning of current values, the book as a whole is pitched on the plane of high comedy'.[92]

For Sherman the strain of comedy in *St. Mawr* was 'mordantly satirical'. Louis Kronenberger, in the *Saturday Review of Literature*, preferred to call it pervasive irony: 'The treatment in this novel is ironical, the tone is negative, the chief emotions are impotence and disillusionment.'[93] Like many of his fellow American reviewers, Kronenberger felt that *St. Mawr* drew on all of Lawrence's diverse talents. John Crawford summed up this majority opinion in the New York *World* when he wrote that *St. Mawr* offered 'conclusive proof that Lawrence has not stopped developing in the novel and in life'.[94]

The two unfavourable American reviews both echoed the charge heard more repetitively in Britain, that art is sacrificed to idea in *St. Mawr*. In the *New Republic* Robert Littell argued that Lawrence's characters 'are quite subordinate to his idea, which plays havoc with their reality, with their independence'. Only the horse and the New Mexican landscape have a life of their own: the characters, Littell wrote, merely reflect their author's 'irritation' with the world at large.[95] This sentiment is echoed by the belated review in the *Dial*: 'all Mr Lawrence's later work trumpets out in changing cadences the same injunction, an injunction which one finds more artistically expressed in The Fox, or even The Lost Girl.'[96]

Meantime Lawrence's main commitment had shifted to *The Plumed Serpent*, which he had been revising while the reviews of *St. Mawr* were appearing. So it is not surprising to find him writing to Edward McDonald that reviewers of *St. Mawr* like Sherman 'pretend it's one of my best things: it isn't', and going on to claim that *The Plumed Serpent* is his 'chief novel so far'.[97] Similarly he assured Mrs Knopf, who was worried about the length

---

[91] 14 June 1925, p. 3 See R. P. Draper, ed. *D. H. Lawrence: The Critical Heritage* (1970), pp. 256–7.   [92] 14 June 1925, p. 8.
[93] 1 August 1925, p. 4.
[94] 5 July 1925, p. 9. The other favourable review was *Independent*, 4 July 1925, p. 24.
[95] 8 July 1925, p. 184.   [96] November 1925, p. 431.   [97] 29 June 1925.

of *The Plumed Serpent*, that his new novel was not too long; rather '*St. Mawr* was too short.'[98]

'*The Princess*'

'The Princess' was never published in the United States during Lawrence's lifetime, and appeared with the longer *St. Mawr* in Britain. It received scant notice from British reviewers, and none at all in America. With the exception of the *Manchester Guardian* and the *Empire Review*, all the reviewers were negative. Even the *Times Literary Supplement* reviewer, who had noticed *St. Mawr* favourably, concluded that in 'The Princess' 'the peculiarity of the little "princess" and the fantastically brutal catastrophe deprive it of the significance of "St Mawr". It remains an extreme case of fancy.' Louis McQuilland in *G. K.'s Weekly* dismissed it as 'the second story in a rather ludicrous volume'. Edwin Muir considered that '"The Princess" fails also. It is an unrestrained exercise in the romantic.' H. C. Harwood in *Calendar of Modern Letters*, while impressed by Lawrence's powerful writing in this story, concluded: 'The creative Mr Lawrence has not in these novelettes been busily enough engaged.'

Only John Sydenham in the *Empire Review* wrote positively at any length on 'The Princess': 'It has the advantage as a story of ending closer to its point of climax than *St. Mawr*; and an intense climax it is. The Princess's,' he continued, 'is the universal conflict between the desire for experience and the loathing of it.' To Sydenham, Lawrence's story 'proves...that for short stretches of imaginative intensity on a tragic plane he has few equals among living novelists' (p. 84).

'*The Overtone*'

By the time 'The Overtone' was published in *The Lovely Lady* at the beginning of 1933 the climate of critical opinion had altered. In noticing this posthumous collection of short stories, the *New Outlook* referred to 'the Lawrence cult that is growing rapidly'.[99] Ben Ray Redman in the *Saturday Review of Literature* similarly asked: 'Would these seven tales, for instance, which comprise "The Lovely Lady", without a signature command the same interest and respectful attention that they do bearing the now magical name of D. H. Lawrence?'[100] Whatever their verdict, almost all the reviewers of

98   23 November 1925.   99   February 1933, p. 60.
100   11 March 1933, p. 478.

The Lovely Lady treated this volume as the work of a man of outstanding talent. In particular, Lawrence's exploration of the unconscious areas of the mind was much more widely understood. Percy Hutchinson in the *New York Times Book Review* discerned a common theme running through the book – 'the not consciously expressed psychology – of sex'; while Fanny Butcher in the *Chicago Daily Tribune* hailed the Lawrence of these stories as 'a sturdy pioneer' in the 'human wilderness... of man's mind'.[101]

Opinions varied more widely on whether *The Lovely Lady* was representative or not. Most reviewers, like the *Forum*'s, thought that the majority of the stories, with one or two exceptions, were 'distinctly mediocre'.[102] One of the exceptions frequently cited was 'The Overtone'. Arthur Ball in the London *Bookman* was effusive in its praise. Singling out its 'mood of deep, musing half-fantasy', he declared that 'the success of the method should not be doubted for a moment. This is one of the finest stories in the language.'[103] Geoffrey West in the *Criterion* also called 'The Overtone' 'a beautiful tale' which 'gives expression to Lawrence's view of full being as a balance, tension, harmony, dynamic not static, between opposed infinites or forces – in this case symbolized as Pan and Christ, more broadly expressed as Flesh, or Matter, and Spirit'.[104] Not all the English reviewers who mentioned this story by name were complimentary. The *Times Literary Supplement* reviewer thought that 'The Overtone' ('the one story... where Lawrence directly expresses his physical mysticism') 'is not much of a success'.[105] The *Manchester Guardian* reviewer also felt that 'The Overtone' was among the 'less subtle stories of ill-mating' in the book.[106]

In America the only adverse mention of 'The Overtone' appeared in the *Nation*. Seeing the stories as mere 'chips left over from his novels' and misinformed about the true dating of his short fiction, the reviewer saw 'The Overtone' as simply 'a bit of addendum to "The Escaped Cock"'.[107] On the other hand L. P. Herring in *New York Herald Tribune Books*[108] and Redman in the *Saturday Review of Literature* both thought that 'The Overtone' was the finest of the stories in this posthumous collection. As the latter wrote: '"The Overtone": – A tale that runs from prose to poetry; a hymn to the flesh that is itself full of overtones... In this story, and this alone of the seven, we might possibly read the name of Lawrence without having it spelled out for us.'[109]

---

[101] 12 February 1933, p. 6, and 18 February 1933, p. 12, respectively.
[102] April 1933, p. vi.   [103] February 1933, p. 442.   [104] April 1933, p. 501.
[105] 19 January 1933, p. 37.   [106] 3 February 1933, p. 5.
[107] 22 March 1933, p. 324.   [108] 12 February 1933, p. 3.
[109] Other reviews specifically mentioning 'The Overtone' were *New Republic*, 7 June 1933, p. 104 and *Bookman* (New York), March 1933, p. 290.

'The Flying-Fish'

By the time 'The Flying-Fish' appeared, three years later, in Edward McDonald's collection of Lawrence's posthumous papers, *Phoenix*, critical respect for Lawrence's work had consolidated. As a result, all those reviewers of *Phoenix* who singled out 'The Flying-Fish' for special mention followed the lead McDonald gave in his 'Introduction' where he wrote that 'in this colourful fabric of rich and varied prose are beautifully fused the finest and highest qualities of D. H. Lawrence as writer and artist' (p. xxvii). Harry T. Moore in the *Nation* called 'The Flying-Fish' 'one of the most important keys to Lawrence and one of the finest things he ever wrote'.[110] The *Yale Review* labelled it 'a superb fragment of fiction'.[111]

Most reviewers especially admired the description of the flying-fish in section 2: 'The Gulf'. The *Observer* reviewer called this passage 'a description...that surely stands among the finest pieces of descriptive writing'.[112] The *Times Literary Supplement* attributed the power of this passage to the way in which Lawrence transformed the fish into 'symbols of the joyful living which is his constant theme'.[113] David Garnett in the *New Statesman*, the only reviewer to suggest that '["The Flying-Fish"] starts horribly with a lot of falsity about an old country house and an ancient family', went on that it 'then burst into passages of lyrical beauty – Lawrence at his best'.[114] The reviewer in the *Criterion* attempted to explain the stylistic technique which made this passage one 'of outstanding loveliness': 'the theme is mentioned, passed over, returned to, dodged again, and then steadily expanded, built up with the eddying, strengthening, accumulating sentences, so reminiscent of Tudor English, which seem to take possession of the mind and dominate the whole horizon'.[115]

Most complimentary of all the reviewers was Lawrence's first patron, Edward Garnett in the *London Mercury*. He claimed that in 'The Flying-Fish' 'the poet emerges in all his genius', and went on: 'The description of the marvellous joy of life, of the flying fish, and the school of porpoises speeding through the water with the ship, is one of the most beautiful things Lawrence wrote, but the whole, indeed, is a prose poem revealing Lawrence's genius in its purest essence.'[116]

[110] (New York), 24 October 1936, p. 493.
[112] 13 December 1936, p. 19.
[114] 21 November 1936, p. 814.
[116] December 1936, pp. 159–60.
[111] June 1937, p. 848.
[113] 21 November 1936, p. 956.
[115] July 1937, p. 749.

Publishing history

The publishing histories of the stories collected in this volume hold no suprises. First editions approximated in varying degrees to Lawrence's textual intentions; transmission-errors accumulated in subsequent reprints and editions. In particular, no new edition of any of these stories was based on either a comparison of American with English first editions, or, where appropriate, a comparison of both with magazine publication or extant manuscripts.

In the case of *St. Mawr* most of the errors concern punctuation and spelling, the result of heavy house-styling, especially in the American editions, although the British paperback edition by Penguin Books did revert to Secker's first edition,[117] but unwittingly perpetuated the unauthorised deletion by Secker from page 65. Five omissions in 'The Princess' mentioned above, as well as the usual effects of house-styling, have been reproduced in all subsequent editions of the story in Britain and America.[118] The same is true of 'The Overtone', where the omission of three sentences of dialogue in the first and all subsequent editions represents either an act of unauthorised censorship on Secker's part, or an omission by the typesetter.[119] Even Edward McDonald, a professional bibliographer, was responsible for considerable editorial intervention in matters of spelling (which he Americanised) and punctuation when he first published 'The Flying-Fish' in *Phoenix*.[120]

This edition is the first to shed the effects of house-styling of these various first editions and to approximate as closely as available evidence permits to Lawrence's final version of the texts.

---

[117] Secker reprinted September 1927, June 1930 and January 1933. Further editions containing *St. Mawr* include in addition to those mentioned above: pocket edition, Secker, 1928; *St. Mawr and The Man Who Died*, Vintage Books, New York, 1928 (repr. 1950, 1953, 1959); *The Tales of D. H. Lawrence*, Secker, 1934 (repr. Heinemann, 1934, 1948, 1949); *The Spirit of Place*, Heinemann, 1935 (repr. 1938); *The Later D. H. Lawrence*, Knopf, 1952 (repr. 1969); *The Short Novels of D. H. Lawrence*, vol. II, Heinemann, 1956 (re-issued, Heron Books, 1969).

[118] Further editions containing 'The Princess' include in addition to those in the previous note: *Full Score, Twenty Tales by D. H. Lawrence*, Reprint Society, London, 1943; *The Complete Short Stories of D. H. Lawrence*, vol. II, Heinemann, 1955 (re-issued, Heron Books, 1968; and as *The Collected Short Stories*, Heinemann, 1974); also as a Compass paperback, Viking Press, New York, 1961 (repr., Penguin, New York, 1977); *The Princess and Other Stories*, Penguin, 1971 (repr. 1972 on).

[119] Further editions containing 'The Overtone' include: *The Complete Short Stories of D. H. Lawrence*, vol. III, and as a Compass paperback; *The Princess and Other Stories*.

[120] 'The Flying-Fish' was also included in *The Princess and Other Stories*.

ST. MAWR AND OTHER STORIES

Note on the texts

The base-texts used for this volume are as follows:

'The Overtone': autograph manuscript, 12 pages, UT.

St. Mawr: corrected ribbon copy typescript, 181 pages, Lazarus.

'The Princess': autograph manuscript, 51 pages, UT. This has been emended wherever the text published by *The Calendar of Modern Letters* i (March, April, May 1925), pp. 2–22, 122–32, 226–35, and the English first edition of *St. Mawr Together with The Princess* (Martin Secker, 1925) differ in substance (but not normally in the case of punctuation) from the manuscript.

'The Wilful Woman': autograph manuscript, 7 pages, UCB.

'The Flying-Fish': uncorrected ribbon copy typescript, 34 pages, UCB.

The apparatus records all textual variants, except for the following silent emendations:

1. Clearly accidental spelling errors by DHL or his typists and obvious typesetter's mistakes have been corrected.

2. The English and American texts of 'The Overtone' and *St. Mawr*, the English editions of 'The Princess' (*Per*, *E1*) and the first edition of 'The Flying-Fish' (*A1*) consistently printed 'to-day', 'to-morrow', 'to-night', 'good-bye' and 'good-night' whereas DHL wrote these as one unhyphenated word; the American edition of *St. Mawr* and the first edition of 'The Flying-Fish' house-styled '-ise' to '-ize', e.g. DHL's 'civilise' became 'civilize'. In all these instances, DHL's practice has been preserved.

3. Inadvertent omissions, apostrophes in contractions, possessives and 'o'clock', incomplete quotation marks and full stops omitted at the end of sentences where no other punctuation exists have all been supplied.

4. DHL usually wrote 'Mr' and 'Mrs' without a full stop; his printers supplied one (except for *E1* of 'The Overtone'). DHL's practice has been adopted throughout. On the other hand 'St.' in 'St. Mawr' was consistently typed with the full stop, which has been retained.

5. Where consecutive paragraphs of monologue or letters occur, DHL placed inverted commas only before the first paragraph and after the final one, e.g. 12:9–13:5, 113:20–33. The convention of placing opening inverted commas before each paragraph, followed by the typesetters, has been retained.

6. In 'The Overtone', 'The Princess' and 'The Flying-Fish' DHL often followed a full stop, question mark or exclamation mark with a dash before beginning the next sentence with a capital letter (e.g. 'life.—It' at 6:23). His typists occasionally and the typesetters consistently omitted these dashes (with one exception at 219:1–2). They have been restored in this edition.

Supplementary points to the note on the texts have been supplied preceding each story as needed.

2

THE OVERTONE

The Overtone

His wife was talking to two other women. He lay on the lounge pretending to read. The lamps shed a golden light, and through the open door, the night was lustrous, and a white moon went like a woman,* unashamed and naked across the sky. His wife, her dark hair, tinged with grey, looped low on her white neck, fingered as she talked the pearl that hung in a heavy, naked drop against the bosom of her dress. She still was a beautiful woman, and one who dressed like the night, for harmony. Her gown was of silk lace, all in flakes, as if the fallen, pressed petals of black and faded-red poppies were netted together with gossamer about her. She was fifty one, and he was fifty two. It seemed impossible. He felt his love cling round her like her dress, like a garment of dead leaves.

She was talking to a quiet woman about the suffrage.* The other girl, tall, rather aloof, sat listening in her chair, with the posture of one who neither accepts nor rejects, but who allows things to go on around her, and will know what she thinks only when she must act. She seemed to be looking away into the night. A scent of honeysuckle came through the open door. Then a large grey moth blundered into the light.

It was very still, almost too silent, inside the room. Mrs Renshaw's quiet, musical voice continued:

"But think of a case like Mrs Mann's now. She is a clever woman. If she had slept in my cradle, and I in hers, she would have looked a greater lady than I do at this minute. But she married Mann, and she has seven children by him, and goes out charring. Her children she can never leave. So she must stay with a dirty, drunken brute like Mann. If she had an income of two pounds a week, she could say to him 'Sir, goodbye to you,' and she would be well rid. But no, she is tied to him for ever—"

They were discussing the State-endowment of mothers.* She and Mrs Hankin were bitterly keen upon it. Elsa Laskell sat and accepted their talk as she did the scent of the honeysuckle or the blundering adventure of the moth round the silk: it came burdened, not with the meaning of the words, but with the feeling of the woman's heart as she spoke. Perhaps she heard a nightingale in the park outside—perhaps she did. And then this talk inside drifted also to the girl's heart, like

5

a sort of inarticulate music. Then she was vaguely aware of the man
sprawled in his homespun* suit upon the lounge. He had not changed
for dinner:* he was called unconventional.

She knew he was old enough to be her father, and yet he looked
young enough to be a lover. They all seemed young, the beautiful
hostess too, but with a meaningless youth that cannot ripen, like an
unfertilised flower which lasts a long time. He was a man she classed
as a Dane—with fair, almost sandy hair, blue eyes, long, loose limbs,
and a boyish activity. But he was fifty two—and he lay looking out
on the night, with one of his hands swollen from hanging so long inert,
silent. The women bored him.

Elsa Laskell sat in a sort of dreamy state, and the feelings of her
hostess, and the feeling of her host, drifted like iridescence upon the
quick of her soul, among the white touch of that moon out there, and
the exotic heaviness of the honeysuckle, and the strange flapping of
the moth. So still, it was, behind the murmur of talk: a silence of being.
Of the third woman, Mrs Hankin, the girl had no sensibility. But the
night and the moon, the moth, Will Renshaw and Edith Renshaw and
herself were all in full being, a harmony.

To him it was six months after his marriage, and the sky was the
same, and the honeysuckle in the air. He was living again his crisis,
as we all must, fretting and fretting against our failure, till we have
worn away the thread of our life.—It was six months after his marriage,
and they were down at the little bungalow on the bank of the Soar.*
They were comparatively poor, though her father was rich, and his
was well-to-do. And they were alone in the little, two-roomed
bungalow that stood on its wild bank over the river, among the
honeysuckle bushes. He had cooked the evening meal, they had eaten
the omelette and drunk the coffee, and all was settling into stillness.

He sat outside, by the remnants of the fire, looking at the country
lying level and lustrous grey opposite him. Trees hung like vapour in
a perfect calm under the moonlight. And that was the moon, so
perfectly naked and unfaltering, going her errand simply through the
night. And that was the river faintly rustling! And there, down the
darkness, he saw a flashing of activity white betwixt black twigs. It
was the water mingling and thrilling with the moon. So! It made him
quiver, and reminded him of the starlit rush of a hare. There was
vividness then in all this lucid night, things flashing and quivering with
being, almost as the soul quivers in the darkness of the eye. He could
feel it. The night's great circle was the pupil of an eye, full of the

mystery, and the unknown fire of life, that does not burn away, but flickers unquenchable.

So he rose, and went to look for his wife. She sat with her dark head bent into the light of a reading-lamp, in the little hut. She wore a white dress, and he could see her shoulders' softness and curve through the lawn. Yet she did not look up when he moved. He stood in the doorway, knowing that she felt his presence. Yet she gave no sign. "Will you come out?" he asked.

She looked up at him as if to find out what he wanted, and she was rather cold to him. But when he had repeated his request, she had risen slowly to acquiesce, and a tiny shiver had passed down her shoulders. So he unhung from its peg her beautiful Paisley* shawl, with its tempered colours that looked as if they had filtered through the years and now were here in their essence, and put it round her. They sat again outside the little hut, under the moonlight. He held both her hands. They were heavy with rings. But one ring was his wedding-ring. He had married her, and there was nothing more to own. He owned her, and the night was the pupil of her eye, in which was everything. He kissed her fingers, but she sat and made no sign. It was as he wished. He kissed her fingers again.

Then a corncrake began to call in the meadow across the river, a strange, dispassionate sound, that made him feel not quite satisfied, not quite sure. It was not all achieved. The moon, in her white and naked candour, was beyond him. He felt a little numbness, as one who has gloves on. He could not feel that clear, clean moon. There was something betwixt him and her, as if he had gloves on. Yet he ached for the clear touch, skin to skin—even of the moonlight. He wanted a further purity, a newer cleanness and nakedness.* The corncrake cried it too. And he watched the moon, and he watched her light on his hands. It was like a butterfly on his glove, that he could see, but not feel. And he wanted to unglove himself. Quite clear, quite, quite bare to the moon, the touch of everything, he wanted to be. And after all, his wife was everything—moon, vapour of trees, trickling water and drift of perfume—it was all his wife. The moon glistened on her fingertips as he cherished them,* and a flash came out of a diamond, among the darkness. So, even here in the quiet harmony, life was at a flash with itself.

"Come with me to the top of the red hill," he said to his wife quietly.
"But why?" she asked.
"Do come."

And dumbly, she acquiesced, and her shawl hung gleaming above the white flash of her skirt. He wanted to hold her hand, but she was walking apart from him, in her long shawl. So he went at her side, humbly. And he was humble, but he felt it was great. He had looked
5 into the whole of the night, as into a pupil of an eye. And now, he would come perfectly clear out of all his embarrassments of shame and darkness, clean as the moon who walked naked across the night, so that the whole night was as an effluence from her, the whole of it was hers, held in her effluence of moonlight, which was her perfect
10 nakedness, uniting her to everything. Covering was barrier, like cloud across the moon.

The red hill was steep, but there was a tiny path from the bungalow, which he had worn himself. And in the effort of climbing, he felt he was struggling nearer and nearer to himself. Always he looked half
15 round, where, just behind him, she followed, in the lustrous obscurity of her shawl. Her steps came with a little effort up the steep hill, and he loved her feet, he wanted to kiss them as they strove upwards in the gloom. He put aside the twigs and branches. There was a strong scent of honeysuckle like a thick strand of gossamer over his mouth.
20 He knew a place on the ledge of the hill, on the lip of the cliff, where the trees stood back and left a little dancing-green,* high up above the water, there in the midst of miles of moonlit, lonely country. He parted the boughs, sure as a fox that runs to its lair. And they stood together on this little dancing-green presented towards the moon, with the red
25 cliff cumbered with bushes going down to the river below, and the haze of moon-dust on the meadows, and the trees behind them, and only the moon could look straight down into the form he had chosen.*

She stood always a little way behind him. He saw her face all compounded of shadows and moonlight, and he dared not kiss her yet.
30 "Will you," he said, "will you take off your things and love me here?"

"I can't," she said.

He looked away to the moon. It was difficult to ask her again, yet it meant so much to him. There was not a sound in the night. He put
35 his hand to his throat and began to unfasten his collar.

"Take off all your things and love me," he pleaded.

For a moment she was silent.

"I can't," she said.

Mechanically, he had taken off his flannel collar and pushed it into
40 his pocket. Then he stood on the edge of the land, looking down into

all that gleam, as into the living [pupil] of an eye.* He was bareheaded to the moon. Not a breath of air ruffled his bare throat. Still, in the dropping folds of her shawl, she stood, a thing of dusk and moonlight, a little back. He ached with the earnestness of his desire. All he wanted was to give himself, clean and clear, into this night, this time. Of which she was all, she was everything. He could go to her now, under the white candour of the moon, without shame or shadow, but in his completeness loving her completeness, without a stain, without a shadow between them such as even a flower could cast. For this he yearned as never in his life he could yearn more deeply.

"Do take me," he said, gently parting the shawl on her breast. But she held it close, and her voice went hard.

"No—I can't," she said.

"Why?"

"I can't—let us go back."

He looked again over the countryside of dimness, saying in a low tone, his back towards her:

"But I love you—and I want you so much—like that, here and now. I'll never ask you anything again," he said quickly, passionately, as he turned to her. "Do this for me," he said. "I'll never trouble you for anything again. I promise."

"I can't," she said stubbornly, with some hopelessness in her voice.

"Yes—" he said, "yes. You trust me, don't you?"

"I don't want it. You wouldn't have me if I don't want to, would you?" she said.

"Do have me," he said. "Have me then without taking your things off."*

"Not here—not now," she said.

"Do," he said. "Yes."

"You can have me in the bungalow—why do you want me here?" she asked.

"But I do. Have me, Edith. Have me now."

"No," she said, turning away. "I want to go down."

"And you won't?"

"No—I can't."

There was something like fear in her voice. They went down the hill together. And he did not know how he hated her, as if she had kept him out of the promised land* that was justly his. He thought he was too generous to bear her a grudge. So he had always held himself deferential to her. And later that evening he had loved her. But she hated it, it had been really his hate ravaging her. Why had he lied calling it love? Ever since, it had seemed the same, more or less. So that he had ceased to come to her, gradually. For* one night she had said:

5   " I think a man's body is ugly—all in parts with mechanical joints—"
And now he had scarcely had her for some years. For she thought him an ugliness. And there were no children.

Now that everything was essentially over, for both of them, they lived on the surface, and had good times. He drove to all kinds of
10   unexpected places, in his motor car, bathed where he liked, said what he liked, did what he liked. But nobody minded very much his often aggressive unconventionality. It was only fencing with the foils.* There was no danger in his thrusts. He was a castrated bear. So he prided himself on being a bear, on being known as an uncouth bear.

15   It was not often he lay and let himself drift. But always when he did, he held it against her that on the night when they climbed the red bank, she refused to have him. There were perhaps many things he might have held against her, but this was the only one that remained: his real charge against her on the Judgment Day.* Why had
20   she done it? It had been, he might almost say, a holy desire on his part. It had been almost like taking off his shoes before God. Yet she had refused, she who was his religion to him. Perhaps she had been afraid, she who was so good—afraid of the big righteousness of it—as if she could not trust herself so near the Burning Bush, dared not go
25   near for transfiguration, afraid for herself.*

It was a thought he could not bear. Rising softly, because she was still talking, he went out into the night.*

Elsa Laskell stirred uneasily in her chair. Mrs Renshaw went on talking like a somnambule, not because she really had anything to say
30   about the State-endowment of mothers, but because she had a weight on her heart that she wanted to talk away. The girl heard, and lifted her hand, and stirred her fingers uneasily in the dark-purple porphyry bowl, where pink rose leaves and crimson, thrown this morning from the stem, lay gently shrivelling. There came a slight acrid scent of new
35   rose-petals. And still the girl lifted her long white fingers among the red and pink in the dark bowl, as if they stirred in blood.

And she felt the nights behind like a purple bowl into which the woman's heart-beats were shed, like rose leaves fallen and left to wither and go brown. For Mrs Renshaw had waited for him. During happy
40   days of stillness and blueness she had moved, while the sunshine

glancing through her blood made flowers in her heart, like blossoms underground thrilling with expectancy, lovely fragrant things that would have delight to appear. And all day long she had gone secretly and quietly, saying: "Tonight—tonight they will blossom for him. Tonight I shall be a bed of blossom for him, all narcissi and fresh fragrant things shaking for joy, when he comes with his deeper sunshine, when he turns the darkness like mould, and brings them forth with his sunshine for spade. There* are two suns: him in the sky, and that other, warmer one whose beams are our radiant bodies. He is a sun to me, shining full on my heart when he comes, and everything stirs." But he had come like a bitter morning. He had never bared the sun of himself to her—a sullen day he had been on her heart, covered with cloud impenetrable. She had waited* so heavy anxious, with such a wealth of possibility. And he in his blindness had never known. He could never let the real rays of his love through the cloud of fear, and mistrust. For once she had denied him.—And all her flowers had been shed inwards, so that her heart was like a heap of leaves, brown, withered, almost scentless petals that had never given joy to anyone. And yet again she had come to him pregnant with beauty and love, but he had been afraid. When she lifted her eyes to him, he had looked aside. The kisses she needed like warm raindrops he dared not give, till she was parched and gone hard, and did not want them. Then he gave kisses enough. But he never trusted himself. When she was open and eager to him, he was afraid. When she was shut, it was like playing at pride, to pull her petals apart, a game that gave him pleasure.

So they had been mutually afraid of each other, but he most often. Whenever she had needed him at some mystery of love, he had overturned her censers and her sacraments, and made profane love in her sacred place. Which was why, at last, she had hated his body; but perhaps she had hated it at first, or feared it so much, it was hate.

And he had said to her: "If *we* don't have children, you might have them by another man—" which was surely one of the cruellest things a woman ever heard from her husband. For so little was she his, that he would give her to a caller and not mind. This was all the wife she was to him. He was a free and easy man, and brought home to dinner any man who pleased him, from a beggar.* And his wife was to be as public as his board.

Nay, to the very bowl of her heart, any man might put his lips, and

he would not mind. And so, she sadly set down the bowl from between
her two hands of offering, and went always empty, and aloof.

Yet they were married, they were good friends. It was said, they
were the most friendly married couple in the county. And this was it.

5 And all the while, like a scent, the bitter psalm of the woman filled
the room:

"Like a garden in winter, I was full of bulbs and roots, I was full
of little flowers, all conceived inside me.

"And they were all shed away unborn, little abortions of flowers.

10 "Every day I went like a bee gathering honey from the sky and
among the stars I rummaged for yellow honey, filling it in my comb.

"Then I broke the comb, and put it to your lips. But you turned
your mouth aside, and said 'You have made my face unclean, and
smeared my mouth.'

15 "And week after week my body was a vineyard, my veins were vines.
And as the grapes, the purple drops grew full and sweet, I crushed
them in a bowl, I treasured the wine.

"Then when the bowl was full I came with joy to you. But you in
fear started away, and the bowl was thrown from my hands, and broke

20 in pieces at my feet.

"Many times, and many times, I said 'The hour is striking' but
he answered 'Not yet.'

"Many times and many times he has heard the cock-crow, and gone
out and wept, he knew not why.*

25 "I was a garden, but he ran in me as in grass.

"I was a stream, and he threw his waste in me.

"I held the rainbow balanced on my outspread hands, and he said
'You open your hands and give me nothing.'

"What am I now but a bowl of withered leaves, but a kaleidoscope

30 of broken beauties, but an empty bee-hive, yea, a rich garment rusted
that no-one has worn, a dumb singer, with the voice of a nightingale
yet making discord.

"And it is over with me, and my hour is gone. And soon like a barren
sea-shell on the strand, I shall be crushed underfoot to dust.

35 "But meanwhile I sing to those that listen with their ear against me,
of the sea that gave me form and being, the everlasting. Yea, and in
my song is nothing but bitterness, for of the fluid life of the sea I have
no more, but am to be dust, that powdery stuff the sea knows not. I
am to be dead, who was born of life, silent who was made a mouth,

40 formless, who was all of beauty.

"Yea I was a seed that held the heavens lapped up in bud, with a whirl of stars and a steady moon.

"And the seed is crushed that never sprouted, there is a heaven lost, and stars and a moon that never came forth.

"I was a bud that was never discovered, and in my shut chalice, skies and lake water and brooks lie crumbling, and stars and the sun are smeared out, and birds are a little powdery dust, and their singing is dry air, and I am a dark, shut chalice."*

And the girl, hearing her hostess talk, still talk, and yet her voice like the sound of a sea-shell whispering hoarsely of despair, rose and went out into the garden, timidly, beginning to cry. For what should she do for herself.

Renshaw, leaning on the wicket that led to the paddock, called: "Come on, don't be alarmed—Pan is dead."*

And then she bit back her tears. For when he said 'Pan is dead' he meant Pan was dead in his own long, loose Dane's body. Yet she was a nymph still, and if Pan were dead, she ought to die. So with tears she went up to him.

"It's all right out here," he said. "By Jove, when you see a night like this, how can you say that life's a tragedy—or death either, for that matter?"

"What is it then?" she asked.

"Nay, that's one too many—a joke, eh?"

"I think," she said, "one has no business to be irreverent."

"Who?" he asked.

"You," she said, "and me, and all of us."

Then he leaned on the wicket, thinking till he laughed.

"Life's a real good thing," he said.

"But why protest it?" she answered.

And again he was silent.

"If the moon came nearer and nearer," she said, "and were a naked woman, what would you do?"

"Fetch her a wrap probably," he said.

"Yes—you would do that," she answered.

"And if he were a man ditto?" he teased.

"If a star came nearer and were a naked man, I should look at him."

"That is surely very improper," he mocked, with still a tinge of yearning.

"If he were a star come near—" she answered.

Again he was silent.

"You are a queer fish of a girl," he said.

They stood at the gate, facing the silver-grey paddock. Presently their hostess came out, a long shawl hanging from her shoulders.

"So you are here," she said. "Were you bored?"

5 "I was," he replied amiably. "But there, you know I always am."

"And I forgot," replied the girl.

"What were you talking about?" asked Mrs Renshaw, simply curious. She was not afraid of her husband's running loose.

"We were just saying 'Pan is dead,'" said the girl.

10 "Isn't that rather trite?" asked the hostess.

"Some of us miss him fearfully," said the girl.

"For what reason?" asked Mrs Renshaw.

"Those of us who are nymphs—just lost nymphs among farm-lands and suburbs. I wish Pan were alive."

15 "Did he die of old age?" mocked the hostess.

"Don't they say, when Christ was born, a voice was heard in the air saying 'Pan is dead.' I wish Christ needn't have killed Pan."

"I wonder how he managed it," said Renshaw.

"By disapproving of him, I suppose," replied his wife. And her
20 retort cut herself, and gave her a sort of fakir pleasure.*

"The men are all women now," she said, "since the fauns died in a frost one night."

"A frost of disapproval," said the girl.

"A frost of fear," said Renshaw.

25 There was a silence.

"Why was Christ afraid of Pan?" said the girl suddenly.

"Why was Pan so much afraid of Christ, that he died," asked Mrs Renshaw bitterly.

"And all his fauns in a frost one night," mocked Renshaw. Then
30 a light dawned on him. "Christ was woman, and Pan was man," he said. It gave him real joy to say this, bitterly, keenly—a thrust into himself, and into his wife.

"But the fauns and satyrs are there—you have only to look under* the surplices that all men wear nowadays."

35 "Nay," said Mrs Renshaw, "it is not true—the surplices have grown into their limbs, like Hercules' garment."*

"That his wife put on him," said Renshaw.

"Because she was afraid of him—not because she loved him," said the girl.

40 "She imagined that all her lonely wasted hours wove him a robe

of love," said Mrs Renshaw. "It was to her horror she was mistaken.
You can't weave love out of waste."

"When I meet a man," said the girl, "I shall look down the pupil
of his eye, for a faun. And after a while it will come, skipping—"

"Perhaps a satyr," said Mrs Renshaw bitterly. 5

"No," said the girl, "because satyrs are old, and I have seen some
fearfully young men."

"Will is young even now—quite a boy," said his wife.

"Oh no!" cried the girl. "He says that neither life nor death is a
tragedy. Only somebody very old could say that." 10

There was a tension in the night. The man felt something give way
inside him.

"Yes Edith," he said, with a quiet, bitter joy of cruelty, "I am old."

The wife was frightened.

"You are always preposterous," she said quickly, crying inside 15
herself. She knew she herself had been—never young.

"I shall look in the eyes of my man for the faun," the girl continued
in a singsong, "and I shall find him. Then I shall pretend to run away
from him. And both our surplices, and all the crucifix, will be outside
the wood. Inside nymph and faun, Pan and his satyrs—ah yes: for 20
Christ and the cross is only for daytime, and bargaining. Christ came
to make us deal honorably.

"But love is no deal, nor merchant's bargaining, and Christ neither
spoke of it nor forbade it. He was afraid of it. If once his faun, the
faun of the young Jesus had run free, seen one white nymph's brief 25
breast, he would not have been content to die on a cross*—and then
the men would have gone on cheating the women in life's business,
all the time. Christ made one bargain in mankind's business—and he
made it for the women's sake—I suppose for his mother's, since he
was fatherless. And Christ made a bargain for me, and I shall avail 30
myself of it.

"I won't be cheated by my man. When between my still hands I
weave silk out of the air, like a cocoon, he shall not take it to pelt me
with. He shall draw it forth and weave it up. For I want to finger the
sunshine I have drawn through my body, stroke it, and have joy of 35
the fabric.

"And when I run wild on the hills with Dionysos,* and shall come
home like a bee that has rolled in floury crocuses, he must see the
wonder on me, and make bread of it.

"And when I say to him 'It is harvest in my soul,' he shall look 40 in my eyes and lower his nets where the shoal moves in a throng in the dark, and lift out the living blue silver for me to see, and know, and taste.

"All this, my faun in commerce, my faun at traffic with me.

5 "And if he cheat me, he must take his chance.

"But I will not cheat him, in his hour, when he runs like a faun after me. I shall flee, but only to be overtaken. I shall flee, but never out of the wood to the crucifix. For that is to deny I am a nymph; since how can a nymph cling at the crucifix. Nay, the cross is the sign 10 I have on my money, for honesty.

"In the morning, when we come out of the wood, I shall say to him: 'Touch the cross, and prove you will deal fairly,' and if he will not, I will set the dogs of anger and judgment on him, and they shall chase him.* But if, perchance some night he contrive to crawl back into the 15 wood, beyond the crucifix, he will be faun and I nymph, and I shall have no knowledge what happened outside, in the realm of the crucifix. But in the morning, I shall say:

'Touch the cross, and prove you will deal fairly.' And being renewed, he will touch the cross.

20 "Many a dead faun I have seen, like dead rabbits poisoned lying about the paths, and many a dead nymph, like swans that could not fly and the dogs destroyed.

"But I am a nymph and a woman, and Pan is for me, and Christ is for me.

25 "For Christ I cover myself in my robe, and weep, and vow my vow of honesty.

"For Pan I throw my coverings down and run headlong through the leaves, because of the joy of running.

"And Pan will give me my children and joy, and Christ will give 30 me my pride.

"And Pan will give me my man, and Christ my husband.

"To Pan I am nymph, to Christ I am woman.

"And Pan is in the darkness, and Christ in the pale light.

"And night shall never be day, and day shall never be night.

35 "But side by side they shall go, day and night, night and day, for ever apart, for ever together.

"Pan and Christ, Christ and Pan.

"Both moving over me, so when in the sunshine I go in my robes among my neighbours, I am a christian. But when I run robe-less 40 through the dark-scented woods alone, I am a Pan's nymph.

"Now I must go, for I want to run away. Not run away from myself, but to myself.

"For neither am I a lamp that stands in the way in the sunshine. "Nor am I a sundial foolish at night.

"I am myself, running through light and shadow for ever, a nymph and a christian, I, not two things, but an apple with a gold side and a red, a freckled deer, a stream that tinkles and a pool where light is drowned; I, no fragment, no half-thing like the day, but a black bird with a white breast and underwings, a peewit, a wild thing, beyond understanding."

"I wonder if we shall hear the nightingale tonight," said Mrs Renshaw.

"He's a gurgling fowl—I'd rather hear a linnet," said Renshaw.— "Come a drive with me tomorrow, Miss Laskell."

And the three went walking back to the house. And Elsa Laskell was glad to get away from them.*

ST. MAWR

Supplementary note on the text

See note on the texts, p. 2. Additional silent emendations in this story are the following:

1. The English first edition printed 'Santa Fé', the American first edition printed 'Negro' and 'connexion', and both first editions printed 'Phœnix', whereas the typescript has 'Santa Fe', 'negro', 'connection' and 'Phoenix'. In these instances, DHL's practice has been preserved.

2. Dorothy Brett typed the closing quotation marks for a single word or a short phrase before, after or over the punctuation, e.g. "knowledge", (22:12); "enjoying oneself." (41:9); "charming", (40:39). In the two instances of DHL's handwritten revision or addition of this form of emphasis, he has placed the quotation marks *after* the punctuation (41:31; 132:22); this was also the form used in both first editions. DHL's practice has been followed.

St. Mawr

Lou Witt had had her own way so long, that by the age of twenty-five
she didn't know where she was. Having one's own way landed one
completely at sea.

To be sure for a while she had failed in her grand love affair with   5
Rico. And then she had had something really to despair about. But even
that had worked out as she wanted. Rico had come back to her, and
was dutifully married to her. And now, when she was twenty-five and
he was three months older, they were a charming married couple. He
flirted with other women still, to be sure. He wouldn't be the handsome   10
Rico if he didn't. But she had "got" him. Oh yes! You had only
to see the uneasy backward glance at her, from his big blue eyes: just
like a horse that is edging away from its master: to know how
completely he was mastered.

She, with her odd little *museau*,* not exactly pretty, but very   15
attractive; and her quaint air of playing at being well-bred, in a sort
of charade game; and her queer familiarity with foreign cities and
foreign languages; and the lurking sense of being an outsider everywhere, like a sort of gipsy, who is at home anywhere and nowhere:
all this made up her charm and her failure. She didn't quite belong.   20

Of course she was American: Louisiana family, moved down to
Texas. And she was moderately rich, with no close relation except her
mother. But she had been sent to school in France when she was twelve,
and since she had finished school, she had drifted from Paris to
Palermo, Biarritz to Vienna and back via Munich to London, then   25
down again to Rome. Only fleeting trips to her America.

So what sort of American was she, after all?

And what sort of European was she either? She didn't "belong"
anywhere. Perhaps most of all in Rome, among the artists and the
Embassy people.   30

It was in Rome she had met Rico. He was an Australian, son of a
government official in Melbourne, who had been made a baronet. So
one day Rico would be Sir Henry, as he was the only son. Meanwhile
he floated round Europe on a very small allowance—his father wasn't
rich in capital—and was being an artist.   35

They met in Rome when they were twenty-two, and had a love affair
in Capri. Rico was handsome, elegant, but mostly he had spots of paint

21

on his trousers and he ruined a necktie pulling it off. He behaved in a most floridly elegant fashion, fascinating to the Italians. But at the same time he was canny and shrewd and sensible as any young poser could be, and on principle, good-hearted, anxious. He was anxious
5 for his future, and anxious for his place in the world, he was poor, and suddenly wasteful in spite of all his tension of economy, and suddenly spiteful in spite of all his ingratiating efforts, and suddenly ungrateful in spite of all his burden of gratitude, and suddenly rude in spite of all his good manners, and suddenly detestable in spite of
10 all his suave, courtier-like amiability.

He was fascinated by Lou's quaint aplomb, her experiences, her "knowledge," her *gamine* knowingness, her aloneness, her pretty clothes that were sometimes an utter failure, and her southern "drawl" that was sometimes so irritating. That sing-song which was so
15 American. Yet she used no Americanisms at all, except when she lapsed into her odd spasms of acid irony, when she was very American indeed!

And she was fascinated by Rico. They played to each other like two butterflies at one flower. They pretended to be very poor in Rome—he *was* poor: and very rich in Naples. Everybody stared their eyes out
20 at them. And they had that love affair in Capri.

But they reacted badly on each other's nerves. She became ill. Her mother appeared. He couldn't stand Mrs Witt, and Mrs Witt couldn't stand him. There was a terrible fortnight. Then Lou was popped into a convent nursing-home in Umbria, and Rico dashed off to Paris.
25 Nothing would stop him. He must go back to Australia.

He went to Melbourne, and while there, his father died, leaving him a baronet's title and an income still very moderate. Lou visited America once more, as the strangest of strange lands to her. She came away disheartened, panting for Europe, and of course, doomed to meet
30 Rico again.

They couldn't get away from one another, even though in the course of their rather restrained correspondence, he informed her that he was "probably" marrying a very dear girl, friend of his childhood, only daughter of one of the oldest families in Victoria. Not saying much.
35 He didn't commit the probability, but reappeared in Paris, wanting to paint his head off, terribly inspired by Cezanne and by old Renoir. He dined at the Rotonde* with Lou and Mrs Witt, who, with her queer democratic New Orleans sort of conceit looked round the drinking-hall with savage contempt, and at Rico as part of the show. "Certainly,"
40 she said, "when these people here have got any money, they fall in

love on a full stomach. And when they've got no money, they fall in love with a full pocket. I never was in a more disgusting place. They take their love like some people take after-dinner pills."

She would watch with her arching, full, strong grey eyes, sitting there erect and silent in her well-bought American clothes. And then 5 she would deliver some such charge of grape-shot.* Rico always writhed.

Mrs Witt hated Paris: "this sordid, unlucky city," she called it. "Something unlucky is bound to happen to me in this sinister, unclean town," she said. "I feel it in the air. I* feel *contagion* in the air of 10 this place. For heaven's sake, Louise, let us go to Morocco or somewhere."

"No mother dear, I can't now. Rico has proposed to me, and I have accepted him. Let us think about a wedding, shall we?"

"There!" said Mrs Witt. "I said it was an unlucky city!" 15

And the peculiar look of extreme New Orleans annoyance came round her sharp nose. But Lou and Rico were both twenty-four years old, and beyond management. And anyhow, Lou would be Lady Carrington. But Mrs Witt was exasperated beyond exasperation. She would almost rather have preferred Lou to elope with one of the great, 20 evil porters at Les Halles.* Mrs Witt was at the age when the malevolent male in man, the old Adam, begins to loom above all the social tailoring. And yet—and yet—it was better to have Lady Carrington for a daughter, seeing Lou was that sort.

There was a marriage, after which Mrs Witt departed to America, 25 Lou and Rico leased a little old house in Westminster, and began to settle into a certain layer of English society. Rico was becoming an almost fashionable portrait painter. At least, *he* was almost fashionable, whether his portraits were or not. And Lou too was almost fashionable: almost a hit. There was some flaw somewhere. In spite of their 30 appearances, both Rico and she would never quite go down, in any society. They were the drifting artist sort. Yet neither of them was content to be of the drifting artist sort. They wanted to fit in, to make good.

Hence the little house in Westminster, the portraits, the dinners, 35 the friends, and the visits. Mrs Witt came and sardonically established herself in a suite in a quiet but good-class hotel not far off. Being on the spot. And her terrible grey eyes with the touch of a leer looked on at the hollow mockery of things. As if *she* knew of anything better!

Lou and Rico had a curious exhausting effect on one another: 40

neither knew why. They were fond of one another. Some inscrutable
bond held them together. But it was a strange vibration of the nerves,
rather than of the blood. A nervous attachment, rather than a sexual
love. A curious tension of will, rather than a spontaneous passion. Each
5 was curiously under the domination of the other. They were a
pair—they had to be together. Yet quite soon they shrank from one
another. This attachment of the will and the nerves was destructive.
As soon as one felt strong, the other felt ill. As soon as the ill one
recovered strength, down went the one who had been well.

10 And soon, tacitly, the marriage became more like a friendship,
Platonic. It was a marriage, but without sex. Sex was shattering and
exhausting, they shrank from it, and became like brother and sister.
But still they were husband and wife. And the lack of physical relation
was a secret source of uneasiness and chagrin to both of them. They
15 would neither of them accept it. Rico looked with contemplative,
anxious eyes at other women.

Mrs Witt kept track of everything, watching as it were from outside
the fence, like a potent well-dressed demon, full of uncanny energy
and a shattering sort of sense. She said little: but her small, occasionally
20 biting remarks revealed her attitude of contempt for the ménage.

Rico entertained clever and well-known people. Mrs Witt would
appear, in her New York gowns and few good jewels. She was
handsome, with her vigorous grey hair. But her heavy-lidded grey eyes
were the despair of any hostess. They looked too many shattering
25 things. And it was but too obvious that these clever, well-known
English people got on her nerves terribly, with their finickiness and
their fine-drawn discriminations. She wanted to put her foot through
all these fine-drawn distinctions. She thought continually of the house
of her girlhood, the plantation, the negroes, the planters: the sardonic
30 grimness that underlay all the big, shiftless life. And she wanted to
cleave with some of this grimness of the big, dangerous America, into
the safe, finicky drawing-rooms of London. So naturally she was not
popular.

But being a woman of energy, she had to do *something*. During the
35 latter part of the war, she had worked in the American Red Cross in
France, nursing. She loved men—real men. But, on close contact, it was
difficult to define what she meant by "real" men. She never met any.

Out of the débâcle of the war she had emerged with an odd piece
of débris, in the shape of Geronimo Trujillo. He was an American,
40 son of a Mexican father and a Navajo Indian mother, from Arizona.

When you knew him well, you recognised the real half-breed, though at a glance he might pass as a sunburnt citizen of any nation, particularly of France. He looked like a certain sort of Frenchman, with his curiously-set dark eyes, his straight black hair, his thin black moustache, his rather long cheeks, and his almost slouching, diffident, sardonic bearing. Only when you knew him, and looked right into his eyes, you saw that unforgettable glint of the Indian.

He had been badly shell-shocked, and was for a time a wreck. Mrs Witt, having nursed him into convalescence, asked him where he was going next. He didn't know. His father and mother were dead, and he had nothing to take him back to Phoenix, Arizona. Having had an education in one of the Indian high-schools, the unhappy fellow had now no place in life at all. Another of the many misfits.

There was something of the Paris *Apache** in his appearance: but he was all the time withheld, and nervously shut inside himself. Mrs Witt was intrigued by him.

"Very well, Phoenix," she said, refusing to adopt his Spanish name, "I'll see what I can do."

What she did was to get him a place on a sort of manor farm, with some acquaintances of hers. He was very good with horses, and had a curious success with turkeys and geese and fowls.

Some time after Lou's marriage, Mrs Witt reappeared in London, from the country, with Phoenix in tow, and a couple of horses. She had decided that she would ride in the Park in the morning, and see the world that way. Phoenix was to be her groom.

So, to the great misgiving of Rico, behold Mrs Witt in splendidly tailored habit and perfect boots, a smart black hat on her smart grey hair, riding a grey gelding as smart as she was, and looking down her conceited, inquisitive, scornful, aristocratic-democratic Louisiana nose at the people in Piccadilly, as she crossed to the Row,* followed by the taciturn shadow of Phoenix, who sat on a chestnut with three white feet as if he had grown there.

Mrs Witt, like many other people, always expected to find the real *beau monde* and the real *grand monde* somewhere or other. She didn't quite give in to what she saw in the Bois de Boulogne, or in Monte Carlo, or on the Pincio:* all a bit shoddy, and not very *beau* and not at all *grand*. There she was, with her grey eagle eye, her splendid complexion and her weapon-like health of a woman of fifty, dropping her eyelids a little, very slightly nervous, but completely prepared to despise the *monde* she was entering in Rotten Row.

In she sailed, and up and down that regatta-canal of horsemen and
horsewomen under the trees of the Park.—And yes, there were lovely
girls with fair hair down their backs, on happy ponies. And awfully
well-groomed papas, and tight mamas who looked as if they were going
5   to pour tea between the ears of their horses, and converse with banal
skill, one eye on the teapot, one on the visitor with whom she was
talking, and all the rest of her hostess' argus-eyes* upon everybody in
sight. That alert argus capability of the English matron was startling
and a bit horrifying. Mrs Witt would at once think of the old negro
10   mammies, away in Louisiana. And her eyes became dagger-like as she
watched the clipped, shorn, mincing young Englishmen. She refused
to look at the prosperous Jews.

It was still the days before motor-cars were allowed in the Park, but
Rico and Lou, sliding round Hyde Park Corner and up Park Lane in
15   their car would watch the steely horsewoman and the saturnine groom
with a sort of dismay. Mrs Witt seemed to be pointing a pistol at the
bosom of every other horseman or horsewoman, and announcing: *Your
virility or your life!*—*Your femininity or your life!* She didn't know
herself what she really wanted them to be: but it was something as
20   democratic as Abraham Lincoln and as aristocratic as a Russian Czar,
as highbrow as Arthur Balfour,* and as taciturn and unideal as
Phoenix. Everything at once.

There was nothing for it: Lou had to buy herself a horse and ride
at her mother's side, for very decency's sake. Mrs Witt was *so* like a
25   smooth, levelled, gun-metal pistol, Lou had to be a sort of sheath. And
she really looked pretty, with her clusters of dark, curly, New Orleans
hair, like grapes, and her quaint brown eyes that didn't quite match,
and that looked a bit sleepy and vague, and at the same time quick
as a squirrel's. She was slight and elegant, and a tiny bit rakish, and
30   somebody suggested she might be on the movies.

Nevertheless, they were in the society columns next morning—*two
new and striking figures in the Row this morning were Lady Henry
Carrington and her mother Mrs Witt* etc: And Mrs Witt liked it, let
her say what she might. So did Lou. Lou liked it immensely. She
35   simply luxuriated in the sun of publicity.

"Rico dear, you must get a horse."

The tone was soft and southern and drawling, but the overtone had
a decisive finality. In vain Rico squirmed—he had a way of writhing
and squirming which perhaps he had caught at Oxford. In vain he
40   protested that he couldn't ride, and that he didn't care for riding. He

got quite angry, and his handsome arched nose tilted and his upper lip lifted from his teeth, like a dog that is going to bite. Yet daren't quite bite. And that was Rico. He daren't quite bite. Not that he was really afraid of the others. He was afraid of himself, once he let himself go. He might rip up in an eruption of life-long anger all this pretty-pretty picture of a charming young wife and a delightful little home and a fascinating success as a painter of fashionable, and at the same time "great" portraits: with colour, wonderful colour, and at the same time, form, marvellous form. He had composed this little *tableau vivant* with great effort. He didn't want to erupt like some suddenly wicked horse—Rico was really more like a horse than a dog, a horse that might go nasty any moment. For the time, he was good, very good, dangerously good.

"Why, Rico dear, I thought you used to ride so much, in Australia, when you were young? Didn't you tell me all about it, hm?"—and as she ended on that slow, singing *hm?*, which acted on him like an irritant and a drug, he knew he was beaten.

Lou kept the sorrel mare in a mews* just behind the house in Westminster, and she was always slipping round to the stables. She had a funny little nostalgia for the place: something that really surprised her. She had never had the faintest notion that she cared for horses and stables and grooms. But she did. She was fascinated. Perhaps it was her childhood's Texas associations come back. Whatever it was, her life with Rico in the elegant little house, and all her social engagements seemed like a dream, the substantial reality of which was those mews in Westminster, her sorrel mare, the owner of the mews, Mr Saintsbury, and the grooms he employed. Mr Saintsbury was a horsey elderly man like an old maid, and he loved the sound of titles.

"Lady Carrington!—well I never! You've come to us for a bit of company again, I see. I don't know whatever we shall do if you go away, we shall be that lonely!" and he flashed his old-maid's smile at her. "No matter how grey the morning, your Ladyship* would make a beam of sunshine. Poppy* is all right, I think..."

Poppy was the sorrel mare with the no white feet and the startled eye, and she was all right. And Mr Saintsbury was smiling with his old-maid's mouth, and showing all his teeth.

"Come across with me, Lady Carrington, and look at a new horse just up from the country? I think he's worth a look, and I believe you have a moment to spare, your Ladyship."

Her Ladyship had too many moments to spare. She followed the sprightly, elderly, cleanshaven man across the yard to a loose box, and waited while he opened the door.

5 In the inner dark she saw a handsome bay horse with his clean ears pricked like daggers from his naked head as he swung handsomely round to stare at the open doorway. He had big, black, brilliant eyes, with a sharp questioning glint, and that air of tense, alert quietness which betrays an animal that can be dangerous.

"Is he quiet?" Lou asked.

10 "Why—yes—my Lady! He's quiet, with those that know how to handle him. *Cup! my boy! Cup my beauty! Cup then! St. Mawr!*"*

Loquacious even with the animals, he went softly forward and laid his hand on the horse's shoulder, soft and quiet as a fly settling. Lou saw the brilliant skin of the horse crinkle a little in apprehensive
15 anticipation, like the shadow of the descending hand on a bright red-gold liquid. But then the animal relaxed again.

"Quiet with those that know how to handle him, and a bit of a ruffian with those that don't. Isn't that the ticket,* eh, St. Mawr?"

"What is his name?" Lou asked.

20 The man repeated it, with a slight Welsh twist—"He's from the Welsh borders, belonging to a Welsh gentleman, Mr Griffith Edwards. But they're wanting to sell him."

"How old is he?" asked Lou.

"About seven years—seven years and five months," said Mr
25 Saintsbury, dropping his voice as if it were a secret.

"Could one ride him in the Park—"

"Well—yes! I should say a gentleman who knew how to handle him could ride him very well and make a very handsome figure in the Park—"

30 Lou at once decided that this handsome figure should be Rico's. For she was already half in love with St. Mawr. He was of such a lovely red-gold colour, and a dark, invisible fire seemed to come out of him. But in his big black eyes there was a lurking afterthought. Something told her that the horse was not quite happy: that somewhere deep in
35 his animal consciousness lived a dangerous, half-revealed resentment, a diffused sense of hostility. She realised that he was sensitive, in spite of his flaming, healthy strength, and nervous with a touchy uneasiness that might make him vindictive.

"Has he got any tricks?" she asked.

40 "Not that I know of, my Lady: not tricks exactly. But he's one of

these temperamental creatures, as they say. Though *I* say, every horse is temperamental, when you come down to it.—But this one, it is as if he was a trifle raw somewhere. Touch this raw spot, and there's no answering for him."

"Where is he raw?" asked Lou, somewhat mystified. She thought he might really have some physical sore.

"Why, that's hard to say, my Lady. If he was a human being, you'd say something had gone wrong in his life. But with a horse, it's not that, exactly. A high-bred animal like St. Mawr needs understanding, and I don't know as anybody has quite got the hang of him. I confess I haven't myself. But I do realise that he is a special animal and needs a special sort of touch, and I'm willing he should have it, did I but know exactly what it is."

She looked at the glowing bay horse, that stood there with his ears back, his face averted, but attending as if he were some lightning conductor. He was a stallion. When she realised this, she became more afraid of him.

"Why does Mr Griffith Edwards want to sell him?" she asked.

"Well—my Lady—They raised him for stud purposes—but he didn't answer. There are horses like that: don't seem to fancy the mares, for some reason.—Well anyway, they couldn't keep him for the stud. And as you see, he's a powerful, beautiful hackney, clean as a whistle, and eaten up with his own power. But there's no putting him between the shafts. He won't stand it. He's a fine saddle-horse, beautiful action, and lovely to ride.—But he's got to be handled, and there you are."

Lou felt there was something behind the man's reticence.

"Has he ever made a break?" she asked, apprehensive.

"Made a break?" replied the man. "Well, if I must admit it, he's had two accidents. Mr Griffith Edwards' son rode him a bit wild, away there in the forest of Dean, and the young fellow had his skull smashed in, against a low oak bough. Last Autumn, that was. And some time back, he crushed a groom against the side of the stall—injured him fatally.—But they were both accidents, my Lady. Things will happen."

The man spoke in a melancholy, fatalistic way. The horse, with his ears laid back, seemed to be listening tensely, his face averted. He looked like something finely bred and passionate, that has been judged and condemned.

"May I say *how do you do?*" she said to the horse, drawing a little

nearer in her white, summery dress, and lifting her hand, that glittered
with emeralds and diamonds.

He drifted away from her, as if some wind blew him. Then he ducked
his head, and looked sideways at her, from his black, full eye.

5   "I think I'm all right," she said, edging nearer, while he watched
her.

She laid her hand on his side, and gently stroked him. Then she
stroked his shoulder, and then the hard, tense arch of his neck. And
she was startled to feel the vivid heat of his life come through to her,
10   through the lacquer of red-gold gloss. So slippery with vivid, hot life!

She paused, as if thinking, while her hand rested on the horse's
sun-arched neck. Dimly, in her weary young-woman's soul, an ancient
understanding seemed to flood in.

She wanted to buy St. Mawr.

15   "I think," she said to Saintsbury, "if I can, I will buy him."

The man looked at her long and shrewdly.

"Well my Lady," he said at last. "There shall be nothing kept
from you. But what would your Ladyship do with him, if I may make
so bold?"

20   "I don't know," she replied, vaguely. "I might take him to
America."

The man paused once more, then said:

"They say it's been the making of some horses, to take them over
the water, to Australia or such places. It might repay you—you never
25   know."

She wanted to buy St. Mawr. She wanted him to belong to her. For
some reason the sight of him, his power, his alive, alert intensity, his
unyieldingness, made her want to cry.

She never did cry: except sometimes with vexation, or to get her
30   own way. As far as weeping went, her heart felt as dry as a Christmas
walnut.* What was the good of tears, anyhow? You had to keep on
holding on, in this life, never give way, and never give in. Tears only
left one weakened and ragged.

But now, as if that mysterious fire of the horse's body had split some
35   rock in her, she went home and hid herself in her room, and just cried.
The wild, brilliant, alert head of St. Mawr seemed to look at her out
of another world. It was as if she had had a vision, as if the walls of
her own world had suddenly melted away, leaving her in a great
darkness, in the midst of which the large, brilliant eyes of that horse
40   looked at her with demonish question, while his naked ears stood up

like daggers from the naked lines of his inhuman head, and his great
body glowed red with power.*

What was it? Almost like a god looking at her terribly out of the
everlasting dark, she had felt the eyes of that horse; great, glowing,
fearsome eyes, arched with a question, and containing a white blade 5
of light like a threat. What was his non-human question, and his
uncanny threat? She didn't know. He was some splendid demon, and
she must worship him.

She hid herself away from Rico. She could not bear the triviality
and superficiality of her human relationships. Looming like some god 10
out of the darkness was the head of that horse, with the wide, terrible,
questioning eyes. And she felt that it forbade her to be her ordinary,
commonplace self. It forbade her to be just Rico's wife, young Lady
Carrington, and all that.

It haunted her, the horse. It had looked at her as she had never been 15
looked at before: terrible, gleaming, questioning eyes arching out of
darkness, and backed by all the fire of that great ruddy body. What
did it mean, and what ban did it put upon her? She felt it put a ban
on her heart: wielded some uncanny authority over her, that she dared
not, could not understand. 20

No matter where she was, what she was doing, at the back of her
consciousness loomed a great, over-aweing figure out of a dark
background: St. Mawr, looking at her without really seeing her, yet
gleaming a question at her, from his wide terrible eyes, and gleaming
a sort of menace, doom. Master of doom, he seemed to be! 25

"You are thinking about something, Lou dear!" Rico said to her
that evening.

He was so quick and sensitive to detect her moods—so exciting in
this respect. And his big slightly prominent blue eyes, with the whites
a little bloodshot, glanced at her quickly, with searching, and anxiety, 30
and a touch of fear. As if his conscience were always uneasy.—He
too was rather like a horse—but forever quivering with a sort of cold,
dangerous mistrust, which he covered with anxious love.

At the middle of his eyes was a central powerlessness, that left him
anxious. It used to touch her to pity, that central look of powerlessness 35
in him. But now, since she had seen the full, dark, passionate blaze
of power and of different life, in the eyes of the thwarted horse, the
anxious powerlessness of the man drove her mad. Rico was so handsome,
and he was so self-controlled, he had a gallant sort of kindness and a
real worldly shrewdness. One had to admire him: at least *she* had to. 40

But after all, and after all, it was a bluff, an attitude. He kept it all working in himself, deliberately. It was an attitude. She read psychologists who said that everything was an attitude. Even the best of everything.—But now she realised that, with men and women, everything is an attitude only when something else is lacking. Something is lacking and they are thrown back on their own devices. That black fiery flow in the eyes of the horse was not "attitude." It was something much more terrifying, and real, the only thing that was real. Gushing from the darkness in menace and question, and blazing out in the splendid body of the horse.

"Was I thinking about something?" she replied, in her slow, amused, casual fashion. As if everything was so casual and easy to her. And so it was, from the hard, polished side of herself. But that wasn't the whole story.

"I think you were, Loulina. May we offer the penny?"*

"Don't trouble," she said. "I was thinking, if I was thinking of anything, about a bay horse called St. Mawr."—Her secret *almost* crept into her eyes.

"The name is awfully attractive," he said with a laugh.

"Not so attractive as the creature himself. I'm going to buy him."

"Not really!" he said. "But why?"

"He *is* so attractive. I'm going to buy him for you."

"For *me*! *Darling*! how you do take me for granted. He may not be in the least attractive to me. As you know, I have hardly any feeling for horses at all.—Besides, how much does he cost?"

"That I don't know, Rico dear. But I'm sure you'll love him, for my sake."—She felt, now, she was merely playing for her own ends.

"Lou dearest, *don't* spend a fortune on a horse for me, which I *don't* want. Honestly, I prefer a car."

"Won't you ride with me in the Park, Rico?"

"Honestly, dear Lou, I don't want to."

"Why not, dear boy? You'd look so beautiful. I wish you would.— And anyhow, come with me to look at St. Mawr."

Rico was divided. He had a certain uneasy feeling about horses. At the same time, he *would* like to cut a handsome figure in the Park.

They went across to the mews. A little Welsh groom was watering the brilliant horse.

"Yes dear, he certainly *is* beautiful: such a marvellous colour! Almost orange! But rather large, I should say, to ride in the Park."

"No, for you he's perfect. You are so tall."

"He'd be marvellous in a composition. That colour!"

And all Rico could do was to gaze with the artist's eye at the horse, with a glance at the groom.

"Don't you think the man is rather fascinating too?" he said, nursing his chin artistically and penetratingly.

The groom, Lewis, was a little, quick, rather bow-legged, loosely-built fellow of indeterminate age, with a mop of black hair and a little black beard. He was grooming the brilliant St. Mawr, out in the open. The horse was really glorious: like a marigold, with a pure golden sheen, a shimmer of green-gold lacquer, upon a burning red-orange. There on the shoulder you saw the yellow lacquer glisten. Lewis, a little scrub of a fellow, worked absorbedly, unheedingly at the horse, with an absorption that was almost ritualistic. He seemed the attendant shadow of the ruddy animal.

"He goes with the horse," said Lou. "If we buy St. Mawr we get the man thrown in."

"They'd be *so* amusing to paint: such an extraordinary contrast! But darling, I *hope* you won't insist on buying the horse. It's so frightfully expensive."

"Mother will help me.—You'd look so well on him, Rico."

"If ever I dared take the liberty of getting on his back—!"

"Why not?" She went quickly across the cobbled yard.

"Good morning Lewis. How is St. Mawr?"

Lewis straightened himself and looked at her from under the falling mop of his black hair.

"All right," he said.

He peered straight at her from under his overhanging black hair. He had pale grey eyes, that looked phosphorescent, and suggested the eyes of a wild cat peering intent from under the darkness of some bush where it lies unseen. Lou, with her brown, unmatched, oddly perplexed eyes, felt herself found out.—"He's a common little fellow," she thought to herself. "But he knows a woman and a horse, at sight."—Aloud she said, in her southern drawl:

"How do you think he'd be with Sir Henry?"

Lewis turned his remote, coldly watchful eyes on the young baronet. Rico was tall and handsome and balanced on his hips. His face was long and well-defined, and with the hair taken straight back from the brow. It seemed as well-made as his clothing, and as perpetually presentable. You could not imagine his face dirty, or scrubby and unshaven, or bearded, or even moustached. It was perfectly prepared

for social purposes. If his head had been cut off, like John the Baptist's, it would have been a thing complete in itself, would not have missed the body in the least. The body was perfectly tailored. The head was one of the famous "talking heads" of modern youth, with eyebrows
5 a trifle Mephistophelian, large blue eyes a trifle bold, and curved mouth thrilling to death to kiss.

Lewis, the groom, staring from between his bush of hair and his beard, watched like an animal from the underbrush. And Rico was still sufficiently a colonial to be uneasily aware of the underbrush, uneasy
10 under the watchfulness of the pale grey eyes, and uneasy in that man-to-man exposure which is characteristic of the democratic colonies and of America. He knew he must ultimately be judged on his merits as a man, alone without a background: an ungarnished colonial.

This lack of background, this defenceless man-to-man business
15 which left him at the mercy of every servant, was bad for his nerves. For he was *also* an artist. He bore up against it in a kind of desperation, and was easily moved to rancorous resentment. At the same time he was free of the Englishman's water-tight *suffisance.** He really was aware that he would have to hold his own all alone, thrown alone on
20 his own defences in the universe. The extreme democracy of the Colonies had taught him this.

And this, the little aboriginal Lewis recognised in him. He recognised also Rico's curious hollow misgiving, fear of some deficiency in himself, beneath all his handsome, young-hero appearance.
25 "He'd be all right with anybody as would meet him half way," said Lewis, in the quick Welsh manner of speech, impersonal.

"You hear, Rico!" said Lou in her sing-song, turning to her husband.

"Perfectly, darling!"
30 "Would you be willing to meet St. Mawr half way, hmm?"

"All the way, darling! Mahomet would go *all* the way, to that mountain.* Who would dare do otherwise?"

He spoke with a laughing, yet piqued sarcasm.

"Why, I think St. Mawr would understand perfectly," she said in
35 the soft voice of a woman haunted by love. And she went and laid her hand on the slippery, life-smooth shoulder of the horse. He, with his strange equine head lowered, its exquisite fine lines reaching a little snake-like forward, and his ears a little back, was watching her sideways, from the corner of his eye. He was in a state of absolute
40 mistrust, like a cat crouching to spring.

"St. Mawr!" she said. "St. Mawr! What is the matter? Surely you and I are all right!"

And she spoke softly, dreamily stroked the animal's neck. She could feel a response gradually coming from him. But he would not lift up his head. And when Rico suddenly moved nearer, he sprang with a 5 sudden jerk backwards, as if lightning exploded in his four hoofs. The groom spoke a few low words in Welsh. Lou, frightened, stood with lifted hand arrested. She had been going to stroke him.

"Why did he do that?" she said.

"They gave him a beating once or twice," said the groom in a 10 neutral voice, "and he doesn't forget."

She could hear a neutral sort of judgement in Lewis' voice. And she thought of the "raw spot."

Not any raw spot at all. A battle between two worlds. She realised that St. Mawr drew his hot breaths in another world from Rico's, from 15 our world. Perhaps the old Greek horses had lived in St. Mawr's world. And the old Greek heroes, even Hippolytus,* had known it.

With their strangely naked equine heads, and something of a snake in their way of looking round, and lifting their sensitive, dangerous muzzles, they moved in a prehistoric twilight where all things loomed 20 phantasmagoric, all on one plane, sudden presences suddenly jutting out of the matrix. It was another world, an older, heavily potent world. And in this world the horse was swift and fierce and supreme, undominated and unsurpassed.—"Meet him half way," Lewis said. But half way across from our human world to that terrific equine 25 twilight was not a small step. It was a step, she knew, that Rico could never take. She knew it. But she was prepared to sacrifice Rico.

St. Mawr was bought, and Lewis was hired along with him. At first, Lewis rode him behind Lou, in the Row, to get him going. He behaved perfectly. 30

Phoenix, the half-Indian, was very jealous when he saw the black-bearded Welsh groom on St. Mawr.

"What horse you got there?" he asked, looking at the other man with the curious unseeing stare in his hard, Navajo eyes, in which the Indian glint moved like a spark upon a dark chaos. In Phoenix's high- 35 boned face there was all the race-misery of the dispossessed Indian, with an added blankness left by shell-shock. But at the same time, there was that unyielding, save to death, which is characteristic of his tribe; his mother's tribe. Difficult to say what subtle thread bound him to the Navajo, and made his destiny a Red Man's destiny still. 40

They were a curious pair of grooms, following the correct, and yet extraordinary, pair of American mistresses. Mrs Witt and Phoenix both rode with long stirrups and straight leg, sitting close to the saddle, without posting.* Phoenix looked as if he and the horse were all one piece, he never seemed to rise in the saddle at all, neither trotting nor galloping, but sat like a man riding bareback. And all the time he stared around, at the riders in the Row, at the people grouped outside the rail, chatting, at the children walking with their nurses, as if he were looking at a mirage, in whose actuality he never believed for a moment. London was all a sort of dark mirage to him. His wide, nervous-looking brown eyes, with a smallish brown pupil that showed the white all round, seemed to be focussed on the far distance, as if he could not see things too near. He was watching the pale deserts of Arizona shimmer with moving light, the long mirage of a shallow lake ripple, the great pallid concave of earth and sky expanding with interchanged light. And a horse-shape loom large and portentous in the mirage, like some pre-historic beast.

That was real to him: the phantasm of Arizona. But this London was something his eye passed over, as a false mirage.

He looked too smart in his well-tailored groom's clothes, so smart, he might have been one of the satirised new-rich. Perhaps it was a sort of half-breed physical assertion that came through his clothing, the savage's physical assertion of himself. Anyhow, he looked "common," rather horsey and loud.

Except his face. In the golden suavity of his high-boned Indian face, that was hairless, with hardly any eyebrows, there was a blank, lost look that was almost touching. The same startled blank look was in his eyes. But in the smallish dark pupils the dagger-point of light still gleamed unbroken.

He was a good groom, watchful, quick, and on the spot in an instant, if anything went wrong. He had a curious quiet power over the horses, unemotional, unsympathetic, but silently potent. In the same way, watching the traffic of Piccadilly with his blank, glinting eye, he would calculate everything instinctively, as if it were an enemy, and pilot Mrs Witt by the strength of his silent will. He threw around her the tense watchfulness of her own America, and made her feel at home.

"Phoenix," she said, turning abruptly in her saddle as they walked the horses past the sheltering policeman at Hyde Park Corner, "I can't tell you how glad I am to have something a hundred per-cent American at the back of me, when I go through these gates."

She looked at him from dangerous grey eyes as if she meant it indeed, in vindictive earnest. A ghost of a smile went up to his high cheek-bones, but he did not answer.

"Why mother?" said Lou, sing-song. "It feels to me so friendly—!"

"Yes Louise, it does. *So* friendly! That's why I mistrust it so entirely—"

And she set off at a canter up the Row, under the green trees, her face like the face of Medusa* at fifty, a weapon in itself. She stared at everything and everybody, with that stare of cold dynamite waiting to explode them all. Lou posted trotting at her side, graceful and elegant, and faintly amused. Behind came Phoenix, like a shadow, with his yellowish, high-boned face still looking sick. And at his side, on the big brilliant bay horse, the smallish, black-bearded Welshman.

Between Phoenix and Lewis there was a latent, but unspoken and wary sympathy. Phoenix was terribly impressed by St. Mawr, he could not leave off staring at him. And Lewis rode the brilliant, handsome-moving stallion so very quietly, like an insinuation.

Of the two men, Lewis looked the darker, with his black beard coming up to his thick black eyebrows. He was swarthy, with a rather short nose, and the uncanny pale-grey eyes that watched everything and cared about nothing. He cared about nothing in the world, except, at the present, St. Mawr. People did not matter to him. He rode his horse and watched the world from the vantage ground of St. Mawr, with a final indifference.

"You been with that horse long?" asked Phoenix.

"Since he was born."

Phoenix watched the action of St. Mawr as they went. The bay moved proud and springy, but with perfect good sense, among the stream of riders. It was a beautiful June morning, the leaves overhead were thick and green, there came the first whiff of lime-tree scent. To Phoenix, however, the city was a sort of nightmare mirage, and to Lewis, it was a sort of prison. The presence of people he felt as a prison around him.

Mrs Witt and Lou were turning, at the end of the Row, bowing to some acquaintances. The grooms pulled aside. Mrs Witt looked at Lewis with a cold eye.

"It seems an extraordinary thing to me, Louise," she said, "to see a groom with a beard."

"It isn't usual, mother," said Lou. "Do you mind?"

"Not at all. At least, I think I don't. I get very tired of modern bare-faced young men, *very*! The clean, pure boy, don't you know! Doesn't it make you tired?—No, I think a groom with a beard is quite attractive."

She gazed into the crowd defiantly, perching her finely shod toe with
5 warlike firmness on the stirrup-iron. Then suddenly she reined in, and turned her horse towards the grooms.

"Lewis!" she said. "I want to ask you a question. Supposing, now, that Lady Carrington wanted you to shave off that beard, what should you say?"
10 Lewis instinctively put up his hand to the said beard.

"They've wanted me to shave it off, Mam," he said. "But I've never done it."

"But why? Tell me why?"

"It's part of me, Mam."
15 Mrs Witt pulled on again.

"Isn't that extraordinary, Louise?" she said. "Don't you like the way he says *Mam*? It sounds so impossible to me. Could any woman think of herself as Mam? Never!—Since Queen Victoria. But, do you know it hadn't occurred to me that a man's beard was really part of
20 him. It always seemed to me that men wore their beards, like they wear their neckties, for show. I shall always remember Lewis for saying his beard was part of him. Isn't it curious, the way he rides? He seems to sink himself in the horse. When I speak to him, I'm not sure whether I'm speaking to a man or to a horse."
25 A few days later, Rico himself appeared on St. Mawr, for the morning ride. He rode self-consciously, as he did everything, and he was just a little nervous. But his mother-in-law was benevolent. She made him ride between her and Lou, like three ships slowly sailing abreast.

And that very day, who should come driving in an open carriage
30 through the Park, but the Queen Mother! Dear old Queen Alexandra,* there was a flutter everywhere. And she bowed expressly to Rico, mistaking him, no doubt, for somebody else.

"Do you know," said Rico as they sat at lunch, he and Lou and Mrs Witt, in Mrs Witt's sitting-room in the dark, quiet hotel in
35 Mayfair; "I really like riding St. Mawr *so* much. He really is a noble animal.—If ever I am made a Lord—which heaven forbid!—I shall be Lord St. Mawr."

"You mean," said Mrs Witt, "his real lordship would be the horse?"
40 "Very possible, I admit," said Rico, with a curl of his long upper lip.

"Don't you think mother," said Lou, "there *is* something quite noble about St. Mawr? He strikes me as the first noble thing I have ever seen."

"Certainly I've not seen any *man* that could compare with him. Because these English noblemen—well! I'd rather look at a negro Pullman-boy, if I was looking for what *I* call nobility."

Poor Rico was getting crosser and crosser. There was a devil in Mrs Witt. She had a hard, bright devil inside her, that she seemed to be able to let loose at will.

She let it loose the next day, when Rico and Lou joined her in the Row. She was silent but deadly with the horses, balking them in every way. She suddenly crowded over against the rail, in front of St. Mawr, so that the stallion had to rear, to pull himself up. Then, having a clear track, she suddenly set off at a gallop, like an explosion, and the stallion, all on edge, set off after her.

It seemed as if the whole Park, that morning, were in a state of nervous tension. Perhaps there was thunder in the air. But St. Mawr kept on dancing and pulling at the bit, and wheeling sideways up against the railing, to the terror of the children and the onlookers, who squealed and jumped back suddenly, sending the nerves of the stallion into a rush like rockets. He reared and fought as Rico pulled him round.

Then he went on: dancing, pulling, springily progressing sideways, possessed with all the demons of perversity. Poor Rico's face grew longer and angrier. A fury rose in him, which he could hardly control. He hated his horse, and viciously tried to force him to a quiet, straight trot. Up went St. Mawr on his hind legs, to the terror of the Row. He got the bit in his teeth, and began to fight.

But Phoenix, cleverly, was in front of him.

"You get off, Rico!" called Mrs Witt's voice, with all the calm of her wicked exultance.

And almost before he knew what he was doing, Rico had sprung lightly to the ground, and was hanging on to the bridle of the rearing stallion.

Phoenix also lightly jumped down, and ran to St. Mawr, handing his bridle to Rico. Then began a dancing and a splashing, a rearing and a plunging. St. Mawr was being wicked. But Phoenix, the indifference of conflict in his face, sat tight and immovable, without any emotion, only the heaviness of his impersonal will settling down like a weight, all the time, on the horse. There was, perhaps, a curious barbaric exultance in bare, dark will, devoid of emotion or personal feeling.

So they had a little display in the Row for almost five minutes, the brilliant horse rearing and fighting. Rico, with a stiff long face, scrambled on to Phoenix's horse, and withdrew to a safe distance. Policemen came, and an officious mounted police rode up to save the situation. But it was obvious that Phoenix, detached and apparently unconcerned, but barbarically potent in his will, would bring the horse to order.

Which he did, and rode the creature home. Rico was requested not to ride St. Mawr in the Row any more, as the stallion was dangerous to public safety. The authorities knew all about him.

Where ended the first fiasco of St. Mawr.

"We didn't get on very well with his lordship this morning," said Mrs Witt triumphantly.

"No, he didn't like his company *at all!*" Rico snarled back.

He wanted Lou to sell the horse again.

"I doubt if anyone would buy him, dear," she said. "He's a known character."

"Then make a gift of him—to your mother," said Rico with venom.

"Why to mother?" asked Lou innocently.

"She might be able to cope with him—or he with her!" The last phrase was deadly. Having delivered it, Rico departed.

Lou remained at a loss. She felt almost always a little bit dazed, as if she could not see clear nor feel clear. A curious deadness upon her, like the first touch of death. And through this cloud of numbness, or deadness, came all her muted experiences.

Why was it? She did not know. But she felt that in some way it came from a battle of wills. Her mother, Rico, herself, it was always an unspoken, unconscious battle of wills, which was gradually numbing and paralysing her. She knew Rico meant nothing but kindness by her. She knew her mother only wanted to watch over her. Yet always there was this tension of will, that was so numbing. As if at the depths of him, Rico were always angry, though he seemed so "happy" on top. And Mrs Witt was organically angry. So they were like a couple of bombs, timed to explode someday, but ticking on like two ordinary timepieces, in the meanwhile.

She had come definitely to realise this: that Rico's anger was wound up tight at the bottom of him, like a steel spring that kept his works going, while he himself was "charming," like a bomb-clock with Sevres paintings or Dresden figures on the outside. But his very charm was a sort of anger, and his love was a destruction in itself. He just couldn't help it.

And she? Perhaps she was a good deal the same herself. Wound up tight inside, and enjoying herself being "lovely." But wound up tight on some tension that, she realised now with wonder, was really a sort of anger. This, the main-spring that drove her on the round of "joys." She used really to enjoy the tension, and the *élan* it gave her. While she knew nothing about it. So long as she felt it really was life and happiness, this *élan*, this tension and excitement of "enjoying oneself."

Now suddenly she doubted the whole show. She attributed to it the curious numbness that was overcoming her, as if she couldn't feel any more.

She wanted to come unwound. She wanted to escape this battle of wills.

Only St. Mawr gave her some hint of the possibility. He was so powerful, and so dangerous. But in his dark eye, that looked, with its cloudy brown pupil, a cloud within a dark fire, like a world beyond our world, there was a dark vitality glowing, and within the fire, another sort of wisdom. She felt sure of it: even when he put his ears back, and bared his teeth, and his great eyes came bolting out of his naked horse's head, and she saw demons upon demons in the chaos of his horrid eyes.

Why did he seem to her like some living background, into which she wanted to retreat? When he reared his head and neighed from his deep chest, like deep wind-bells resounding, she seemed to hear the echoes of another, darker, more spacious, more dangerous, more splendid world than ours, that was beyond her. And there she wanted to go.

She kept it utterly a secret, to herself. Because Rico would just have lifted his long upper lip, in his bare face, in a condescending sort of "understanding." And her mother would, as usual, have suspected her of side-stepping. People, all the people she knew, seemed so entirely contained within their cardboard lets-be-happy world. Their wills were fixed like machines on happiness, or fun, or the-best-ever. This ghastly cheery-o! touch, that made all her blood go numb.

Since she had really seen St. Mawr looming fiery and terrible in an outer darkness, she could not believe the world she lived in. She could not believe it was actually happening, when she was dancing in the afternoon at Claridge's, or in the evening at the Carlton,* sliding about with some suave young man who wasn't like a man at all to her. Or

down in Sussex for the weekend with the Enderley's:—the talk, the
eating and drinking, the flirtation, the endless dancing: it all seemed
far more bodiless and, in a strange way, wraith-like, than any fairy
story. She seemed to be eating Barmecide food,* that had been
5 conjured up out of thin air, by the power of words. She seemed to
be talking to handsome young bare-faced unrealities, not men at all:
as she slid about with them, in the perpetual dance, they too seemed
to have been conjured up out of air, merely for this soaring, slithering
dance-business. And she could not believe that, when the lights went
10 out, they wouldn't melt back into thin air again, and complete
nonentity. The strange nonentity of it all! Everything just conjured
up, and nothing real. "*Isn't this the best ever!*" they would beamingly
assert, like the wraiths of enjoyment, without any genuine substance.
And she would beam back: "*Lots of fun!*"
15 She was thankful the season* was over, and everybody was leaving
London. She and Rico were due to go to Scotland, but not till August.
In the meantime they would go to her mother.
Mrs Witt had taken a cottage in Shropshire, on the Welsh border,
and had moved down there with Phoenix and her horses. The open,
20 heather-and-bilberry-covered hills were splendid for riding.
Rico consented to spend the month in Shropshire, because for near
neighbours Mrs Witt had the Manbys, at Corrabach Hall. The Manbys
were rich Australians returned to the old country and set up as Squires,
all in full blow. Rico had known them in Victoria: they were of good
25 family: and the girls made a great fuss of him.
So down went Lou and Rico, Lewis, Poppy and St. Mawr, to
Shrewsbury, then out into the country. Mrs Witt's "cottage" was a
tall red-brick Georgian house looking straight on to the churchyard,
and the dark, looming, big Church.*
30 "I never knew what a comfort it would be," said Mrs Witt, "to
have grave-stones under my drawing-room windows, and funerals for
lunch."
She really did take a strange pleasure in sitting in her panelled room,
that was painted grey, and watching the Dean or one of the curates*
35 officiating at the graveside, among a group of black country mourners
with black-bordered handkerchiefs luxuriantly in use.
"Mother!" said Lou. "I think it's gruesome!"
She had a room at the back, looking over the walled garden and
the stables. Nevertheless there was the *boom!* *boom!* of the passing-
40 bell, and the chiming and pealing on Sundays. The shadow of the

Church, indeed! A very audible shadow, making itself heard insistently.

The Dean was a big, burly, fat man with a pleasant manner. He was a gentleman, and a man of learning in his own line. But he let Mrs Witt know that he looked down on her just a trifle—as a parvenu American, a Yankee—though she never was a Yankee: and at the same time he had a sincere respect for her, as a rich woman. Yes, a sincere respect for her, as a rich woman.

Lou knew that every Englishman, especially of the upper classes, has a wholesome respect for riches. But then, who hasn't?

The Dean was more *impressed* by Mrs Witt than by little Lou. But to Lady Carrington he was charming: she was *almost* "one of us," you know. And he was very gracious to Rico: "your father's splendid colonial service."

Mrs Witt had now a new pantomime to amuse her: the Georgian house, her own pew in Church—it went with the old house: a village of thatched cottages—some of them with corrugated iron over the thatch: the cottage people, farm laborers and their families, with a few, very few outsiders: the wicked little group of cottagers down at Mile End, famous for ill-living. The Mile-Enders were all Allisons and Jephsons, and in-bred, the Dean said: result of working through the centuries at the Quarry, and living isolated there at Mile End.

Isolated! Imagine it! A mile and a half from the railway station, ten miles from Shrewsbury. Mrs Witt thought of Texas, and said:

"Yes they are *very* isolated, away down there!"

And the Dean never for a moment suspected sarcasm.

But there she had the whole thing staged complete for her: English village life. Even miners breaking in to shatter the rather stuffy, unwholesome harmony.—All the men touched their caps to her, all the women did a bit of a reverence,* the children stood aside for her, if she appeared in the Street.

They were all poor again: the laborers could no longer afford even a glass of beer in the evenings, since the Glorious war.

"Now I think that *is* terrible." said Mrs Witt. "Not to be able to get away from those stuffy, squalid, picturesque cottages for an hour in the evening, to drink a glass of beer."

"It's a pity, I do agree with you, Mrs Witt. But Mr Watson has organised a men's reading-room, where the men can smoke and play dominoes, and read if they wish."

"But that" said Mrs Witt, "is not the same as that cosy parlour in the *Moon and Stars.*"

"I quite agree," said the Dean. "It isn't."

Mrs Witt marched to the landlord of the *Moon and Stars*, and asked for a glass of cider.

"I want," she said, in her American accent, "these poor laborers to have their glass of beer in the evenings."

"They want it themselves," said Harvey.

"Then they must have it—"

The upshot was, she decided to supply one large barrel of beer per week and the landlord was to sell it to the laborers at a penny a glass.

"My own country has gone dry,"* she asserted. "But not because we can't *afford* it."

By the time Lou and Rico appeared, she was deep in. She actually interfered very little: the barrel of beer was her one public act. But she *did* know everybody by sight, already, and she *did* know everybody's circumstances. And she had attended one prayer-meeting, one mother's meeting, one sewing-bee, one "social," one Sunday School meeting, one Band of Hope meeting,* and one Sunday School treat. She ignored the poky little Wesleyan and Baptist chapels, and was true-blue episcopalian.

"How strange these picturesque old villages are, Louise!" she said, with a duskiness around her sharp, well-bred nose. "How *easy* it all seems, all on a definite pattern. And how false! And underneath, *how corrupt!*"

She gave that queer, triumphant leer from her grey eyes, and queer demonish wrinkles seemed to twitter on her face.

Lou shrank away. She was beginning to be afraid of her mother's insatiable curiosity, that always looked for the snake under the flowers. Or rather, for the maggots.

Always this same morbid interest in other people and their doings, their privacies, their dirty linen. Always this air of alertness for personal happenings, personalities, personalities, personalities. Always this subtle criticism and appraisal of other people, this analysis of other people's motives. If anatomy pre-supposes a corpse, then psychology pre-supposes a world of corpses. Personalities, which means personal criticism and analysis, pre-supposes a whole world-laboratory of human psyches waiting to be vivisected. If you cut a thing up, of course it will smell. Hence, nothing raises such an infernal stink, at last, as human psychology.

Mrs Witt was a pure psychologist, a fiendish psychologist. And Rico, in his way, was a psychologist too. But he had a formula. "Let's *know* the worst, dear! But let's look on the bright side, and believe the best."
"Isn't the Dean a priceless old darling!" said Rico at breakfast. And it had begun. Work had started in the psychic vivisection laboratory.

"Isn't he wonderful!" said Lou vaguely.

"So delightfully worldly!—*Some of us are not born to make money, dear boy. Luckily for us, we can marry it.*"—Rico made a priceless face.

"Is Mrs Vyner so rich?" asked Lou.

"She is, quite a wealthy woman—in coal," replied Mrs Witt. "But the Dean is surely worth his weight, even in gold.* And he's a massive figure. I can imagine there would be great satisfaction in having him for a husband."

"Why, mother?" asked Lou.

"Oh, such a presence! One of these old Englishmen, that nobody can put in their pocket. You can't imagine his wife asking him to thread her needle. Something after all so *robust*! So different from *young* Englishmen, who all seem to me like ladies, perfect ladies."

"*Somebody* has to keep up the tradition of the perfect lady," said Rico.

"I know it," said Mrs Witt. "And if the women won't do it, the young gentlemen take on the burden. They bear it very well."

It was in full swing, the cut and thrust. And poor Lou, who had reached the point of stupefaction in the game, felt she did not know what to do with herself.

Rico and Mrs Witt were deadly enemies, yet neither could keep clear of the other. It might have been they who were married to one another, their duel and their duet were so relentless.

But Rico immediately started the social round: first the Manbys: then motor twenty miles to luncheon at Lady Tewkesbury's: then young Mr Burns came flying down in his aeroplane from Chester: then they must motor to the sea, to Sir Edward Edwards' place, where there was a moonlight bathing party. Everything intensely thrilling, and so innerly wearisome, Lou felt.

But back of it all was St. Mawr, looming like a bonfire in the dark. He really was a tiresome horse to own. He worried the mares, if they were in the same paddock with him, always driving them round. And with any other horse he just fought with definite intent to kill. So he had to stay alone.

"That St. Mawr, he's a bad horse," said Phoenix.

"Maybe!" said Lewis.

"You don' like quiet horses?" said Phoenix.

"Most horses *is* quiet," said Lewis. "St. Mawr, he's different."

"Why don't he never get any foals?"

"Doesn't want to, I should think. Same as me."

"What good is a horse like that? Better shoot him, before he kill somebody."

"What good'll they get, shooting St. Mawr?" said Lewis.

"If he kills somebody!—" said Phoenix.

But there was no answer.

The two grooms both lived over the stables, and Lou, from her window, saw a good deal of them. They were two quiet men, yet she was very much aware of their presence, aware of Phoenix's rather high square shoulders and his fine, straight, vigorous black hair that tended to stand up assertively on his head, as he went quietly, drifting about his various jobs. He was not lazy, but he did everything with a sort of diffidence, as if from a distance, and handled his horses carefully, cautiously, and cleverly, but without sympathy. He seemed to be holding something back, all the time, unconsciously, as if in his very being there was some secret. But it was a secret of *will*. His quiet, reluctant movements, as if he never really wanted to do anything; his his long flat-stepping stride; the permanent challenge in his high cheek-bones, the Indian glint in his eyes, and his peculiar stare, watchful and yet unseeing, made him unpopular with the women servants.

Nevertheless, women had a certain fascination for him: he would stare at the pretty young maids with an intent blank stare, when they were not looking. Yet he was rather overbearing, domineering with them, and they resented him. It was evident to Lou that he looked upon himself as belonging to the master, not to the servant class. When he flirted with the maids, as he very often did, for he had a certain crude ostentatiousness, he seemed to let them feel that he despised them as inferiors, servants, while he admired their pretty charms, as fresh, country maids.

"I'm fair nervous of that Phoenix," said Fanny, the fair-haired maid. "He makes you feel what he'd do to you if he could."

"He'd better not try with me," said Mabel. "I'd scratch his cheeky eyes out. Cheek!—for it's nothing else! He's nobody—Common as they're made!"

"He makes you feel you was there for him to trample on," said Fanny.

"Mercy, you *are* soft! If anybody's that it's him. Oh my, Fanny, you've no right to let a fellow make you feel like *that*! Make *them* feel that *they're* dirt, for you to trample on: which they are!" 5

Fanny, however, being a shy little blonde thing, wasn't good at assuming the trampling rôle. She was definitely nervous of Phoenix. And he enjoyed it. An invisible smile seemed to creep up his cheek-bones, and the glint moved in his eyes as he teased her. He tormented her by his very presence, as he knew. 10

He would come silently up when she was busy, and stand behind her perfectly still, so that she was unaware of his presence. Then, silently, he would *make* her aware. Till she glanced nervously round, and with a scream, saw him.

One day Lou watched this little play. Fanny had been picking over 15 a bowl of black currants, sitting on the bench under the maple tree in a corner of the yard. She didn't look round till she had picked up her bowl to go to the kitchen. Then there was a scream and a crash.

When Lou came out Phoenix was crouching down silently gathering up the currants, which the little maid, scarlet and trembling, was 20 collecting into another bowl. Phoenix seemed to be smiling down his back.

"Phoenix!" said Lou. "I wish you wouldn't startle Fanny!"

He looked up, and she saw the glint of ridicule in his eyes.

"Who, me?" he said. 25

"Yes, you. You go up behind Fanny, to startle her. You're not to do it."

He slowly stood erect, and lapsed into his peculiar invisible silence. Only for a second his eyes glanced at Lou's, and then she saw the cold anger, the gleam of malevolence and contempt. He could not bear being 30 commanded, or reprimanded, by a woman.

Yet it was even worse with a man.

"What's that, Lou?" said Rico, appearing all handsome and in the picture,* in white flannels* with an apricot silk shirt.

"I'm telling Phoenix he's not to torment Fanny!" 35

"Oh!"—and Rico's voice immediately became his father's, the important government official's. "Certainly *not*! Most certainly *not*!" He looked at the scattered currants and the broken bowl. Fanny melted into tears.—"This, I suppose, is some of the results!—Now look here, Phoenix, you're to leave the maids strictly alone. I shall ask them 40 to report to me whenever, or *if* ever, you interfere with them. But I hope you *won't* interfere with them—in any way. You understand?"

As Rico became more and more Sir Henry and the Government Official, Lou's bones melted more and more into discomfort. Phoenix stood in his peculiar silence, the invisible smile on his cheek-bones.

"You understand what I'm saying to you?" Rico demanded, in intensified acid tones.

But Phoenix only stood there, as it were behind a cover of his own will, and looked back at Rico with a faint smile on his face and the glint moving in his eyes.

"Do you intend to answer?" Rico's upper lip lifted nastily.

"Mrs Witt is my boss," came from Phoenix.

The scarlet flew up Rico's throat and flushed his face, his eyes went glaucous. Then quickly his face turned yellow.

Lou looked at the two men: her husband, whose rages, over-controlled, were organically terrible: the half-breed, whose dark-coloured lips were widened in a faint smile of derision, but in whose eyes caution and hate were playing against one another. She realised that Phoenix would accept *her* reprimand, or her mother's, because he could despise the two of them as mere women. But Rico's bossiness aroused murder pure and simple.

She took her husband's arm.

"Come dear!" she said, in her half plaintive way. "I'm sure Phoenix understands. We all understand.—Go to the kitchen, Fanny, never mind the currants There are plenty more in the garden."

Rico was always thankful to be drawn quickly, submissively away from his own rage. He was afraid of it. He was afraid lest he should fly at the groom in some horrible fashion. The very thought horrified him. But in actuality he came very near to it.

He walked stiffly, feeling paralysed by his own fury. And those words, *Mrs Witt is my boss*, were like hot acid in his brain. An insult!

"By the way, Belle-Mère!"* he said when they joined Mrs Witt—she hated being called Belle-Mère, and once said: "If I'm the bell-mare, are you one of the colts?"—She also hated his voice of smothered fury—"I had to speak to Phoenix about persecuting the maids. He took the liberty of informing me that you were his boss, so perhaps you had better speak to him."

"I certainly will. I believe they're my maids, and nobody else's, so its my duty to look after them. Who was he persecuting?"

"I'm the responsible one, mother," said Lou———

Rico disappeared in a moment. He must get out: get away from the house. How? Something was wrong with the car. Yet he must get away, away. He would go over to Corrabach. He would ride St. Mawr. He had been talking about the horse, and Flora Manby was dying to see him. She had said: "Oh, I can't *wait* to see that marvellous horse of yours."   5
He would ride him over. It was only seven miles. He found Lou's maid Elena, and sent her to tell Lewis. Meanwhile, to soothe himself, he dressed himself most carefully in white riding-breeches and a shirt of purple silk crape, with a flowing black tie spotted red like a ladybird,   10
and black riding-boots. Then he took a *chic* little white hat with a black band.

St. Mawr was saddled and waiting, and Lewis had saddled a second horse.

"Thanks, Lewis, I'm going alone!" said Rico.   15

This was the first time he had ridden St. Mawr in the country, and he was nervous. But he was also in the hell of a smothered fury. All his careful dressing had not really soothed him. So his fury consumed his nervousness.

He mounted with a swing, blind and rough. St. Mawr reared.   20
"Stop that!" snarled Rico, and put him to the gate.

Once out in the village street, the horse went dancing sideways. He insisted on dancing at the sidewalk, to the exaggerated terror of the children. Rico, exasperated, pulled him across. But no, he wouldn't go down the centre of the village street. He began dancing and edging   25
on to the other sidewalk, so the foot-passengers fled into the shops in terror.

The devil was in him. He would turn down every turning where he was not meant to go. He reared with panic at a furniture van. He *insisted* on going down the wrong side of the road. Rico was riding him   30
with a martingale, and he could see the rolling, bloodshot eye.

"Damn you, *go*!" said Rico, giving him a dig with the spurs.

And away they went, down the high-road, in a thunderbolt. It was a hot day, with thunder threatening, so Rico was soon in a flame of heat. He held on tight, with fixed eyes, trying all the time to rein in   35
the horse. What he really was afraid of was that the brute would shy suddenly, as he galloped. Watching for this, he didn't care when they sailed past the turning to Corrabach.

St. Mawr flew on, in a sort of *élan*. Marvellous the power and life in the creature. There was really a great joy in the motion. If only   40

he wouldn't take the corners at a gallop, nearly swerving Rico off!
Luckily the road was clear. To ride to ride at this terrific gallop, on
into eternity!

After several miles, the horse slowed down, and Rico managed to
pull him into a lane that might lead to Corrabach. When all was said
and done, it was a wonderful ride. St. Mawr could go like the wind,
but with that luxurious heavy ripple of life which is like nothing else
on earth. It seemed to carry one at once into another world, away from
the life of the nerves.

So Rico arrived after all something of a conqueror, at Corrabach.
To be sure, he was perspiring, and so was his horse. But he was a hero
from another, heroic world.

"Oh, such a hot ride!" he said, as he walked on to the lawn at
Corrabach Hall. "Between the sun and the horse, really!—between
two fires!"

"Don't you trouble, you're looking dandy, a bit hot and flushed-
like!" said Flora Manby. "Let's go and see your horse."

And her exclamation was: "Oh, he's *lovely*! He's *fine*! I'd love to
try him once—"

Rico decided to accept the invitation to stay overnight at Corrabach.
Usually he was very careful, and refused to stay, unless Lou was with
him. But they telephoned to the post office at Chomesbury, would Mr
Jones please send a message to Lady Carrington that Sir Henry was
staying the night at Corrabach Hall, but would be home next day. Mr
Jones received the request with unction, and said he would go over
himself to give the message to Lady Carrington.

Lady Carrington was in the walled garden. The peculiarity of Mrs
Witt's house was that, for grounds proper, it had the churchyard.

"I never thought, Louise, that one day I should have an old English
church-yard for my lawns and shrubbery and park, and funeral
mourners for my herds of deer. It's curious. For the first time in my
life, a funeral has become a real thing to me. I feel I could write a
book on them."

But Louise only felt intimidated.

At the back of the house was a flagged courtyard, with stables and
a maple tree in a corner, and big doors opening on to the village street.
But at the side was a walled garden, with fruit trees and currant bushes
and a great bed of rhubarb, and some tufts of flowers, peonies, pink
roses, sweet williams. Phoenix, who had a certain taste for gardening,
would be out there thinning the carrots or tying up the lettuce. He

was not lazy. Only he would not take work seriously, as a job. He would be quite amused, tying up lettuces, and would tie up head after head, quite prettily. Then, becoming bored, he would abandon his task, light a cigarette, and go and stand on the threshold of the big doors, in full view of the street, watching, and yet completely indifferent.

After Rico's departure on St. Mawr, Lou went into the garden. And there she saw Phoenix working in the onion bed. He was bending over, in his own silence, busy with nimble, amused fingers among the grassy young onions. She thought he had not seen her, so she went down another path, to where a swing bed hung under the apple trees. There she sat with a book and a bundle of magazines. But she did not read.

She was musing vaguely. Vaguely, she was glad that Rico was away for a while. Vaguely, she felt a sense of bitterness, of complete futility: the complete futility of her living. This left her drifting in a sea of utter chagrin. And Rico seemed to her the symbol of the futility. Vaguely, she was aware that something else existed, but she didn't know where it was or what it was.

In the distance she could see Phoenix's dark, rather tall-built head, with its black, fine, intensely-living hair tending to stand on end, like a brush with long, very fine black bristles. His hair, she thought, betrayed him as an animal of a different species. He was growing a little bored by weeding onions: that also she could tell. Soon he would want some other amusement.

Presently Lewis appeared. He was small, energetic, a little bit bow-legged, and he walked with a slight strut. He wore khaki riding-breeches, leather gaiters, and a blue shirt. And like Phoenix, he rarely had any cap or hat on his head. His thick black hair was parted at the side and brushed over heavily sideways, dropping on his forehead at the right. It was very long, a real mop, under which his eyebrows were dark and steady.

"Seen Lady Carrington?" he asked of Phoenix.

"Yes, she's sitting on that swing over there—she's been there quite a while."

The wretch—he had seen her from the very first!

Lewis came striding over, looking towards her with his pale grey eyes, from under his mop of hair.

"Mr Jones from the post office wants to see you, my Lady, with a message from Sir Henry."

Instantly alarm took possession of Lou's soul.

"Oh!—Does he want to see me personally?—What message? Is

anything wrong?—" And her voice trailed out over the last word, with a sort of anxious nonchalance.

"I don't think it's anything amiss," said Lewis reassuringly.

"Oh! You don't!" the relief came into her voice. The she looked at Lewis with a slight, winning smile in her unmatched eyes. "I'm so afraid of St. Mawr, you know." Her voice was soft and cajoling. Phoenix was listening in the distance.

"St. Mawr's all right, if you don't do nothing to him," Lewis replied.

"I'm sure he is!—But how is one to know when one is doing something to him—?—Tell Mr Jones to come here, please," she concluded, on a changed tone.

Mr Jones, a man of forty-five, thick-set, with a fresh complexion and rather foolish brown eyes, and a big brown moustache, came prancing down the path, smiling rather fatuously, and doffing his straw hat with a gorgeous bow the moment he saw Lou sitting in her slim white frock on the coloured swing bed under the trees with their hard green apples.

"Good morning Mr Jones!"

"Good morning Lady Carrington—If I may say so, what a picture you make—a beautiful picture—"

He beamed under his big brown moustache like the greatest lady-killer.

"Do I!—Did Sir Henry say he was all right?"

"He didn't *say* exactly, but I should expect he is all right———" and Mr Jones delivered his message, in the mayonnaise of his own unction.

"Thank you so much, Mr Jones. It's awfully good of you to come and tell me. Now I shan't worry about Sir Henry *at all*."

"It's a great pleasure to come and deliver a satisfactory message to Lady Carrington.—But it won't be kind to Sir Henry if you don't worry about him *at all* in his absence. We all enjoy being worried about by those we love—so long as there is nothing to worry about of course!—"

"Quite!" said Lou. "Now won't you take a glass of port and a biscuit—or a whisky and soda? And thank you ever so much."

"Thank *you*, my Lady.—I might drink a whisky and soda, since you are so good."

And he beamed fatuously.

"Let Mr Jones mix himself a whisky and soda, Lewis," said Lou.

"Heavens!" she thought, as the postmaster retreated a little
uncomfortably down the garden path, his bald spot passing in and out
of the sun, under the trees: "How ridiculous everything is, how
ridiculous, ridiculous!" Yet she didn't really dislike Mr Jones and his
interlude.   5

Phoenix was melting away out of the garden. He had to follow the fun.

"Phoenix!" Lou called. "Bring me a glass of water, will you? Or
send somebody with it."

He stood in the path looking round at her.

"All right!" he said.   10
And he turned away again.

She did not like being alone in the garden. She liked to have the
men working somewhere near. Curious how pleasant it was to sit there
in the garden when Phoenix was about, or Lewis. It made her feel she
could never be lonely or jumpy. But when Rico was there, she was   15
all aching nerve.

Phoenix came back with a glass of water, lemon juice, sugar, and
a small bottle of brandy. He knew Lou liked a spoonful of brandy in
her iced lemonade.

"How thoughtful of you Phoenix!" she said. "Did Mr Jones get   20
his whisky?"

"He was just getting it."

"That's right.—By the way, Phoenix, I wish you wouldn't get
mad, if Sir Henry speaks to you. He is *really* so kind."—

She looked up at the man. He stood there watching her in silence,   25
the invisible smile on this face, and the inscrutable Indian glint moving
in his eyes. What was he thinking? There was something passive and
almost submissive about him, but underneath this, an unyielding
resistance and cruelty: yes, even cruelty. She felt that, on top, he was
submissive and attentive, bringing her her lemonade as she liked it,   30
without being told: thinking for her quite subtly. But underneath,
there was an unchanging hatred. He submitted circumstantially, he
worked for a wage. And even circumstantially, he *liked* his mistress—*la
patrona*—and her daughter. But much deeper than any circumstance
or any circumstantial liking, was the categorical hatred upon which he   35
was founded, and with which he was powerless. His liking for Lou
and for Mrs Witt, his serving them and working for a wage, was all
side-tracking his own nature, which was grounded on hatred of their
very existence. But what was he to do? He had to live. Therefore he
had to serve, to work for a wage, and even to be faithful.   40

And yet *their* existence made his own existence negative. If he was to exist, positively, they would have to cease to exist. At the same time, a fatal sort of tolerance made him serve these women, and go on serving.

5   "Sir Henry is *so* kind to everybody," Lou insisted.

The half-breed met her eyes, and smiled uncomfortably.

"Yes, he's a kind man," he replied, as if sincerely.

"Then why do you mind, if he speaks to you?"

"I don't mind," said Phoenix glibly.

10   "But you do. Or else you wouldn't make him so angry."

"Was he angry?—I don't know," said Phoenix.

"He was very angry. And you *do* know."

"No I don't know if he's angry. I don't know," the fellow persisted. And there was a glib sort of satisfaction in his tone.

15   "That's awfully unkind of you, Phoenix," she said, growing offended in her turn.

"No, I don't know if he's angry. I don't want to make him angry. I don't know"—

He had taken on a tone of naive ignorance, which at once gratified 20 her pride as a woman, and deceived her.

"Well, you believe me when I tell you you *did* make him angry, don't you?"

"Yes, I believe when you tell me."

"And you promise me, won't you, not to do it again? It's *so* bad 25 for him—so bad for his nerves, and for his eyes. It makes them inflamed, and injures his eyesight. And you know, as an artist, it's terrible if anything happens to his eyesight—"

Phoenix was watching her closely, to take it in. He still was not good at understanding continuous, logical statement. Logical connection in 30 speech seemed to stupefy him, make him stupid. He understood in disconnected assertions of fact. But he had gathered what she said. "He gets mad at you. When he gets mad, it hurts his eyes. His eyes hurt him. He can't see, because his eyes hurt him. He want to paint a picture, he can't. He can't paint a picture, he can't see clear—"

35   Yes, he had understood. She saw he had understood. The bright glint of satisfaction moved in his eyes.

"So now promise me, won't you, you won't make him mad again: you won't make him angry?"

"No, I won't make him angry. I don't do anything to make him 40 angry," Phoenix answered, rather glibly.

"And you do understand, don't you? You do know how kind he is: how he'd do a good turn to anybody?"

"Yes, he's a kind man," said Phoenix.

"I'm so glad you realise.—There, that's luncheon! How nice it is to sit here in the garden, when everybody is nice to you! No, I can carry the tray, don't you bother."

But he took the tray from her hand, and followed her to the house. And as he walked behind her, he watched the slim white nape of her neck, beneath the clustering of her bobbed hair, something as a stoat watches a rabbit he is following.

In the afternoon Lou retreated once more to her place in the garden. There she lay, sitting with a bunch of pillows behind her, neither reading nor working, just musing. She had learned the new joy: to do absolutely nothing, but to lie and let the sunshine filter through the leaves, to see the bunch of red-hot-poker flowers pierce scarlet into the afternoon, beside the comparative neutrality of some fox gloves. The mere colour of hard red, like the big oriental poppies that had fallen, and these poker flowers, lingered in her consciousness like a communication.

Into this peaceful indolence, when even the big, dark-grey tower of the church beyond the wall and the yew-trees, was keeping its bells in silence, advanced Mrs Witt, in a broad panama hat and a white dress.

"Don't you want to ride, or do something, Louise?" she asked ominously.

"Don't you want to be peaceful, Mother?" retorted Louise.

"Yes—an *active* peace.—I can't *believe* that my daughter can be content to lie on a hammock and do *nothing*, not even read or improve her mind, the greater part of the day."

"Well, your daughter *is* content to do that. It's her greatest pleasure."

"I know it. I can see it. And it surprises me *very* much. When I was your age, I was never still. I had so much *go*— "

"'*Those maids thank God*
  Are 'neath the sod,
  And all their generation.'*—No but, mother, I only take life differently. Perhaps you used up that sort of *go*. I'm the harem type, mother: only I never want the men inside the lattice."

"Are you really my daughter?—Well! A woman never knows what will happen to her.—I'm an *American* woman, and I suppose I've got to remain one, no matter where I am.—What did you want, Lewis?"

The groom had approached down the path.

"If I am to saddle Poppy?" said Lewis.

"No, apparently *not!*" replied Mrs Witt. "Your mistress prefers the hammock to the saddle."

5 "Thank you, Lewis. What mother says is true this afternoon, at least." And she gave him a peculiar little cross-eyed smile.

"Who," said Mrs Witt to the man, "has been cutting at your hair?" There was a moment of silent resentment.

"I did it myself, Mam! Sir Henry said it was too long."

10 "He certainly spoke the truth.—But I believe there's a barber in the village on Saturdays—or you could ride over to Shrewsbury.—Just turn round, and let me look at the back. Is it the money?"

"No Mam. I don't like these fellows touching my head."

He spoke coldly, with a certain hostile reserve that at once piqued
15 Mrs Witt.

"Don't you really!" she said. "But it's quite *impossible* for you to go about as you are. It gives you a half-witted appearance. Go now into the yard, and get a chair and a dust-sheet. I'll cut your hair."

20 The man hesitated, hostile.

"Don't be afraid, I know how it's done. I've cut the hair of many a poor wounded boy in hospital: and shaved them too. *You've got such a touch, nurse!* Poor fellow, he was dying, though none of us knew it.—Those are the compliments I value, Louise.—Get that chair now,
25 and a dust-sheet. I'll borrow your hair-scissors from Elena, Louise."

Mrs Witt, happily on the war-path, was herself again. She didn't care for work, actual work. But she loved trimming. She loved arranging unnatural and pretty salads, devising new and piquant-looking ice-creams, having a turkey stuffed exactly as she knew a
30 stuffed turkey in Louisiana, with chestnuts and butter and stuff, or showing a servant how to turn waffles on a waffle-iron, or to bake a ham with brown sugar and cloves and a moistening of rum. She liked pruning rose-trees, or beginning to cut a yew hedge into shape. She liked ordering her own and Louise's shoes, with an exactitude and a
35 knowledge of shoe-making that sent the salesmen crazy. She was a demon in shoes. Reappearing from America, she would pounce on her daughter. "Louise, throw those shoes away. Give them to one of the maids."—"But mother, they are some of the best French shoes. I like them."—"Throw them away. A shoe has only two excuses for
40 existing: perfect comfort or perfect appearance. Those have neither.

I have brought you some shoes."—Yes, she had brought ten pairs of shoes from New York. She knew her daughter's foot as she knew her own.

So now she was in her element, looming behind Lewis as he sat in the middle of the yard swathed in a dust-sheet. She had on an overall and a pair of wash-leather gloves, and she poised a pair of long scissors like one of the fates.* In her big hat she looked curiously young, but with the youth of a by-gone generation. Her heavy-lidded, laconic grey eyes were alert, studying the groom's black mop of hair. Her eyebrows made thin, uptilting black arches on her brow. Her fresh skin was slightly powdered, and she was really handsome, in a bold, by-gone, eighteenth-century style. Some of the curious, adventurous stoicism of the eighteenth-century: and then a certain blatant American efficiency.

Lou, who had strayed into the yard to see, looked so much younger and so many thousand of years older than her mother, as she stood in her wisp-like diffidence, the clusters of grape-like bobbed hair* hanging beside her face, with its fresh colouring and its ancient weariness, her slightly squinting eyes, that were so disillusioned they were becoming faun-like.

"Not too short, mother, not too short!" she remonstrated, as Mrs Witt, with a terrific flourish of efficiency, darted at the man's black hair, and the thick flakes fell like black snow.

"Now Louise, I'm right in this job, please don't interfere.—Two things I hate to see: a man with his wool in his neck and ears and a bare-faced young man who looks as if he'd bought his face as well as his hair from a men's beauty-specialist."

And efficiently she bent down, clip—clip—clipping! while Lewis sat utterly immobile, with sunken head, in a sort of despair.

Phoenix stood against the stable door, with his restless, eternal cigarette. And in the kitchen doorway the maids appeared and fled, appeared and fled in delight. The old gardener, a fixture who went with the house, creaked in and stood with his legs apart, silent in intense condemnation.

"First time I ever see such a thing!" he muttered to himself, as he creaked on into the garden. He was a bad-tempered old soul, who thoroughly disapproved of the household, and would have given notice, but that he knew which side his bread was buttered: and there was butter unstinted on his bread, in Mrs Witt's kitchen.

Mrs Witt stood back to survey her handywork, holding those

terrifying shears with their beak erect. Lewis lifted his head and looked
stealthily round, like a creature in a trap.

"Keep still!" she said. "I haven't finished."

And she went for his front hair, with vigour, lifting up long layers
and snipping off the ends artistically: till at last he sat with a black
aureole upon the floor, and his ears standing out with curious new
alertness from the sides of his clean-clipped head.

"Stand up," she said, "and let me look."

He stood up, looking absurdly young, with the hair all cut away from
his neck and ears, left thick only on top. She surveyed her work with
satisfaction.

"You look so much younger," she said; "you would be surprised.—
Sit down again."

She clipped the back of his neck with the shears, and then, with
a very slight hesitation, she said:

"Now about the beard!"

But the man rose suddenly from the chair, pulling the dust-cloth
from his neck with desperation.

"No, I'll do that myself," he said, looking her in the eyes with a
cold light in his pale grey, uncanny eyes.

She hesitated in a kind of wonder at his queer male rebellion.

"Now listen, I shall do it much better than you—and besides—"
she added hurriedly, snatching at the dust-cloth he was flinging on
the chair—"I haven't quite finished round the ears."

"I think I shall do," he said, again looking her in the eyes, with
a cold white gleam of finality. "Thank you for what you've done."

And he walked away to the stable.

"You'd better sweep up here," Mrs Witt called.

"Yes Mam," he replied, looking round at her again with an odd
resentment, but continuing to walk away.

"However!" said Mrs Witt. "I suppose he'll do."

And she divested herself of gloves and overall, and walked indoors
to wash and to change. Lou went indoors too.

"It is extraordinary, what hair that man has!" said Mrs Witt. "Did
I tell you when I was in Paris, I saw a woman's face in the hotel,
that I thought I knew? I couldn't place her, till she was coming towards
me. *Aren't you Rachel Fannière?* she said. *Aren't you Janette Leroy?*
We hadn't seen each other since we were girls of twelve and thirteen,
at school in New Orleans. *Oh!* she said to me. *Is every illusion doomed
to perish? You had such wonderful golden curls! All my life I've said,*

*Oh, if only I had such lovely hair as Rachel Fannière! I've seen those
beautiful golden curls of yours all my life. And now I meet you, you're
grey!* Wasn't that terrible, Louise? Well, that man's hair made me think
of it—so thick and curious. It's strange, what a difference there is in
hair. I suppose it's because he's just an animal—no mind! There's
nothing I admire in a man like a good *mind*. Your father was a very
clever man, and all the men I've admired have been clever. But isn't
it curious, now, I've never cared much to touch their hair. How
strange life is! If it gives one thing, it takes away another.—And even
those poor boys in hospital: I have shaved them, or cut their hair, like
a mother, never thinking anything of it. Lovely, intelligent, clean boys,
most of them were. Yet it never did anything to me. I never knew before
that something could happen to one from a person's *hair*! Like to
Janette Leroy from my curls when I was a child. And now I'm grey,
as she says.—I wonder how old a man Lewis is, Louise! Didn't he look
absurdly young with his ears pricking up?"

"I think Rico said he was forty or forty-one."

"And never been married?"

"No—not as far as I know."

"Isn't that curious now!—just an animal! no mind! A man with
no mind! I've always thought that the *most* despicable thing. Yet such
wonderful hair to touch. Your Henry has quite a good mind, yet I
would simply shrink from touching his hair.—I suppose one likes
stroking a cat's fur, just the same. Just the animal in man. Curious
that I never seem to have met it, Louise. Now I come to think of it,
he has the eyes of a human cat: a human tom-cat. Would you call him
stupid? Yes, he's very stupid."

"No mother, he's not stupid. He only doesn't care about our sort
of* things."

"Like an animal! But what a strange look he has in his eyes! a
strange sort of intelligence! and a confidence in himself. Isn't that
curious, Louise, in a man with as little mind as he has? Do you know,
I should say he could see through a woman pretty well."

"Why mother!" said Lou impatiently. "I think one gets so tired
of your men with mind, as you call it. There are so many of that sort
of clever men. And there are lots of men who aren't very clever, but
are rather nice: and lots are stupid. It seems to me there's something
else besides mind and cleverness, or niceness or cleanness. Perhaps it
is the animal. Just think of St. Mawr! I've thought so much about him.
We call him an animal, but we never know what it means. He seems

a far greater mystery to me, than a clever man. He's a horse. Why can't one say in the same way, of a man: *He's a man?* There seems no mystery in being a man. But there's a terrible mystery in St. Mawr."

Mrs Witt watched her daughter quizzically.

5   "Louise," she said. "You won't tell me that the mere animal is all that counts in a man. I will never believe it. Man is wonderful because he is able to *think*."

"But is he?" cried Lou, with sudden exasperation. "Their thinking seems to me all so childish: like stringing the same beads over and over
10   again. Ah, Men! They and their thinking are all so *paltry*. How can you be impressed?"

Mrs Witt raised her eyebrows sardonically.

"Perhaps I'm not—any more," she said with a grim smile.

"But," she added, "I still can't see that I am to be impressed by
15   the mere animal in man. The animals are the same as we are. It seems to me they have the same feelings and wants as we do, in a commonplace way. The only difference is that they have no minds: no human minds, at least. And no matter what you say, Louise, lack of mind makes the commonplace."

20   Lou knitted her brows nervously.

"I suppose it does, mother.—But men's minds *are* so commonplace: look at Dean Vyner and his mind! Or look at Arthur Balfour, as a shining example. Isn't *that* commonplace, that cleverness? I would hate St. Mawr to be spoilt by such a mind."

25   "Yes Louise, so would I. Because the men you mention are really old women, knitting the same pattern over and over again. Nevertheless, I shall never alter my belief, that real mind is all that matters in a man, and it's *that* that we women love."

"Yes mother!—But what *is* real mind? The old woman who knits
30   the most complicated pattern? Oh, I can hear all their needles clicking, the clever men! As a matter of fact, mother, I believe Lewis has far more real mind than Dean Vyner or any of the clever ones. He has a good intuitive mind, he knows things without thinking them."

"That may be, Louise! But he is a servant. He is *under*. A real man
35   should never be under.—And then you could never be intimate with a man like Lewis."*

"I don't want intimacy, mother. I'm too tired of it all. I love St. Mawr because he isn't intimate. He stands where one can't get at him. And he burns with life. And where does his life come from, to him?
40   That's the mystery. That great burning life in him, which never is

dead. Most men have a deadness in them, that frightens me so, because of my own deadness. Why can't men get their life straight, like St. Mawr, and then think? Why can't they think quick, mother: quick as a woman: only farther than we do? Why isn't men's thinking quick like fire, mother? Why is it so slow, so dead, so deadly dull?" 5

"I can't tell you, Louise. My own opinion of the men of today has grown very small. But I can live in spite of it."*

"No mother. We seem to be living off old fuel, like the camel when he lives off his hump. Life doesn't rush into us, as it does even into St. Mawr, and he's a dependent animal. I can't live, mother. I just 10 can't."

"I don't see why not? *I'm* full of life."

"I know you are, mother. But I'm not, and I'm your daughter.—And don't misunderstand me, mother. I don't want to be an animal like a horse or a cat or a lioness, though they all fascinate me, the way they 15 get their life *straight*, not from a lot of old tanks, as we do. I don't admire the cave man, and that sort of thing. But think mother, if we could get our lives straight from the source, as the animals do, and still be ourselves. You don't like men, yourself. But you've no idea how men just tire me out: even the very thought of them. You say 20 they are too animal. But they're not, mother. It's the animal in them has gone perverse, or cringing, or humble, or domesticated, like dogs. I don't know one single man who is a proud living animal. I know they've left off really thinking. But then men always do leave off really thinking, when the last bit of wild animal dies in them." 25

"Because we have minds—"

"We have no minds once we are tame, mother. Men are all women, knitting and crochetting words together."

"I can't altogether agree, you know, Louise."*

"I know you don't.—You like clever men. But clever men are mostly 30 such unpleasant *animals*. As animals, so very unpleasant. And in men like Rico, the animal has gone queer and wrong. And in those nice clean boys you liked so much in the war, there is no wild animal left in them. They're all tame dogs, even when they're brave and well-bred. They're all tame dogs, mother, with human masters. There's no 35 mystery in them."

"What do you want, Louise? You *do* want the cave man, who'll knock you on the head with a club."

"Don't be silly, mother. That's much more your subconscious line, you admirer of Mind.—I don't consider the cave man is a real human 40

animal at all. He's a brute, a degenerate. A pure animal man would
be as lovely as a deer or a leopard, burning like a flame fed straight
from underneath. And he'd be part of the unseen, like a mouse is, even.
And he'd never cease to wonder, he'd breathe silence and unseen
5 wonder, as the partridges do, running in the stubble. He'd be all the
animals in turn, instead of one, fixed, automatic thing, which he is
now, grinding on the nerves.—Ah no, mother, I want the wonder back
again, or I shall die. I don't want to be like you, just criticizing and
annihilating these dreary people, and enjoying it."

10   "My dear daughter, whatever else the human animal might be, he'd
be a dangerous commodity."

"I wish he would, mother. I'm dying of these empty, dangerless
men, who are only sentimental and spiteful."

"Nonsense, you're not dying."

15   "I am, mother. And I should be dead, if there weren't St. Mawr
and Phoenix and Lewis in the world."

"St. Mawr and Phoenix and Lewis, I thought you said they were
servants!"

"That's the worst of it. If only they were masters! If only there were
20 some men with as much natural life as they have, and then brave quick
minds that commanded instead of serving!"

"There are no such men," said Mrs Witt, with a certain grim
satisfaction.

"I know it. But I'm young, and I've got to live. And the thing that
25 is offered me as life just starves me, starves me to death, mother. What
am I to do? You enjoy shattering people like Dean Vyner. But I am
young, I can't live that way."*

"That may be."

It had long ago struck Lou, how much more her mother realised
30 and understood, than ever Rico did. Rico was afraid, always afraid
of realising. Rico, with his good manners and his habitual kindness,
and that peculiar imprisoned sneer of his.

He arrived home next morning on St. Mawr, rather flushed and
gaudy, and over-kind, with an *empressé** anxiety about Lou's welfare
35 which spoke too many volumes. Especially as he was accompanied by
Flora Manby, and by Flora's sister Elsie, and Elsie's husband,
Frederick Edwards. They all came on horseback.

"Such awful ages since I saw you!" said Flora to Lou. "Sorry if
we burst in on you. We're only just saying *How do you do*! and going
40 on to the inn. They've got rooms all ready for us there. We thought

we'd stay just one night over here, and ride tomorrow to the Devil's Chair.* Won't you come? Lots of fun! Isn't Mrs Witt at home?"

Mrs Witt was out for the moment. When she returned, she had on her curious stiff face, yet she greeted the newcomers with a certain cordiality: she felt it would be diplomatic, no doubt.

"There *are* two rooms here," she said, "and if you care to poke into them, why we shall be *delighted* to have you. But I'll show them to you first, because they are poor, inconvenient rooms, with no running water and *miles* from the baths."

Flora and Elsie declared that they were "perfectly darling sweet rooms—not overcrowded."—

"Well," said Mrs Witt. "The conveniences certainly don't fill up much space. But if you like to take them for what they are—"

"Why we feel absolutely overwhelmed, don't we Elsie!—But we've no clothes—!"

Suddenly the silence had turned into a house-party. The Manby girls appeared to lunch in fine muslin dresses, bought in Paris, fresh as daisies. Women's clothing take up so little space, especially in summer! Fred Edwards was one of those blond Englishmen with a little brush moustache and those strong blue eyes which were always attempting the sentimental, but which Lou, in her prejudice, considered cruel: upon what grounds, she never analysed. However, he took a gallant tone with her at once, and she had to seem to simper. Rico, watching her, was so relieved when he saw the simper coming.

It had begun again, the whole clockwork of "lots of fun!"

"Isn't Fred flirting perfectly outrageously with Lady Carrington—! She looks so *sweet!*" cried Flora, over her coffee-cup. "Don't you mind, Harry!"

They called Rico "Harry"! His boy-name.

"Only a very little," said Harry. "*L'uomo é cacciatore.*"

"Oh now, what does that mean?" cried Flora, who always thrilled to Rico's bits of affectation.

"It means," said Mrs Witt, leaning forward and speaking in her most suave voice, "that man is a hunter."

Even Flora shrank under the smooth acid of the irony.

"Oh well now!" she cried. "If he is, then what is woman?"

"The hunted," said Mrs Witt, in a still smoother acid.

"At least," said Rico, "she is always *game!*"

"Ah, is she though!" came Fred's manly, well-bred tones. "I'm not so sure."

Mrs Witt looked from one man to the other, as if she were dropping them down the bottomless pit.*

Lou escaped to look at St. Mawr. He was still moist where the saddle had been. And he seemed a little bit extinguished, as if virtue had gone out of him.*

But when he lifted his lovely naked head, like a bunch of flames, to see who it was had entered, she saw he was still himself. Forever sensitive and alert, his head lifted like the summit of a fountain. And within him the clean bones striking to the earth, his hoofs intervening between him and the ground like lesser jewels.

He knew her and did not resent her. But he took no notice of her. He would never "respond." At first she had resented it. Now she was glad. He would never be intimate, thank heaven.

She hid herself away till teatime: but she could not hide from the sound of voices. Dinner was early, at seven. Dean Vyner came—Mrs Vyner was an invalid—and also an artist who had a studio in the village and did etchings. He was a man of about thirty-eight, and poor, just beginning to accept himself as a failure, as far as making money goes. But he worked at his etchings and studied esoteric matters like astrology and alchemy. Rico patronised him, and was a little afraid of him. Lou could not quite make him out. After knocking about Paris and London and Munich, he was trying to become staid, and to persuade himself that English village life, with squire and dean in the background, humble artist in the middle, and laborer in the common foreground, was a genuine life. His self-persuasion was only moderately successful. This was betrayed by the curious arrest in his body: he seemed to have to force himself into move-ment: and by the curious duplicity in his yellow-grey, twinkling eyes, that twinkled and expanded like a goat's, with mockery, irony, and frustration.*

"Your face is curiously like Pan's," said Lou to him at dinner.

It was true, in a commonplace sense. He had the tilted eyebrows, the twinkling goaty look, and the pointed ears of a goat-Pan.

"People have said so," he replied. "But I'm afraid it's not the face of the Great God Pan. Isn't it rather the Great Goat Pan!"

"I say, that's good!" cried Rico. "The Great Goat Pan!"

"I have always found it difficult," said the Dean, "to see the Great God Pan in that goat-legged old father of satyrs. He may have a good deal of influence—the world will always be full of goaty old satyrs. But we find them somewhat vulgar. Even our late King Edward.* The goaty old satyrs are too comprehensible to me, to be venerable, and I fail to see a Great God in the father of them all."

"Your ears should be getting red," said Lou to Cartwright.—She too had an odd squinting smile that suggested nymphs, so irresponsible and unbelieving.

"Oh no, nothing personal!" cried the Dean.

"I am not sure," said Cartwright, with a small smile. "But don't you imagine Pan once *was* a great god, before the anthropomorphic Greeks turned him into half a man?"

"Ah!—maybe. That is very possible. But—I have noticed the limitation in myself—my mind has no grasp whatsoever of Europe before the Greeks arose. Mr Wells' Outline* does not help me there, either," the Dean added with a smile.

"But what was Pan before he was a man with goat legs?" asked Lou.

"Before he looked like me?" said Cartwright with a faint grin. "I should say he was the God that is hidden in everything. In those days you saw the thing, you never saw the God in it: I mean in the tree or the fountain or the animal. If you ever saw the God instead of the thing, you died. If you saw it with the naked eye, that is. But in the night you might see the God. And you knew it was there."

"The modern pantheist not only sees the God in everything, he takes photographs of it," said the Dean.

"Oh, and the divine pictures he paints!" cried Rico.

"Quite!" said Cartwright.

"But if they never *saw* the God in the thing, the old ones, how did they know he was there? How did they have any Pan at all?" said Lou.

"Pan was the hidden mystery—the hidden cause. That's how it was a great God. Pan wasn't *he* at all: not even a great God. He was Pan, All: what you see when you see in full. In the daytime you see the thing. But if your third eye* is open, which sees only the things that can't be seen, you may see Pan within the thing, hidden: you may see with your third eye, which is darkness."

"Do you think I might see Pan in a horse, for example?"

"Easily. In St. Mawr!"—Cartwright gave her a knowing look.

"But," said Mrs Witt, "it would be difficult, I should say, to open the third eye and see Pan in a man."

"Probably," said Cartwright smiling. "In man he is over-visible: the old satyr: the fallen Pan."

"Exactly!" said Mrs Witt. And she fell into a muse. "The fallen

Pan!" she re-echoed. "Wouldn't a man be wonderful, in whom Pan hadn't fallen!"

Over the coffee in the grey drawing-room, she suddenly asked:

"Supposing, Mr Cartwright, one *did* open the third eye and see Pan
5 in an actual man—I wonder what it would be like?"

She half lowered her eyelids and tilted her face in a strange way, as if she were tasting something, and not quite sure.

"I wonder!" he said, smiling his enigmatic smile. But she could see he did not understand.

10 "Louise!" said Mrs Witt at bedtime. "Come into my room for a moment, I want to ask you something."

"What is it, mother?"

"You, you *get* something from what Mr Cartwright said, about seeing Pan with the third eye? Seeing Pan in something?"

15 Mrs Witt came rather close, and tilted her face with strange insinuating question, at her daughter.

"I think I do, mother."

"In what?"—The question came as a pistol-shot.

"I think, mother," said Lou reluctantly, "in St. Mawr."

20 "In a horse!"—Mrs Witt contracted her eyes slightly. "Yes, I can see that. I know what you mean. It *is* in St. Mawr. It *is*! But in St. Mawr it makes me *afraid*—" she dragged out the word. Then she came a step closer. "But Louise, did you ever see it in a man?"

"What, mother?"

25 "Pan. Did you ever see Pan in a man, as you see Pan in St. Mawr?"

Louise hesitated.

"No mother, I don't think I did. When I look at men with my third eye, as you call it—I think I see—mostly—a sort of—pan-cake." She uttered the last word with a despairing grin, not knowing quite what
30 to say.

"Oh Louise, isn't that it! Doesn't one always see a pancake!—Now listen, Louise. Have you ever been in love?"

"Yes, as far as I understand it."

"Listen now. Did you ever see Pan in the man you loved? Tell me
35 if you did?"

"As I see Pan in St. Mawr?—no mother." And suddenly her lips began to tremble and the tears came to her eyes.

"Listen Louise.—I've been in love innumerable times—and *really* in love twice. Twice!—yet for fifteen years I've left off wanting to have
40 anything to do with a man, really. For fifteen years! And why?—Do

you know?—Because I couldn't see that peculiar hidden Pan in any
of them. And I became that I needed to. I needed it. But it wasn't
there. Not in any man. Even when I was in love with a man, it was
for other things: because I *understood* him so well, or he understood
me, or we had such sympathy. Never the hidden Pan.—Do you
understand what I mean? Unfallen Pan!"

"More or less, mother."

"But now my third eye is coming open, I believe. I am tired of all
these men like breakfast cakes, with a tea-spoonful of mind or a
tea-spoonful of spirit in them, for baking powder. Isn't it extraordinary, that young man Cartwright talks about Pan, but he knows
nothing of it all. He knows nothing of the unfallen Pan: only the fallen
Pan with goat legs and a leer—and that sort of power, don't you
know—"

"But what do you know of the unfallen Pan, mother?"

"Don't ask me, Louise! I feel all of a tremble, as if I was just on
the verge."

She flashed a little look of incipient triumph, and said goodnight.

An excursion on horseback had been arranged for the next day, to
two old groups of rocks, called the Angel's Chair and the Devil's Chair,
which crowned the moor-like hills looking into Wales, ten miles away.
Everybody was going—they were to start early in the morning, and
Lewis would be the guide, since no-one exactly knew the way.

Lou got up soon after sunrise. There was a summer scent in the
trees of early morning, and monkshood flowers stood up dark and tall,
with shadows. She dressed in the green linen riding-skirt her maid had
put ready for her, with a close bluish smock.

"Are you going out already, dear?" called Rico from his room.

"Just to smell the roses before we start, Rico."

He appeared in the doorway in his yellow silk pyjamas. His large
blue eyes had that rolling irritable look and the slightly bloodshot
whites which made her want to escape.

"Booted and spurred!—the *energy*!" he cried.

"It's a lovely day to ride," she said.

"A lovely day to do anything *except* ride!" he said. "Why spoil the
day riding!"—A curious bitter-acid escaped into his tone. It was
evident he hated the excursion.

"Why, we needn't go if you don't want to, Rico."

"Oh, I'm sure I shall love it, once I get started. It's all this business
of *starting*, with horses and paraphernalia—"

Lou went into the yard. The horses were drinking at the trough
under the pump, their colours strong and rich in the shadow of the
tree.

"You're not coming with us, Phoenix?" she said.

"Lewis, he's riding my horse."

She could tell Phoenix did not like being left behind.

By half-past seven, everybody was ready. The sun was in the yard,
the horses were saddled. They came swishing their tails. Lewis
brought out St. Mawr from his separate box, speaking to him very
quietly, in Welsh: a murmuring, soothing little speech. Lou, alert,
could see that he was uneasy.

"How is St. Mawr this morning?" she asked.

"He's all right. He doesn't like so many people. He'll be all right
once he's started."

The strangers were in the saddle: they moved out to the deep shade
of the village road outside. Rico came to his horse, to mount. St. Mawr
jumped away as if he had seen the devil.

"Steady, fool!" cried Rico.

The bay stood with his four feet spread, his neck arched, his big
dark eye glancing sideways with that watchful, frightening look.

"You shouldn't be irritable with him, Rico!" said Lou. "Steady
then, St. Mawr! Be steady."

But a certain anger rose also in her. The creature was so big, so
brilliant, and so stupid, standing there with his hind legs spread, ready
to jump aside or to rear terrifically, and his great eye glancing with
a sort of suspicious frenzy. What was there to be suspicious of, after
all?—Rico would do him no harm.

"No-one will harm you, St. Mawr," she reasoned, a bit
exasperated.

The groom was talking quietly, murmuringly, in Welsh. Rico was
slowly advancing again, to put his foot in the stirrup. The stallion was
watching from the corner of his eye, a strange glare of suspicious frenzy
burning stupidly. Any moment, his immense physical force might be
let loose in a frenzy of panic—or malice. He was really very irritating.

"Probably he doesn't like that apricot shirt," said Mrs Witt,
"although it tones into him wonderfully well."

She pronounced it *ap*—ricot, and it irritated Rico terribly.

"Ought we to have *asked* him, before we put it on?" he flashed,
his upper lip lifting venomously.

"I should say you should," replied Mrs Witt coolly.

Rico turned with a sudden rush to the horse. Back went the great animal, with a sudden splashing crash of hoofs on the cobble-stones, and Lewis hanging on like a shadow. Up went the fore-feet, showing the belly.

"The thing is accursed," said Rico, who had dropped the reins in sudden shock, and stood marooned. His rage overwhelmed him like a black flood.

"Nothing in the world is so irritating as a horse that is acting up," thought Lou.

"Say Harry!" called Flora from the road. "Come out here into the road to mount him."

Lewis looked at Rico and nodded. Then soothing the big, quivering animal, he led him springily out to the road under the trees, where the three friends were waiting. Lou and her mother got quickly into the saddle, to follow. And in another moment Rico was mounted and bouncing down the road in the wrong direction, Lewis following on the chestnut. It was some time before Rico could get St. Mawr round. Watching him from behind, those waiting could judge how the young Baronet hated it.

But at last they set off—Rico ahead, unevenly but quietly, with the two Manby girls, Lou following with the fair young man, who had been in a cavalry regiment, and who kept looking round for Mrs Witt.

"Don't look round for me," she called. "I'm riding behind, out of the dust."

Just behind Mrs Witt came Lewis. It was a whole cavalcade trotting in the morning sun past the cottages and the cottage gardens, round the field that was the recreation ground, into the deep hedges of the lane.

"Why is St. Mawr so bad at starting? Can't you get him into better shape?" she asked over her shoulder.

"Beg your pardon Mam!"

Lewis trotted a little nearer. She glanced over her shoulder at him, at his dark, unmoved face, his cool little figure.

"I think *Mam*! is so ugly. Why not leave it out!" she said. Then she repeated her question.

"St. Mawr doesn't trust anybody," Lewis replied.

"Not you?"

"Yes, he trusts me—mostly."

"Then why not other people?"

"They're different."

"All of them?"

"About all of them."

"How are they different?"

He looked at her with his remote, uncanny grey eyes.

5   "Different," he said, not knowing how else to put it.

They rode on slowly, up the steep rise of the wood, then down into a glade where ran a little railway built for hauling some mysterious mineral out of the hill, in war-time, and now already abandoned. Even on this countryside, the dead hand of the war lay like a corpse 10   decomposing.

They rode up again, past the fox gloves under the trees. Ahead, the brilliant St. Mawr, and the sorrel and grey horses were swimming like butterflies through the sea of bracken, glittering from sun to shade, shade to sun. Then once more they were on a crest, and through the 15   thinning trees could see the slopes of the moors beyond the next dip.

Soon they were in the open, rolling hills, golden in the morning and empty save for a couple of distant bilberry-pickers, whitish figures pick—pick—picking with curious, rather disgusting assiduity. The horses were on an old trail, which climbed through the pinky tips of 20   heather and ling, across patches of green bilberry. Here and there were tufts of hare-bells blue as bubbles.

They were out, high on the hills. And there to west lay Wales, folded in crumpled folds, goldish in the morning light, with its moor-like slopes and patches of corn uncannily distinct. Between was a hollow wide valley of summer haze, showing white farms among trees, and 25   grey slate roofs.

"Ride beside me," she said to Lewis. "Nothing makes me want to go back to America like the old look of these little villages.—You have never been to America?"

30   "No Mam."

"Don't you ever want to go?"

"I wouldn't mind going."

"But you're not just crazy to go?"

"No Mam."

35   "Quite content as you are?"

He looked at her, and his pale, remote eyes met hers.

"I don't fret myself." he replied.

"Not about anything at all—ever?"

His eyes glanced ahead, at the other riders.

40   "No Mam!" he replied, without looking at her.

She rode a few moments in silence.

"What is that over there?" she asked, pointing across the valley. "What is it called?"

"Yon's Montgomery."

"Montgomery! And is that *Wales*—?" she trailed the ending curiously.

"Yes Mam."

"Where you come from?"

"No Mam! I come from Merionetn."

"Not from Wales? I thought you were Welsh?"

"Yes Mam. Merioneth *is* Wales."

"And you are Welsh?"

"Yes Mam."

"I had a Welsh grandmother. But I come from Louisiana, and when I go back home, the negroes still call me Miss Rachel. *Oh, my, it's little Miss Rachel come back home! Why, ain't I mighty glad to see you—u, Miss Rachel!* That gives me such a strange feeling, you know."

The man glanced at her curiously, especially when she imitated the negroes.

"Do you feel strange when you go home?" she asked.

"I was brought up by an aunt and uncle," he said. "I never go to see them."

"And you don't have any home?"

"No Mam."

"No wife nor anything?"

"No Mam."

"But what do you do with your life?"

"I keep to myself."

"And care about nothing?"

"I mind St. Mawr."

"But you've not always had St. Mawr—and you won't always have him.—Were you in the war?"

"Yes Mam."

"At the front?"

"Yes Mam—but I was a groom."

"And you came out all right?"

"I lost my little finger from a bullet."

He held up his small, dark left hand, from which the little finger was missing.

"And did you like the war—or didn't you?"

"I didn't like it."

Again his pale grey eyes met hers, and they looked so non-human and uncommunicative, so without connection, and inaccessible, she was troubled.

5   "Tell me," she said. "Did you never want a wife and a home and children, like other men?"

"No Mam. I never wanted a home of my own."

"Nor a wife of your own?"

"No Mam."

10   "Nor children of your own?"

"No Mam."

She reined in her horse.

"Now wait a minute," she said. "Now tell me why."

His horse came to standstill, and the two riders faced one another.

15   "Tell me why—I must know why you never wanted a wife and children and a home. I must know why you're not like other men."

"I never felt like it," he said. "I made my life with horses."

"Did you hate people very much? Did you have a very unhappy time as a child."

20   "My aunt and uncle didn't like me, and I didn't like them."

"So you've never liked anybody?"

"Maybe not," he said. "Not to get as far as marrying them."

She touched her horse and moved on.

"Isn't that curious!" she said. "I've loved people, at various times.

25   But I don't believe *I've* ever liked anybody, except a few of our negroes. I don't like Louise, though she's my daughter and I love her. But I don't really *like* her.—I think you're the first person I've ever liked since I was on our plantation, and we had some *very fine* negroes.—And I think that's very curious.—Now I want to know if

30   you like *me*."

She looked at him searchingly, but he did not answer.

"Tell me," she said. "I don't mind if you say no. But tell me if you like me. I feel I must know."

The flicker of a smile went over his face—a very rare thing with

35   him.

"Maybe I do," he said. He was thinking that she put him on a level with a negro slave on a plantation: in his idea, negroes were still slaves. But he did not care where she put him.

"Well, I'm glad—I'm glad if you like me. Because you *don't* like

40   most people, I know that."

They had passed the hollow where the old Aldecar Chapel* hid in damp isolation, beside the ruined mill, over the stream that came down from the moors. Climbing the sharp slope, they saw the folded hills like great shut fingers, with steep, deep clefts between. On the near sky-line was a bunch of rocks: and away to the right, another bunch.

"Yon's the Angel's Chair," said Lewis, pointing to the nearer rocks.

"And yon's the Devil's Chair, where we're going."

"Oh!" said Mrs Witt. "And aren't we going to the Angel's Chair?"

"No Mam!"

"Why not?"

"There's nothing to see there. The other's higher, and bigger, and that's where folks mostly go."

"Is that so!—They give the Devil the higher seat in this country, do they? I think they're right.—" And as she got no answer, she added: "You believe in the Devil, don't you?"

"I never met him," he answered, evasively.

Ahead, they could see the other horses twinkling in a cavalcade up the slope, the black, the bay, the two greys and the sorrel, sometimes bunching, sometimes straggling. At a gate all waited for Mrs Witt. The fair young man fell in beside her, and talked hunting at her. He had hunted the fox over these hills, and was vigorously excited locating the spot where the hounds first gave cry, etc.

"Really!" said Mrs Witt, "*Really!* Is that so!"

If irony could have been condensed to prussic acid, the fair young man would have ended his life's history with his reminiscences.

They came at last, trotting in file along a narrow track between heather, along the saddle of a hill, to where the knot of pale granite suddenly cropped out. It was one of those places where the spirit of aboriginal England still lingers, the old savage England, whose last blood flows still in a few Englishmen, Welshmen, Cornishmen. The rocks, whitish with weather of all the ages, jutted against the blue August sky, heavy with age-moulded roundnesses.

Lewis stayed below with the horses, the party scrambled rather awkwardly, in their riding-boots, up the foot-worn boulders. At length they stood in the place called the Chair, looking west, west towards Wales, that rolled in golden folds upwards. It was neither impressive nor a very picturesque landscape: the hollow valley with farms, and then the rather bare upheaval of hills, slopes with corn and moor and pasture, rising like a barricade, seemingly high, slantingly. Yet it had a strange effect on the imagination.

"Oh mother," said Lou, "doesn't it make you feel old, old, older than anything ever was?"

"It certainly does seem aged," said Mrs Witt.

"It makes me want to die," said Lou. "I feel we've lasted almost
5 too long."

"Don't say that, Lady Carrington. Why you're a spring chicken yet: or shall I say an unopened rosebud," remarked the fair young man.

"No," said Lou. "All these millions of ancestors have used all the life up. We're not really alive, in the sense that they were alive."

10 "But who?" said Rico. "Who are *they*?"

"The people who lived on these hills, in the days gone by."

"But the same people still live on the hills, darling. It's just the same stock."

"No Rico. That old fighting stock that worshipped devils among
15 these stones—I'm sure they did—"

"But look here, do you mean they were any better than we are?" asked the fair young man.

Lou looked at him quizzically.

"We don't exist," she said, squinting at him oddly.

20 "I jolly well know *I* do," said the fair young man.

"I consider these days are the best ever, especially for girls," said Flora Manby. "And anyhow they're our own days, so I don't jolly well see the use of crying them down."

They were all silent, with the last echoes of emphatic *joie de vivre*
25 trumpeting on the air, across the hills of Wales.

"Spoken like a brick,* Flora," said Rico. "Say it again, we may not have the Devil's Chair for a pulpit next time."

"I do," reiterated Flora. "I think this is the best age there ever was, for a girl to have a good time in. I read all through H. G. Wells' history,
30 and I shut it up and thanked my stars I live in nineteen-twenty odd, not in some other beastly date when a woman had to cringe before mouldy domineering men."

After this, they turned to scramble to another part of the rocks, to the famous Needle's Eye.

35 "Thank you so much, I am really better without help," said Mrs Witt to the fair young man, as she slid downwards till a piece of grey silk stocking showed above her tall boot. But she got her toe in a safe place, and in a moment stood beside him, while he caught her arm protectively. He might as well have caught the paw of a mountain lion
40 protectively.

"I should like *so* much to know," she said suavely, looking into his eyes with a demonish straight look, "what makes you so certain that you exist?"

He looked back at her, and his jaunty blue eyes went baffled. Then a slow, hot, salmon-coloured flush stole over his face, and he turned abruptly round.

The Needle's Eye was a hole in the ancient grey rock, like a window, looking to England; England at the moment in shadow. A stream wound and glinted in the flat shadow, and beyond that, the flat, insignificant hills heaped in mounds of shade. Cloud was coming—the English side was in shadow. Wales was still in the sun, but the shadow was spreading. The day was going to disappoint them. Lou was a tiny bit chilled, already.

Luncheon was still several miles away. The party hastened down to the horses. Lou picked a few sprigs of ling, and some hare-bells, and some straggling yellow flowers: not because she wanted them, but to distract herself. The atmosphere of "enjoying ourselves" was becoming cruel to her: it sapped all the life out of her. "Oh, if only I needn't enjoy myself," she moaned inwardly. But the Manby girls were enjoying themselves so much. "I think it's frantically lovely up here," said the other one—not Flora—Elsie.

"It *is* beautiful, isn't it! I'm *so* glad you like it," replied Rico. And he was really relieved and gratified, because the other one said she was enjoying it so frightfully. He dared not say to Lou, as he wanted to: "I'm afraid, Lou darling, you don't love it as much as we do."—He was afraid of her answer: "No dear, I don't love it at all! I want to be away from these people."

Slightly piqued, he rode on with the Manby group, and Lou came behind with her mother. Cloud was covering the sky with grey. There was a cold wind. Everybody was anxious to get to the farm for luncheon, and be safely home before rain came.

They were riding along one of the narrow little foot-tracks, mere grooves of grass between heather and bright green bilberry. The blond young man was ahead, then his wife, then Flora, then Rico. Lou, from a little distance, watched the glossy, powerful haunches of St. Mawr swaying with life, always too much life, like a menace. The fair young man was whistling a new dance tune.

"That's an awfully attractive tune," Rico called. "Do whistle it again, Fred, I should like to memorise it."

Fred began to whistle it again.

At that moment St. Mawr exploded again, shied sideways as if a bomb had gone off, and kept backing through the heather.

"Fool!" cried Rico, thoroughly unnerved: he had been terribly sideways in the saddle, Lou had feared he was going to fall. But he got his seat, and pulled the reins viciously, to bring the horse to order, and put him on the track again. St. Mawr began to rear: his favourite trick. Rico got him forward a few yards, when up he went again.

"Fool!" yelled Rico, hanging in the air.

He pulled the horse over backwards, on top of him.

Lou gave a loud, unnatural, horrible scream: she heard it herself, at the same time as she heard the crash of the falling horse. Then she saw a pale gold belly, and hoofs that worked and flashed in the air, and St. Mawr writhing, straining his head terrifically upwards, his great eyes starting from the naked lines of his nose. With a great neck arching cruelly from the ground, he was pulling frantically at the reins, which Rico still held tight.—Yes, Rico, lying strangely sideways, his eyes also starting from his yellow-white face, among the heather, still clutched the reins.

Young Edwards was rushing forward, and circling round the writhing, immense horse, whose pale-gold inverted bulk seemed to fill the universe.

"Let him get up, Carrington! Let him get up!" he was yelling, darting warily near, to get the reins.—Another spasmodic convulsion of the horse.

Horror! The young man reeled backwards with his face in his hands. He had got a kick in the face. Red blood running down his chin!

Lewis was there, on the ground, getting the reins out of Rico's hands. St. Mawr gave a great curve like a fish, spread his fore-feet on the earth and reared his head, looking round in a ghastly fashion. His eyes were arched, his nostrils wide, his face ghastly in a sort of panic. He rested thus, seated with his fore-feet planted and his face in panic, almost like some terrible lizard, for several moments. Then he heaved sickeningly to his feet, and stood convulsed, trembling.

There lay Rico, crumpled and rather sideways, staring at the heavens from a yellow, dead-looking face. Lewis, glancing round in a sort of horror, looked in dread at St. Mawr again. Flora had been hovering.— She now rushed screeching to the prostrate Rico:

"Harry! Harry! you're not dead! Oh Harry! Harry! Harry!"

Lou had dismounted—She didn't know when. She stood a little way off, as if spell-bound, while Flora cried *Harry! Harry! Harry!*

Suddenly Rico sat up.

"Where is the horse?" he said.

At the same time an added whiteness came on his face, and he bit his lip with pain, and he fell prostrate again in a faint. Flora rushed to put her arm round him.

Where was the horse? He had backed slowly away, in an agony of suspicion, while Lewis murmured to him in vain. His head was raised again, the eyes still starting from their sockets, and a terrible guilty, ghost-like look on his face. When Lewis drew a little nearer he twitched and shrank like a shaken steel spring, away—not to be touched. He seemed to be seeing legions of ghosts, down the dark avenues of all the centuries that have lapsed since the horse became subject to man.

And the other young man? He was still standing, at a little distance, with his face in his hands, motionless, the blood falling on his white shirt, and his wife at his side, pleading distracted.

Mrs Witt too was there, as if cast in steel, watching. She made no sound and did not move, only, from a fixed, impassive face, watched each thing.

"Do tell me what you think is the matter?" Lou pleaded, distracted, to Flora, who was supporting Rico and weeping torrents of unknown tears.

Then Mrs Witt came forward and began in a very practical manner to unclose the shirt-neck and feel the young man's heart. Rico opened his eyes again, said "*Really!*" and closed his eyes once more.

"It's fainting!" said Mrs Witt. "We have no brandy."

Lou, too weary to be able to feel anything, said:

"I'll go and get some."

She went to her alarmed horse, who stood among the others with her head down, in suspense. Almost unconsciously Lou mounted, set her face ahead, and was riding away.

Then Poppy shied too, with a sudden start, and Lou pulled up. "Why?" she said to her horse. "Why did you do that?"

She looked round, and saw in the heather a glimpse of yellow and black.

"A snake!" she said wonderingly.

And she looked closer.

It was a dead adder that had been drinking at a reedy pool in a little depression just off the road, and had been killed with stones. There it lay, also crumpled, its head crushed, its gold-and-yellow back still glittering dully, and a bit of pale-blue belly showing, killed that morning!

Lou rode on, her face set towards the farm. An unspeakable weariness had overcome her. She could not even suffer. Weariness of
5   spirit left her in a sort of apathy.

And she had a vision, a vision of evil. Or not strictly a vision. She became aware of evil, evil, evil, rolling in great waves over the earth. Always she had thought there was no such thing—only a mere negation of good. Now, like an ocean to whose surface she had risen, she saw
10   the dark-grey waves of evil rearing in a great tide.

And it had swept mankind away without mankind's knowing. It had caught up the nations as the rising ocean might lift the fishes, and was sweeping them on in a great tide of evil. They did not know. The people did not know. They did not even wish it. They wanted to be good
15   and to have everything joyful and enjoyable. Everything joyful and enjoyable: for everybody. This was what they wanted, if you asked them.

But at the same time, they had fallen under the spell of evil. It was a soft, subtle thing, soft as water, and its motion was soft and
20   imperceptible, as the running of a tide is invisible to one who is out on the ocean. And they were all out on the ocean, being borne along in the current of the mysterious evil, creatures of the evil principle, as fishes are creatures of the sea.

There was no relief. The whole world was enveloped in one great
25   flood. All the nations, the white, the brown, the black, the yellow, all were immersed in the strange tide of evil that was subtly, irresistibly rising. No-one, perhaps, deliberately wished it. Nearly every individual wanted peace and a good time all round: everybody to have a good time.

30   But some strange thing had happened, and the vast, mysterious force of positive evil was let loose. She felt that from the core of Asia the evil welled up, as from some strange pole, and slowly was drowning earth.

It was something horrifying, something you could not escape from.
35   It had come to her as in a vision, when she saw the pale gold belly of the stallion upturned, the hoofs working wildly, the wicked curved hams of the horse, and then the evil straining of that arched, fish-like neck, with the dilated eyes of the head. Thrown backwards, and working its hoofs in the air. Reversed, and purely evil.

40   She saw the same in people. They were thrown backwards, and

writhing with evil. And the rider, crushed, was still reining them
down.

What did it mean? Evil, evil, and a rapid return to the sordid chaos.
Which was wrong, the horse or the rider? Or both?

She thought with horror of St. Mawr, and of the look on his face.
But she thought with horror, a colder horror, of Rico's face as he
snarled *Fool*! His fear, his impotence as a master, as a rider, his
presumption. And she thought with horror of those other people, so
glib, so glibly evil.

What did they want to do, those Manby girls? Undermine,
undermine, undermine. They wanted to undermine Rico, just as that
fair young man would have liked to undermine her. Believe in nothing,
care about nothing: but keep the surface easy, and have a good time.
*Let us undermine one another. There is nothing to believe in, so let us
undermine everything. But look out! No scenes, no spoiling the game. Stick
to the rules of the game. Be sporting, and don't do anything that would
make a commotion. Keep the game going smooth and jolly, and bear your
bit like a sport. Never, by any chance, injure your fellow man openly. But
always injure him secretly. Make a fool of him, and undermine his nature.
Break him up by undermining him, if you can. It's good sport.*

The evil! The mysterious potency of evil. She could see it all the
time, in individuals, in society, in the press. There it was in socialism
and bolshevism: the same evil. But bolshevism made a mess of the
outside of life, so turn it down. Try fascism. Fascism would keep the
surface of life intact, and carry on the undermining business all the
better. All the better sport. Never draw blood. Keep the hemorrhage
internal, invisible.

And as soon as fascism makes a break—which it is bound to, because
all evil works up to a break—then turn it down. With gusto, turn it
down.

Mankind, like a horse, ridden by a stranger, smooth-faced, evil rider.
Evil himself, smooth-faced and pseudo-handsome, riding mankind
past the dead snake, to the last break.

Mankind no longer its own master. Ridden by this pseudo-handsome
ghoul of outward loyalty, inward treachery, in a game of betrayal,
betrayal, betrayal. The last of the gods of our era, Judas supreme!

People performing outward acts of loyalty, piety, self-sacrifice. But
inwardly bent on undermining, betraying. Directing all their subtle
evil will against any positive living thing. Masquerading as the ideal,
in order to poison the real.

Creation destroys as it goes, throws down one tree for the rise of another. But ideal mankind would abolish death, multiply itself million upon million, rear up city upon city, save every parasite alive, until the accumulation of mere existence is swollen to a horror. But go on
5 saving life, the ghastly salvation army of ideal mankind. At the same time secretly, viciously, potently undermine the natural creation, betray it with kiss after kiss, destroy it from the inside, till you have the swollen rottenness of our teeming existences.—But keep the game going. Nobody's going to make another bad break, such as Germany
10 and Russia made.

Two bad breaks the secret evil has made: in Germany and in Russia. Watch it! Let evil keep a policeman's eye on evil! The surface of life must remain unruptured. Production must be heaped upon production. And the natural creation must be betrayed by many more kisses, yet.
15 Judas is the last God, and by heaven, the most potent.

But even Judas made a break: hanged himself, and his bowels gushed out. Not long after his triumph.

Man must destroy as he goes, as trees fall for trees to rise. The accumulation of life and things means rottenness. Life must destroy
20 life, in the unfolding of creation. We save up life at the expense of the unfolding, till all is full of rottenness. Then at last, we make a break.

What's to be done? Generally speaking, nothing. The dead will have to bury their dead, while the earth stinks of corpses. The individual
25 can but depart from the mass, and try to cleanse himself. Try to hold fast to the living thing, which destroys as it goes, but remains sweet. And in his soul fight, fight, fight to preserve that which is life in him from the ghastly kisses and poison-bites of the myriad evil ones. Retreat to the desert, and fight. But in his soul adhere to that which
30 is life itself, creatively destroying as it goes: destroying the stiff old thing to let the new bud come through. The one passionate principle of creative being, which recognises the natural good, and has a sword for the swarms of evil. Fights, fights, fights to protect itself. But with itself, is strong and at peace.

35 Lou came to the farm, and got brandy, and asked the men to come out to carry in the injured.

It turned out that the kick in the face had knocked a couple of young Edward's teeth out, and would disfigure him a little.

"To go through the war, and then get this!" he mumbled, with a
40 vindictive glance at St. Mawr.

And it turned out that Rico had two broken ribs and a crushed ankle.
Poor Rico, he would limp for life.

"I want St. Mawr *shot!*" was almost his first word, when he was
in bed at the farm and Lou was sitting beside him.

"What good would that do, dear?" she said.   5

"The brute is evil. I want him *shot!*"

Rico could make the last word sound like the spitting of a bullet.

"Do you want to shoot him yourself?"

"No. But I want to have him shot. I shall never be easy till I know
he has a bullet through him. He's got a wicked character. I don't feel   10
you are safe, with him down there. I shall get one of the Manbys'
game-keepers to shoot him. You might tell Flora—or I'll tell her
myself, when she comes."

"Don't talk about it now, dear. You've got a temperature."

Was it true, St. Mawr was evil? She would never forget him   15
writhing and lunging on the ground, nor his awful face when he reared
up. But then that noble look of his: surely he was not mean? Whereas
all evil had an inner meanness, mean! Was he mean! Was he meanly
treacherous? Did he know he could kill, and meanly wait his
opportunity?   20

She was afraid. And if this were true, then he *should* be shot. Perhaps
he ought to be shot.

This thought haunted her. Was there something mean and
treacherous in St. Mawr's spirit, the vulgar evil? If so, then have him
shot. At moments, an anger would rise in her, as she thought of his   25
frenzied rearing, and his mad, hideous writhing on the ground, and
in the heat of her anger she would want to hurry down to her mother's
house, and have the creature shot at once. It would be a satisfaction, and a vindication of human rights. Because after all, Rico
was so considerate of the brutal horse. But not a spark of con-   30
sideration did the stallion have for Rico. No, it was the slavish
malevolence of a domesticated creature that kept cropping up in St.
Mawr. The slave, taking his slavish vengeance, then dropping back
into subservience.

All the slaves of this world, accumulating their preparations for   35
slavish vengeance, and then, when they have taken it, ready to drop
back into servility. Freedom! Most slaves can't be freed, no matter how
you let them loose. Like domestic animals, they are, in the long run,
more afraid of freedom than of masters: and freed by some generous
master, they will at last crawl back to some mean boss, who will have   40

no scruples about kicking them. Because, for them, far better kicks and
servility than the hard, lonely responsibility of real freedom.

The wild animal is at every moment intensely self-disciplined,
poised in the tension of self-defence, self-preservation, and self-
5   assertion. The moments of relaxation are rare and most carefully
chosen. Even sleep is watchful, guarded, unrelaxing, the wild courage
pitched one degree higher than the wild fear. Courage, the wild thing's
courage to maintain itself alone and living in the midst of a diverse
universe.

10   Did St. Mawr have this courage?

And did Rico?

Ah Rico! He was one of mankind's myriad conspirators, who
conspire to live in absolute physical safety, whilst willing the minor
disintegration of all positive living.

15   But St. Mawr? Was it the natural wild thing in him which caused
these disasters? Or was it the slave, asserting himself for vengeance?

If the latter, let him be shot. It would be a great satisfaction to see
him dead.

But if the former—

20   When she could leave Rico with the nurse, she motored down to
her mother for a couple of days. Rico lay in bed at the farm.

Everything seemed curiously changed. There was a new silence
about the place, a new coolness. Summer had passed with several
thunderstorms, and the blue, cool touch of autumn was about the
25   house. Dahlias and perennial yellow sunflowers were out, the yellow
of ending summer, the red coals of early autumn. First mauve tips of
michaelmas daisies were showing. Something suddenly carried her
away to the great bare spaces of Texas, the blue sky, the flat, burnt
earth, the miles of sunflowers. Another sky, another silence, towards
30   the setting sun.

And suddenly, she craved again for the more absolute silence of
America. English stillness was so soft, like an inaudible murmur of
voices, of presences. But the silence in the empty spaces of America
was still unutterable, almost cruel.

35   St. Mawr was in a small field by himself: she could not bear that
he should be always in stable. Slowly she went through the gate
towards him. And he stood there looking at her, the bright bay
creature.

She could tell he was feeling somewhat subdued, after his late
40   escapade. He was aware of the general human condemnation: the

human damning. But something obstinate and uncanny in him made him not relent.

"Hello! St. Mawr!" she said, as she drew near, and he stood watching her, his ears pricked, his big eyes glancing sideways at her. But he moved away when she wanted to touch him. 5

"Don't trouble," she said, "I don't want to catch you or do anything to you."

He stood still, listening to the sound of her voice, and giving quick, small glances at her. His underlip trembled. But he did not blink. His eyes remained wide and unrelenting. There was a curious malicious 10 obstinacy in him which roused her anger.

"I don't want to touch you," she said. "I only want to look at you, and even you can't prevent that."

She stood gazing hard at him, wanting to know, to settle the question of his meanness or his spirit. A thing with a brave spirit is not mean. 15

He was uneasy, as she watched him. He pretended to hear something, the mares two fields away, and he lifted his head and neighed. She knew the powerful, splendid sound so well: like bells made of living membrane. And he looked so noble again, with his head tilted up, listening, and his male eyes looking proudly over the 20 distance, eagerly.

But it was all a bluff.

He knew, and became silent again. And as he stood there a few yards away from her, his head lifted and wary, his body full of power and tension, his face slightly averted from her, she felt a great animal 25 sadness come from him. A strange animal atmosphere of sadness, that was vague and disseminated through the air, and made her feel as though she breathed grief. She breathed it into her breast, as if it were a great sigh down the ages, that passed into her breast. And she felt a great woe: the woe of human unworthiness. The race of men judged 30 in the consciousness of the animals they have subdued, and there found unworthy, ignoble.

Ignoble men, unworthy of the animals they have subjugated, bred the woe in the spirit of their creatures. St. Mawr, that bright horse, one of the kings of creation in the order below man, it had been a 35 fulfilment for him to serve the brave, reckless, perhaps cruel men of the past, who had a flickering, rising flame of nobility in them. To serve that flame of mysterious further nobility. Nothing matters, but that strange flame, of inborn nobility that obliges men to be brave, and onward plunging. And the horse will bear him on. 40

But now where is the flame of dangerous, forward-pressing nobility in men? Dead, dead, guttering out in a stink of self-sacrifice whose feeble light is a light of exhaustion and *laisser-faire.*

And the horse, is he to go on carrying man forward into this?—this gutter?

No! Man wisely invents motor-cars and other machines, automobile and locomotive. The horse is superannuated, for man.

But alas, man is even more superannuated, for the horse.

Dimly in a woman's muse, Lou realised this, as she breathed the horse's sadness, his accumulated vague woe from the generations of latter-day ignobility. And a grief and a sympathy flooded her, for the horse. She realised now how his sadness recoiled into these frenzies of obstinacy and malevolence. Underneath it all was grief, an unconscious, vague, pervading animal grief, which perhaps only Lewis understood, because he felt the same. The grief of the generous creature which sees all ends turning to the morass of ignoble living.

She did not want to say any more to the horse: she did not want to look at him any more. The grief flooded her soul, that made her want to be alone. She knew now what it all amounted to. She knew that the horse, born to serve nobly, had waited in vain for some one noble to serve. His spirit knew that nobility had gone out of men. And this left him high and dry, in a sort of despair.

As she walked away from him, towards the gate, slowly he began to walk after her.

Phoenix came striding through the gate towards her.

"You not afraid of that horse?" he asked sardonically, in his quiet, subtle voice.

"Not at the present moment," she replied, even more quietly, looking direct at him. She was not in any mood to be jeered at.

And instantly the sardonic grimace left his face, followed by the sudden blankness, and the look of race-misery in the keen eyes.

"Do you want me to be afraid?" she said, continuing to the gate.

"No, I don't want it," he replied, dejected.

"Are you afraid of him yourself?" she said, glancing round. St. Mawr had stopped, seeing Phoenix, and had turned away again.

"I'm not afraid of no horses," said Phoenix.

Lou went on quietly. At the gate, she asked him:

"Don't you like St. Mawr, Phoenix?"

"I like him. He's a very good horse."

"Even after what he's done to Sir Henry?"

"That don't make no difference to him being a good horse."

"But suppose he'd done it to you?"

"I don't care. I say it my own fault."

"Don't you think he is wicked?"

"I don't think so. He don't kick anybody. He don't bite anybody. He don't pitch, he don't buck, he don't do nothing."

"He rears," said Lou.

"Well, what is rearing!" said the man, with a slow, contemptuous smile.

"A good deal, when a horse falls back on you."

"That horse don't want to fall back on you, if you don't make him. If you know how to ride him.—That horse want his own way sometime. If you don't let him, you got to fight him. Then look out!"

"Look out he doesn't kill you, you mean!"

"Look out you don't let him," said Phoenix, with his slow, grim, sardonic smile.

Lou watched the smooth, golden face with its thin line of moustache and its sad eyes with the glint in them. Cruel—there was something cruel in him, right down in the abyss of him. But at the same time, there was an aloneness, and a grim little satisfaction in a fight, and the peculiar courage of an inherited despair. People who inherit despair may at last turn it into greater heroism. It was almost so with Phoenix. Three-quarters of his blood was probably Indian and the remaining quarter, that came through the Mexican father, had the Spanish-American despair to add to the Indian. It was almost complete enough to leave him free to be heroic.

"What are we going to do with him, though?" she asked.

"Why don't you and Mrs Witt go back to America—you never been west. You go west."

"Where, to California?"

"No. To Arizona or New Mexico or Colorado or Wyoming, anywhere. Not to California."

Phoenix looked at her keenly, and she saw the desire dark in him. He wanted to go back. But he was afraid to go back alone, empty-handed, as it were. He had suffered too much, and in that country his sufferings would overcome him, unless he had some other background. He had been too much in contact with the white world, and his own world was too dejected, in a sense, too hopeless for his own hopelessness. He needed an alien contact to give him relief.

But he wanted to go back. His necessity to go back was becoming too strong for him.

"What is it like in Arizona?" she asked. "Isn't it all pale-coloured sand and alkali, and a few cactuses, and terribly hot and deathly?"

"No!" he cried. "I don't take you there. I take you to the mountains,—Trees—" he lifted up his hand and looked at the sky—"big trees—Pine! *Pino real* and *pinavete*, smell good. And then you come down, *piñón*, not very tall, and *cedro*,* cedar, smell good in the fire. And then you see the desert, away below, go miles and miles, and where the canyon go, the crack where it look red! I know, I been there, working a cattle ranch."

He looked at her with a haunted glow in his dark eyes. The poor fellow was suffering from nostalgia. And as he glowed at her in that queer mystical way, she too seemed to see that country, with its dark, heavy mountains holding in their lap the great stretches of pale, creased, silent desert that still is virgin of idea, its word unspoken.

Phoenix was watching her closely and subtly. He wanted something of her. He wanted it intensely, heavily, and he watched her as if he could force her to give it him. He wanted her to take him back to America, because, rudderless, he was afraid to go back alone. He wanted her to take him back: avidly he wanted it. She was to be the means to his end.

Why shouldn't he go back by himself? Why should he crave for her to go too? Why should he want her there?

There was no answer, except that he did.

"Why, Phoenix," she said. "I might possibly go back to America. But you know, Sir Henry would never go there. He doesn't like America, though he's never been. But I'm sure he'd never go there to live."

"Let him stay here," said Phoenix abruptly, the sardonic look on his face as he watched her face. "You come, and let him stay here."

"Ah, that's a whole story!" she said, and moved away.

As she went, he looked after her, standing silent and arrested and watching as an Indian watches.—It was not love. Personal love counts so little when the greater griefs, the greater hopes, the great despairs and the great resolutions come upon us.

She found Mrs Witt rather more silent, more firmly closed within herself, than usual. Her mouth was shut tight, her brows were arched rather more imperiously than ever, she was revolving some inward problem about which Lou was far too wise to enquire.

In the afternoon Dean Vyner and Mrs Vyner came to call on Lady Carrington.

"What bad luck this is, Lady Carrington!" said the Dean. "Knocks Scotland on the head for you this year, I'm afraid. How did you leave your husband?"

"He seems to be doing as well as he could do!" said Lou.

"But how *very* unfortunate!" murmured the invalid Mrs Vyner. "Such a handsome young man, in the bloom of youth! Does he suffer much pain?"

"Chiefly his foot," said Lou.

"Oh, I *do* so hope they'll be able to restore the ankle. Oh how dreadful, to be lamed at his age!"

"The doctor doesn't know. There *may* be a limp," said Lou.

"That horse has certainly left his mark on two good-looking young fellows," said the Dean. "If you don't mind my saying so, Lady Carrington, I think he's a bad egg."

"Who, St. Mawr?" said Lou, in her American sing-song.

"Yes, Lady Carrington," murmured Mrs Vyner, in her invalid's low tone. "Don't you think he ought to be put away? He seems to me the incarnation of cruelty. His neigh! It goes through me like knives. Cruel! Cruel! Oh, I think he should be put away."

"How put away?" murmured Lou, taking on an invalid's low tone herself.

"Shot, I suppose," said the Dean.

"It is quite painless. He'll know nothing," murmured Mrs Vyner hastily. "And think of the harm he has done already! Horrible! Horrible!" she shuddered. "Poor Sir Henry lame for life, and Eddy Edwards disfigured. Besides all that has gone before. Ah no, such a creature ought not to live!"

"To live, and have a groom to look after him and feed him," said the Dean. "It's a bit thick,* while he's smashing up the very people that give him bread—or oats, since he's a horse.—But I suppose you'll be wanting to get rid of him?"

"Rico does," murmured Lou.

"Very naturally. So should I. A vicious horse is worse than a vicious man—except that you are free to put him six feet underground, and end his vice finally, by your own act."

"Do you think St. Mawr is vicious?" said Lou.

"Well, of course—if we're driven to definitions—! I *know* he's dangerous."

"And do you think we ought to shoot everything that is dangerous?"
asked Lou, her colour rising.

"But Lady Carrington, have you consulted your husband? Surely
his wish should be law, in a matter of this sort! And on such an
occasion! For *you*, who are a woman, it is enough that the horse is cruel,
cruel, evil! I felt it long before anything happened. That evil male
cruelty! Ah!" and she clasped her hands convulsively.

"I suppose," said Lou slowly, "that St. Mawr is really Rico's horse:
I gave him to him, I suppose. But I don't believe I could let him shoot
him, for all that."

"Ah Lady Carrington," said the Dean breezily. "You can shift
the responsibility. The horse is a public menace, put it at that. We
can get an order* to have him done away with, at the public expense.
And among ourselves we can find some suitable compensation for you,
as a mark of sympathy. Which, believe me, is very sincere! One hates
to have to destroy a fine looking animal. But I would sacrifice a dozen
rather than have our Rico limping."

"Yes indeed!" murmured Mrs Vyner.

"Will you excuse me one moment, while I see about tea," said Lou,
rising and leaving the room. Her colour was high, and there was a glint
in her eye. These people almost roused her to hatred. Oh, these awful,
house-bred, house-inbred human-beings, how repulsive they were!

She hurried to her mother's dressing room. Mrs Witt was very
carefully putting a touch of red on her lips.

"Mother, they want to shoot St. Mawr," she said.

"I know," said Mrs Witt, as calmly as if Lou had said tea was ready.

"Well—" stammered Lou, rather put out. "Don't you think it
cheek?"

"It depends, I suppose, on the point of view," said Mrs Witt
dispassionately, looking closely at her lips. "I don't think the English
climate agrees with me. I need something to stand up against, no matter
whether it's great heat or great cold. This climate, like the food and
the people, is most always lukewarm or tepid, one or the other. And
the tepid and the lukewarm are not really my line." She spoke with a
slow drawl.

"But they're in the drawing-room, mother, trying to force me to
have St. Mawr killed."

"What about tea?" said Mrs Witt.

"I don't care," said Lou.

Mrs Witt worked the bell-handle.

"I suppose, Louise," she said, in her most beaming eighteenth-century manner, "that these are your guests, so you will preside over the ceremony of pouring out."

"No mother, you do it. I can't smile today."

"I can," said Mrs Witt.   5

And she bowed her head slowly, with a faint, ceremoniously-effusive smile, as if handing a cup of tea.

Lou's face flickered to a smile.

"Then you pour out for them. You can stand them better than I can."   10

"Yes," said Mrs Witt. "I saw Mrs Vyner's hat coming across the churchyard. It looks so like a crumpled cup and saucer, that I have been saying to myself ever since: *Dear Mrs Vyner, can't I fill your cup!*—and then pouring tea into that hat. And I hear the Dean responding: *My head is covered with cream, my cup runneth over**—That   15 is the way they make *me* feel."

They marched downstairs, and Mrs Witt poured tea with that devastating correctness which made Mrs Vyner, who was utterly impervious to sarcasm, pronounce her "indecipherably vulgar."

But the Dean was the old bull-dog, and he had set his teeth in a   20 subject.

"I was talking to Lady Carrington about that stallion, Mrs Witt."

"Did you say stallion?" asked Mrs Witt, with perfect neutrality.

"Why, yes, I presume that's what he is."

"I presume so," said Mrs Witt colourlessly.   25

"I'm afraid Lady Carrington is a little sensitive on the wrong score," said the Dean.

"I beg your pardon," said Mrs Witt, leaning forward in her most colourless polite manner. "You mean the stallion's score?"

"Yes," said the Dean testily. "The horse St. Mawr."   30

"The stallion St. Mawr," echoed Mrs Witt, with utmost mild vagueness. She completely ignored Mrs Vyner, who felt plunged like a specimen into methylated spirit. There was a moment's full stop.

"Yes?" said Mrs Witt naively.

"You agree that we can't have any more of these accidents to your   35 young men?" said the Dean rather hastily.

"I certainly do!" Mrs Witt spoke very slowly, and the Dean's lady began to look up. She might find a loop-hole through which to wriggle into the contest. "You know, Dean, that my son-in-law calls me, for preference, *belle mère*! It sounds so awfully English when he says it,   40

I always see myself as an old grey mare with a bell round her neck,
leading a bunch of horses." She smiled a prim little smile, *very*
conversationally. "Well!" and she pulled herself up from the aside.
"Now as the bell-mare of the bunch of horses, I shall see to it that
5   my son-in-law doesn't go too near that stallion again. That stallion
won't stand mischief."

She spoke so earnestly, that the Dean looked at her with round wide
eyes, completely taken aback.

"We all know, Mrs Witt, that the author of the mischief is St. Mawr
10 himself." he said, in a loud tone.

"Really! you think *that?*" Her voice went up in American surprise.
"Why how *strange*—!" and she lingered over the last word.

"Strange, eh?—After what's just happened?" said the Dean, with
a deadly little smile.

15 "Why yes! Most strange! I saw with my own eyes my son-in-law
pull that stallion over backwards, and hold him down with the reins
as tight as he could hold them; pull St. Mawr's head backwards on
to the ground, till the groom had to crawl up and force the reins out
of my son-in-law's hands. Don't you think that was mischievous on
20 Sir Henry's part?"

The Dean was growing purple. He made an apoplectic movement
with his hand. Mrs Vyner was turned to a seated pillar of salt,*
strangely dressed up.

"Mrs Witt, you are playing on words."

25 "No Dean Vyner, I am not. My son-in-law pulled that horse over
backwards and pinned him down with the reins."

"I am sorry for the horse." said the Dean, with heavy sarcasm.

"I am *very*," said Mrs Witt, "sorry for that stallion: *very!*"

Here Mrs Vyner rose as if a chair-spring had suddenly propelled
30 her to her feet. She was streaky pink in the face.

"Mrs Witt," she panted, "you misdirect your sympathies. That
poor young man—in the beauty of youth—"

"Isn't he *beautiful*—" murmured Mrs Witt, extravagantly in
sympathy. "He's my daughter's husband!" And she looked at the
35 petrified Lou.

"Certainly!" panted the Dean's wife. "And you can defend
that—that—"

"That stallion," said Mrs Witt. "But you see, Mrs Vyner," she
added, leaning forward female and confidential, "if the old grey mare
40 doesn't defend the stallion, who will? All the blooming young ladies

will defend my beautiful son-in-law. You feel so *warmly* for him yourself! I'm an American woman, and I always have to stand up for the accused. And I stand up for that stallion. I say it is not right. He was pulled over backwards and then pinned down by my son-in-law—who may have meant to do it, or may not. And now people abuse him.—Just tell everybody, Mrs Vyner and Dean Vyner—" She looked round at the Dean—"that the belle-mère's sympathies are with the stallion."

She looked from one to the other with a faint and gracious little bow, her black eyebrows arching in her eighteenth-century face like black rainbows, and her full, bold grey eyes absolutely incomprehensible.

"Well, it's a peculiar message to have to hand round, Mrs Witt," the Dean began to boom, when she interrupted him by laying her hand on his arm and leaning forward, looking up into his face like a clinging pleading female:

"Oh, but *do* hand it, Dean, *do* hand it," she pleaded, gazing intently into his face.

He backed uncomfortably from that gaze.

"Since you wish it," he said, in a chest voice.

"I most certainly *do*—" she said, as if she were wishing the sweetest wish on earth. Then turning to Mrs Vyner:

"Goodbye Mrs Vyner. We *do* appreciate your coming, my daughter and I."

"I came out of kindness—" said Mrs Vyner.

"Oh, I know it, I know it," said Mrs Witt. "Thank you *so* much. Goodbye! Goodbye Dean! Who is taking the morning service on Sunday. I hope it is you, because I want to come."

"It *is* me," said the Dean. "Goodbye! Well, goodbye Lady Carrington. I shall be going over to see our young man tomorrow, and will gladly take you or anything you have to send."

"Perhaps Mother would like to go," said Lou, softly, plaintively.

"Well, we shall see," said the Dean. "Goodbye for the present!"

Mother and daughter stood at the window watching the two cross the churchyard. Dean and wife knew it, but daren't look round, and daren't admit the fact to one another.

Lou was grinning with a complete grin that gave her an odd, dryad or faun look, intensified.

"It was almost as good as pouring tea into her hat," said Mrs Witt serenely. "People like that tire me out. I shall take a glass of sherry."

"So will I, mother.—It was even better than pouring tea in her

hat.—You meant, didn't you, if you poured tea in her hat, to put cream
and sugar in first?"

"I did," said Mrs Witt.

But after the excitement of the encounter had passed away, Lou felt
5   as if her life had passed away too. She went to bed, feeling she could
stand no more.

In the morning she found her mother sitting at a window watching
a funeral. It was raining heavily, so that some of the mourners even
wore mackintosh coats. The funeral was in the poorer corner of the
10 churchyard, where another new grave was covered with wreaths of
sodden, shrivelling flowers.—The yellowish coffin stood on the wet
earth, in the rain: the curate held his hat, in a sort of permanent salute,
above his head, like a little umbrella, as he hastened on with the service.
The people seemed too wet to weep more wet.

15 It was a long coffin.

"Mother, do you really *like* watching?" asked Lou irritably, as Mrs
Witt sat in complete absorption.

"I do, Louise, I really enjoy it."

"Enjoy, mother!"—Lou was almost disgusted.

20 "I'll tell you why. I imagine I'm the one in the coffin—this is a girl
of eighteen, who died of consumption—and those are my relatives, and
I'm watching them put me away. And you know, Louise, I've come
to the conclusion that hardly anybody in the world really lives, and
so hardly anybody really dies. They may well say *Oh Death where*
25 *is thy sting-a-ling-a-ling?** Even Death can't sting those that have never
really lived.—I always used to want that—to die without death
stinging me.—And I'm sure the girl in the coffin is saying to herself:
Fancy Aunt Emma putting on a drab slicker, and wearing it while they*
bury me. Doesn't show much respect. But then my mother's family always
30 *were common!* I feel there should be a solemn burial of a roll of
newspapers containing the account of the death and funeral, next week.
It would be just as serious: the grave of all the world's remarks—"

"I don't want to think about it, mother. One ought to be able to
laugh at it. I want to laugh at it."

35 "Well, Louise, I think it's just as great a mistake to laugh at
everything as to cry at everything. Laughter's not the one panacea,
either. I should *really* like, before I do come to be buried in a box,
to know where I am. That young girl in that coffin never was
anywhere—any more than the newspaper remarks on her death and
40 burial. And I begin to wonder if I've ever been anywhere. I seem to

have been a daily sequence of newspaper remarks, myself. I'm sure I never really conceived you and gave you birth. It all happened in newspaper notices. It's a newspaper fact that you are my child, and that's about all there is to it."

Lou smiled as she listened.

"I always knew you were philosophic, mother. But I never dreamed it would come to elegies in a country churchyard,* written to your motherhood."

"*Exactly*, Louise! Here I sit and sing the elegy to my own motherhood. I never had any motherhood, except in newspaper fact. I never was a wife, except in newspaper notices. I never was a young girl, except in newspaper remarks. Bury everything I ever said or that was said about me, and you've buried *me*. But since Kind Words Can Never Die,* I can't be buried, and death has no sting-aling-aling for *me*!—Now listen to me, Louise: I want death to be real to me—not as it was to that young girl. I *want* it to hurt me, Louise. If it hurts me enough, I shall know I was alive."

She set her face and gazed under half-dropped lids at the funeral, stoic, fate-like, and yet, for the first time, with a certain pure wistfulness of a young, virgin girl. This frightened Lou very much. She was so used to the matchless Amazon* in her mother, that when she saw her sit there, still, wistful, virginal, tender as a girl who has never taken armour, wistful at the window that only looked on graves, a serious terror took hold of the young woman. The terror of *too late*!

Lou felt years, centuries older than her mother, at that moment, with the tiresome responsibility of youth to protect and guide their elders.

"What can we do about it, mother?" she asked protectively.

"Do nothing, Louise. I'm not going to have anybody wisely steering my canoe, now I feel the rapids are near. I shall go with the river. Don't you pretend to do anything for me. I've done enough mischief myself, that way. I'm going down the stream, at last."

There was a pause.

"But in actuality, what?" asked Lou a little ironically.

"I don't quite know. Wait a while."

"Go back to America?"

"That is possible."

"I may come too."

"I've always waited for you to go back of your own will."

Lou went away, wandering round the house. She was so unutterably tired of everything—weary of the house, the graveyard, weary of the thought of Rico. She would have to go back to him tomorrow, to nurse him. Poor old Rico, going on like an amiable machine from day to day. It wasn't his fault. But his life was a rattling nullity, and her life rattled in null correspondence. She had hardly strength

5 enough to stop rattling and be still. Perhaps she had not strength enough.

She did not know. She felt so weak, that unless something carried her away, she would go on rattling her bit in the great machine of human life, till she collapsed, and her rattle rattled itself out, and there

10 was a sort of barren silence where the sound of her had been.

She wandered out in the rain, to the coach house where Lewis and Phoenix were sitting facing one another, one on a bin, the other on the inner doorstep.

"Well," she said, smiling oddly. "What's to be done?"

15 The two men stood up. Outside the rain fell steadily on the flagstones of the yard, past the leaves of trees. Lou sat down on the little iron step of the dogcart.

"That's cold," said Phoenix. "You sit here." And he threw a yellow horse-blanket on the box where he had been sitting.

20 "I don't want to take your seat," she said.

"All right, you take it."

He moved across and sat gingerly on the shaft of the dogcart.—Lou seated herself, and loosened her soft tartan shawl. Her face was pink and fresh, and her dark hair curled almost merrily in the damp. But

25 under her eyes were the finger-prints of deadly weariness.

She looked up at the two men, again smiling in her odd fashion. "What are we going to do?" she asked.

They looked at her closely, seeking her meaning.

"What about?" said Phoenix, a faint smile reflecting on his face,

30 merely because she smiled.

"Oh, everything," she said, hugging her shawl again. "You know what they want? They want to shoot St. Mawr."

The two men exchanged glances.

"Who want it?" said Phoenix.

35 "Why—all our *friends!*" she made a little *moue.* "Dean Vyner does."

Again the men exchanged glances. There was a pause. Then Phoenix said, looking aside:

"The boss is selling him."

40 "Who?"

"Sir Henry."—The half-breed always spoke the title with difficulty, and with a sort of sneer. "He sell him to Miss Manby."

"How do you know?"

"The man from Corrabach told me last night. Flora, she say it." Lou's eyes met the sardonic, empty-seeing eyes of Phoenix direct. There was too much sarcastic understanding. She looked aside.

"What else did he say?" she asked.

"I don't know," said Phoenix, evasively. "He say they cut him—else shoot him. Think they cut him—and if he die, he die."

Lou understood. He meant they would geld St. Mawr—at his age. She looked at Lewis. He sat with his head down, so she could not see his face.

"Do you think it is true?" she asked. "Lewis? Do you think they would try to geld St. Mawr—to make him a gelding?"

Lewis looked up at her. There was a faint deadly glimmer of contempt on his face.

"Very likely, Mam," he said.

She was afraid of his cold, uncanny pale eyes, with their uneasy grey dawn of contempt. These two men, with their silent, deadly inner purpose, were not like other men. They seemed like two silent enemies of all the other men she knew. Enemies in the great white camp, disguised as servants, waiting the incalculable opportunity. What the opportunity might be, none knew.

"Sir Henry hasn't mentioned anything to me, about selling St. Mawr to Miss Manby," she said.

The derisive flicker of a smile came on Phoenix's face.

"He sell him first, and tell you then," he said, with his deadly impassive manner.

"But do you really think so?" she asked.

It was extraordinary, how much corrosive contempt Phoenix could convey, saying nothing. She felt it almost as an insult. Yet it was a relief to her.

"You know, I can't believe it. I can't believe Sir Henry would want to have St. Mawr mutilated. I believe he'd rather shoot him."

"You think so?" said Phoenix, with a faint grin.

Lou turned to Lewis.

"Lewis, will you tell me what you truly think."

Lewis looked at her with a hard, straight, fearless British stare.

"That man Philips was in the *Moon and Stars* last night. He said Miss Manby told him, she was buying St. Mawr, and she asked him, if he thought it would be safe to cut him, and make a horse of him. He said it would be better, take some of the nonsense out of him. He's no good for a sire, anyhow—"

Lewis dropped his head again, and tapped a tattoo with the toe of his rather small foot.

"And what do you think?" said Lou.—It occurred to her how sensible and practical Miss Manby was, so much more so than the Dean.

Lewis looked up at her with his pale eyes.

"It won't have anything to do with me," he said. "I shan't go to Corrabach Hall."

"What will you do, then?"

Lewis did not answer. He looked at Phoenix.

"Maybe him and me go to America," said Phoenix, looking at the void.

"Can he get in?" said Lou.

"Yes, he can. I know how," said Phoenix.

"And the money?" she said.

"We got money."

There was a silence, after which she asked of Lewis:

"You'd leave St. Mawr to his fate?"

"I can't help his fate," said Lewis. "There's too many people in the world, for me to help anything."

"Poor St. Mawr!"

She went indoors again, and up to her room: then higher, to the top rooms of the tall Georgian house. From one window she could see the fields in the rain. She could see St. Mawr himself, alone as usual, standing with his head up looking across the fences. He was streaked dark with rain. Beautiful, with his poised head and massive neck, and his supple hindquarters. He was neighing to Poppy. Clear on the wet wind came the sound of his bell-like, stallion's calling, that Mrs Vyner called cruel. It was a strange noise, with a splendour that belonged to another world-age. The mean cruelty of Mrs Vyner's humanitarianism, the barren cruelty of Flora Manby, the eunuch cruelty of Rico. Our whole eunuch civilisation, nasty-minded as eunuchs are, with their kind of sneaking, sterilising cruelty.

Yet even she herself, seeing St. Mawr's conceited march along the fence, could not help addressing him:

"Yes my boy! If you knew what Miss Flora Manby was preparing for you! *She'll* sharpen a knife that will settle you."

And Lou called her mother.

The two American women stood high at the window, overlooking the wet, close, hedged-and-fenced English landscape. Everything enclosed, enclosed, to stifling. The very apples on the trees looked so shut in, it was impossible to imagine any speck of "Knowledge" lurking inside them.* Good to eat, good to cook, good even for show. But the wild sap of untameable and inexhaustible knowledge—no! Bred out of them. Geldings, even the apples.

Mrs Witt listened to Lou's half-humorous statements.

"You must admit, mother, Flora is a sensible girl," she said.

"I admit it, Louise."

"She goes straight to the root of the matter."

"And eradicates the root. Wise girl! And what is your answer?"

"I don't know, mother. What would you say?"

"I know what *I* should say."

"Tell me."

"I should say: *Miss Manby, you may have my husband, but not my horse. My husband won't need emasculating, and my horse I won't have you meddle with. I'll preserve one last male thing in the museum of this world, if I can.*"

Lou listened, smiling faintly.

"That's what I will say," she replied at length. "The funny thing is, mother, they think all their men with their bare faces or their little quotation-mark's moustaches *are* so tremendously male. That fox-hunting one!"

"I know it. Like little male motor-cars. Give him a little gas, and start him on the low gear, and away he goes: all his male gear rattling, like a cheap motor-car."

"I'm afraid I dislike men altogether, mother."

"You may, Louise. Think of Flora Manby, and how you love the fair sex."

"After all, St. Mawr is better. And I'm glad if he gives them a kick in the face."

"Ah Louise!" Mrs Witt suddenly clasped her hands with wicked passion. "*Ay, qué gozo!** as our Juan used to say, on your father's ranch in Texas." She gazed in a sort of wicked ecstasy out of the window.

They heard Lou's maid softly calling Lady Carrington from below. Lou went to the stairs.

"What is it?"

"Lewis wants to speak to you, my Lady."

"Send him into the sitting-room."

The two women went down.

"What is it, Lewis?" asked Lou.

"Am I to bring in St. Mawr, in case they send for him from
5   Corrabach?"

"No," said Lou swiftly.

"Wait a minute," put in Mrs Witt. "What makes you think they
will send for St. Mawr from Corrabach, Lewis?" she asked, suave as
a grey leopard cat.

10   "Miss Manby went up to Flints Farm with Dean Vyner this
morning, and they've just come back. They stopped the car, and
Miss Manby got out at the field gate, to look at St. Mawr. I'm
thinking, if she made the bargain with Sir Henry, she'll be sending
a man over this afternoon, and if I'd better brush St. Mawr down a
15   bit, in case."

The man stood strangely still, and the words came like shadows of
his real meaning. It was a challenge.

"I see," said Mrs Witt slowly.

Lou's face darkened. She too saw.

20   "So that is her game," she said. "That is why they got me down
here."

"Never mind, Louise," said Mrs Witt. Then to Lewis: "Yes, please
bring in St. Mawr. You wish it, don't you, Louise?"

"Yes," hesitated Lou. She saw by Mrs Witt's closed face that a
25   counter-move was prepared.

"And Lewis," said Mrs Witt. "My daughter may wish you to ride
St. Mawr this afternoon—not to Corrabach Hall."

"Very good, Mam."

Mrs Witt sat silent for some time, after Lewis had gone, gathering
30   inspiration from the wet, grisly gravestones.

"Don't you think it's time we made a move, daughter?" she asked.

"Any move," said Lou desperately.

"Very well then.—My dearest friends, and my *only* friends, in this
country, are in Oxfordshire. I will set off to *ride* to Merriton this
35   afternoon, and Lewis will ride with me on St. Mawr."

"But you can't ride to Merriton in an afternoon." said Lou.

"I know it. I shall ride across country. I shall *enjoy* it, Louise.—
Yes.—I shall consider I am on my way back to America. I am most
deadly tired of this country. From Merriton I shall make my
40   arrangements to go to America, and take Lewis and Phoenix and St.

Mawr along with me. I think they want to go.—You will decide for yourself."

"Yes, I'll come too," said Lou casually.

"Very well. I'll start immediately after lunch, for I can't *breathe* in this place any longer. Where are Henry's automobile maps?"

Afternoon saw Mrs Witt, in a large waterproof cape, mounted on her horse, Lewis, in another cape, mounted on St. Mawr, trotting through the rain, splashing in the puddles, moving slowly southwards. They took the open country, and would pass quite near to Flints Farm. But Mrs Witt did not care. With great difficulty she had managed to fasten a small waterproof roll behind her, containing her night things. She seemed to breathe the first breath of freedom.

And sure enough, an hour or so after Mrs Witt's departure, arrived Flora Manby in a splashed up motor-car, accompanied by her sister, and bringing a groom and a saddle.

"Do you know, Harry sold me St. Mawr," she said. "I'm just wild to get that horse in hand."

"How?" said Lou.

"Oh, I don't know. There are ways. Do you mind if Philips rides him over now, to Corrabach?—Oh, I forgot, Harry sent you a note."

"*Dearest Loulina: Have you been gone from here two days or two years. It seems the latter. You are terribly missed. Flora wanted so much to buy St. Mawr, to save us further trouble, that I have sold him to her. She is giving me what we paid: rather, what you paid; so of course the money is yours. I am thankful we are rid of the animal, and that he falls into competent hands—I asked her please to remove him from your charge today. And I can't tell how much easier I am in my mind, to think of him gone. You are coming back to me tomorrow aren't you? I shall think of nothing else but you, till I see you. A rivederci, darling dear! R.*"

"I'm so sorry," said Lou. "Mother went on horseback to see some friends, and Lewis went with her on St. Mawr. He knows the road."

"She'll be back this evening?" said Flora.

"I don't know. Mother is so uncertain. She may be away a day or two."

"Well, here's the cheque for St. Mawr."

"No, I won't take it now—No thank you—not till mother comes back with the goods."

Flora was chagrined. The two women knew they hated one another. The visit was a brief one.

Mrs Witt rode on in the rain, which abated as the afternoon wore

down, and the evening came without rain, and with a suffusion of pale
yellow light. All the time she had trotted in silence, with Lewis just
behind her. And she scarcely saw the heather-covered hill with the
deep clefts between them, nor the oak-woods, nor the lingering fox
gloves, nor the earth at all. Inside herself she felt a profound
repugnance for the English country: she preferred even the crudeness
of Central Park in New York.

And she felt an almost savage desire to get away from Europe, from
everything European. Now she was really *en route*, she cared not a straw
for St. Mawr or for Lewis or anything. Something just writhed inside
her, all the time, against Europe. That closeness, that sense of
cohesion, that sense of being fused into a lump with all the rest—no
matter how much distance you kept—this drove her mad. In America
the cohesion was a matter of choice and will. But in Europe it was
organic, like the helpless particles of one sprawling body. And the great
body in a state of incipient decay.

She was a woman of fifty-one: and she seemed hardly to have lived
a day. She looked behind her—the thin trees and swamps of Louisiana,
the sultry, sub-tropical excitement of decaying New Orleans, the vast
bare dryness of Texas, with mobs of cattle in an illumined dust! The
half-European thrills of New York! The false stability of Boston! A
clever husband, who was a brilliant lawyer, but who was far more
thrilled by his cattle ranch than by his law: and who drank heavily,
and died. The years of first widowhood in Boston, consoled by a
self-satisfied sort of intellectual courtship from clever men.—For
curiously enough, while she wanted it, she had always been able to
compel men to pay court to her. All kinds of men.—Then a rather
dashing time in New York—when she was in her early forties. Then
the long *visual* philandering in Europe. She left off "loving," save
through the eye, when she came to Europe. And when she made her
trips to America, she found it was finished there also, her "loving."

What was the matter? Examining herself, she had long ago decided
that her nature was a destructive force. But then, she justified herself,
she had only destroyed that which was destructible. If she could have
found something indestructible, especially in men, though she would
have fought against it, she would have been glad at last to be defeated
by it.

That was the point. She really wanted to be defeated, in her own
eyes. And nobody had ever defeated her. Men were never really her
match. A woman of terrible strong health, she felt even that in her

strong limbs there was far more electric power than in the limbs of any man she had met. That curious fluid electric force, that could make any man kiss her hand, if she so willed it. A queen, as far as she wished. And not having been very clever at school, she always had the greatest respect for the mental powers. Her own were not mental powers. 5 Rather electric, as of some strange physical dynamo within her. So she had been ready to bow before Mind.

But alas! After a brief time, she had found Mind, at least the man who was supposed to have the mind, bowing before her. Her own peculiar dynamic force was stronger than the force of Mind. She could 10 make Mind kiss her hand.

And not by any sensual tricks. She did not really care about sensualities, especially as a younger woman. Sex was a mere adjunct. She cared about the mysterious, intense, dynamic sympathy that could flow between her and some "live" man—a man who was highly 15 conscious, a real live wire. That she cared about.

But she had never rested until she had made the man she admired: and admiration was the root of her attraction to any man: made him kiss her hand. In both senses, actual and metaphorical. Physical and metaphysical. Conquered his country. 20

She had always succeeded. And she believed that, if she cared, she always *would* succeed. In the world of living men. Because of the power that was in her, in her arms, in her strong shapely, but terrible hands, in all the great dynamo of her body.

For this reason she had been so terribly contemptuous of Rico, and 25 of Lou's infatuation. Ye Gods! what was Rico in the scale of men!

Perhaps she despised the younger generation too easily. Because she did not see its sources of power, she concluded it was powerless. Whereas perhaps the power of accommodating oneself to any circumstance and committing oneself to no circumstance is the last triumph 30 of mankind.

Her generation had had its day. She had had her day. The world of her men had sunk into a sort of insignificance. And with a great contempt she despised the world that had come into place instead: the world of Rico and Flora Manby, the world represented, to her, by the 35 Prince of Wales.*

In such a world, there was nothing even to conquer. It gave everything and gave nothing to everybody and anybody all the time. *Dio benedetto!** as Rico would say. A great complicated tangle of nonentities ravelled in nothingness. So it seemed to her. 40

Great God! This was the generation she had helped to bring into the world.

She had had her day. And, as far as the mysterious battle of life went, she had won all the way. Just as Cleopatra, in the mysterious 5 business of a woman's life, won all the way.

Though that bald tough Caesar had drawn his iron from the fire without losing much of its temper. And he had gone his way. And Antony surely was splendid to die with.

In her life there had been no tough Caesar to go his way in cold 10 blood, away from her. Her men had gone from her like dogs on three legs, into the crowd. And certainly there was no gorgeous Antony to die for and with.

Almost she was tempted in her heart to cry: "Conquer me, Oh God, before I die!"—But then she had a terrible contempt for the God that 15 was supposed to rule this universe. She felt she could make *him* kiss her hand. Here she was a woman of fifty-one, past the change of life. And her great dread was to die an empty, barren death. Oh, if only Death might open dark wings of mystery and consolation. To die an easy, barren death. To pass out as she had passed in, without mystery 20 or the rustling of darkness! That was her last, final, ashy dread.

"Old!" she said to herself. "I am not *old*! I have lived many years, that is all. But I am as timeless as an hourglass that turns morning and night, and spills the hours of sleep one way, the hours of consciousness the other way, without itself being affected. Nothing in 25 all my life has ever truly affected me.—I believe Cleopatra only tried the asp, as she tried her pearls in wine,* to see if it would really, really have any effect on her. Nothing had ever really had any effect on her, neither Caesar nor Antony nor any of them. Never once had she really been lost, lost to herself. Then try death, see if that trick would work. 30 If she would lose herself to herself that way.—Ah death—!"

But Mrs Witt mistrusted death too. She felt she might pass out as a bed of asters passes out in autumn, to mere nothingness.—And something in her longed to die, at least, *positively*: to be folded then at last into throbbing wings of mystery, like a hawk that goes to 35 sleep. Not like a thing made into a parcel and put into the last rubbish-heap.

So she rode trotting across the hills, mile after mile, in silence. Avoiding the roads, avoiding everything, avoiding everybody, just trotting forwards, towards night.

40 And by nightfall they had travelled twenty-five miles. She had

motored around this country, and knew the little towns and the inns. She knew where she would sleep.

The morning came beautiful and sunny. A woman so strong in health, why should she ride with the face of death before her eyes? But she did.

Yet in sunny morning she must do something about it.

"Lewis!" she said. "Come here and tell me something, please! Tell me," she said, "do you believe in God?"

"In God!" he said, wondering. "I never think about it."

"But do you say your prayers?"

"No Mam!"

"Why don't you?"

He thought about it for some minutes.

"I don't like religion. My aunt and uncle were religious."

"You don't like religion," she repeated. "And you don't believe in God.—Well then—"

"Nay!" he hesitated. "I never said I didn't believe in God.—Only I'm sure I'm not a Methodist. And I feel a fool in a proper church.—And I feel a fool saying my prayers.—And I feel a fool when ministers and parsons come getting at me.—I never think about God, if folks don't try to make me." He had a small, sly smile, almost gay.

"And you don't like feeling a fool?" She smiled rather patronisingly.

"No Mam."

"Do I make you feel a fool?" she asked, drily.

He looked at her without answering.

"Why don't you answer?" she said, pressing.

"I think you'd like to make a fool of me sometimes," he said.

"Now?" she pressed.

He looked at her with that slow, distant look.

"Maybe!" he said, rather unconcernedly.

Curiously, she couldn't touch him. He always seemed to be watching her from a distance, as if from another country. Even if she made a fool of him, something in him would all the time be far away from her, not implicated.

She caught herself up in the personal game, and returned to her own isolated question. A vicious habit made her start the personal tricks. She didn't want to really.

There was something about this little man—sometimes, to herself, she called him *Little Jack Horner, Sat in a corner*—that irritated her and made her want to taunt him. His peculiar little inaccessibility, that was so tight and easy.

Then again, there was something, his way of looking at her as if he looked from out of another country, a country of which he was an inhabitant, and where she had never been: this touched her strangely. Perhaps behind this little man was the mystery. In spite of the fact that in actual life, in her world, he was only a groom, almost chétif,* with his legs a little bit horsey and bowed; and of no education, saying *Yes Mam!* and *No Mam!* and accomplishing nothing, simply nothing at all on the face of the earth. Strictly a nonentity.

And yet, what made him perhaps the only real entity to her, his seeming to inhabit another world than hers. A world dark and still, where language never ruffled the growing leaves, and seared their edges like a bad wind.

Was it an illusion, however? Sometimes she thought it was. Just bunkum, which she had faked up, in order to have something to mystify about.

But then, when she saw Phoenix and Lewis silently together, she knew there *was* another communion, silent, excluding her. And sometimes when Lewis was alone with St. Mawr: and once, when she saw him pick up a bird that had stunned itself against a wire: she had realised another world, silent, where each creature is alone in its own aura of silence, the mystery of power: as Lewis had power with St. Mawr, and even with Phoenix.

The visible world, and the invisible. Or rather, the audible and the inaudible. She had lived so long, and so completely, in the visible, audible world. She would not easily admit that other, inaudible. She always wanted to jeer, as she approached the brink of it.

Even now, she wanted to jeer at the little fellow, because of his holding himself inaccessible within the inaudible, silent world. And she knew he knew it.

"Did you never want to be rich, and be a gentleman, like Sir Henry?" she asked.

"I would many times have liked to be rich. But I never exactly wanted to be a gentleman," he said.

"Why not?"

"I can't exactly say. I should be uncomfortable if I was like they are."

"And are you comfortable now?"

"When I'm let alone."

"And do they let you alone? Does the world let you alone?"

"No, they don't."

"Well then—!"

"I keep to myself all I can."

"And are you comfortable, as you call it, when you keep to yourself?"

"Yes, I am."

"But when you keep to yourself, what do you keep to? What precious treasure have you to keep to?"

He looked, and saw she was jeering.

"None," he said. "I've got nothing of that sort."

She rode impatiently on ahead.

And the moment she had done so, she regretted it. She might put the little fellow, with contempt, out of her reckoning. But no, she would not do it.

She had put so much out of her reckoning: soon she would be left in an empty circle, with her empty self at the centre.

She reined in again.

"Lewis!" she said. "I don't want you to take offence at anything I say."

"No Mam."

"I don't want you to say just *No Mam!* all the time!" she cried impulsively. "Promise me."

"Yes Mam!"

"But really! Promise me you won't be offended at whatever I say."

"Yes Mam!"

She looked at him searchingly. To her surprise, she was almost in tears. A woman of her years! And with a servant!

But his face was blank and stony, with a stony, distant look of pride that made him inaccessible to her emotions.

He met her eyes again: with that cold, distant look, looking straight into her hot, confused, pained self. So cold and as if merely refuting her. He didn't believe her, nor trust her, nor like her even. She was an attacking enemy to him. Only he stayed really far away from her, looking down at her from a sort of distant hill where her weapons could not reach: not quite.

And at the same time, it hurt him in a dumb, living way, that she made these attacks on him. She could see the cloud of hurt in his eyes, no matter how distantly he looked at her.

They bought food in a village shop, and sat under a tree near a field

where men were already cutting oats, in a warm valley. Lewis had
stabled the horses for a couple of hours, to feed and rest. But he came
to join her under the tree, to eat.—He sat at a little distance from her,
with the bread and cheese in his small brown hands, eating silently,
and watching the harvesters. She was cross with him, and therefore
she was stingy, would give him nothing to eat but dry bread and cheese.
Herself, she was not hungry.—So all the time he kept his face a little
averted from her. As a matter of fact, he kept his whole being averted
from her, away from her. He did not want to touch her, nor to be
touched by her. He kept his spirit there, alert, on its guard, but out
of contact. It was as if he had unconsciously accepted the battle, the
old battle. He was her target, the old object of her deadly weapons.
But he refused to shoot back. It was as if he caught all her missiles
in full flight, before they touched him, and silently threw them on the
ground behind him. And in some essential part of himself he ignored
her, staying in another world.

That other world! Mere male armour of artificial imperviousness!
It angered her.

Yet she knew, by the way he watched the harvesters, and the
grasshoppers popping into notice, that it was another world. And when
a girl went by, carrying food to the field, it was at him she glanced.
And he gave that quick, animal little smile that came from him
unawares. Another world!

Yet also, there was a sort of meanness about him: a *suffisance*! A
keep-yourself-for-yourself, and don't give yourself away.

Well!—she rose impatiently.

It was hot in the afternoon, and she was rather tired. She went to
the inn and slept, and did not start again till teatime.

Then they had to ride rather late. The sun sank, among a smell of
cornfields, clear and yellow-red behind motionless dark trees. Pale
smoke rose from cottage chimneys. Not a cloud was in the sky, which
held the upward-floating light like a bowl inverted on purpose. A new
moon sparkled and was gone. It was beginning of night.

Away in the distance, they saw a curious pinkish glare of fire,
probably furnaces. And Mrs Witt thought she could detect the scent
of furnace smoke, or factory smoke. But then she always said that of
the English air: it was never quite free of the smell of smoke, coal-smoke.

They were riding slowly on a path through fields, down a long slope.
Away below was a puther* of lights. All the darkness seemed full of
half-spent crossing lights, a curious uneasiness. High in the sky a star

seemed to be walking. It was an aeroplane with a light. Its buzz rattled
above. Not a space, not a speck of this country that wasn't humanised,
occupied by the human claim. Not even the sky.

They descended slowly through a dark wood, which they had
entered through a gate. Lewis was all the time dismounting and
opening gates, letting her pass, shutting the gate and mounting again.

So, in a while she came to the edge of the wood's darkness, and saw
the open pale concave of the world beyond. The darkness was never
dark. It shook with the concussion of many invisible lights, lights of
towns, villages, mines, factories, furnaces, squatting in the valleys and
behind all the hills.

Yet, as Rachel Witt drew rein at the gate emerging from the wood,
a very big, soft star fell in heaven, cleaving the hubbub of this human
night with a gleam from the greater world.

"See! a star falling!" said Lewis, as he opened the gate.

"I saw it," said Mrs Witt, walking her horse past him.

There was a curious excitement of wonder, or magic, in the little
man's voice. Even in this night something strange had stirred awake
in him.

"You ask me about God," he said to her, walking his horse
alongside in the shadow of the wood's-edge, the darkness of the old
Pan, that kept our artificially-lit world at bay. "I don't know about
God. But when I see a star fall like that out of long-distance places
in the sky: and the moon sinking saying Goodbye! Goodbye!
Goodbye! and nobody listening: I think I hear something, though I
wouldn't call it God."

"What then?" said Rachel Witt.

"And you smell the smell of oak-leaves now," he said, "now the
air is cold. They smell to me more alive than people. The trees hold
their bodies hard and still, but they watch and listen with their leaves.
And I think they say to me: *Is that you passing there, Morgan Lewis?
All right, you pass quickly, we shan't do anything to you. You are like
a holly-bush.*"

"Yes," said Rachel Witt, drily. "*Why?*"

"All the time, the trees grow, and listen. And if you cut a tree down
without asking pardon, trees will hurt you some time in your life, in
the night time."

"I suppose," said Rachel Witt, "that's an old superstition."

"They say that ash-trees don't like people. When the other people
were most in the country—I mean like what they call fairies, that have

all gone now—they liked ash-trees best. And you know the little green
things with little small nuts in them, that come flying down from
ash-trees—*pigeons*, we call them—they're the seeds—the other people
used to catch them and eat them before they fell to the ground. And
5   that made the people so they could hear trees living and feeling
things.—But when all these people that there are now came to
England, they liked the oak-trees best, because their pigs ate the
acorns. So now you can tell the ash-trees are mad, they want to kill
all these people. But the oak-trees are many more than the ash-trees."
10   "And do you eat the ash-tree seeds?" she asked.
"I always ate them, when I was little. Then I wasn't frightened
of ash-trees, like most of the others. And I wasn't frightened of the
moon. If you didn't go near the fire all day, and if you didn't eat any
cooked food nor anything that had been in the sun, but only things
15 like turnips or radishes or pig-nuts, and then went without any clothes
on, in the full moon, then you could see the people in the moon, and
go with them. They never have fire, and they never speak, and their
bodies are clear almost like jelly. They die in a minute if there's a bit
of fire near them. But they know more than we. Because unless fire
20 touches them, they never die. They see people live and they see people
perish, and they say, people are only like twigs on a tree, you break
them off the tree, and kindle fire with them. You make a fire of them,
and they are gone, the fire is gone, everything is gone. But the people
of the moon don't die, and fire is nothing to them. They look at it from
25 the distance of the sky, and see it burning things up, people all
appearing and disappearing like twigs that come in spring and you cut
them in autumn and make a fire of them and they are gone. And they
say: what do people matter? If you want to matter, you must become
a moon-boy. Then all your life, fire can't blind you and people can't
30 hurt you. Because at full moon you can join the moon people, and go
through the air and pass any cool places, pass through rocks and
through the trunks of trees, and when you come to people lying warm
in bed, you punish them."
"How?"
35   "You sit on the pillow where they breathe, and you put a web across
their mouth, so they can't breathe the fresh air that comes from the
moon. So they go on breathing the same air again and again, and that
makes them more and more stupefied. The sun gives out heat, but
the moon gives out fresh air. That's what the moon people do: they
40 wash the air clean with moonlight."

He was talking with a strange eager naïveté that amused Rachel Witt, and made her a little uncomfortable in her skin. Was he after all no more than a sort of imbecile?

"Who told you all this stuff?" she asked abruptly.

And, as abruptly, he pulled himself up.

"We used to say it, when we were children."

"But you don't believe it? It *is* only childishness, after all."

He paused a moment or two.

"No," he said, in his ironical little day-voice. "I know I shan't make anything but a fool of myself, with that talk. But all sorts of things go through our heads, and some seem to linger, and some don't.* But you asking me about God put it into my mind, I suppose. I don't know what sort of things I believe in: only I know it's not what the chapel-folks believe in.* We none of us believe in them when it comes to earning a living, or, with you people, when it comes to spending your fortune. Then we know that bread costs money, and even your sleep you have to pay for.—That's work. Or, with you people, it's just owning property and seeing you get your value for your money.—But a man's mind is always full of things. And some people's minds, like my aunt and uncle, are full of religion and hell for everybody except themselves. And some people's minds are all money, money, money, and how to get hold of something they haven't got hold of yet. And some people, like you, are always curious about what everybody else in the world is after. And some people are all for enjoying themselves and being thought much of, and some, like Lady Carrington, don't know what to do with themselves. Myself, I don't want to have in my mind the things other people have in their minds. I'm one that likes my own things best. And if, when I see a bright star fall, like tonight, I think to myself: *There's movement in the sky. The world is going to change again. They're throwing something to us from the distance, and we've got to have it, whether we want it or not. Tomorrow there will be a difference for everybody, thrown out of the sky upon us, whether we want it or not:* then that's how I want to think, so let me please myself."

"You know what a shooting star actually is, I suppose?—and that there are always many in August, because we pass through a region of them?"

"Yes Mam, I've been told. But stones don't come at us from the sky for nothing. Either it's like when a man tosses an apple to you out of his orchard, as you go by. Or it's like when somebody shies a stone at you, to cut your head open. You'll never make me believe the sky

is like an empty house with a slate falling from the roof. The world
has its own life, the sky has a life of its own, and never is it like stones
rolling down a rubbish heap and falling into a pond. Many things
twitch and twitter within the sky, and many things happen beyond
5   us. My own way of thinking is my own way."
    "I never knew you talk so much."
    "No Mam. It's your asking me that about God. Or else it's the
night-time.—I don't believe in God and being good and going to
Heaven. Neither do I worship idols, so I'm not a heathen as my aunt
10 called me. Never from a boy did I want to believe the things they kept
grinding in their guts at home, and at Sunday School, and at school.
A man's mind has to be full of something, so I keep to what we used
to think as lads. It's childish nonsense, I know it. But it suits me. Better
than other people's stuff. Your man Phoenix is about the same, when
15 he lets on.—Anyhow, it's my own stuff, that we believed as lads, and
I like it better than other people's stuff.—You asking about God made
me let on. But I would never belong to any club, or trades-union, and
God's the same to my mind."
    With this he gave a little kick to his horse, and St. Mawr went
20 dancing excitedly along the highway they now entered, leaving Mrs
Witt to trot after as rapidly as she could.
    When she came to the hotel, to which she had telegraphed for rooms,
Lewis disappeared, and she was left thinking hard.
    It was not till they were twenty miles from Merriton, riding through
25 a slow morning mist, and she had a rather far-away, wistful look on
her face, unusual for her, that she turned to him in the saddle and said:
    "Now don't be surprised, Lewis, at what I am going to say. I am
going to ask you, now, supposing I wanted to marry you, what should
you say?"
30 He looked at her quickly, and was at once on his guard.
    "That you didn't mean it," he replied hastily.
    "Yes"—she hesitated, and her face looked wistful and tired.—
"Supposing I *did* mean it. Supposing I did *really*, from my heart, want
to marry you and be a wife to you—" she looked away across the
35 fields—"then what should you say?"
    Her voice sounded sad, a little broken.
    "Why Mam!" he replied, knitting his brow and shaking his head
a little. "I should say you didn't mean it, you know. Something would
have come over you."
40 "But supposing I *wanted* something to come over me?"

He shook his head.

"It would never do, Mam! Some people's flesh and blood is kneaded like bread: and that's me. And some are rolled like fine pastry, like Lady Carrington. And some are mixed with gunpowder. They're like a cartridge you put in a gun, Mam."*

She listened impatiently.

"Don't talk," she said, "about bread and cakes and pastry, it all means nothing. You used to answer short enough, *Yes Mam! No Mam!* That will do now. Do you mean *Yes!* or *No?*"

His eyes met hers. She was again hectoring.

"No Mam!" he said, quite neutral.

"Why?"

As she waited for his answer, she saw the foundations of his loquacity dry up, his face go distant and mute again, as it always used to be, till these last two days, when it had had a funny touch of inconsequential merriness.

He looked steadily into her eyes, and his look was neutral, sombre, and hurt. He looked at her as if infinite seas, infinite spaces divided him and her. And his eyes seemed to put her away beyond some sort of fence. An anger congealed cold like lava, set impassive* against her and all her sort.

"No Mam. I couldn't give my body to any woman who didn't respect it."

"But I do respect it, I do!"—she flushed hot like a girl.

"No Mam. Not as *I* mean it," he replied.

There was a touch of anger against her in his voice, and a distance of distaste.

"And how do *you* mean it?" she replied, the full sarcasm coming back into her tones. She could see that, as a woman to touch and fondle, he saw her as repellant: only repellant.

"I have to be a servant to women now," he said, "even to earn my wage. I could never touch with my body a woman whose servant I was."

"You're not my servant: my daughter pays your wages.—And all that is beside the point, between a man and a woman."

"No woman who I touched with my body should ever speak to me as you speak to me, or think of me as you think of me," he said.

"But!—" she stammered. "I think of you—with love. And can you be so unkind as to notice the way I speak? You know it's only my way."

"You, as a woman," he said, "you have no respect for a man."
"Respect! Respect!" she cried. "I'm likely to lose what respect I
have left. I know I can *love* a man. But whether a man can love a
woman—"

5 "No," said Lewis. "I never could, and I think I never shall.
Because I don't want to. The thought of it makes me feel shame."
"What do you mean?" she cried.

"Nothing in the world," he said, "would make me feel such shame
as to have a woman shouting at me, or mocking at me, as I see women
10 mocking and despising the men they marry. No woman shall touch
my body, and mock me or despise me. No woman."
"But men must be mocked, or despised even, sometimes."
"No. Not this man. Not by the woman I touch with my body."
"Are you perfect?"

15 "I don't know. But if I touch a woman with my body, it must put
a lock on her, to respect what I will never have despised: never!"
"What will you never have despised?"
"My body! And my touch upon the woman."
"Why insist so on your body?"—And she looked at him with a
20 touch of contemptuous mockery, raillery.

He looked her in the eyes, steadily, and coldly, putting her away
from him, and himself far away from her.
"Do you expect that any woman will stay your humble slave,
today?" she asked cuttingly.

25 But he only watched her, coldly, distant, refusing any connection.
"Between men and women, it's a question of give and take. A man
can't expect *always* to be humbly adored."

He watched her still, cold, rather pale, putting her far from him.
Then he turned his horse and set off rapidly along the road, leaving
30 her to follow.

She walked her horse and let him go, thinking to herself:
"There's a little bantam cock. And a groom! Imagine it! Thinking
he can dictate to a woman!"

She was in love with him. And he, in an odd way, was in love with
35 her. She had known it by the odd, uncanny merriment in him, and
his unexpected loquacity. But he would not have her come physically
near him. Unapproachable there as a cactus, guarding his "body" from
her contact. As if contact with her would be mortal insult and fatal
injury to his marvellous "body."

40 What a little cock-sparrow!

Let him ride ahead. He would have to wait for her somewhere. She found him at the entrance to the next village. His face was pallid and set. She could tell he felt he had been insulted, so he had congealed into stiff insentience.

"At the bottom of all men is the same," she said to herself: "an empty, male conceit of themselves."

She too rode up with a face like a mask, and straight on to the hotel.

"Can you serve dinner to myself and my servant?" she asked at the inn: which, fortunately for her, accommodated motorists, otherwise they would have said *No*!

"I think," said Lewis as they came in sight of Merriton, "I'd better give Lady Carrington a week's notice."

A complete little stranger! And an impudent one.

"Exactly as you please," she said.

She found several letters from her daughter at Marshal Place.

"Dear Mother: No sooner had you gone off than Flora appeared, not at all in the bud, but rather in full blow. She demanded her victim; Shylock demanding the pound of flesh: and wanted to hand over the shekels.*

"Joyfully I refused them. She said 'Harry' was much better, and invited him and me to stay at Corrabach Hall till he was quite well: it would be less strain on your household, while he was still in bed and helpless. So the plan is, that he shall be brought down on Friday, if he is really fit for the journey, and we drive straight to Corrabach. I am packing his bags and mine, clearing up our traces: his trunks to go to Corrabach, mine to stay here and make up their minds.—I am going to Flints Farm again tomorrow, dutifully, though I am no flower for the bedside.—I do so want to know if Rico has already called her Fiorita: or perhaps Florecita.* It reminds me of old William's joke: *Now yuh tell me, little Missy: which is the best posey that grow?* And the hushed whisper in which he said the answer: *The Collyposy!* Oh dear, I am so tired of feeling spiteful, but how else is one to feel.

"You looked most prosaically romantic, setting off in a rubber cape, followed by Lewis. Hope the roads were not very slippery, and that you had a good time, à la *Mademoiselle de Maupin*.* Do remember, dear, not to devour little Lewis before you have got half way—"

"Dear Mother: I half expected word from you before I left, but nothing came. Forrester drove me up here just before lunch. Rico seems much better: almost himself, and a little more than that. He broached our staying at Corrabach very tactfully. I told him Flora had

asked me, and it seemed a good plan. Then I told him about St. Mawr.
He was a little piqued, and there was a pause of very disapproving
silence. Then he said: *Very well, darling. If you wish to keep the animal,
do so by all means. I make a present of him again.* Me: *That's so good
of you, Rico. Because I know revenge is sweet.* Rico: *Revenge, Loulina!
I don't think I was selling him for vengeance! Merely to get rid of him
to Flora, who can keep better hold over him.*—Me: *But you know, dear,
she was going to geld him!* Rico: *I don't think anybody knew it. We only
wondered if it were possible, to make him more amenable. Did she tell you?*
Me: *No—Phoenix did. He had it from a groom.* Rico: *Dear me! A
concatenation of grooms! So your mother rode off with Lewis, and carried
St. Mawr out of danger! I understand! Let us hope worse won't befall.*
Me: *Whom?* Rico: *Never mind, dear! It's so lovely to see you. You are
looking rested. I thought those Countess of Witton roses the most
marvellous things in the world, till you came, now they're quite in the
background.* He had some very lovely red roses, in a crystal bowl: the
room smelled of roses. Me: *Where did they come from?* Rico: *Oh Flora
brought them!* Me: *Bowl and all?* Rico: *Bowl and all! Wasn't it dear
of her?* Me: *Why yes! But then she's the goddess of flowers,* isn't she?
Poor darling, he was offended that I should twit him while he is ill,
so I relented. He has had a couple of marvellous invalid's bed-jackets
sent from London: one a pinkish yellow, with rose-arabesque facings:
this one in fine cloth. But unfortunately he has already dropped soup
on it. The other is a lovely silvery and blue and green soft brocade.
He had that one on to receive me, and I at once complimented him
on it. He has got a new ring too: sent by Aspasia Weingartner: a rather
lovely intaglio of Priapus* under an apple bough, at least, so he says
it is. He made a naughty face, and said: *The Priapus stage is rather
advanced for poor me.* I asked what the Priapus stage was, but he said
Oh nothing! Then nurse said: *There's a big classical dictionary that Miss
Manby brought up, if you wish to see it.* So I have been studying the
Classical Gods. The world always was a queer place. It's a very queer
one when Rico is the god Priapus. He would go round the orchard
painting life-like apples on the trees, and inviting nymphs to come
and eat them. And the nymphs would pretend they were real: *Why,
Sir Prippy, what stunningly naughty apples!* There's nothing so artificial
as sinning nowadays. I suppose it once was real.

"I'm bored here: wish I had my horse."

"Dear Mother: I'm so glad you are enjoying your ride. I'm sure
it is like riding into history, like the Yankee at the Court of King

Arthur,* in those old bye-lanes and Roman roads. They still fascinate me: at least, more before I get there than when I am actually there. I begin to feel real American and to resent the past. Why doesn't the past decently bury itself, instead of sitting waiting to be admired by the present?

"Phoenix brought Poppy. I am so fond of her: rode for five hours yesterday. I was glad to get away from this farm. The doctor came, and said Rico would be able to go down to Corrabach tomorrow. Flora came to hear the bulletin, and sailed back full of zest. Apparently Rico is going to do a portrait of her, sitting up in bed. What a mercy the bedclothes won't be mine, when Priapus wields his palette from the pillow.

"Phoenix thinks you intend to go to America with St. Mawr, and that I am coming too, leaving Rico this side.—I wonder. I feel so unreal, nowadays, as if I too were nothing more than a painting by Rico on a millboard. I feel almost too unreal even to make up my mind to anything. It is terrible when the life-flow dies out of one, and everything is like cardboard, and oneself is like cardboard. I'm sure it is worse than being dead. I realised it yesterday when Phoenix and I had a picnic lunch by a stream. You see I must imitate you in all things. He found me some water-cresses, and they tasted so damp and *alive*, I knew how deadened I was. Phoenix wants us to go and have a ranch in Arizona, and raise horses, with St. Mawr, if willing, for Father Abraham.* I wonder if it matters what one does: if it isn't all the same thing over again? Only Phoenix, his funny blank face, makes my heart melt and go sad. But I believe he'd be cruel too. I saw it in his face when he didn't know I was looking. Anything, though, rather than this deadness and this paint-Priapus business. Au revoir, mother dear! Keep on having a good time—"

"Dear Mother—I had your letter from Merriton: am so glad you arrived safe and sound in body and temper. There was such a funny letter from Lewis, too: I enclose it. What makes him take this extraordinary line? But I'm writing to tell him to take St. Mawr to London, and wait for me there. I have telegraphed Mrs Squire to get the house ready for me. I shall go straight there.

"Things developed here, as they were bound to. I just couldn't bear it. No sooner was Rico put in the automobile than a self-conscious importance came over him, like when the wounded hero is carried into the middle of the stage. *Why so solemn, Rico dear?* I asked him, trying to laugh him out of it. *Not solemn, dear, only feeling a little transient.*

I don't think he knew himself what he meant. Flora was on the steps as the car drew up, dressed in severe white. She only needed an apron, to become a nurse: or a veil, to become a bride. Between the two, she had an unbearable air of a woman in seduced circumstances, as the *Times* said. She ordered two menservants about in subdued, you would have said hushed, but competent tones. And then I saw there was a touch of the priestess about her as well: Cassandra preparing for her violation: Iphigenia, with Rico for Orestes, on a stretcher: he looking like Adonis, fully prepared to be an unconscionable time in dying.*
They had given him a lovely room, downstairs, with doors opening on to a little garden all of its own. I believe it was Flora's boudoir. I left nurse and the men to put him to bed. Flora was hovering anxiously in the passage outside. *Oh what a marvellous room! Oh how colourful, how beautiful!* came Rico's tones, the hero behind the scenes.
I must say, it was like a harvest festival, with roses and gaillardias in the shadow, and cornflowers in the light, and a bowl of grapes, and nectarines among leaves. *I'm so anxious that he should be happy*, Flora said to me in the passage. *You know him best. Is there anything else I could do for him?* Me: *Why, if you went to the piano and sang, I'm sure he'd love it. Couldn't you sing: Oh my love is like a rred rred rrose!**—You know how Rico imitates Scotch!
"Thank goodness I have a bedroom upstairs: nurse sleeps in a little ante-chamber to Rico's room. The Edwards are still here, the blonde young man with some very futuristic plaster on his face. *Awfully good of you to come!* he said to me, looking at me out of one eye, and holding my hand fervently. *How's that for cheek? It's awfully good of Miss Manby to let me come*, said I. He: *Ah, but Flora is always a sport, a topping good sport!*
"I don't know what's the matter, but it just all put me into a fiendish temper. I felt I couldn't sit there at luncheon with that bright youthful company, and hear about their tennis and their polo and their hunting and have their flirtatiousness making me sick. So I asked for a tray in my room. Do as I might, I couldn't help being horrid.
"Oh, and Rico! He really is too awful. Lying there in bed with every ear open, like Adonis waiting to be persuaded not to die. Seizing a hushed moment to take Flora's hand and press it to his lips, murmuring: *How awfully good you are to me, dear Flora!* And Flora: *I'd be better, if I knew how, Harry!* So cheerful with it all! No, it's too much. My sense of humour is leaving me: which means, I'm getting into too bad a temper to be able to ridicule it all. I suppose

I feel in the minority. It's an awful thought, to think that most all the
young people in the world are like this: so bright and cheerful, and
sporting, and so brimming with libido. How awful!
"I said to Rico: *You're very comfortable here, aren't you?* He:
Comfortable! It's comparative heaven. Me: *Would you mind if I went   5
away?* A deadly pause. He is deadly afraid of being left alone with
Flora. He feels safe so long as I am about, and he can take refuge in
his marriage ties. He: *Where do you want to go, dear?* Me: *To Mother.
To London. Mother is planning to go to America, and she wants me to
go.* Rico: *But you don't want to go t-he-e-re-e!* You know, Mother, how   10
Rico can put a venomous emphasis on a word, till it suggests pure
poison. It nettled me. *I'm not sure,* I said. Rico: *Oh, but you can't stand
that awful America.* Me: *I want to try again.* Rico: *But Lou dear, it
will be winter before you get there. And this is absolutely the wrong moment
for me to go over there. I am only just making headway over here. When   15
I am absolutely sure of a position in England, then we can nip across the
Atlantic and scoop in a few dollars, if you like. Just now, even when I
am well, would be fatal. I've only just sketched in the outline of my success
in London, and one ought to arrive in New York ready-made as a famous
and important Artist.* Me: *But Mother and I didn't think of going to   20
New York. We thought we'd sail straight to New Orleans—if we could:
or to Havana. And then go west to Arizona.* The poor boy looked at
me in such distress. *But Loulina darling, do you mean you want to leave
me in the lurch for the winter season? You can't mean it. We're just getting
on so splendidly, really!*—I was surprised at the depth of feeling in his   25
voice: how tremendously his career as an artist—a popular artist—
matters to him. I can never believe it.—You know, Mother, you and
I feel alike about daubing paint on canvas: every possible daub that
can be daubed has already been done, so people ought to leave off.
Rico is so shrewd. I always think he's got his tongue in his cheek, and   30
I'm always staggered once more to find that he takes it absolutely
seriously. His career! The Modern British Society of Painters: perhaps
even the Royal Academy! Those people we see in London, and those
portraits Rico does! He may even be a second László, or a thirteenth
Orpen,* and die happy! Oh! Mother! How can it really matter to   35
anybody!
    "But I was really rather upset, when I realised how his heart was
fixed on his career, and that I might be spoiling everything for him.
So I went away to think about it. And then I realised how unpopular
you are, and how unpopular I shall be myself, in a little while. A sort   40

of hatred for people has come over me. I hate their ways and their
bunk, and I feel like kicking them in the face, as St. Mawr did that
young man. Not that I should ever do it. And I don't think I should
ever have made my final announcement to Rico, if he hadn't been such
5   a beautiful pig in clover,* here at Corrabach Hall. He has known the
Manbys all his life, they and he are sections of one engine. He would
be far happier with Flora: or I won't say happier, because there is
something in him which rebels: but he would on the whole fit much
better. I myself am at the end of my limit, and beyond it. I can't 'mix'
10 any more, and I refuse to. I feel like a bit of eggshell in the mayonnaise:
the only thing is to take it out, you can't beat it in. I *know* I shall cause
a fiasco, even in Rico's career, if I stay. I shall go on being rude and
hateful to people as I am at Corrabach, and Rico will lose all his nerve.
    "So I have told him. I said this evening, when no-one was about:
15 *Rico dear, listen to me seriously. I can't stand these people. If you ask
me to endure another week of them, I shall either become ill, or insult them,
as mother does. And I don't want to do either.* Rico: *But darling, isn't
everybody perfect to you!* Me: *I tell you, I shall just make a break, like
St. Mawr, if I don't get out. I simply can't stand people.*—The poor
20 darling, his face goes so blank and anxious. He knows what I mean,
because, except that they tickle his vanity all the time, he hates them
as much as I do. But his vanity is the chief thing to him. He: *Lou
darling, can't you wait till I get up, and we can go away to the Tyrol
or somewhere for a spell?* Me: *Won't you come with me to America, to
25 the South-West? I believe it's marvellous country.*—I saw his face switch
into hostility; quite vicious. He: *Are you so keen on spoiling everything
for me? Is that what I married you for? Do you do it deliberately?* Me:
*Everything is already spoilt for me. I tell you I can't stand people, your
Floras and your Aspasias, and your forthcoming young Englishmen. After
30 all, I am an American, like mother, and I've got to go back.* He: *Really!
And am I to come along as part of the luggage? Labelled Cabin!* Me:
You do as you wish, Rico. He: *I wish to God you did as you wished, Lou
dear. I'm afraid you do as Mrs Witt wishes. I always heard that the holiest
thing in the world was a mother.* Me: *No dear, it's just that I can't stand
35 people.* He (with a snarl): *And I suppose I'm lumped in as* PEOPLE! And
when he'd said it, it was true. We neither of us said anything for a
time. Then he said, calculating: *Very well, dear! You take a trip to the
land of stars and stripes, and I'll stay here and go on with my work. And
when you've seen enough of their stars and tasted enough of their stripes,
40 you can come back and take your place again with me.*—We left it at that.

"You and I are supposed to have important business connected with our estates in Texas—it sounds so well—so we are making a hurried trip to the States, as they call them. I shall leave for London early next week—"

Mrs Witt read this long letter with satisfaction. She herself had one strange craving: to get back to America. It was not that she idealised her native country: she was a tartar of restlessness there, quite as much as in Europe. It was not that she expected to arrive at any blessed abiding place. No, in America she would go on fuming and chafing the same. But at least she would be in America, in her own country. And that was what she wanted.

She picked up the sheet of poor paper, that had been folded in Lou's letter. It was the letter from Lewis, quite nicely written. "Lady Carrington, I write to tell you and Sir Henry that I think I better quit your service, as it would be more comfortable all round. If you will write and tell me what you want me to do with St. Mawr, I will do whatever you tell me. With kind regards to Lady Carrington and Sir Henry, I remain, Your obedient servant, Morgan Lewis."

Mrs Witt put the letter aside, and sat looking out of the window. She felt, strangely, as if already her soul had gone away from her actual surroundings. She was there, in Oxfordshire, in the body, but her spirit had departed elsewhere. A listlessness was upon her. It was with an effort she roused herself, to write to her lawyer in London, to get her release from her English obligations. Then she wrote to the London hotel.

For the first time in her life, she wished she had a maid, to do little things for her. All her life, she had had too much energy to endure anyone hanging round her, personally. Now she gave up. Her wrists seemed numb, as if the power in her were switched off.

When she went down, they said Lewis had asked to speak to her. She had hardly seen him since they had arrived at Merriton.

"I've had a letter from Lady Carrington, Mam. She says will I take St. Mawr to London and wait for her there. But she says I am to come to you, Mam, for definite orders."

"Very well, Lewis. I shall be going to London in a few days' time. You arrange for St. Mawr to go up one day this week, and you will take him to the Mews. Come to me for anything you want. And don't talk of leaving my daughter. We want you to go with St. Mawr to America, with us and Phoenix."

"And your horse, Mam?"

"I shall leave him here at Merriton. I shall give him to Miss Atherton."

"Very good Mam!"

"Dear Daughter: I shall be in my old quarters in Mayfair next
5   Saturday, calling the same day at your house to see if everything is
ready for you. Lewis has fixed up with the railway: he goes to town
tomorrow. The reason of his letter was that I had asked him if he would
care to marry me, and he turned me down with emphasis. But I will
tell you about it. You and I are the scribe and the Pharisee; I never
10 could write a letter, and you could never leave off—"

"Dearest Mother: I smelt something rash, but I know it's no use
saying: How *could* you? I only wonder, though, that you should think
of marriage. You know, dear, I ache in every fibre to be left alone,
from all that sort of thing. I feel all bruises, like one who has been
15 assassinated. I do so understand why Jesus said: *Noli me tangere.*
Touch me not, I am not yet ascended unto the Father. Everything had
hurt him so much, wearied him so beyond endurance, he felt he could
not bear one little human touch on his body. I am like that. I can hardly
bear even Elena to hand me a dress. As for a man—and marriage—ah
20 no! *Noli me tangere, homine!** I am not yet ascended unto the Father.
Oh, leave me alone, leave me alone! That is all my cry to all the world.

"Curiously, I feel that Phoenix understands what I feel. He leaves
me so understandingly alone, he almost gives me my sheath of
aloneness: or at least, he protects me in my sheath. I am grateful for
25 him.

"Whereas Rico feels my aloneness as a sort of shame to himself.
He wants at least a blinding *pretence* of intimacy. Ah intimacy! The
thought of it fills me with aches, and the pretence of it exhausts me
beyond myself.

30 "Yes, I long to go away to the west, to be away from the world
like one dead and in another life, in a valley that life has not yet entered.

"Rico asked me: What are you doing with St. Mawr? When I said
we were taking him with us, he said: *Oh, the Corpus delicti!** Whether
that means anything I don't know. But he has grown sarcastic beyond
35 my depth.

"I shall see you tomorrow—"

Lou arrived in town, at the dead end of August, with her maid and
Phoenix. How wonderful it seemed, to have London empty of all her
set: her own little house to herself, with just the housekeeper and her
40 own maid. The fact of being alone in those surroundings was so

wonderful. It made the surroundings themselves seem all the more
ghostly. Everything that had been actual to her was turning ghostly:
even her little drawing-room was the ghost of a room, belonging to
the dead people who had known it, or to all the dead generations that
had brought such a room into being, evolved it out of their quaint   5
domestic desires. And now, in herself, those desires were suddenly
spent: gone out like a lamp that suddenly dies. And then she saw her
pale, delicate room with its little green agate bowl and its two little
porcelain birds and its soft, roundish chairs, turned into something
ghostly, like a room set out in a museum. She felt like fastening little   10
labels on the furniture: *Lady Louise Carrington Lounge Chair, Last used
August 1923*. Not for the benefit of posterity: but to remove her own
self into another world, another realm of existence.

"My house, my house, my house, how can I ever have taken so much
pains about it!" she kept saying to herself. It was like one of her old   15
hats, suddenly discovered neatly put away in an old hatbox. And what
a horror: an old "fashionable" hat!

Lewis came to see her, and he sat there in one of her delicate mauve
chairs, with his feet on a delicate old carpet from Turkestan, and she
just wondered. He wore his leather gaiters and khaki breeches as usual,   20
and a faded blue shirt. But his beard and hair were trimmed, he was
tidy. There was a certain fineness of contour about him, a certain subtle
gleam, which made him seem, apart from his rough boots, not at all
gross, or coarse, in that setting of rather silky, oriental furnishings.
Rather he made the Asiatic, sensuous exquisiteness of her old rugs and   25
her old white Chinese figures seem a weariness. Beauty! What was
beauty, she asked herself? The Oriental exquisiteness seemed to her
all like dead flowers whose hour had come, to be thrown away.

Lou could understand her mother's wanting, for a moment, to marry
him. His detachedness and his acceptance of something in destiny   30
which people cannot accept. Right in the middle of him he accepted
something from destiny, that gave him a quality of eternity. He did
not care about persons, people, even events. In his own odd way, he
was an aristocrat, inaccessible in his aristocracy. But it was the
aristocracy of the invisible powers, the greater influences, nothing to   35
do with human society.

"You don't really want to leave St. Mawr, do you?" Lou asked him.
"You don't really want to quit, as you said?"

He looked at her steadily, from his pale grey eyes, without
answering, not knowing what to say.   40

"Mother told me what she said to you.—But she doesn't mind, she says you are entirely within your rights. She has a real regard for you. But we mustn't let our regards run us into actions which are beyond our scope, must we? That makes everything unreal. But you will come
5 with us to America with St. Mawr, won't you? We depend on you."

"I don't want to be uncomfortable," he said.

"Don't be," she smiled. "I myself hate unreal situations—I feel I can't stand them anymore. And most marriages are unreal situations. But apart from anything exaggerated, you like being with mother and
10 me, don't you?"

"Yes, I do. I like Mrs Witt as well. But not—"

"I know. There won't be any more of that—"

"You see, Lady Carrington," he said, with a little heat, "I'm not by nature a marrying man. And I should feel I was selling myself."
15 "Quite!—Why do you think you are not a marrying man, though?"

"Me! I don't feel myself after I've been with women." He spoke in a low tone looking down at his hands. "I feel messed up. I'm better to keep to myself.—Because—" and here he looked up with a flare in his eyes: "women—they only want to make you give in to them,
20 so that they feel almighty, and you feel small."

"Don't you like feeling small?" Lou smiled. "And don't you want to make them give in to you?"

"Not me," he said. "I don't want nothing. Nothing, I want."

"Poor mother!" said Lou. "She thinks if she feels moved by a man,
25 it must result in marriage—or that kind of thing. Surely she makes a mistake. I think you and Phoenix and mother and I might live somewhere in a far-away wild place, and make a good life: so long as we didn't begin to mix up marriage, or love or that sort of thing into it. It seems to me men and women have really hurt one another so
30 much, nowadays, that they had better stay apart till they have learned to be gentle with one another again. Not all this forced passion and destructive philandering. Men and women should stay apart, till their hearts grow gentle towards one another again. Now, it's only each one fighting for his own—or her own—underneath the cover of
35 tenderness."

"*Dear!—darling!—Yes my love!*" mocked Lewis, with a faint smile of amused contempt.

"Exactly. People always say *dearest!* when they hate each other most."
40 Lewis nodded, looking at her with a sudden sombre gloom in his

eyes. A queer bitterness showed on his mouth. But even then, he was
so still and remote.

The housekeeper came and announced The Honorable Laura
Ridley.* This was like a blow in the face to Lou. She rose hurriedly—
and Lewis rose, moving to the door.

"Don't go please, Lewis," said Lou—and then Laura Ridley
appeared in the doorway. She was a woman a few years older than Lou,
but she looked younger. She might have been a shy girl of twenty-two,
with her fresh complexion, her hesitant manner, her round, startled
brown eyes, her bobbed hair.

"Hello!" said the newcomer. "Imagine your being back! I saw you
in Paddington."

Those sharp eyes would see everything.

"I thought everyone was out of town," said Lou. "This is Mr
Lewis."

Laura gave him a little nod, then sat on the edge of her chair.

"No," she said. "I did go to Ireland to my people, but I came back.
I prefer London when I can be more or less alone in it. I thought I'd
just run in for a moment, before you're gone again.—Scotland, isn't
it?"

"No, Mother and I are going to America."

"America! Oh, I thought it was Scotland."

"It was. But we have suddenly to go to America."

"I see!—And what about Rico?"

"He is staying on in Shropshire. Didn't you hear of his accident?"
Lou told about it briefly.

"But how awful!" said Laura. "But there! I knew it! I had a
premonition, when I saw that horse. We had a horse that killed a man.
Then my father got rid of it. But ours was a mare, that one. Yours
is a boy."

"A full grown man I'm afraid."

"Yes of course, I remember.—But how awful! I suppose you won't
ride in the Row. The awful people that ride there nowadays, anyhow!
Oh, aren't they awful! Aren't people monstrous, really! My word,
when I see the horses crossing Hyde Park Corner, on a wet day, and
coming down smash on those slippery stones, giving their riders a
fractured skull!—No joke!"

She enquired details of Rico.

"Oh, I suppose I shall see him when he gets back," she said. "But
I'm sorry you are going. I shall miss you, I'm afraid. Though you won't

be staying long in America. No one stays there longer than they can help."

"I think the winter through, at least," said Lou.

"Oh, all the winter! So long? I'm sorry to hear *that*. You're one of the few, very few people one can talk *really* simply with. Extraordinary, isn't it, how few really simple people there are! And they get fewer and fewer. I stayed a fortnight with my people, and a week of that I was in bed. It was really horrible. They really try to take the life out of one, *really*! Just because one won't be as they are, and play their game. I simply refused, and came away."

"But you can't cut yourself off altogether," said Lou.

"No, I suppose not. One has to see somebody. Luckily one has a few artists for friends. They're the only real People, anyhow—" She glanced round inquisitively at Lewis, and said, with a slight, impertinent elvish smile on her virgin face:

"Are you an artist?"

"No Mam!" he said. "I'm a groom."

"Oh, I see!" she looked him up and down.

"Lewis is St. Mawr's master," said Lou.

"Oh, the horse! the terrible horse!" She paused a moment. Then again she turned to Lewis with that faint smile, slightly condescending, slightly impertinent, slightly flirtatious.

"Aren't you afraid of him?" she asked.

"No Mam."

"Aren't you *really*!—And can you always master him?"

"Mostly. He knows me."

"Yes! I suppose that's it."—She looked him up and down again, then turned away to Lou.

"What have you been painting lately?" said Lou. Laura was not a bad painter.

"Oh, hardly anything. I haven't been able to get on at all. This is one of my bad intervals."

Here Lewis rose, and looked at Lou.

"All right," she said. "Come in after lunch, and we'll finish those arrangements."

Laura gazed after the man, as he dived out of the room, as if her eyes were gimlets that could bore into his secret.

In the course of the conversation she said:

"What a curious little man that was!"

"Which?"

"The groom who was here just now. *Very* curious! Such peculiar eyes. I shouldn't wonder if he had psychic powers."

"What sort of psychic powers?" said Lou.

"Could *see* things.—And hypnotic too. He might have hypnotic powers."

"What makes you think so?"

"He gives me that sort of feeling. Very curious! Probably he hypnotises the horse.—Are you leaving the horse here, by the way, in stable?"

"No, taking him to America."

"Taking him to America! How extraordinary!"

"It's mother's idea. She thinks he might be valuable as a stock horse on a ranch. You know we still have interest in a ranch in Texas."

"Oh, I see! Yes, probably he'd be very valuable, to improve the breed of the horses over there.—My father has some very lovely hunters. Isn't it disgraceful, he would never let me ride!"

"Why?"

"Because we girls weren't important, in his opinion.—So you're taking the horse to America! With the little man?"

"Yes, St. Mawr will hardly behave without him."

"I see!—I see—ee—ee! Just you and Mrs Witt and the little man. I'm sure you'll find he has psychic powers."

"I'm afraid I'm not so good at finding things out," said Lou.

"Aren't you? No, I suppose not. I am. I have a flair. I sort of *smell* things.—Then the horse is already here, is he? When do you think you'll sail?"

"Mother is finding a merchant boat that will go to Galveston, Texas, and take us along with the horse. She knows people who will find the right thing. But it takes time."

"What a much nicer way to travel, than on one of those great liners! Oh, how awful they are! So vulgar! Floating palaces they call them! My word, the people inside the palaces!—Yes, I should say that would be a much pleasanter way of travelling: on a cargo boat."

Laura wanted to go down to the Mews to see St. Mawr. The two women went together.

St. Mawr stood in his box, bright and tense as usual.

"Yes!" said Laura Ridley, with a slight hiss, "Yes! Isn't he beautiful. Such very perfect legs!"—She eyed him round with those gimlet-sharp eyes of hers. "Almost a pity to let him go out of

England. We need some of his perfect *bone*, I feel.—But his eye! Hasn't he got a look in it, my word!"

"I can never see that he looks wicked," said Lou.

"Can't you!"—Laura had a slight hiss in her speech, a sort of aristocratic decision in her enunciation, that got on Lou's nerves.—"He looks wicked to me!"

"He's not *mean*," said Lou. "He'd never do anything mean to you."

"Oh, mean! I daresay not. No! I'll grant him that, he gives fair warning. His eye says *Beware*!—But isn't he a beauty, *isn't* he!" Lou could feel the peculiar reverence for St. Mawr's breeding, his show qualities. Herself, all she cared about was the horse himself, his real nature. "Isn't it extraordinary," Laura continued, "that you never get a *really*, perfectly satisfactory animal! There's always something wrong. And in men too. Isn't it curious? there's always something—something wrong—or something missing. Why is it?"

"I don't know," said Lou. She felt unable to cope with any more. And she was glad when Laura left her.

The days passed slowly, quietly, London almost empty of Lou's acquaintances. Mrs Witt was busy getting all sorts of papers and permits: such a fuss! The battle light was still in her eye. But about her nose was a dusky, pinched look that made Lou wonder.

Both women wanted to be gone: they felt they had already flown in spirit, and it was weary, having the body left behind.

At last all was ready: they only awaited the telegram to say when their cargo-boat would sail. Trunks stood there packed, like great stones locked for ever. The Westminster house seemed already a shell. Rico wrote and telegraphed, tenderly, but there was a sense of relentless effort in it all, rather than of any real tenderness. He had taken his position.

Then the telegram came, the boat was ready to sail.

"There now!" said Mrs Witt, as if it had been a sentence of death.

"Why do you look like that, mother?"

"I feel I haven't an ounce of energy left in my body."

"But how queer, for you, mother. Do you think you are ill?"

"No Louise. I just feel that way: as if I hadn't an ounce of energy left in my body."

"You'll feel yourself again, once you are away."

"Maybe I shall."

After all, it was only a matter of telephoning. The hotel and the railway porters and taxi-men would do the rest.

It was a grey, cloudy day, cold even. Mother and daughter sat in a cold first-class carriage and watched the little, Hampshire country-side go past: little, old, unreal it seemed to them both, and passing away like a dream whose edges only are in consciousness. Autumn! Was this autumn? Were these trees, fields, villages? It seemed but the 5 dim, dissolving edges of a dream, without inward substance.

At Southampton it was raining: and just a chaos, till they stepped on to a clean boat, and were received by a clean young captain, quite sympathetic, and quite a gentleman. Mrs Witt, however, hardly looked at him, but went down to her cabin and lay down in her bunk. 10

There, lying concealed, she felt the engines start, she knew the voyage had begun. But she lay still. She saw the clouds and the rain, and refused to be disturbed.

Lou had lunch with the young captain, and she felt she ought to be flirty. The young man was so polite and attentive. And she wished 15 so much she were alone.

Afterwards, she sat on deck and saw the Isle of Wight pass shadowily, in a misty rain. She didn't know it was the Isle of Wight. To her, it was just the lowest bit of the British Isles. She saw it fading away: and with it, her life, going like a clot of shadow in a mist of 20 nothingness. She had no feelings about it, none: neither about Rico, nor her London house, nor anything. All passing in a grey curtain of rainy drizzle, like a death, and she, with not a feeling left.

They entered the Channel, and felt the slow heave of the sea. And soon, the clouds broke in a little wind. The sky began to clear. By 25 mid-afternoon it was blue summer, on the blue, running waters of the Channel. And soon, the ship steering for Santander, there was the coast of France, the rocks twinkling like some magic world.

The magic world! And back of it, that post-war Paris, which Lou knew only too well, and which depressed her so thoroughly. Or that 30 post-war Monte Carlo, the Riviera still more depressing even than Paris. No no, one must not land, even on magic coasts. Else you found yourself in a railway station and a "centre of civilisation" in five minutes.

Mrs Witt hated the sea, and stayed, as a rule, practically the whole 35 time of the crossing, in her bunk. There she was now, silent, shut up like a steel trap, as in her tomb. She did not even read. Just lay and stared at the passing sky. And the only thing to do was to leave her alone.

Lewis and Phoenix hung on the rail, and watched everything. Or 40 they went down to see St. Mawr. Or they stood talking in the doorway of the wireless operator's cabin. Lou begged the Captain to give them jobs to do.

5   The queer, transitory, unreal feeling, as the ship crossed the great, heavy Atlantic. It was rather bad weather. And Lou felt, as she had felt before, that this grey, wolf-like, cold-blooded Ocean hated men and their ships and their smoky passage. Heavy grey waves, a low-sagging sky: rain: yellow, weird evenings with snatches of sun: so it went on. Till they got way south, into the westward-running

10 stream. Then they began to get blue weather and blue water.

To go south! Always to go south, away from the arctic horror as far as possible! That was Lou's instinct. To go out of the clutch of greyness and low skies, of seeping rain, and of slow, blanketing snow. Never again to see the mud and rain and snow of a northern winter,

15 nor to feel the idealistic, Christianised tension of the now irreligious north.

As they neared Havana, and the water sparkled at night with phosphorus, and the flying-fishes came like drops of bright water, sailing out of the massive-slippery waves, Mrs Witt emerged once

20 more. She still had that shut-up, deathly look on her face. But she prowled round the deck, and manifested at least a little interest in affairs not her own. Here at sea, she hardly remembered the existence of St. Mawr or Lewis or Phoenix. She was not very deeply aware even of Lou's existence.—But of course, it would all come back, once they

25 were on land.

They sailed in hot sunshine out of a blue, blue sea, past the castle into the harbour at Havana. There was a lot of shipping: and this was already America. Mrs Witt had herself and Lou put ashore immediately. They took a motor-car and drove at once to the great

30 boulevard that is the centre of Havana. Here they saw a long rank of motor-cars, all drawn up ready to take a couple of hundred American tourists for one more tour. There were the tourists, all with badges in their coats, lest they should get lost.

"They get so drunk by night," said the driver in Spanish, "that

35 the policemen find them lying in the road—turn them over, see the badge—and, hup!—carry them to their hotel." He grinned sardonically.

Lou and her mother lunched at the Hotel d'Angleterre, and Mrs Witt watched transfixed while a couple of her countrymen, a stout

40 successful man and his wife, lunched abroad. They had cocktails—then

lobster—and a bottle of hock—then a bottle of champagne—then a half-bottle of port—And Mrs Witt rose in haste as the liqueurs came. For that successful man and his wife had gone on imbibing with a sort of fixed and deliberate will, apparently tasting nothing, but saying to themselves: Now we're drinking Rhine wine! Now we're drinking 1912 champagne. Yah, Prohibition!* Thou canst not put it over me.—Their complexions became more and more lurid. Mrs Witt fled, fearing a Havana débâcle. But she said nothing.

In the afternoon, they motored into the country, to see the great brewery gardens, the new villa suburb, and through the lanes past the old, decaying plantations with palm-trees. In one lane they met the fifty motor-cars with the two hundred tourists all with badges on their chests and self-satisfaction on their faces. Mrs Witt watched in grim silence.

"Plus ça change, plus c'est la même chose," said Lou, with a wicked little smile. "On n'est pas mieux ici,* mother."

"I know it," said Mrs Witt.

The hotels by the sea were all shut up: it was not yet the "season." Not till November. And then!—Why then Havana would be an American city, in full leaf of green dollar bills. The green leaf of American prosperity shedding itself recklessly, from every roaming sprig of a tourist, over this city of sunshine and alcohol. Green leaves unfolded in Pittsburgh and Chicago, showering in winter downfall in Havana.

Mother and daughter drank tea in a corner of the Hotel d'Angleterre once more, and returned to the ferry.

The Gulf of Mexico was blue and rippling, with the phantom of islands on the south. Great porpoises rolled and leaped, running in front of the ship in the clear water, diving, travelling in perfect motion, straight, with the tip of the ship touching the tip of their tails, then rolling over, cork-screwing and showing their bellies as they went. Marvellous! The marvellous beauty and fascination of natural wild things! The horror of man's unnatural life, his heaped-up civilisation!

The flying-fishes burst out of the sea in clouds of silvery, transparent motion. Blue above and below, the Gulf seemed a silent, empty, timeless place where man did not really reach. And Lou was again fascinated by the glamour of the universe.*

But bump! She and her mother were in a first-class hotel again, calling down the telephone for the bell-boy and ice-water. And soon they were in a Pullman, off towards San Antonio.

It was America, it was Texas. They were at their ranch, on the great
level of yellow autumn, with the vast sky above. And after all, from
the hot wide sky, and the hot, wide, red earth, there *did* come
something new, something not used-up. Lou *did* feel exhilarated.

5 The Texans were there, tall blonde people, ingenuously cheerful,
ingenuously, childishly intimate, as if the fact that you had never seen
them before was as nothing compared to the fact that you'd all been
living in one room together all your lives, so that nothing was hidden
from either of you. The one room being the mere shanty of the world
10 in which we all live. Strange, uninspired cheerfulness, filling, as it were,
the blank of complete incomprehension.

And off they set in their motor-cars, chiefly high-legged Fords,
rattling away down the red trails between yellow sunflowers or sere grass
or dry cotton, away, away into great distances, cheerfully raising the
15 dust of haste. It left Lou in a sort of blank amazement. But it left her
amused, not depressed. The old screws of emotion and intimacy that
had been screwed down so tightly upon her fell out of their holes, here.
The Texan intimacy weighed no more on her than a postage stamp,
even if, for the moment, it stuck as close. And there was a certain
20 underneath recklessness, even a stoicism in all the apparently childish
people, which left one free. They might appear childish: but they
stoically depended on themselves alone, in reality. Not as in England,
where every man waited to pour the burden of himself upon you.

St. Mawr arrived safely, a bit bewildered. The Texans eyed him
25 closely, struck silent, as ever, by anything pure-bred and beautiful. He
was somehow too beautiful, too perfected, in this great open country.
The long-legged Texan horses, with their elaborate saddles, seemed
somehow more natural.

Even St. Mawr felt himself strange, as it were naked and singled
30 out, in this rough place. Like a jewel among stones, a pearl before
swine,* maybe. But the swine were no fools. They knew a pearl from
a grain of maize, and a grain of maize from a pearl. And they knew
what they wanted. When it was pearls, it was pearls: though chiefly,
it was maize. Which shows good sense. They could see St. Mawr's
35 points. Only he needn't draw the point too fine, or it would just not
pierce the tough skin of this country.

The ranch-man mounted him—just threw a soft skin over his back,
jumped on, and away down the red trail, raising the dust among the
tall wild yellow of sunflowers, in the hot wild sun. Then back again
40 in a fume, and the man slipped off.

"He's got the stuff in him, he sure has," said the man.

And the horse seemed pleased with this rough handling. Lewis looked on in wonder, and a little envy.

Lou and her mother stayed a fortnight on the ranch. It was all so queer: so crude, so rough, so easy, so artificially civilised, and so meaningless. Lou could not get over the feeling that it all meant nothing. There were no roots of reality at all. No consciousness below the surface, no meaning in anything save the obvious, the blatantly obvious. It was like life enacted in a mirror. Visually, it was wildly vital. But there was nothing behind it. Or like a cinematograph: flat shapes, exactly like men, but without any substance of reality, rapidly rattling away with talk, emotions, activity, all in the flat, nothing behind it. No deeper consciousness at all.—So it seemed to her.

One moved from dream to dream, from phantasm to phantasm.

But at least, this Texan life, if it had no bowels, no vitals, at least it could not prey on one's own vitals. It was this much better than Europe.

Lewis was silent, and rather piqued. St. Mawr had already made advances to the boss' long-legged, arched-necked, glossy-maned Texan mare. And the boss was pleased.

What a world!

Mrs Witt eyed it all shrewdly. But she failed to participate. Lou was a bit scared at the emptiness of it all, and the queer, phantasmal self-consciousness. Cowboys just as self-conscious as Rico, far more sentimental, inwardly vague and unreal. Cowboys that went after their cows in black Ford motor-cars: and who self-consciously saw Lady Carrington falling to them, as elegant young ladies from the East fall to the noble cowboy of the films, or in Zane Grey.* It was all film-psychology.

And at the same time, these boys led a hard, hard life, often dangerous and gruesome. Nevertheless, inwardly they were self-conscious film-heroes. The boss himself, a man over forty, long and lean and with a great deal of stringy energy, showed off before her in a strong silent manner, existing for the time being purely in his imagination of the sort of picture he made to her, the sort of impression he made on her.

So they all were, coloured up like a Zane Grey book-jacket, all of them living in the mirror. The kind of picture they made to somebody else.

And at the same time, with energy, courage, and a stoical grit getting their work done, and putting through what they had to put through. It left Lou blank with wonder. And in the face of this strange cheerful living in the mirror—a rather cheap mirror at that—England
5 began to seem real to her again.

Then she had to remember herself back in England. And no, oh God, England was not real either, except poisonously.

What was real? What under heaven was real?

Her mother had gone dumb and, as it were, out of range. Phoenix
10 was a bit assured and bouncy, back more or less in his own conditions. Lewis was a bit impressed by the emptiness of everything, the *lack* of concentration. And St. Mawr followed at the heels of the boss' long-legged black Texan mare, almost slavishly.

What, in heaven's name, was one to make of it all?

15 Soon, she could not stand this sort of living in a film-setting, with the mechanical energy of "making good," that is, making money, to keep the show going. The mystic duty to "make good," meaning to make the ranch pay a laudable interest on the "owners'" investment. Lou herself being one of the owners. And the interest that came to
20 her, from her father's will, being the money she spent to buy St. Mawr and to fit up that house in Westminster. Then also the mystic duty to "feel good." Everybody had to *feel good, fine!* "How are you this morning, Mr Latham?"—"*Fine!* Eh! Don't you feel good out here, eh? Lady Carrington?"—"*Fine!*"—Lou pronounced it with the
25 same ringing conviction. It was Coué* all the time!

"Shall we stay here long, mother?" she asked.

"Not a day longer than you want to, Louise. I stay entirely for your sake."

"Then let us go, mother."

30 They left St. Mawr and Lewis. But Phoenix wanted to come along. So they motored to San Antonio, got into the Pullman, and travelled as far as El Paso. Then they changed to go north. Santa Fe would be at least "easy." And Mrs Witt had acquaintances there.

They found the fiesta over in Santa Fe: Indians, Mexicans, artists
35 had finished their great effort to amuse and attract the tourists. *Welcome Mr Tourist* said a great board on one side of the high-road. And on the other side, a little nearer to town: *Thank You, Mr Tourist.*

"Plus ça change—" Lou began.

"Ça ne change jamais*—except for the worse!" said Mrs Witt, like
40 a pistol going off. And Lou held her peace, after she had sighed to

herself, and said in her own mind: "*Welcome Also Mrs and Miss Tourist!*"

There was no getting a word out of Mrs Witt, these days. Whereas Phoenix was becoming almost loquacious.

They stayed a while in Santa Fe, in the clean, comfortable, "homely" hotel, where "every room had its bath": a spotless white bath, with very hot water night and day. The tourists and commercial travellers sat in the big hall down below, everybody living in the mirror! And of course, they knew Lady Carrington down to her shoe-soles. And they all expected her to know them down to their shoe-soles. For the only object of the mirror is to reflect images.

For two days mother and daughter ate in the mayonnaise intimacy of the dining-room. Then Mrs Witt struck, and telephoned down every meal-time, for her meal in her room. She got to staying in bed later and later, as on the ship. Lou became uneasy. This was worse than Europe.

Phoenix was still there, as a sort of half-friend, half-servant retainer. He was perfectly happy, roving round among the Mexicans and Indians, talking Spanish all day, and telling about England and his two mistresses, rolling the ball of his own importance.

"I'm afraid we've got Phoenix for life," said Lou.

"Not unless we wish," said Mrs Witt indifferently. And she picked up a novel which she didn't want to read, but which she was going to read.

"What shall we do next, mother?" Lou asked.

"As far as I am concerned, there is no next," said Mrs Witt.

"Come mother! Let's go back to Italy or somewhere, if it's as bad as that."

"Never again, Louise, shall I cross that water. I have come home to die."

"I don't see much home about it—the Gonzalez Hotel in Santa Fe."

"Indeed not! But as good as anywhere else, to die in."

"Oh mother, don't be silly! Shall we look for somewhere where we can be by ourselves?"

"I leave it to you, Louise. I have made my last decision."

"What is that, mother."

"Never, never to make another decision."

"Not even to decide to die?"

"No, not even that."

"Or *not* to die?"

"Not that either."

Mrs Witt shut up like a trap. She refused to rise from her bed that day.

Lou went to consult Phoenix. The result was, the two set out to look at a little ranch that was for sale.

It was autumn, and the loveliest time in the South-West, where there is no spring, snow blowing into the hot lap of summer: and no real summer, hail falling in thick ice, from the thunderstorms: and even no very definite winter, hot sun melting the snow and giving an impression of spring at any time. But autumn there is, when the winds of the desert are almost still, and the mountains fume no clouds. But morning comes cold and delicate, upon the wild sunflowers and the puffing, yellow-flowered greasewood. For the desert blooms in autumn. In spring it is grey ash all the time, and only the strong breath of the summer sun, and the heavy splashing of thunder rain succeed at last, by September, in blowing it into soft, puffy yellow fire.

It was such a delicate morning when Lou drove out with Phoenix towards the mountains, to look at this ranch that a Mexican wanted to sell. For the brief moment, the high mountains had lost their snow: it would be back again in a fortnight: and stood dim and delicate with autumn haze. The desert stretched away pale, as pale as the sky, but silvery and sere, with hummock-mounds of shadow, and long wings of shadow, like the reflection of some great bird. The same eagle-shadows came like rude paintings of the outstretched bird, upon the mountains, where the aspens were turning yellow. For the moment, the brief moment, the great desert-and-mountain landscape had lost its certain cruelty, and looked tender, dreamy. And many, many birds were flickering around.

Lou and Phoenix bumped and hesitated over a long trail: then wound down into a deep canyon: and then the car began to climb, climb, climb, in steep rushes, and in long heart-breaking, uneven pulls. The road was bad, and driving was no joke. But it was the sort of road Phoenix was used to. He sat impassive and watchful, and kept on, till his engine boiled. He was *himself* in this country: impassive, detached, self-satisfied and silently assertive. Guarding himself at every moment, but, on his guard, sure of himself. Seeing no difference at all between Lou or Mrs Witt and himself, except that they had money and he had none, while he had a native importance which they lacked. He depended on them for money, they on him for the power to live out here in the West. Intimately, he was as good as they. Money was their only advantage.

As Lou sat beside him in the front seat of the car, where it bumped less than behind, she felt this. She felt a peculiar tough-necked arrogance in him, as if he were asserting himself to put something over her. He wanted her to allow him to make advances to her, to allow him to suggest that he should be her lover. And then, finally, she would marry him, and he would be on the same footing as she and her mother.

In return, he would look after her, and give her his support and countenance, as a man, and stand between her and the world. In this sense, he would be faithful to her, and loyal. But as far as other women went, Mexican women or Indian women: why, that was none of her business. His marrying her would be a pact between two aliens, on behalf of one another, and he would keep his part of it all right. But himself, as a private man and a predative alien-blooded male, this had nothing to do with her. It didn't enter into her scope and count. She was one of these nervous white women with lots of money. She was very nice too. But as a *squaw*—as a real woman in a shawl whom a man went after for the pleasure of the night—why, she hardly counted. One of these white women who talk clever and know things like a man. She could hardly expect a half-savage male to acknowledge her as his female counterpart.—No! She had the bucks! And she had all the paraphernalia of the white man's civilisation, which a savage can play with and so escape his own hollow boredom. But his own real female counterpart?—Phoenix would just have shrugged his shoulders, and thought the question not worth answering. How could there be any answer in *her*, to the phallic male in him? Couldn't! Yet it would flatter his vanity and his self-esteem immensely, to possess her. That would be possessing the very clue to the white man's overwhelming world. And if she would let him possess her, he would be absolutely loyal to her, as far as affairs and appearances went. Only, the aboriginal phallic male in him simply couldn't recognise her as a woman at all. In this respect, she didn't exist. It needed the shawled Indian or Mexican women, with their squeaky, plaintive voices, their shuffling, watery humility, and the dark glances of their big, knowing eyes. When an Indian woman looked at him from under her black fringe, with dark, half-secretive suggestion in her big eyes: and when she stood before him hugged in her shawl, in such apparently complete quiescent humility: and when she spoke to him in her mousey squeak of a high, plaintive voice, as if it were difficult for her female bashfulness even

to emit so much sound: and when she shuffled away with her legs wide apart, because of her wide-topped, white, high buckskin boots with tiny white feet, and her dark-knotted hair so full of hard, yet subtle lure: and when he remembered the almost watery softness of the
5 Indian woman's dark, warm flesh: then he was a male, an old, secretive, rat-like male. But before Lou's straightforwardness and utter sexual incompetence, he just stood in contempt. And to him, even a French cocotte* was utterly devoid of the right sort of sex. She couldn't really move him. She couldn't satisfy the furtiveness in him. He needed this
10 plaintive, squeaky, dark-fringed Indian quality. Something furtive and soft and rat-like, really to rouse him.

Nevertheless he was ready to trade his sex, which, in his opinion, every white woman was secretly pining for, for the white woman's money and social privileges. In the daytime, all the thrill and
15 excitement of the white man's motor-cars and moving-pictures and ice-cream sodas and so forth. In the night, the soft, watery-soft warmth of an Indian or half-Indian woman. This was Phoenix's idea of life for himself.

Meanwhile, if a white woman gave him the privileges of the white
20 man's world, he would do his duty by her as far as all that went.

Lou, sitting very very still beside him as he drove the car: he was not a very good driver, not quick and marvellous as some white men are, particularly some French chauffeurs she had known, but usually a little behind-hand in his movements: she knew more or less all that
25 he felt. More or less she divined as a woman does. Even from a certain rather assured stupidity of his shoulders, and a certain rather stupid assertiveness of his knees, she knew him.

But she did not judge him too harshly. Somewhere deep, deep in herself she knew she too was at fault. And this made her sometimes
30 inclined to humble herself, as a woman, before the furtive assertiveness of this underground, "knowing" savage. He was so different from Rico.

Yet, after all, *was* he? In his rootlessness, his drifting, his real meaninglessness, was he different from Rico? And his childish,
35 spellbound absorption in the motor-car, or in the moving-pictures, or in an ice-cream soda—was it very different from Rico? Anyhow, was it really any better? Pleasanter, perhaps, to a woman, because of the childishness of it.

The same with his opinion of himself as a sexual male! So childish,
40 really, it was almost thrilling to a woman. But then, so stupid also,

with that furtive lurking in holes and imagining it could not be detected. He imagined he kept himself dark, in his sexual rat-holes. He imagined he was not detected!*

No no, Lou was not such a fool as she looked, in his eyes anyhow. She knew what she wanted. She wanted relief from the nervous tension and irritation of her life, she wanted to escape from the friction which is the whole stimulus in modern social life. She wanted to be still: only that, to be very, very still, and recover her own soul.

When Phoenix presumed she was looking for some secretly sexual male such as himself, he was ridiculously mistaken. Even the illusion of the beautiful St. Mawr was gone. And Phoenix, roaming round like a sexual rat in promiscuous back yards!—*Merci, mon cher!** For that was all he was: a sexual rat in the great barn-yard of man's habitat, looking for female rats!

Merci, mon cher! You are had.

Nevertheless, in his very mistakenness, he was a relief to her. His mistake was amusing rather than impressive. And the fact that one half of his intelligence was a complete dark blank, that too was a relief.

Strictly, and perhaps in the best sense, he was a servant. His very unconsciousness and his very limitation served as a shelter, as one shelters within the limitations of four walls. The very decided limits to his intelligence were a shelter to her. They made her feel safe.

But that feeling of safety did not deceive her. It was the feeling one derived from having a *true* servant attached to one, a man whose psychic limitations left him incapable of anything but service, and whose strong flow of natural life, at the same time, made him *need* to serve.

And Lou, sitting there so very still and frail, yet self-contained, had not lived for nothing. She no longer wanted to fool herself. She had no desire at all to fool herself into thinking that a Phoenix might be a husband and a mate. No desire that way at all. His obtuseness was a servant's obtuseness. She was grateful to him for serving, and she paid him a wage. Moreover, she provided him with something to do, to occupy his life. In a sense, she gave him his life, and rescued him from his own boredom. It was a balance.

He did not know what she was thinking. There was a certain physical sympathy between them. His obtuseness made him think it was also a sexual sympathy.

"It's a nice trip, you and me!" he said suddenly, turning and looking her in the eyes with an excited look, and ending on a foolish little laugh.

She realised that she should have sat in the back seat.

5   "But it's a bad road," she said. "Hadn't you better stop and put the sides of the hood up, your engine is boiling."

He looked away with a quick switch of interest to the red thermometer in front of his machine.

"She's boiling," he said, stopping, and getting out with a quick 10   alacrity to go to look at the engine.

Lou got out also, and went to the back seat, shutting the door decisively.

"I think I'll ride at the back," she said, "it gets so frightfully hot in front, when the engine heats up.—Do you think she needs some 15   water? Have you got some in the canteen?"

"She's full," he said, peering into the steaming valve.

"You can run a bit out, if you think there's any need. I wonder if it's much further!"

"*Quién sabe!*"* said he, slightly impertinent.

20   She relapsed into her own stillness. She realised how careful, how very careful she must be of relaxing into sympathy, and reposing, as it were, on Phoenix. He would read it as a sexual appeal. Perhaps he couldn't help it. She had only herself to blame. He was obtuse, as a man and a savage. He had only one interpretation, sex, for any woman's 25   approach to him.

And she knew, with the last clear knowledge of weary disillusion, that she did not want to be mixed up in Phoenix's sexual promiscuities. The very thought was an insult to her. The crude, clumsy servant-male: no no, not that. He was a good fellow, a very good fellow, as far as 30   he went. But he fell far short of physical intimacy.

"No no," she said to herself, "I was wrong to ride in the front seat with him. I must sit alone, just alone. Because sex, mere sex, is repellant to me. I will never prostitute myself again. Unless something touches my very spirit, the very quick of me, I will stay alone, just 35   alone. Alone, and give myself only to the unseen presences, serve only the other, unseen presences."

She understood now the meaning of the Vestal Virgins, the Virgins of the holy fire in the old temples.* They were symbolic of herself, of woman weary of the embrace of incompetent men, weary, weary, 40   weary of all that, turning to the unseen gods, the unseen spirits, the hidden fire, and devoting herself to that, and that alone. Receiving thence her pacification and her fulfilment.

Not these little, incompetent, childish self-opinionated men! Not these to touch her. She watched Phoenix's rather stupid shoulders, as he drove the car on between the piñón trees and the cedars of the narrow mesa* ridge, to the mountain foot. He was a good fellow. But let him run among women of his own sort. Something was beyond him. And this something must remain beyond him, never allow itself to come within his reach. Otherwise he would paw it and mess it up, and be as miserable as a child that has broken its father's watch.

No no! She had loved an American, and lived with him for a fortnight. She had had a long, intimate friendship with an Italian. Perhaps it was love on his part. And she had yielded to him. Then her love and marriage to Rico.

And what of it all? Nothing. It was almost nothing. It was as if only the outside of herself, her top layers, were human. This inveigled her into intimacies. As soon as the intimacy penetrated, or attempted to penetrate inside her, it was a disaster. Just a humiliation and a breaking down.

Within these outer layers of herself lay the successive inner sanctuaries of herself. And these were inviolable. She accepted it.

"I am not a marrying woman," she said to herself. "I am not a lover nor a mistress nor a wife. It is no good. Love can't really come into me from the outside, and I can never, never mate with any man, since the mystic new man will never come to me. No no, let me know myself and my rôle. I am one of the eternal Virgins, serving the eternal fire. My dealings with men have only broken my stillness and messed up my doorways. It has been my own fault. I ought to stay virgin and still, very, very still, and serve the most perfect service. I want my temple and my loneliness and my Apollo mystery of the inner fire.* And with men, only the delicate, subtler, more remote relations. No coming near. A coming near only breaks the delicate veils, and broken veils, like broken flowers, only lead to rottenness."

She felt a great peace inside herself as she made this realisation. And a thankfulness. Because, after all, it seemed to her that the hidden fire was alive and burning in this sky, over the desert, in the mountains. She felt a certain latent holiness in the very atmosphere, a young, spring-fire of latent holiness, such as she had never felt in Europe, or in the East. "For me," she said, as she looked away at the mountains

in shadow and the pale-warm desert beneath, with wings of shadow
upon it: "For me, this place is sacred. It is blessed."

But as she watched Phoenix: as she remembered the motor-cars and
tourists, and the rather dreary Mexicans of Santa Fe, and the lurking,
invidious Indians, with something of a rat-like secretiveness and
defeatedness in their bearing, she realised that the latent fire of the
vast landscape struggled under a great weight of dirt-like inertia. She
had to mind the dirt, most carefully and vividly avoid it and keep it
away from her, here in this place that at last seemed sacred to her.

The motor-car climbed up, past the tall pine-trees, to the foot of
the mountains, and came at last to a wire gate, where nothing was to
be expected. Phoenix opened the gate, and they drove on, through
more trees, into a clearing where dried up bean-plants were yellow.

"This man got no water for his beans," said Phoenix. "Not got
much beans this year."

They climbed slowly up the incline, through more pine-trees, and
out into another clearing, where a couple of horses were grazing. And
there they saw the ranch itself, little low cabins with patched roofs,
under a few pine-trees, and facing the long twelve-acre clearing, or
field, where the michaelmas daisies were purple mist, and spangled
with clumps of yellow flowers.

"Not got no alfalfa here neither!" said Phoenix, as the car waded
past the flowers. "Must be a dry place, up here. Got no water, sure
they haven't."

Yet it was the place Lou wanted. In an instant, her heart sprang
to it. The instant the car stopped, and she saw the two cabins inside
the rickety fence, the rather broken corral beyond, and behind all, tall,
blue balsam pines, the round hills, the solid uprise of the mountain
flank: and getting down, she looked across the purple and gold of the
clearing, downwards at the ring of pine-trees standing so still, so crude
and untameable, the motionless desert beyond the bristles of the pine
crests, a thousand feet below: and beyond the desert, blue mountains,
and far, far-off blue mountains in Arizona: "*This is the place*," she
said to herself.

This little tumble-down ranch, only a homestead of a hundred-
and-sixty acres, was, as it were, man's last effort towards the wild heart
of the Rockies, at this point. Sixty years before, a restless schoolmaster
had wandered out from the East, looking for gold among the
mountains. He found a very little, then no more. But the mountains
had got hold of him, he could not go back.

There was a little trickling spring of pure water, a thread of treasure perhaps better than gold. So the schoolmaster took up a homestead on the lot where this little spring arose. He struggled, and got himself his log cabin erected, his fence put up, sloping at the mountain-side through the pine-trees and dropping into the hollows where the ghost-white mariposa lilies stood leafless and naked in flower, in spring, on tall invisible stems. He made the long clearing for alfalfa.

And fell so into debt, that he had to trade his homestead away, to clear his debt. Then he made a tiny living teaching the children of the few American prospectors who had squatted in the valleys, beside the Mexicans.

The trader who got the ranch tackled it with a will. He built another log cabin, and a big corral, and brought water from the canyon two miles and more across the mountain slope, in a little runnel ditch, and more water, piped a mile or more down the little canyon immediately above the cabins. He got a flow of water for his houses: for being a true American, he felt he could not *really* say he had conquered his environment till he had got running water, taps, and wash-hand basins inside his house.

Taps, running water and wash-hand basins he accomplished. And, undaunted through the years, he prepared the basin for a fountain in the little fenced-in enclosure, and he built a little bath-house. After a number of years, he sent up the enamelled bath-tub to be put in the little log bath-house on the little wild ranch hung right against the savage Rockies, above the desert.

But here the mountains finished him. He was a trader down below, in the Mexican village. This little ranch was, as it were, his hobby, his ideal. He and his New England wife spent their summers there: and turned on the taps in the cabins and turned them off again, and felt really that civilisation had conquered.

All this plumbing from the savage ravines of the canyons—one of them nameless to this day—cost, however, money. In fact, the ranch cost a great deal of money. But it was all to be got* back. The big clearing was to be irrigated for alfalfa, the little clearing for beans, and the third clearing, under the corral, for potatoes. All these things the trader could trade to the Mexicans, very advantageously.

And moreover, since somebody had started a praise of the famous goat's cheese made by Mexican peasants in New Mexico, goats there should be.

Goats there were: five hundred of them, eventually. And they fed chiefly in the wild mountain hollows, the no-man's-land. The Mexicans call them fire-mouths, because everything they nibble dies. Not because of their flaming mouths, really, but because they nibble a live plant down, down to the quick, till it can put forth no more.

5   So, the energetic trader, in the course of five or six years, had got the ranch ready. The long three-roomed cabin was for him and his New England wife. In the two-roomed cabin lived the Mexican family who really had charge of the ranch. For the trader was mostly fixed to his store, seventeen miles away, down in the Mexican village.*

10   The ranch lay over eight thousand feet up, the snows of winter came deep and the white goats, looking dirty yellow, swam in snow with their poor curved horns poking out like dead sticks. But the corral had a long, cosy, shut-in goat-shed all down one side, and into this crowded the five-hundred, their acrid goat-smell rising like hot acid over the

15   snow. And the thin, pock-marked Mexican threw them alfalfa out of the log barn. Until the hot sun sank the snow again, and froze the surface, when patter-patter went the two-thousand little goat-hoofs, over the silver-frozen snow, up at the mountain. Nibble, nibble, nibble, the fire-mouths, at every tender twig. And the goat-bell climbed, and

20   the baa-ing came from among the dense and shaggy pine-trees. And sometimes, in a soft drift under the trees, a goat, or several goats went through, into the white depths, and some were lost thus, to reappear dead and frozen at the thaw.

By evening, they were driven down again, like a dirty yellowish-white

25   stream carrying dark sticks on its yeasty surface, tripping and bleating over the frozen snow, past the bustling dark green pine-trees, down to the trampled mess of the corral. And everywhere, everywhere over the snow, yellow stains and dark pills of goat-droppings melting into the surface crystal. On still, glittering nights, when the frost was hard,

30   the smell of goats came up like some uncanny acid fire, and great stars sitting on the mountain's edge seemed to be watching like the eyes of a mountain lion, brought by the scent. Then the coyotes in the near canyon howled and sobbed, and ran like shadows over the snow. But the goat corral had been built tight.

35   In the course of years, the goat-herd had grown from fifty to five hundred, and surely that was increase. The goat-milk cheeses sat drying on their little racks. In spring, there was a great flowing and skipping of kids. In summer and early autumn, there was a pest of flies, rising from all that goat-smell and that cast-out whey of goats-milk,

40   after the cheese making. The rats came, and the pack-rats, swarming.

And after all, it was difficult to sell or trade the cheeses, and little profit to be made. And in dry summers, no water came down in the narrow ditch-channel, that straddled in wooden runnels over the deep clefts in the mountain-side. No water meant no alfalfa. In winter the goats scarcely drank at all. In summer they could be watered at the little spring. But the thirsty land was not so easy to accommodate.

Five hundred fine white angora goats, with their massive handsome padres!* They were beautiful enough. And the trader made all he could of them. Come summer, they were run down into the narrow tank filled with the fiery dipping fluid. Then their lovely white wool was clipped. It was beautiful, and valuable, but comparatively little of it.

And it all cost, cost, cost. And a man was always let down. At one time no water. At another a poison-weed. Then a sickness. Always, some mysterious malevolence fighting, fighting against the will of man. A strange invisible influence coming out of the livid rock-fastnesses in the bowels of those uncreated Rocky Mountains, preying upon the will of man, and slowly wearing down his resistance, his onward-pushing spirit. The curious, subtle thing, like a mountain fever, got into the blood, so that the men at the ranch, and the animals with them, had bursts of queer, violent, half-frenzied energy, in which, however, they were wont to lose their wariness. And then, damage of some sort. The horses ripped and cut themselves, or they were struck by lightning, the men had great hurts, or sickness. A curious disintegration working all the time, a sort of malevolent breath, like a stupefying, irritant gas, coming out of the unfathomed mountains.

The pack-rats with their bushy tails and big ears, came down out of the hills, and were jumping and bouncing about: symbols of the curious debasing malevolence that was in the spirit of the place. The Mexicans in charge, good honest men, worked all they could. But they were like most of the Mexicans in the South-West, as if they had been pithed, to use one of Kipling's words.* As if the invidious malevolence of the country itself had slowly taken all the pith of manhood from them, leaving a hopeless sort of corpus of a man.

And the same happened to the white men, exposed to the open country. Slowly, they were pithed. The energy went out of them. And more than that, the interest. An inertia of indifference invading the soul, leaving the body healthy and active, but wasting the soul, the living interest, quite away.

It was the New England wife of the trader who put most energy into the ranch. She looked on it as her home. She had a little white fence put all round the two cabins: the bright brass water-taps she kept shining in the two kitchens: outside the kitchen door she had a little kitchen garden and nasturtiums, after a great fight with invading animals, that nibbled everything away. And she got so far as the preparation of the round concrete basin which was to be a little pool, under the few enclosed pine-trees between the two cabins, a pool with a tiny fountain jet.

But this, with the bath-tub, was her limit, as the five hundred goats were her man's limit. Out of the mountains came two breaths of influence: the breath of the curious, frenzied energy, that took away one's intelligence as alcohol or any other stimulus does: and then the most strange invidiousness that ate away the soul. The woman loved her ranch, almost with passion. It was she who felt the stimulus, more than the men. It seemed to enter her like a sort of sex passion, intensifying her ego, making her full of violence and of blind female energy. The energy, and the blindness of it! A strange blind frenzy, like an intoxication while it lasted. And the sense of beauty that thrilled her New England woman's soul.

Her cabin faced the slow downslope of the clearing, the alfalfa field: her long, low cabin, crouching under the great pine-tree that threw up its trunk sheer in front of the house, in the yard. That pine-tree was the guardian of the place. But a bristling, almost demonish guardian, from the far-off crude ages of the world. Its great pillar of pale, flakey-ribbed copper rose there in strange callous indifference, and the grim permanence, which is in pine-trees. A passionless, non-phallic column, rising in the shadows of the pre-sexual world, before the hot-blooded ithyphallic column ever erected itself.* A cold, blossomless, resinous sap surging and oozing gum, from that pallid brownish bark. And the wind hissing in the needles, like a vast nest of serpents. And the pine cones falling plumb as the hail hit them. Then lying all over the yard, open in the sun like wooden roses, but hard, sexless, rigid with a blind will.

Past the column of that pine-tree, the alfalfa field sloped gently down, to the circling guard of pine-trees, from which silent, living barrier isolated pines rose to ragged heights at intervals, in blind assertiveness. Strange, those pine-trees! In some lights all their needles glistened like polished steel, all subtly glittering with a whitish glitter among darkness, like real needles. Then again, at evening, the trunks would flare up orange red, and the tufts would be dark, alert tufts like a wolf's tail touching the air. Again, in the morning sunlight they would be soft and still, hardly noticeable. But all the same, present, and watchful. Never sympathetic, always watchfully on their guard, and resistant, they hedged one in with the aroma and the power and the slight horror of the pre-sexual primeval world. The world where each creature was crudely limited to its own ego, crude and bristling and 5 cold, and then crowding in packs like pine-trees and wolves.

But beyond the pine-trees, ah, there beyond, there was beauty for the spirit to soar in. The circle of pines, with the loose trees rising high and ragged at intervals, this was the barrier, the fence to the foreground. Beyond was only distance, the desert a thousand feet 10 below, and beyond.

The desert swept its great fawn-coloured circle around, away beyond and below like a beach, with a long mountain-side of pure blue shadow closing in the near corner, and strange bluish hummocks of mountains rising like wet rock from a vast strand, away in the middle 15 distance, and beyond, in the farthest distance, pale blue crests of mountains looking over the horizon, from the west, as if peering in from another world altogether.

Ah, that was beauty!—perhaps the most beautiful thing in the world. It was pure beauty, *absolute* beauty! There! That was it. To 20 the little woman from New England, with her tense fierce soul and her egoistic passion of service, this beauty was absolute, a *ne plus ultra*. From her doorway, from her porch, she could watch the vast, eagle-like wheeling of the daylight, that turned as the eagles which lived in the near rocks turned overhead in the blue, turning their luminous, 25 dark-edged-patterned bellies and underwings upon the pure air, like winged orbs. So the daylight made the vast turn upon the desert, brushing the farthest outwatching mountains. And sometimes, the vast strand of the desert would float with curious undulations and exhalations amid the blue fragility of mountains, whose upper edges 30 were harder than the floating bases. And sometimes she would see the little brown adobe* houses of the village Mexicans, twenty miles away, like little cube crystals of insect-houses dotting upon the desert, very distinct, with a cotton-wood tree or two rising near. And sometimes she would see the far-off rocks, thirty miles away, where the canyon 35 made a gateway between the mountains. Quite clear, like an open gateway out of a vast yard, she would see the cut-out bit of the canyon-passage. And on the desert itself, curious puckered folds of mesa-sides. And a blackish crack which in places revealed the otherwise invisible canyon of the Rio Grande. And beyond everything, 40 the mountains like icebergs showing up from an outer sea. Then later, the sun would go down blazing above the shallow cauldron of simmering darkness, and the round mountain of Colorado would lump up into uncanny significance, northwards. That was always rather frightening. But morning came again, with the sun peeping over the mountain slopes and lighting the desert away in the distance long, long before it lighted on her yard. And then she would see another valley, like magic and very lovely, with green fields and long tufts of cotton-wood trees, and a few long-cubical adobe houses, lying floating in shallow light below, like a vision.

Ah: it was beauty, beauty absolute, at any hour of the day: whether the perfect clarity of morning, or the mountains beyond the simmering desert at noon, or the purple lumping of northern mounds under a red sun at night. Or whether the dust whirled in tall columns, travelling across the desert far away, like pillars of cloud by day,* tall, leaning pillars of dust hastening with ghostly haste: or whether, in the early part of the year, suddenly in the morning a whole sea of solid white would rise rolling below, a solid mist from melted snow, ghost-white under the mountain sun, the world below blotted out: or whether the black rain and cloud streaked down, far across the desert, and lightning stung down with sharp white stings on the horizon: or the cloud travelled and burst overhead, with rivers of fluid blue fire running out of heaven and exploding on earth, and hail coming down like a world of ice shattered above: or the hot sun rode in again: or snow fell in heavy silence: or the world was blinding white under a blue sky, and one must hurry under the pine-trees for shelter against that vast, white, back-beating light which rushed up at one and made one almost unconscious, amid the snow.

It was always beauty, *always*! It was always great, and splendid, and, for some reason, natural. It was never grandiose or theatrical. Always, for some reason, perfect. And quite simple, in spite of it all.

So it was, when you watched the vast and living landscape. The landscape lived, and lived as the world of the gods, unsullied and unconcerned. The great circling landscape lived its own life, sumptuous and uncaring. Man did not exist for it.

And if it had been a question simply of living through the eyes, into the *distance*, then this would have been Paradise, and the little New England woman on her ranch would have found what she was always looking for, the earthly paradise of the spirit.

But even a woman cannot live only into the distance, the beyond.

Willy-nilly she finds herself juxtaposed to the near things, the thing in itself. And willy-nilly she is caught up into the fight with the immediate object.

The New England woman had fought to make the nearness as perfect as the distance: for the distance was absolute beauty. She had been confident of success. She had felt quite assured, when the water came running out of her bright brass taps, the wild water of the hills caught, tricked into the narrow iron pipes, and led tamely to her kitchen, to jump out over her sink, into her wash-basin, at her service. *There!* she said. I have tamed the waters of the mountain to my service. So she had, for the moment.

At the same time, the invisible attack was being made upon her. While she revelled in the beauty of the luminous world that wheeled around and below her, the grey, rat-like spirit of the inner mountains was attacking her from behind. She could not keep her attention. And, curiously, she could not keep even her speech. When she was saying something, suddenly the next word would be gone out of her, as if a pack-rat had carried it off. And she sat blank, stuttering, staring in the empty cupboard of her mind, like Mother Hubbard, and seeing the cupboard bare. And this irritated her husband intensely.

Her chickens, of which she was so proud, were carried away. Or they strayed. Or they fell sick. At first she could cope with their circumstances. But after a while, she couldn't. She couldn't care. A drug like numbness possessed her spirit, and at the very middle of her, she couldn't care what happened to her chickens.

The same when a couple of horses were struck by lightning. It frightened her. The rivers of fluid fire that suddenly fell out of the sky and exploded on the earth near by, as if the whole earth had burst like a bomb, frightened her from the very core of her, and made her know, secretly and with cynical certainty, *that there was no merciful God in the heavens.* A very tall, elegant pine-tree just above her cabin took the lightning, and stood tall and elegant as before, but with a white seam spiralling from its crest, all down its tall trunk, to earth. The perfect scar, white and long as lightning itself. And every time she looked at it, she said to herself, in spite of herself: *There is no Almighty loving God. The God there is shaggy as the pine-trees, and horrible as the lightning.* Outwardly, she never confessed this. Openly, she thought of her dear New England Church as usual. But in the violent undercurrent of her woman's soul, after the storms, she would look at that living seamed tree, and the voice would say in her, almost savagely: *What nonsense about Jesus and a God of Love, in a place like this! This is more awful and more splendid. I like it better.* The very chipmunks, in their jerky helter-skelter, the blue jays wrangling in the pine-tree in the dawn, the grey squirrel undulating to the tree-trunk, then pausing to chatter at her and scold her, with a shrewd fearlessness, as if she were the alien, the outsider, the creature that should not be permitted among the trees, all destroyed the illusion she cherished, of love, universal love. There was no love on this ranch. There was life, intense, bristling life, full of energy, but also, with an undertone of savage sordidness.

The black ants in her cupboard, the pack-rats bouncing on her ceiling like hippopotamuses in the night, the two sick goats: there was a peculiar undercurrent of squalor, flowing under the curious *tussle* of wild life. That was it. The wild life, even the life of the trees and flowers, seemed one bristling, hair-raising tussle. The very flowers came up bristly, and many of them were fang-mouthed, like the dead-nettle: and none had any real scent. But they were very fascinating, too, in their very fierceness. In May, the curious columbines of the stream-beds, columbines scarlet outside and yellow in, like the red and yellow of a herald's uniform: farther from the dove* nothing could be: then the beautiful rosy-blue of the great tufts of the flower they called blue-bell, but which was really a flower of the snap-dragon family: these grew in powerful beauty in the little clearing of the pine-trees, followed by the flower the settlers had mysteriously called herb honeysuckle: a tangle of long drops of pure fire-red, hanging from slim invisible stalks of smoke colour. The purest, most perfect vermilion scarlet, cleanest fire-colour, hanging in long drops like a shower of fire-rain that is just going to strike the earth. A little later, more in the open, there came another sheer fire-red flower, sparking, fierce red stars running up a bristly grey ladder, as if the earth's fire-centre had blown out some red sparks, white-speckled and deadly inside, puffing for a moment in the day air.

So it was! The alfalfa field was one raging, seething conflict of plants trying to get hold. One dry year, and the bristly wild things had got hold: the spiky, blue-leaved thistle-poppy with its moon-white flowers, the low clumps of blue nettle-flower, the later rush, after the sereness of June and July, the rush of red sparks and michaelmas daisies, and the tough wild sunflowers, strangling and choking the dark, tender green of the clover-like alfalfa! A battle, a battle, with banners of bright scarlet and yellow.

When a really defenceless flower did issue, like the moth-still, ghost-centred mariposa lily, with its inner moth-dust of yellow, it came invisible. There was nothing to be seen, but a hair of greyish grass near the oak-scrub. Behold, this invisible long stalk was balancing a white, ghostly, three-petalled flower, naked out of nothingness. A mariposa lily!

Only the pink wild roses smelled sweet, like the old world. They were sweet-briar roses. And the dark blue hare-bells among the oak-scrub, like the ice-dark bubbles of the mountain flowers in the Alps, the Alpenglocken.

The roses of the desert are the cactus flowers, crystal of translucent yellow or of rose-colour. But set among spines the devil himself must have conceived in a moment of sheer ecstasy.

Nay, it was a world before and after the God of Love. Even the very humming-birds hanging about the flowering squaw-berry bushes, when the snow had gone, in May, they were before and after the God of Love. And the blue jays were crested dark with challenge, and the yellow-and-dark woodpecker was fearless like a warrior in war-paint, as he struck the wood. While on the fence the hawks sat motionless, like dark fists clenched under heaven, ignoring man and his ways.

Summer, it was true, unfolded the tender cotton-wood leaves, and the tender aspen. But what a tangle and a ghostly aloofness in the aspen thickets high up on the mountains, the coldness that is in the eyes and the long cornelian talons of the bear.

Summer brought the little wild strawberries, with their savage aroma, and the late summer brought the rose-jewel raspberries in the valley cleft. But how lonely, how harsh-lonely and menacing it was, to be alone in that shadowy, steep cleft of a canyon just above the cabins, picking raspberries, while the thunder gathered thick and blue-purple at the mountain tops. The many wild raspberries hanging rose-red in the thickets. But the stream bed below all silent, water-less. And the trees all bristling in silence, and waiting like warriors at an out-post. And the berries waiting for the sharp-eyed, cold, long-snouted bear to come rambling and shaking his heavy sharp fur. The berries grew for the bears, and the little New England woman, with her uncanny sensitiveness to underlying influences, felt all the time she was stealing. Stealing the wild raspberries in the secret little canyon behind her home. And when she had made them into jam, she could almost taste the theft in her preserves.

She confessed nothing of this. She tried even to confess nothing of her dread. But she was afraid. Especially she was conscious of the prowling, intense aerial electricity all the summer, after June. The air was thick with wandering currents of fierce electric fluid, waiting to discharge themselves. And almost every day there was the rage and battle of thunder. But the air was never cleared. There was no relief. However the thunder raged, and spent itself, yet, afterwards, among the sunshine was the strange lurking and wandering of the electric currents, moving invisible, with strange menace, between the atoms of the air. She knew. Oh she knew!

And her love for her ranch turned sometimes into a certain repulsion. The underlying rat-dirt, the everlasting bristling tussle of the wild life, with the tangle and the bones strewing. Bones of horses struck by lightning, bones of dead cattle, skulls of goats with little horns: bleached, unburied bones. Then the cruel electricity of the mountains. And then, most mysterious but worst of all, the animosity of the spirit of place: the crude, half-created spirit of place, like some serpent-bird forever attacking man, in a hatred of man's onward-struggle towards further creation.

The seething caldron of lower life, seething on the very tissue of the higher life, seething the soul away, seething at the marrow. The vast and unrelenting will of the swarming lower life, working forever against man's attempt at a higher life, a further created being.

At last, after many years, the little woman admitted to herself that she was glad to go down from the ranch, when November came with snows. She was glad to come to a more human home, her house in the village. And as winter passed by, and spring came again, she knew she did not want to go up to the ranch again. It had broken something in her. It had hurt her terribly. It had maimed her for ever in her hope, her belief in paradise on earth. Now, she hid from herself her own corpse, the corpse of her New England belief in a world ultimately all for love. The belief, and herself with it, was a corpse. The gods of those inner mountains were grim and invidious and relentless, huger than man, and lower than man. Yet man could never master them.

The little woman in her flower-garden away below, by the stream-irrigated village, hid away from the thought of it all. She would not go to the ranch any more.

The Mexicans stayed in charge, looking after the goats. But the place didn't pay. It didn't pay, not quite. It had paid. It might pay. But the effort, the effort! And as the marrow is eaten out of a man's bones and the soul out of his belly, contending with the strange rapacity of savage life, the lower stage of creation, he cannot make the effort any more.

Then also, the war came, making many men give up their enterprises at civilisation.

Every new stroke of civilisation has cost the lives of countless brave men, who have fallen defeated by the "dragon," in their efforts to win the apples of the Hesperides, or the fleece of gold.* Fallen in their efforts to overcome the old, half-sordid savagery of the lower stages of creation, and win to the next stage.

For all savagery is half-sordid. And man is only himself when he is fighting on and on, to overcome the sordidness.

And every civilisation, when it loses its inward vision and its cleaner energy, falls into a new sort of sordidness, more vast and more stupendous than the old savage sort. An Augean stables of metallic filth.*

And all the time, man has to rouse himself afresh, to cleanse the new accumulations of refuse. To win from the crude wild nature the victory and the power to make another start, and to cleanse behind him the century-deep deposits of layer upon layer of refuse: even of tin cans.

The ranch dwindled. The flock of goats declined. The water ceased to flow. And at length the trader gave it up.

He rented the place to a Mexican, who lived c̯n the handful of beans he raised, and who was being slowly driven out by the vermin.

And now arrived Lou, new blood to the attack. She went back to Santa Fe, saw the trader and a lawyer, and bought the ranch for twelve hundred dollars. She was so pleased with herself.

She went upstairs to tell her mother.

"Mother, I've bought a ranch."

"It is just as well, for I can't stand the noise of automobiles outside here another week."

"It is quiet on my ranch, mother: the stillness simply speaks."

"I had rather it held its tongue. I am simply drugged with all the bad novels I have read. I feel as if the sky was a big cracked bell and a million clappers were hammering human speech out of it."

"Aren't you interested in my ranch, mother?"

"I hope I may be, by and by."

Mrs Witt actually got up the next morning, and accompanied her daughter in the hired motor-car, driven by Phoenix, to the ranch: which was called Las Chivas.* She sat like a pillar of salt, her face

looking what the Indians call a False Face, meaning a mask. She
seemed to have crystallised into neutrality. She watched the desert with
its tufts of yellow greasewood go lurching past: she saw the fallen
apples on the ground in the orchards near the adobe cottages: she
5   looked down into the deep arroyo,* and at the stream they forded in
the car, and at the mountains blocking up the sky ahead, all with
indifference. High on the mountains was snow: lower, blue-grey livid
rock: and below the livid rock the aspens were expiring their daffodil
yellow, this year, and the oak-scrub was dark and reddish, like gore.
10 She saw it all with a sort of stony indifference.
"Don't you think it's lovely?" said Lou.
"I can *see* it is lovely," replied her mother.
The michaelmas daisies in the clearing as they drove up to the ranch
were sharp-rayed with purple, like a coming night.
15 Mrs Witt eyed the two log cabins, one of which was delapidated
and practically abandoned. She looked at the rather ricketty corral,
whose long planks had silvered and warped in the fierce sun. On one
of the roof-planks a pack-rat was sitting erect like an old Indian keeping
watch on a pueblo roof. He showed his white belly, and folded his
20 hands, and lifted his big ears, for all the world like an old immobile
Indian.
"Isn't it for all the world as if *he* were the real boss of the place,
Louise?" she said cynically.
And turning to the Mexican, who was a rag of a man but a pleasant
25 courteous fellow, she asked him why he didn't shoot the rat.
"Not worth a shell!" said the Mexican, with a faint hopeless smile.
Mrs Witt paced round and saw everything: it did not take long. She
gazed in silence at the water of the spring, trickling out of an iron pipe
into a barrel, under the cotton-wood tree in an arroyo.
30 "Well Louise," she said. "I am glad you feel competent to cope
with so much hopelessness and so many rats."
"But mother, you must admit it is beautiful."
"Yes, I suppose it is. But to use one of your Henry's phrases, beauty
is a cold egg,* as far as I am concerned."
35 "Rico never would have said that beauty was a cold egg to him."
"No, he wouldn't. He sits on it like a broody old hen on a china
imitation.—Are you going to bring him here?"
"*Bring* him!—No. But he can come if he likes," stammered Lou.
"*Oh—h*! won't it be beau-ti-ful!" cried Mrs Witt, rolling her head
40 and lifting her shoulders in savage imitation of her son-in-law.

"Perhaps he won't come, mother," said Lou, hurt.

"He will most certainly come, Louise, to see what's doing: unless you tell him you don't want him."

"Anyhow I needn't think about it till spring," said Lou, anxiously pushing the matter aside.

Mrs Witt climbed the steep slope above the cabins, to the mouth of the little canyon. There she sat on a fallen tree, and surveyed the world beyond: a world not of men. She could not fail to be roused.

"What is your idea in coming here, daughter?" she asked.

"I love it here, mother."

"But what do you expect to achieve by it?"

"I was rather hoping, mother, to escape achievement. I'll tell you—and you musn't get cross if it sounds silly. As far as people go, my heart is quite broken. As far as people go, I don't want any more. I can't stand any more. What heart I ever had for it—for life with people—is quite broken. I want to be alone, mother: with you here, and Phoenix perhaps to look after horses and drive a car. But I want to be by myself, really."

"With Phoenix in the background! Are you sure he won't be coming into the foreground before long?"

"No mother, no more of that. If I've got to say it, Phoenix is a servant: he's really placed, as far as I can see. Always the same, playing about in the old back-yard. I can't take those men seriously. I can't fool round with them, or fool myself about them. I can't and I won't fool myself any more, mother, especially about men. They don't count. So why should you want them to pay me out."

For the moment, this silenced Mrs Witt. Then she said:

"Why, *I* don't want it. Why should I! But after all you've got to live. You've never *lived* yet: not in my opinion."

"Neither, mother, in my opinion, have you," said Lou drily.

And this silenced Mrs Witt altogether. She had to be silent, or angrily on the defensive. And the latter she wouldn't be. She couldn't, really, in honesty.

"What do you call life?" Lou continued. "Wriggling half-naked at a public show, and going off in a taxi to sleep with some half-drunken fool who thinks he's a man because—Oh mother, I don't even want to think of it. I know you have a lurking idea that *that is life*. Let it be so then. But leave me out. Men in that aspect simply nauseate me: so grovelling and ratty. Life in that aspect simply drains all my life away. I tell you, for all that sort of thing, I'm broken, absolutely broken: if I wasn't broken to start with."

"Well Louise," said Mrs Witt after a pause. "I'm convinced that ever since men and women were men and women, people who took things seriously, and had time for it, got their hearts broken. Haven't I had mine broken! It's as sure as having your virginity broken: and it amounts to about as much. It's a beginning rather than an end."

"So it is, mother. It's the beginning of something else, and the end of something that's done with. I *know*, and there's no altering it, that I've got to live differently. It sounds silly, but I don't know how else to put it. I've got to live for something that matters, way, way down in me. And I think sex would matter, to my very soul, if it was really sacred. But cheap sex kills me."

"You have had a fancy for rather cheap men, perhaps."

"Perhaps I have. Perhaps I should always be a fool, where people are concerned. Now I want to leave off that kind of foolery. There's something else, mother, that I want to give myself to. I know it. I know it absolutely. Why should I let myself be shouted down any more!"

Mrs Witt sat staring at the distance, her face a cynical mask.

"What is the something bigger? And *pray*, what is it bigger than?" she asked, in that tone of honied suavity which was her deadliest poison. "I want to learn. I am out to know. I'm terribly intrigued by it—Something bigger! Girls in my generation occasionally entered convents, for *something bigger*. I always wondered if they found it. They seemed to me inclined in the imbecile direction, but perhaps that was because I was *something less*—"

There was a definite pause between the mother and daughter, a silence that was a pure breach. Then Lou said:

"You know quite well I'm not conventy, mother, whatever else I am—even a bit of an imbecile. But that kind of religion seems to me the other half of men. Instead of running after them you run away from them, and get the thrill that way. I don't hate men *because* they're men, as nuns do. I dislike them because they're not men enough: babies, and playboys, and poor things showing off all the time, even to themselves. I don't say I'm any better. I only wish, with all my soul, that some men *were* bigger and stronger and *deeper* than I am...."

"How do you know they're not—?" asked Mrs Witt.

"How *do* I know?—" said Lou mockingly.

And the pause that was a breach resumed itself. Mrs Witt was teasing with a little stick the bewildered black ants among the fir-needles.

"And no doubt you are right about men." she said at length. "But at your age, the only sensible thing is to try and keep up the illusion. After all, as you say, you may be no better."

"I may be no better. But keeping up the illusion means fooling myself. And I won't do it. When I see a man who is even a bit attractive to me—even as much as Phoenix—I say to myself: *Would you care for him afterwards? Does he really mean anything to you, except just a sensation?*—And I know he doesn't. No mother, of this I am convinced: either my taking a man shall have a meaning and a mystery that penetrates my very soul, or I will keep to myself.—And what I *know*, is that the time has come for me to keep to myself. No more messing about."

"Very well, daughter. You will probably spend your life keeping to yourself."

"Do you think I mind! There's something else for me, mother. There's something else even that loves me and wants me. I can't tell you what it is. It's a spirit. And it's here, on this ranch. It's here, in this landscape. It's something more real to me than men are, and it soothes me, and it holds me up. I don't know what it is, definitely. It's something wild, that will hurt me sometimes and will wear me down sometimes. I know it. But it's something big, bigger than men, bigger than people, bigger than religion. It's something to do with wild America. And it's something to do with me. It's a mission, if you like. I am imbecile enough for that!—But it's my mission to keep myself for the spirit that is wild, and has waited so long here: even waited for such as me. Now I've come! Now I'm here. Now I am where I want to be: with the spirit that wants me.—And that's how it is. And neither Rico nor Phoenix nor anybody else really matters to me. They are in the world's back-yard. And I am here, right deep in America, where there's a wild spirit wants me, a wild spirit more than men. And it doesn't want to save me either. It needs me. It craves for me. And to it, my sex is deep and sacred, deeper than I am, with a deep nature aware deep down of my sex. It saves me from cheapness, mother. And even you could never do that for me."

Mrs Witt rose to her feet, and stood looking far, far away, at the turquoise ridge of mountains half sunk under the horizon.

"How much did you say you paid for Las Chivas?" she asked.

"Twelve hundred dollars," said Lou, surprised.

"Then I call it cheap, considering all there is to it: even the name!"

THE PRINCESS

The Princess

To her father, she was The Princess.* To her Boston aunts and uncles she was just *Dollie Urquhart, poor little thing*.

Colin Urquhart was just a bit mad. He was of an old Scottish family, and he claimed royal blood. The blood of Scottish kings flowed in his veins. On this point, his American relatives said, he was just a bit "off." They could not bear any more to be told *which* royal blood of Scotland blued his veins. The whole thing was rather ridiculous, and a sore point. The only fact they remembered was that it was not Stuart.*

He was a handsome man, with a wide-open blue eye that seemed sometimes to be looking at nothing, soft black hair brushed rather low on his low, broad brow, and a very attractive body. Add to this a most beautiful speaking voice, usually rather hushed and diffident, but sometimes resonant and powerful like bronze, and you have the sum of his charms. He looked like some old Celtic hero. He looked as if he should have worn a greyish kilt and a sporran, and shown his knees. His voice came direct out of the hushed Ossianic past.*

For the rest, he was one of those gentlemen of sufficient but not excessive means, who fifty years ago wandered vaguely about, never arriving anywhere, never doing anything, and never definitely being anything, yet well received and familiar in the good society of more than one country.

He did not marry till he was nearly forty: and then it was a wealthy Miss Prescott from New England.* Hannah Prescott at twenty-two was fascinated by the man with the soft black hair not yet touched by grey, and the wide, rather vague blue eyes. Many women had been fascinated before her. But Colin Urquhart, by his very vagueness, had avoided any decisive connection.

Mrs Urquhart lived three years in the mist and glamour of her husband's presence. And then it broke her. It was like living with a fascinating spectre. About most things he was completely, even ghostlily oblivious. He was always charming, courteous, perfectly gracious in that hushed, musical voice of his. But absent. When all came to all, he just wasn't there. Not all there, as the vulgar say.

He was the father of the little girl she bore at the end of the first year. But this did not substantiate him the more. His very beauty and his haunting musical quality became dreadful to her after the first few

months. The strange echo: he was like a living echo! His very flesh,
when you touched it, did not seem quite the flesh of a real man.
    Perhaps it was that he was a little bit mad. She thought it definitely
the night her baby was born.

5   "Ah, so my little princess has come at last!" he said, in his throaty,
singing Celtic voice, like a glad chant, swaying absorbed.
    It was a tiny frail baby, with wide, amazed blue eyes. They
christened it Mary Henrietta. She called the little thing: *My Dollie.*
He called it always: *My Princess.*

10   It was useless to fly at him. He just opened his wide blue eyes wider,
and took a childlike silent dignity there was no getting past.
    Hannah Prescott had never been robust. She had no great desire
to live. So when the baby was two years old, she suddenly died.
    The Prescotts felt a deep but unadmitted resentment against Colin

15 Urquhart. They said he was selfish. Therefore they discontinued
Hannah's income, a month after her burial in Florence, after they had
urged the father to give the child over to them, and he had courteously,
musically, but quite finally refused. He treated the Prescotts as if they
were not of his world, not realities to him: just casual phenomena,

20 or gramophones, talking-machines that had to be answered. He
answered them. But of their actual existence he was never once aware.
    They debated having him certified unsuitable to be guardian of his
own child. But that would have created a scandal. So they did the
simplest thing, after all: washed their hands of him. But they wrote

25 scrupulously to the child, and sent her modest presents of money at
Christmas, and on the anniversary of the death of her mother.
    To The Princess her Boston relatives were for many years just a
nominal reality. She lived with her father: and he travelled continually,
though in a modest way, living on his moderate income. And never

30 going to America. The child changed nurses all the time. In Italy it
was a contadina: in India she had an ayah:* in Germany she had a
yellow-haired peasant girl.
    Father and child were inseparable. He was not a recluse. Wherever
he went, he was to be seen paying formal calls, going out to luncheon

35 or to tea, rarely to dinner. And always with the child. People called
her Princess Urquhart, as if that were her christened name.
    She was a quick, dainty little thing with dark gold hair that went
a soft brown, and wide, slightly prominent blue eyes that were at once
so candid and so knowing. She was always grown-up: she never really

40 grew up. Always strangely wise, and always childish.

It was her father's fault.

"My little Princess must never take too much notice of people and the things they say and do," he repeated to her. "People don't know what they are doing and saying. They chatter-chatter, and they hurt one another and they hurt themselves very often, till they cry. But don't take any notice, my little Princess. Because it is all nothing. Inside everybody there is another creature, a demon which doesn't care at all. You peel away all the things they say and do and feel, as cook peels away the outside of the onions. And in the middle of everybody, there is a green demon which you can't peel away. And this green demon never changes, and it doesn't care at all about all the things that happen to the outside leaves of the person, all the chatter-chatter, and all the husbands and wives and children, and troubles and fusses. You peel everything away from people, and there is a green, upright demon in every man and woman: and this demon is a man's real self, and a woman's real self. It doesn't really care about anybody, it belongs to the demons and the primitive fairies who never care—.—But even so, there are big demons and mean demons, and splendid demonish fairies and vulgar ones. But there are no royal fairy women left. Only you, my little Princess. You are the last of the royal race of the old people; the last, my Princess. There are no others. You and I are the last. When I am dead there will be only you.—And that is why, darling, you will never care for any of the people in the world very much. Because their demons are all dwindled and vulgar. They are not royal. Only you are royal, after me. Always remember that. And always remember, it is a *great secret*. If you tell people, they will try to kill you, because they will envy you for being a princess. It is our great secret, darling. I am a prince, and you a princess, of the old, old blood. And we keep our secret between us, all alone. And so, darling, you must treat all people very politely, because *noblesse oblige*.* But you must never forget, that you alone are the last of princesses, and that all others are less than you are: less noble, more vulgar. Treat them politely and gently and kindly, darling. But you are the Princess, and they are commoners. Never try to think of them as if they were like you. They are not. You will find, always, that they are lacking, lacking in the royal touch, which only you have—"*

The Princess learned her lesson early: the first lesson, of absolute reticence, the impossibility of intimacy with any other than her father: the second lesson, of naïve, slightly benevolent politeness. As a small child, something crystallised in her character, making her clear and finished, and as impervious as crystal.

"Dear child!" her hostesses said of her. "She is so quaint and old-fashioned: such a lady, poor little mite!"

She was erect, and very dainty. Always small, nearly tiny in physique, she seemed like a changeling* beside her big, handsome, slightly mad father. She dressed very simply, usually in blues or delicate greys, with little collars of old Milan point,* or very finely-worked linen. She had exquisite little hands, that made the piano sound like a spinet when she played. She was rather given to wearing cloaks and capes, instead of coats, out of doors, and little eighteenth-century sort of hats. Her complexion was pure apple-blossom.

She looked as if she had stepped out of a picture. But no-one, to her dying day, ever knew exactly the strange picture her father had framed her in, and from which she never stepped.

Her grandfather and grandmother and her Aunt Maud demanded twice to see her: once in Rome and once in Paris. Each time they were charmed, piqued, and annoyed. She was so exquisite and such a little virgin. At the same time, so knowing, and so oddly assured. That odd, assured touch of condescension, and the inward coldness, infuriated her American relations.

Only she really fascinated her grandfather. He was spellbound: in a way, in love with the little faultless thing. His wife would catch him brooding, musing over his grandchild, long months after the meeting, and craving to see her again. He cherished to the end the fond hope that she might come to live with him and her grandmother.

"Thank you so much, grandfather. You are so very kind. But Papa and I are such an odd couple, you see, such a crochetty old couple, living in a world of our own."

Her father let her see the world, from the outside. And he let her read. When she was in her teens she read Zola and Maupassant, and with the eyes of Zola and Maupassant she looked on Paris. A little later, she read Tolstoi and Dostoevsky. The latter confused her. The others, she seemed to understand with a very shrewd, canny understanding, just as she understood the Decameron stories as she read them in their old Italian, or the Nibelung poems.* Strange and *uncanny*, she seemed to understand things in a cold light perfectly, with all the flush of fire absent. She was something like a changeling, not quite human.

This earned her, also, strange antipathies. Cabmen and railway-porters, especially in Paris and Rome, would suddenly treat her with

brutal rudeness, when she was alone. They seemed to look on her with
sudden violent antipathy. They sensed in her a curious impertinence,
an easy, sterile impertinence towards the things *they* felt most. She was
so assured, and her flower of maidenhood was so scentless. She could
look at a lusty, sensual Roman cabman as if he were a sort of grotesque   5
to make her smile. She knew all about him, in Zola. And the peculiar
condescension with which she would give him her order, as if she, frail
beautiful thing, were the only reality, and he, coarse monster, were
a sort of Caliban floundering in the mud on the margin of the pool
of the perfect lotus,* would suddenly enrage the fellow, the real   10
Mediterranean, who prided himself on his *beauté mâle*, and to whom
the phallic mystery was still the only mystery. And he would turn a
terrible face on her, bully her in a brutal, coarse fashion, hideous. For
to him, she had only the blasphemous impertinence of her own
sterility.   15
    Encounters like these made her tremble, and made her know she
must have support from the outside. The power of her spirit did not
extend to these low people: and they had all the physical power. She
realised an implacability of hatred in their turning on her. But she did
not lose her head. She quietly paid out money and turned away.   20
    Those were dangerous moments, though, and she learned to be
prepared for them. The Princess she was, and the fairy from the north,
she could never understand the volcanic phallic rage with which
coarse people could turn on her, in a paroxysm of hatred. They never
turned on her father like that. And quite early, she decided it was the   25
New England mother in her whom they hated. Never for one minute
could she see with the old Roman eyes, see herself as sterility, the
barren flower, taken on airs and an intolerable impertinence. This was
what the Roman cabman saw in her. And he longed to crush the barren
blossom. Its sexless beauty and its authority put him in a passion of   30
brutal revolt.
    When she was nineteen her grandfather died, leaving her a
considerable fortune in the safe hands of responsible trustees. They
would deliver her her income, but only on condition that she resided
for six months in the year in the United States.   35
    "Why should they make me conditions!" she said to her father.
"I refuse to be imprisoned six months in the year in the United States.
We will tell them to keep their money."
    "Let us be wise, my little Princess, let us be wise. Now we are
almost poor, and we are never safe from rudeness. I cannot allow   40

anybody to be rude to me. I hate it, I hate it!" His eyes flamed as he said it. "I could kill any man or woman who is rude to me. But we are in exile in the world. We are powerless. If we were really poor, we should be quite powerless, and then I should die.—No, my Princess. Let us take their money, then they will not dare to be rude to us. Let us take it, as we put on clothes, to cover ourselves from their aggressions."

There began a new phase, when the father and daughter spent their summers on the Great Lakes, or in California, or in the South West. The father was something of a poet, the daughter something of a painter. He wrote poems about the Lakes or the redwood trees, and she made dainty drawings. He was physically a strong man, and he loved the out-of-doors. He would go off with her for days, paddling in a canoe and sleeping by a camp-fire. Frail little Princess, she was always undaunted: always undaunted. She would ride with him on horseback over the mountain trails till she was so tired, she was nothing but a bodiless consciousness sitting astride her pony. But she never gave in. And at night he folded her in her blankets on a bed of balsam-pine twigs, and she lay and looked at the stars unmurmuring. She was fulfilling her rôle.

People said to her, as the years passed, and she was a woman of twenty-five, then a woman of thirty, and always the same virgin dainty Princess, "knowing" in a dispassionate way, like an old woman, and utterly intact:

"Don't you ever think what you will do when your father is no longer with you?"

She looked at her interlocutor with that cold, elfin detachment of hers:

"No, I never think of it," she said.

She had a tiny, but exquisite little house in London, and another small, perfect house in Connecticut, each with a faithful housekeeper. Two homes, if she chose. And she knew many interesting literary and artistic people. What more!

So the years passed, imperceptibly. And she had that quality of the sexless fairies, she did not change. At thirty-three she looked twenty-three.

Her father, however, was ageing, and becoming more and more queer. It was now her task to be his guardian in his private madness. He spent the last three years of life in the house in Connecticut. He was very much estranged, sometimes had fits of violence which almost killed the little Princess. Physical violence was horrible to her, it seemed to shatter her heart. But she found a woman a few years younger than herself, well educated and sensitive, to be a sort of nurse-companion to the mad old man. So the fact of madness was never openly admitted. Miss Cummins, the companion, had a passionate loyalty to the Princess, and a curious affection, tinged with love, for the handsome, white-haired, courteous old man who was never at all aware of his fits of violence, once they had passed.

The Princess was thirty-eight years old when her father died: and quite unchanged. She was still tiny, and like a dignified, scentless flower. Her soft brownish hair, almost the colour of beaver fur, was bobbed, and fluffed softly round her apple-blossom face, that was modelled with an arched nose like a proud old Florentine portrait. In her voice, manner, and bearing, she was exceedingly still, like a flower that has blossomed in a shadowy place. And from her blue eyes looked out the Princess' eternal laconic challenge, that grew almost sardonic as the years passed. She was the Princess, and sardonically she looked out on a princeless world.

She was relieved when her father died, and at the same time, it was as if everything had evaporated around her. She had lived in a sort of hot-house, in the aura of her father's madness. Suddenly the hot-house had been removed from around her, and she was in the raw, vast, vulgar open air.

Quoi faire? What was she to do? She seemed faced with absolute nothingness. Only she had Miss Cummins, who shared with her the secret, and almost the passion for her father. In fact the Princess felt that her passion for her mad father had in some curious way transferred itself largely to Charlotte Cummins, during the last years. And now Miss Cummins was the vessel that held the passion for the dead man. She herself, the Princess, was an empty vessel.

An empty vessel, in the enormous warehouse of the world.

Quoi faire? What was she to do? She felt that, since she could not evaporate into nothingness like alcohol from an unstoppered bottle, she must *do* something. Never before in her life had she felt the incumbency. Never, never had she felt she must *do* anything. That was left to the vulgar.

Now her father was dead, she found herself on the *fringe* of the vulgar crowd, sharing their necessity to *do* something. It was a little humiliating. She felt herself becoming vulgarised. At the same time, she found herself looking at men with a shrewder eye: an eye to marriage. Not that she felt any sudden interest in men, or attraction towards them. No! She was still neither interested nor attracted towards men vitally. But *marriage*, that peculiar abstraction, had imposed a sort of spell on her. She thought that *marriage*, in the blank abstract, was the thing she ought to *do*. That marriage implied a man, she also knew. She knew all the facts. But the man seemed a property of her own mind rather than a thing in himself, another being.

Her father died in the summer, the month after her thirty-eighth birthday. When all was over, the obvious thing to do, of course, was to travel. With Miss Cummins. The two women knew each other intimately, but they were always Miss Urquhart and Miss Cummins to one another, and a certain distance was instinctively maintained. Miss Cummins, from Philadelphia, of scholastic stock, and intelligent, but untravelled, four years younger than the Princess, felt herself immensely the junior of her "lady." She had a sort of passionate veneration for the Princess, who seemed to her ageless, timeless. She could not see the rows of tiny, dainty, exquisite shoes in the Princess' cupboard without feeling a stab at the heart, a stab of tenderness and reverence, almost of awe.

Miss Cummins also was virginal: but with a look of puzzled surprise in her brown eyes. Her skin was pale and clear, her features well modelled, but there was a certain blankness in her expression, where the Princess had an odd touch of Renaissance grandeur. Miss Cummins' voice was also hushed almost to a whisper: it was the inevitable effect of Colin Urquhart's room. But the hushedness had a hoarse quality.

The Princess did not want to go to Europe. Her face seemed turned west. Now her father was gone, she felt she would go west, westwards, as if for ever. Following, no doubt, the March of Empire,* which is brought up rather short on the Pacific coast, among swarms of wallowing bathers.

No, not the Pacific coast. She would stop short of that. The South West was less vulgar. She would go to New Mexico.

She and Miss Cummins arrived at the Rancho del Cerro Gordo* towards the end of August, when the crowd was beginning to drift back east. The ranch lay by a stream on the desert some four miles from the foot of the mountains, a mile away from the Indian pueblo of San Cristobal. It was a ranch for the rich: the Princess paid thirty dollars a day for herself and Miss Cummins. But then she had a little cottage to herself, among the apple-trees of the orchard, with an excellent cook. She and Miss Cummins, however, took dinner at evening in the large guest-house. For the Princess still entertained the idea of "marriage."

The guests at the Rancho del Cerro Gordo were of all sorts, except the poor sort. They were practically all rich, and many were romantic. Some were charming, others were vulgar, some were movie people, quite quaint and not unattractive in their vulgarity, and many were Jews. The Princess did not care for Jews, though they were usually the most interesting to *talk* to. So she talked a good deal with the Jews, and painted with the artists, and rode with the young men from College, and had altogether quite a good time. And yet she felt something of a fish out of water, or a bird in the wrong forest. And "marriage" remained still completely in the abstract. No connecting it with any of these young men, even the nice ones.

The Princess looked just twenty-five. The freshness of her mouth, the hushed, delicate-complexioned virginity of her face gave her not a day more. Only a certain laconic look in her eyes was disconcerting.— When she was *forced* to write her age, she put twenty-eight, making the figure *two* rather badly, so that it just avoided being a three.

Men hinted marriage at her. Especially boys from college suggested it from a distance. But they all failed before the look of sardonic ridicule in the Princess' eyes. It always seemed to her rather preposterous, quite ridiculous, and a tiny bit impertinent on their part.

The only man that intrigued her at all was one of the guides, a man called Romero: Domingo Romero. It was he who had sold the ranch itself to the Wilkiesons,* ten years before, for two thousand dollars. He had gone away: then reappeared at the old place. For he was the son of the old Romeros, the last of the Spanish family that had owned miles of land around San Cristobal. But the coming of the white man and the failure of the vast flocks of sheep and the fatal inertia which overcomes all men, at last, on the desert near the mountains, had finished the Romero family. The last descendants were just Mexican peasants.

Domingo, the heir, had spent his two thousand dollars, and was working for white people. He was now about thirty years old, a tall, silent fellow with a heavy closed mouth and black eyes that looked across at one almost sullenly. From behind, he was handsome, with a strong, natural body and the back of his neck very dark and well-shapen, strong with life. But his dark face was long and heavy, almost sinister, with that peculiar heavy meaninglessness in it,

characteristic of the Mexicans of his own locality. They are strong, they seem healthy. They laugh and joke with one another. But their physique and their natures seem static, as if there were nowhere, nowhere at all for their energies to go, and their faces, degenerating
5 to misshapen heaviness, seem to have no *raison d'être*. As if, both as individual men and as a race, they had no *raison d'être*,* no radical meaning. Waiting either to die, or to be aroused into passion and hope. In some of the black eyes, a queer, haunting mystic quality, sombre and a bit gruesome, the skull-and-crossbones look of the Penitentes.*
10 They had found their *raison d'être* in self-torture and death-worship. Unable to wrest a *positive* significance for themselves from the vast, beautiful, but vindictive landscape they were born into, they turned on their own selves, and worshipped death through self-torture. The mystic gloom of this showed in their eyes.
15 But as a rule the dark eyes of the Mexicans were heavy and half-alive, sometimes hostile, sometimes kindly, often with the fatal Indian glaze on them, or the fatal Indian glint.

Domingo Romero was *almost* a typical Mexican to look at, with the typical heavy, dark long face, clean-shaven, with an almost brutally
20 heavy mouth. His eyes were black and Indian looking. Only, at the centre of their hopelessness was a spark of pride, of self-confidence, of dauntlessness. Just a spark in the midst of the blackness of static despair.

But this spark was the difference between him and the mass of men.
25 It gave a certain alert sensitiveness to his bearing, and a certain beauty to his appearance. He wore a low-crowned black hat, instead of the ponderous head-gear of the usual Mexican, and his clothes were thinnish and graceful. Silent, aloof, almost imperceptible in the landscape, he was an admirable guide, with a startling quick intelligence
30 that anticipated difficulties about to arise. He could cook too, crouching over the camp-fire and moving his lean, deft brown hands. The only fault he had was that he was not forthcoming: he wasn't chatty and cosy.

"Oh, don't send Romero with us," the Jews would say. "One can't
35 get any response from him."

Tourists come and go, but they rarely *see* anything, inwardly. None of them ever saw the spark at the middle of Romero's eye: they were not alive enough to see it.

The Princess caught it one day, when she had him for a guide. She
40 was fishing for trout in the canyon, Miss Cummins was reading a book,

the horses were tied under the trees, Romero was fixing a proper fly on her line. He fixed the fly and handed her the line, looking up at her. And at that moment she caught the spark in his eye. And instantly she knew that he was a gentleman, that his "demon," as her father would have said, was a fine demon. And instantly her manner towards him changed.

He had perched her on a rock over a quiet pool, beyond the cottonwood trees. It was early September, and the canyon already cool, but the leaves of the cottonwoods were still green. The Princess stood on her rock, a small but perfectly-formed figure, wearing a soft close grey sweater and neatly cut grey riding-breeches, with tall black boots, her fluffy brown hair straggling from under a little grey felt hat. A woman? Not quite. A changeling of some sort, perched in outline there on the rock, in the bristling wild canyon. She knew perfectly well how to handle a line. Her father had made a fisherwoman of her.

Romero, in a black shirt and with loose black trousers pushed into wide black riding-boots, was fishing a little further down. He had put his hat on a rock behind him, his dark head was bent a little forward, watching the water. He had caught three trout. From time to time he glanced upstream at the Princess, perched there so daintily. He saw she had caught nothing.

Soon he quietly drew in his line and came up to her. His keen eye watched her line, watched her position. Then quietly, he suggested certain changes to her, putting his sensitive brown hand before her. And he withdrew a little, and stood in silence leaning against a tree, watching her. He was helping her across the distance. She knew it, and thrilled. And in a moment she had a bite. In two minutes she had landed a good trout. She looked round at him quickly, her eyes sparkling, the colour heightened in her cheeks. And as she met his eyes a smile of greeting went over his dark face, very sudden, with an odd sweetness.

She knew he was helping her. And she felt in his presence a subtle, insidious male *kindliness* she had never known before, waiting upon her. Her cheek flushed, and her blue eyes darkened.

After this, she always looked for him, and for that curious dark beam of a man's kindliness which he could give her, as it were, from his chest, from his heart. It was something she had never known before.

A vague, unspoken intimacy grew up between them. She liked his voice, his appearance, his presence. His natural language was Spanish, he spoke English like a foreign language, rather slow, with a slight hesitation, but with a sad, plangent sonority lingering over from his Spanish. There was a certain subtle correctness in his appearance, he was always perfectly shaved, his hair was thick and rather long on top, but always carefully groomed behind. And his fine black cashmere shirt, his wide leather belt, his well-cut, wide black trousers going into the embroidered cowboy boots had a certain inextinguishable elegance. He wore no silver rings or buckles. Only his boots were embroidered and decorated at the top with an inlay of white suède. He seemed elegant, slender, yet he was very strong.

And at the same time, curiously, he gave her the feeling that death was not far from him. Perhaps he too was half in love with death.* However that may be, the sense she had that death was not far from him made him "possible" to her.

Small as she was, she was quite a good horsewoman. They gave her at the ranch a sorrel mare, very lovely in colour, and well-made, with a powerful broad neck and the hollow back that betokens a swift runner. Tansy, she was called. Her only fault was the usual mare's failing, she was inclined to be hysterical.

So that every day the Princess set off with Miss Cummins and Romero, on horseback, riding into the mountains. Once they went camping for several days, with two more friends in the party.

"I think I like it better," the Princess said to Romero, "when we three go alone."

And he gave her one of his quick, transfiguring smiles.

It was curious, no white man had ever showed her this capacity for subtle gentleness, this power to *help* her in silence across a distance, if she were fishing without success, or tired on her horse, or if Tansy suddenly got scared. It was as if Romero could send her *from his heart* a dark beam of succour and sustaining. She had never known this before, and it was very thrilling.

Then the smile that suddenly creased his dark face, showing the strong white teeth. It creased his face almost into a savage grotesque. And at the same time there was in it something so warm, such a dark flame of kindliness for her, she was elated into her true Princess self.

Then that vivid, latent spark in his eye, which she had seen, and which she knew he was aware she had seen. It made an inter-recognition between them, silent and delicate. Here he was delicate as a woman, in this subtle inter-recognition.

And yet his presence only put to flight in her the *idée fixe* of "marriage." For some reason, in her strange little brain, the idea of *marrying* him could not enter. Not for any definite reason. He was in himself a gentleman, and she had plenty of money for two. There was no actual obstacle. Nor was she conventional.

No, now she came down to it, it was as if their two "dæmons" could marry, were perhaps married. Only their two *selves*, Miss Urquhart and Señor Domingo Romero, were for some reason incompatible. There was a peculiar subtle intimacy of inter-recognition between them. But she did not see in the least how it could lead to marriage. Almost she could more easily marry one of the nice boys from Harvard or Yale.

The time passed, and she let it pass. The end of September came, with aspens going yellow on the mountain heights, and oak-scrub going red. But as yet, the cottonwoods in the valleys and canyons had not changed.

"When will you go away?" Romero asked her, looking at her fixedly, with a blank black eye.

"By the end of October," she said. "I have promised to be in Santa Barbara at the beginning of November."

He was hiding the spark in his eye from her. But she saw the peculiar sullen thickening of his heavy mouth.

She had complained to him many times that one never saw any wild animals, except chipmunks and squirrels and perhaps a skunk and a porcupine. Never a deer, or a bear, or a mountain lion.

"Are there no bigger animals in these mountains?" she asked, dissatisfied.

"Yes!" he said. "There are deer—I see their tracks. And I saw the tracks of a bear."

"But why can one never see the animals themselves?"—She looked dissatisfied and wistful like a child.

"Why it's pretty hard for you to see them. They won't let you come close. You have to keep still, in a place where they come. Or else you have to follow their tracks, a long way."

"I can't bear to go away till I've seen them: a bear, or a deer—"
The smile came suddenly on his face, indulgent.

"Well what do you want? Do you want to go up into the mountains to some place, to wait till they come?"

"Yes," she said, looking up at him with a sudden naïve impulse of recklessness.

And immediately his face became sombre again, responsible.

"Well," he said, with slight irony, a touch of mockery of her. "You

would have to find a house. It's very cold at night now. You would
have to stay all night in a house."

"And there are no houses up there?" she said.

"Yes," he replied. "There is a little shack that belong to me,what
5 a miner built a long time ago, looking for gold. You can go there and
stay one night, and maybe you see something. Maybe! I don't know.
Maybe nothing come."

"How much chance is there?"

"Well I don't know. Last time when I was there I see three deer
10 come down to drink at the water, and I shot two raccoons. But maybe
this time we don't see anything."

"Is there water there?" she asked.

"Yes, there is a little round pond, you know, below the spruce trees.
And the water from the snow run into it."

15 "Is it far away?" she asked.

"Yes, pretty far. You see that ridge there—" and turning to the
mountains he lifted his arm in the gesture which is somehow so moving,
out in the West, pointing to the distance—"that ridge where there
are no trees, only rock—"—his black eyes were focussed on the
20 distance, his face impassive, but as if in pain—"you go round that
ridge, and along, then you come down through the spruce trees to
where the cabin is. My father, he bought that placer* claim from a
miner who was broke, but nobody ever found any gold or anything,
and nobody ever goes there. Too lonesome!"

25 The Princess watched the massive, heavy-sitting, beautiful bulk of
the Rocky Mountains. It was early in October, and the aspens were
already losing their gold leaves; high up, the spruce and pine seemed
to be growing darker; the great flat patches of oak-scrub on the heights
were red like gore.

30 "Can I go over there?" she asked, turning to him and meeting the
spark in his eye.

His face was heavy with responsibility.

"Yes," he said, "you can go. But there'll be snow over the ridge,
and it's awful cold, and awful lonesome."

35 "I should like to go," she said, persistent.

"All right," he said. "You can go if you want to."

She doubted, though, if the Wilkiesons would let her go: at least,
alone with Romero and Miss Cummins.

Yet an obstinacy characteristic of her nature, an obstinacy tinged
40 perhaps with madness, had taken hold of her. She wanted to look over

the mountains into their secret heart. She wanted to descend to the cabin below the spruce trees, near the tarn of bright green water. She wanted to see the wild animals move about in their wild unconsciousness.

"Let us say to the Wilkiesons that we want to make the trip round the Frijoles canyon,"* she said.

The trip round the Frijoles canyon was a usual thing. It would not be strenuous nor cold nor lonely: they could sleep in the log house that was called an hotel.

Romero looked at her quickly.

"If you want to say that," he replied, "you can tell Mrs Wilkieson. Only I know she'll be mad with me, if I take you up in the mountains to that place.—And I've got to go there first with a pack-horse, to take lots of blankets and some bread. Maybe Miss Cummins can't stand it. Maybe not! It's a hard trip."

He was speaking, and thinking, in the heavy, disconnected Mexican fashion.

"Never mind!"—The Princess was suddenly very decisive and stiff with authority. "I want to do it. I will arrange with Mrs Wilkieson. And we'll go on Saturday."

He shook his head slowly.

"I've got to go up on Sunday with a pack-horse and blankets," he said. "Can't do it before."

"Very well!" she said, rather piqued. "Then we'll start on Monday."

She hated being thwarted even the tiniest bit.

He knew that if he started with the pack on Sunday at dawn he would not be back until late at night. But he consented that they should start on Monday morning at seven. The obedient Miss Cummins was told to prepare for the Frijoles trip. On Sunday Romero had his day off. He had not put in an appearance when the Princess retired on Sunday night, but on Monday morning, as she was dressing, she saw him bringing in the three horses from the corral. She was in high spirits.

The night had been cold. There was ice at the edges of the irrigation ditch, and the chipmunks crawled into the sun and lay with wide, dumb, anxious eyes, almost too numb to run.

"We may be away two or three days," said the Princess.

"Very well. We won't begin to be anxious about you before Thursday, then," said Mrs Wilkieson, who was young and capable:

from Chicago. "Anyway," she added, "Romero will see you through. He's so trustworthy."

The sun was already on the desert as they set off towards the mountains, making the greasewood and the sage pale as pale-grey sands, luminous the great level around them. To the right glinted the shadows of the adobe pueblo, flat and almost invisible on the plain, earth of its earth. Behind lay the ranch and the tufts of tall, plumy cottonwoods, whose summits were yellowing under the perfect blue sky.

Autumn breaking into colour, in the great spaces of the South West.

But the three trotted gently along the trail, towards the sun that sparkled yellow just above the dark bulk of the ponderous mountains. Side-slopes were already gleaming yellow, flaming with a second light, under the coldish blue of the pale sky. The front slopes were in shadow, with submerged lustre of red oak-scrub and dull-gold aspens, blue-black pines and grey-blue rock. While the canyon was full of a deep blueness.

They rode single file, Romero first, on a black horse. Himself in black, he made a flickering black spot in the delicate pallor of the great landscape, where even pine-trees at a distance take a film of blue paler than their green. Romero rode on in silence past the tufts of furry greasewood. The Princess came next, on her sorrel mare. And Miss Cummins, who was not quite happy on horseback, came last, in the pale dust that the others kicked up. Sometimes her horse sneezed, and she started.

But on they went, at a gentle trot. Romero never looked round. He could hear the sound of the hoofs following, and that was all he wanted. For the rest, he held ahead. And the Princess, with that black, unheeding figure always travelling away from her, felt strangely helpless, withal elated.

They neared the pale, round foot-hills, dotted with the round dark piñón and cedar shrubs. The horses clinked and clattered among stones. Occasionally a big round greasewood held out fleecy tufts of flowers, pure gold. They wound into blue shadow, then up a steep stony slope, with the world lying pallid away behind and below. Then they dropped into the shadow of the San Cristobal canyon.*

The stream was running full and swift. Occasionally the horses snatched at a tuft of grass. The trail narrowed and became rocky, the rocks closed in, it was dark and cool as the horses climbed and climbed upwards, and the tree-trunks crowded in, in the shadowy, silent tightness of the canyon. They were among cottonwood trees that ran up straight and smooth and round to an extraordinary height. Above, the tips were gold and it was sun. But away below, where the horses struggled up the rocks and wound among the trunks, there was chill blue shadow by the sound of waters, and an occasional grey festoon 5 of old-man's-beard, and here and there a pale, dipping cranesbill flower among the tangle and the débris of the virgin place. And again the chill entered the Princess' heart, as she realised what a tangle of decay and despair lay in the virgin forests.

They scrambled downwards, splashed across-stream, up rocks and 10 along the trail of the other side. Romero's black horse stopped, looked down quizzically at the fallen trees, then stepped over lightly. The Princess' sorrel followed, carefully. But Miss Cummins' buckskin* made a fuss, and had to be got round.

In the same silence, save for the clinking of the horses and the 15 splashing as the trail crossed stream, they worked their way upwards in the tight, tangled shadow of the canyon. Sometimes, crossing stream, the Princess would glance upwards, and then always her heart caught in her breast. For high up, away in heaven, the mountain heights shone yellow dappled with dark spruce firs, clear almost as 20 speckled daffodils against the pale turquoise blue lying high and serene above the dark-blue shadow where the Princess was. And she would snatch at the blood-red leaves of the oak as her horse crossed a more open slope, not knowing what she felt.

They were getting fairly high, occasionally lifted above the canyon 25 itself, in the low groove below the speckled, gold-sparkling heights which towered beyond. Then again they dipped and crossed stream, the horses stepping gingerly across a tangle of fallen, frail aspen stems, then suddenly floundering in a mass of rocks. The black emerged ahead, his black tail waving. The Princess let her mare find her own 30 footing: then she too emerged from the clatter. She rode on after the black. Then came a great, frantic rattle of the buckskin behind. The Princess was aware of Romero's dark face looking round with a strange, demon-like watchfulness, before she herself looked round, to see the buckskin scrambling rather lamely beyond the rocks, with one 35 of his pale buff knees already red with blood.

"He *almost* went down!" called Miss Cummins.

But Romero was already out of the saddle and hastening down the path. He made quiet little noises to the buckskin, and began examining the cut knee. 40

"Is he hurt?" cried Miss Cummins anxiously, and she climbed hastily down.

"Oh my Goodness!" she cried, as she saw the blood running down the slender buff leg of the horse, in a thin trickle. "Isn't that *awful!*"
5   She spoke in a stricken voice, and her face was white.

Romero was still carefully feeling the knee of the buckskin. Then he made him walk a few paces. And at last he stood up straight and shook his head.

"Not very bad!" he said. "Nothing broken."
10   Again he bent and worked at the knee. Then he looked up at the Princess.

"He can go on," he said. "It's not bad."

The Princess looked down at the dark face in silence.

"What, go on right up here?" cried Miss Cummins. "How many
15   hours?"

"About five," said Romero simply.

"Five hours!" cried Miss Cummins. "A horse with a lame knee! And a steep mountain!—Why-y!—"

"Yes, it's pretty steep up there," said Romero, pushing back his
20   hat and staring fixedly at the bleeding knee. The buckskin stood in a stricken sort of dejection. "But I think he'll make it all right," the man added.

"Oh!" cried Miss Cummins, her eyes bright with sudden passion of unshed tears. "I wouldn't think of it. I wouldn't ride him up there,
25   not for any money."

"Why wouldn't you?" asked Romero.

"It *hurts* him."

Romero bent down again to the horse's knee.

"Maybe it hurts him a little." he said. "But he can make it all right,
30   and his leg won't get stiff—"

"What! Ride him five hours up the steep mountains!" cried Miss Cummins. "I couldn't. I just couldn't do it. I'll lead him a little way and see if he can go. But I *couldn't* ride him again. I couldn't. Let me walk."

"But Miss Cummins dear, if Romero says he'll be all right—?"
35   said the Princess.

"I know it hurts him. Oh, I just couldn't bear it."

There was no doing anything with Miss Cummins. The thought of a hurt animal always put her into a sort of hysterics.

They walked forward a little, leading the buckskin. He limped rather
40   badly. Miss Cummins sat on a rock.

"Why it's agony to see him!" she cried. "It's *cruel!*"

"He won't limp after a bit, if you don't take no notice* of him," said Romero. "Now he plays up, and limps very much, because he wants to make you see."

"I don't think there can be much playing up," said Miss Cummins 5
bitterly. "We can *see* how it must hurt him."

"It don't hurt much," said Romero.

But now Miss Cummins was silent with antipathy.

It was a deadlock. The party remained motionless on the trail, the Princess in the saddle, Miss Cummins seated on a rock, Romero 10
standing black and remote near the drooping buckskin.

"Well!" said the man suddenly at last. "I guess we go back, then."

And he looked up swiftly at his horse, which was cropping at the mountain herbage and treading on the trailing reins.

"No!" cried the Princess. "Oh no!"—Her voice rang with a great 15
wail of disappointment and anger. Then she checked herself.

Miss Cummins rose with energy.

"Let me lead the buckskin home," she said, with cold dignity, "and you two go on."

This was received in silence. The Princess was looking down at her 20
with a sardonic, almost cruel gaze.

"We've only come about two hours," said Miss Cummins. "I don't mind a bit leading him home. But I *couldn't* ride him. I *couldn't* have him ridden, with that knee."

This again was received in dead silence. Romero remained impassive, 25
almost inert.

"Very well then," said the Princess. "You lead him home. You'll be quite all right. Nothing can happen to you, possibly. And say to them that we have gone on and shall be home tomorrow—or the day after—" 30

She spoke coldly and distinctly. For she could not bear to be thwarted.

"Better all go back, and come again another day," said Romero, non-committal.

"There will never *be* another day," cried the Princess. "I *want* to 35
go on."

She looked him square in the eyes, and met the spark in his eye.

He raised his shoulders slightly.

"If you want it," he said. "I'll go on with you. But Miss Cummins 40 can ride my horse to the end of the canyon, and I lead the buckskin. Then I come back to you."

It was arranged so. Miss Cummins had her saddle put on Romero's black horse, Romero took the buckskin's bridle, and they started back.
5   The Princess rode very slowly on, upwards, alone. She was at first so angry with Miss Cummins, that she was blind to everything else. She just let her mare follow her own inclinations.

The peculiar spell of anger carried the Princess on, almost unconscious, for an hour or so. And by this time she was beginning to
10 climb pretty high. Her horse walked steadily all the time. They emerged on a bare slope, and the trail wound through frail aspen-stems. Here a wind swept, and some of the aspens were already bare. Others were fluttering their discs of pure solid yellow, leaves so *nearly* like petals, while the slope ahead was one soft, glowing fleece of daffodil
15 yellow; fleecy like a golden fox-skin, and yellow as daffodils alive in the wind and the high mountain sun.

She paused and looked back. The near great slopes were mottled with gold and the dark hue of spruce, like some unsinged eagle, and the light lay gleaming upon them. Away through the gap of the canyon
20 she could see the pale blue of the egg-like desert, with the crumpled dark crack of the Rio Grande canyon.* And far, far off, the blue mountains like a fence of angels on the horizon.

And she thought of her adventure. She was going on alone with Romero. But then she was very sure of herself, and Romero was not
25 the kind of man to do anything to her, against her will. This was her first thought. And she just had a fixed desire to go over the brim of the mountains, to look into the inner chaos of the Rockies. And she wanted to go with Romero, because he had some peculiar kinship with her, there was some peculiar link between the two of them. Miss
30 Cummins anyhow would have been only a discordant note.

She rode on, and emerged at length in the lap of the summit. Beyond her was a great concave of stone and stark dead-grey trees, where the mountain ended against the sky. But nearer was the dense black, bristling spruce, and at her feet was the lap of the summit, a flat little
35 valley of sere grass and quiet-standing yellow aspens, the stream trickling like a thread across.

It was a little valley or shell from which the stream was gently poured into the lower rocks and trees of the canyon. Around her was a fairy-like gentleness, the delicate sere grass, the groves of delicate-stemmed
40 aspens dropping their flakes like petals. Almost like flowers the aspen

trees stood in thickets, shedding their petals* of bright yellow. And the delicate, quick little stream threading through the wild, sere grass. Here one might expect deer and fawns and wild things, as in a little paradise. Here she was to wait for Romero, and they were to have lunch.

She unfastened her saddle and pulled it to the ground with a crash, letting her horse wander with a long rope. How beautiful Tansy looked, sorrel among the yellow leaves that lay like a patina on the sere ground. The Princess herself wore a fleecy sweater of a pale, sere buff, like the grass, and riding breeches of a pure orange-tawny colour. She felt quite in the picture.

From her saddle-pouches she took the packages of lunch, spread a little cloth, and sat to wait for Romero. Then she made a little fire. Then she ate a devilled egg. Then she ran after Tansy, who was straying across-stream. Then she sat in the sun, in the stillness near the aspens, and waited.

The sky was blue. Her little alp was soft and delicate as fairyland. But beyond and up jutted the great slopes, dark with the pointed feathers of spruce, bristling with grey dead trees among grey rock, or dappled with dark and gold. The beautiful, but fierce, heavy, cruel mountains, with their moments of tenderness.

She saw Tansy start, and begin to run. Two ghostlike figures on horseback emerged from the black of the spruce across the stream. It was two Indians on horseback, swathed like seated mummies in their pale-grey cotton blankets. Their guns jutted beyond the saddles. They rode straight towards her, to her thread of smoke.

As they came near, they unswathed themselves and greeted her, looking at her curiously from their dark eyes. Their black hair was somewhat untidy, the long rolled plaits on their shoulders were soiled. They looked tired.

They got down from their horses near her little fire—a camp was a camp—swathed their blankets round their hips, pulled the saddles from their ponies and turned them loose, then sat down. One was a young Indian whom she had met before, the other was an older man.

"You all alone?" said the younger man.

"Romero will be here in a minute," she said, glancing back along the trail.

"Ah Romero! You with him? Where you going?"

"Round the ridge," she said. "Where are you going?"

"We going down to Pueblo."

"Been out hunting? How long have you been out?"

"Yes. Been out five days." The young Indian gave a little, meaningless laugh.

"Got anything?"

5 "No, we see tracks of two deer—but not got nothing."

The Princess noticed a suspicious-looking bulk under one of the saddles: surely a folded-up deer. But she said nothing.

"You must have been cold," she said.

"Yes, very cold in the night. And hungry. Got nothing to eat since

10 yesterday. Eat it all up."—And again he laughed his little meaningless laugh.

Under their dark skins, the two men looked peaked and hungry. The Princess rummaged for food among the saddle-bags. There was a lump of bacon—the regular stand-back*—and some bread.

15 She gave them this, and they began toasting slices of it on long sticks at the fire. Such was the little camp Romero saw as he rode down the slope: the Princess in her orange breeches, her head tied in a blue and brown silk kerchief, sitting opposite the two dark-headed Indians across the camp-fire, while one of the Indians was

20 leaning forward toasting bacon, his two plaits of braid-swathed hair dangling as if wearily.

Romero rode up, his face expressionless. The Indians greeted him in Spanish. He unsaddled his horse, took food from the bags, and sat down at the camp to eat. The Princess went to the stream for water,

25 and to wash her hands.

"Got coffee?" asked the Indians.

"No coffee this outfit," said Romero.

They lingered an hour or more in the warm midday sun. Then Romero saddled the horses. The Indians still squatted by the fire.

30 Romero and the Princess rode away, calling *Adios!* to the Indians, over the stream and into the dense spruce whence the two strange figures had emerged.

When they were alone, Romero turned and looked at her curiously, in a way she could not understand, with such a hard glint in his eyes.

35 And for the first time, she wondered if she was rash.

"I hope you don't mind going alone with me," she said.

"If you want it," he replied.

They emerged at the foot of the great bare slope of rocky summit, where dead spruce trees stood sparse and bristling like bristles on a

40 grey, dead hog. Romero said the Mexicans, twenty years back, had

fired the mountains, to drive out the whites.* This grey concave slope
of summit was corpse-like.

The trail was almost invisible. Romero watched for the trees which
the Forest Service had blazed. And they climbed the stark corpse
slope, among dead spruce fallen and ash-grey, into the wind. The   5
wind came rushing from the west, up the funnel of the canyon, from
the desert. And there was the desert, like a vast mirage tilting slowly
upwards towards the west, immense and pallid, away beyond the funnel
of the canyon. The Princess could hardly look.

For an hour their horses rushed the slope, hastening with a great   10
working of the haunches upwards, and halting to breathe, scrambling
again, and rowing their way up length by length, on the livid, slanting
wall. While the wind blew like some vast machine.

After an hour they were working their way on the incline, no longer
forcing straight up. All was grey and dead around them, the horses   15
picked their way over the silver-grey corpses of the spruce. But they
were near the top, near the ridge.

Even the horses made a rush for the last bit. They had worked round
to a scrap of spruce forest, near the very top. They hurried in, out
of the huge, monstrous, mechanical wind, that whistled inhumanly and   20
was palely cold. So, stepping through the dark screen of trees, they
emerged over the crest.

In front now was nothing but mountains, ponderous, massive,
down-sitting mountains, in a huge and intricate knot, empty of life or
soul. Under the bristling black feathers of spruce near by lay patches   25
of white snow. The lifeless valleys were concaves of rock and spruce,
the rounded summits and the hog-backed summits of grey rock
crowded one behind the other, like some monstrous herd in arrest.

It frightened the Princess, it was *so* inhuman. She had not thought
it could be so inhuman, so, as it were, anti-life. And yet now one of   30
her desires was fulfilled. She had seen it, the massive, gruesome,
repellent core of the Rockies. She saw it there beneath her eyes, in
its gigantic heavy gruesomeness.

And she wanted to go back. At this moment she wanted to turn back.
She had looked down into the intestinal knot of these mountains. She   35
was frightened. She wanted to go back.

But Romero was riding on, on the lee side of the spruce forest, above
the concaves of the inner mountains. He turned round to her, and
pointed at the slope with a dark hand:

"Here a miner has been trying for gold," he said.   40

It was a grey, scratched out heap near a hole—like a great badger hole. And it looked quite fresh.

"Quite lately?" said the Princess.

"No, long ago—twenty, thirty years." He had reined in his horse and was looking at the mountains. "Look!" he said. "There goes the Forest Service trail—along those ridges, on the top, way over there till it come to Lucytown, where is the government road. We go down there—no trail—see, behind that mountain—you see the top, no trees, and some grass?"

His arm was lifted, his brown hand pointing, his dark eyes piercing into the distance, as he sat on his black horse twisting round to her. Strange and ominous, only the demon of himself, he seemed to her. She was dazed and a little sick, at that height, and she could not *see* any more. Only she saw an eagle turning in the air beyond, and the light from the west showed the pattern on him underneath.

"Shall I ever be able to go so far?" asked the Princess faintly, petulantly.

"Oh yes! All easy now. No more hard places."

They worked along the ridge, up and down, keeping on the lee side, the inner side, in the dark shadow. It was cold. Then the trail laddered up again, and they emerged on a narrow ridge-track, with the mountain slipping away enormously on either side. The Princess was afraid. For one moment she looked out, and saw the desert, the desert ridges, more desert, more blue ridges, shining pale and very vast, far below, vastly, palely tilting to the western horizon. It was ethereal and terrifying in its gleaming, pale, half-burnished immensity, tilted at the west. She could not bear it. To the left was the ponderous, involved mass of mountains all kneeling heavily.

She closed her eyes and let her consciousness evaporate away. The mare followed the trail. So on and on, in the wind again.

They turned their backs to the wind, facing inwards to the mountains. She thought they had left the trail: it was quite invisible.

"No," he said, lifting his hand and pointing. "Don't you see the blazed trees?"

And making an effort of consciousness, she was able to perceive on a pale-grey dead spruce stem the old marks where an axe had chipped a piece away. But with the height, the cold, the wind, her brain was numb.

They turned again and began to descend: he told her they had left the trail. The horses slithered in the loose stones, picking their way downward. It was afternoon, the sun stood obtrusive and gleaming in the lower heavens: about four o'clock. The horses went steadily, slowly, but obstinately onwards. The air was getting colder. They were in among the lumpish peaks and steep concave valleys. She was barely conscious at all of Romero. 5

He dismounted and came to help her from her saddle. She tottered, but would not betray her feebleness.

"We must slide down here," he said. "I can lead the horses."

They were on a ridge, and facing a steep bare slope of pallid, tawny mountain grass on which the western sun shone full. It was steep and 10 concave. The Princess felt she might start slipping, and go down like a toboggan, into the great hollow.

But she pulled herself together. Her eye blazed up again with excitement and determination. A wind rushed past her: she could hear the shriek of spruce trees far below. Bright spots came on her cheeks, 15 as her hair blew across. She looked a wild, fairy-like little thing.

"No," she said. "I will take my horse."

"Then mind she doesn't slip down on top of you," said Romero. And away he went, nimbly dropping down the pale, steep incline, making from rock to rock, down the grass, and following any little 20 slanting groove. His horse hopped and slithered after him, and sometimes stopped dead, with forefeet pressed back, refusing to go further. He, below his horse, looked up and pulled the reins gently, and encouraged the creature. Then the horse once more dropped his forefeet, with a jerk, and the descent continued. 25

The Princess set off in blind, reckless pursuit, tottering and yet nimble. And Romero, looking constantly back to see how she was faring, saw her fluttering down like some queer little bird, her orange breeches twinkling like the legs of some duck, and her head, tied in the blue and buff kerchief, bound round and round like the head of some 30 blue-topped bird. The sorrel mare rocked and slipped behind her. But down came the Princess, in a reckless intensity, a tiny, vivid spot on the great hollow flank of the tawny mountain. So tiny! Tiny as a frail bird's egg. It made Romero's mind go blank with wonder.

But they had to get down, out of that cold and drugging wind. The 35 spruce trees stood below, where a tiny stream emerged in stones. Away plunged Romero, zigzagging down. And away behind, up the slope, fluttered the tiny, bright coloured Princess, holding the end of the long reins, and leading the lumbering, four-foot-sliding mare.

At last they were down. Romero sat in the sun, below the wind, 40 beside some squaw-berry bushes. The Princess came near, the colour flaming in her cheeks, her eyes dark blue, much darker than the kerchief on her head, and glowing unnaturally.

"We make it," said Romero.

5   "Yes," said the Princess, dropping the reins and subsiding on to the grass, unable to speak, unable to think.

But thank heaven, they were out of the wind and in the sun.

In a few minutes her consciousness and her control began to come back. She drank a little water. Romero was attending to the saddles.

10   Then they set off again, leading the horses still a little further down the tiny stream-bed. Then they could mount.

They rode down a bank and into a valley grove dense with aspens. Winding through the thin, crowding, pale-smooth stems, the sun shone flickering beyond them, and the disc-like aspen leaves, waving queer

15 mechanical signals, seemed to be splashing the gold light before her eyes. She rode on in a splashing dazzle of gold.

Then they entered shadow and the dark, resinous spruce trees. The fierce boughs always wanted to sweep her off her horse. She had to twist and squirm past.

20   But there was a semblance of an old trail. And all at once they emerged in the sun on the edge of the spruce-grove, and there was a little cabin, and the bottom of a small, naked valley with grey rock and heaps of stones, and a round pool of intense green water, dark green.* The sun was just about to leave it.

25 Indeed, as she stood, the shadow came over the cabin and over herself; they were in the lower gloom, a twilight. Above, the heights still blazed.

It was a little hole of a cabin, near the spruce trees, with an earthen floor and an unhinged door. There was a wooden bed-bunk, three old

30 sawn-off log-lengths, to sit on, as stools, and a sort of fire-place, no room for anything else. The little hole would hardly contain two people. The roof had gone—but Romero had laid on thick spruce-boughs.

The strange squalor of the primitive forest pervaded the place, the squalor of animals and their droppings, the squalor of the wild.

35 The Princess knew the peculiar repulsiveness of it. She was tired and faint.

Romero hastily got a handful of twigs, set a little fire going in the stone grate, and went out to attend to the horses. The Princess vaguely, mechanically put sticks on the fire, in a sort of stupor,

40 watching the blaze stupefied and fascinated. She could not make much

fire—it would set the whole cabin alight. And smoke oozed out of the delapidated mud-and-stone chimney.

When Romero came in with the saddle-pouches and saddles, hanging the saddles on the wall, there sat the little Princess on her stump of wood in front of the delapidated fire-grate, warming her tiny hands at the blaze, while her orange breeches glowed almost like another fire. She was in a sort of stupor.

"You have some whiskey now, or some tea? Or wait for some soup?" he asked.

She rose and looked at him with bright, dazed eyes, half comprehending, the colour glowing hectic in her cheeks.

"Some tea," she said, "with a little whiskey in it. Where's the kettle?"

"Wait," he said. "I'll bring the things."

She took her cloak from the back of her saddle, and followed him into the open. It was a deep cup of shadow. But above, the sky was still shining, and the heights of the mountains were blazing with aspens like fire blazing.

Their horses were cropping the grass among the stones. Romero clambered up a heap of grey stones and began lifting away logs and rocks, till he had opened the mouth of one of the miner's little old workings. This was his cache. He brought out bundles of blankets, pans for cooking, a little petrol camp-stove, an axe: the regular camp outfit. He seemed so quick and energetic and full of force. This quick force dismayed the Princess a little.

She took a saucepan and went down the stones to the water. It was very still and mysterious, and of a deep green colour, yet pure, transparent as glass. How cold the place was! How mysterious and fearful.

She crouched in her dark cloak by the water, rinsing the saucepan, feeling the cold heavy above her, the shadow like a vast weight upon her, bowing her down. The sun was leaving the mountain tops, departing, leaving her under profound shadow. Soon it would crush her down completely.

Sparks?—or eyes looking at her across the water? She gazed hypnotised. And with her sharp eyes she made out in the dusk the pale form of a bob-cat crouching by the water's edge, pale as the stones among which it crouched, opposite. And it was watching her with cold, electric eyes of strange intentness, a sort of cold, icy wonder and fearlessness. She saw its *museau* pushed forward, its tufted ears pricking intensely up. It was watching her with cold, animal curiosity, something demonish and conscienceless.

She made a swift movement, spilling her water. And in a flash the creature was gone, leaping like a cat that is escaping: but strange and soft in its motion, with its little bob tail. Rather fascinating. Yet that cold, intent, demonish watching! She shivered with cold and fear. She knew well enough the dread and repulsiveness of the wild.

Romero carried in the bundles of bedding and the camp outfit. The windowless cabin was already dark inside. He lit a lantern, and then went out again with the axe. She heard him chopping wood as she fed sticks to the fire under her water. When he came in with an armful of oak-scrub faggots, she had just thrown the tea into the water.

"Sit down," she said, "and drink tea."

He poured a little bootleg whiskey* into the enamel cups, and in the silence the two sat on the log-ends, sipping the hot liquid and coughing occasionally from the smoke.

"We burn these oak sticks," he said. "They don't make hardly any smoke."

Curious and remote he was, saying nothing except what had to be said. And she, for her part, was as remote from him. They seemed far, far apart, worlds apart, now they were so near.

He unwrapped one bundle of bedding, and spread the blankets and the sheepskin in the wooden bunk.

"You lie down and rest," he said, "and I make the supper."

She decided to do so. Wrapping her cloak round her, she lay down in the bunk, turning her face to the wall. She could hear him preparing supper over the little petrol stove. Soon she could smell the soup he was heating: and soon she heard the hissing of fried chicken in a pan.

"You eat your supper now?" he said.

With a jerky, despairing movement she sat up in the bunk, tossing back her hair. She felt cornered.

"Give it me here," she said.

He handed her first the cupful of soup. She sat among the blankets, eating it slowly. She was hungry. Then he gave her an enamel plate with pieces of fried chicken, and currant jelly, butter, and bread. It was very good. As they ate the chicken he made the coffee. She said never a word. A certain resentment filled her. She was cornered.

When supper was over he washed the dishes, dried them, and put everything away carefully, else there would have been no room to move, in the hole of a cabin. The oak-wood gave out a good bright heat.

He stood for a few moments at a loss. Then he asked her:
"You want to go to bed soon?"
"Soon," she said. "Where are you going to sleep?" 5
"I make my bed here—" he pointed to the floor along the wall.
"Too cold out of doors."
"Yes," she said. "I suppose it is."
She sat immobile, her cheeks hot, full of conflicting thoughts. And she watched him while he folded the blankets on the floor, a sheepskin 10 underneath. Then she went out into the night.

The stars were big. Mars sat on the edge of a mountain, for all the world like the blazing eye of a crouching mountain lion. But she herself was deep, deep below, in a pit of shadow. In the intense silence she seemed to hear the spruce forest crackling with electricity and cold. 15 Strange, foreign stars floated on that unmoving water. The night was going to freeze. Over the hills came the far sobbing-singing howling of the coyotes. She wondered how the horses would be.

Shuddering a little, she turned to the cabin. Warm light showed through its chinks. She pushed at the ricketty, half opened door. 20
"What about the horses?" she said.
"My black, he won't go away. And your mare will stay with him.—You want to go to bed now?"
"I think I do."
"All right. I feed the horses some oats." 25
And he went out into the night.

He did not come back for some time. She was lying wrapped up tight in the bunk.

He blew out the lantern, and sat down on his bedding to take off his clothes. She lay with her back turned. And soon, in the silence, 30 she was asleep.

She dreamed it was snowing, and the snow was falling on her through the roof, softly, softly, helplessly, and she was going to be buried alive. She was growing colder and colder, the snow was weighing down on her. The snow was going to absorb her. 35

She awoke with a sudden convulsion, like pain. She was really very cold. Perhaps the heavy blankets had numbed her. Her heart seemed unable to beat, she felt she could not move.

With another convulsion she sat up. It was intensely dark. There was not even a spark of fire: the light wood had burned right away. 40

She sat in thick, oblivious darkness. Only through a chink she could
see a star.

"What did she want? Oh, what did she want?"—She sat in bed
and rocked herself wofully. She could hear the steady breathing of
the sleeping man. She was shivering with cold, her heart seemed as
if it could not beat. She wanted warmth, protection, she wanted to be
taken away from herself. And at the same time, perhaps more deeply
than anything she wanted to keep herself intact, intact, untouched,
that no-one should have any power over her, or rights to her. It was
a wild necessity in her: that no-one, particularly no man, should have
any rights or power over her, that no-one and nothing should possess
her.

Yet that other thing! And she was so cold, so shivering, and her
heart could not beat. Oh, would not someone help her heart to beat.
She tried to speak, and could not. Then she cleared her throat.

"Romero," she said strangely. "It is so cold!"

Where did her voice come from, and whose voice was it, in the dark?

She heard him at once sit up, and his voice, startled, with a
resonance that seemed to vibrate against her, saying:

"What? What is it? Eh?"

"I am so cold."

He had risen from his blankets, and stood by the bunk.*

"You want me to make you warm."

"Yes."

As soon as he had lifted her in his arms, she wanted to scream to
him not to touch her. She stiffened herself. Yet she was dumb.

And he was warm, but with a terrible animal warmth that seemed
to annihilate her. He panted like an animal with desire. And she was
given over to this thing.

She had never, never wanted to be given over to this. But she had
willed that it should happen to her. And according to her will, she lay
and let it happen. But she never wanted it. She never wanted to be
thus assailed and handled, mauled. She wanted to keep herself to
herself.

However, she had willed it to happen, and it had happened. She
panted with relief when it was over.

Yet even now she had to lie within the hard, powerful clasp of this
other creature, this man. She dreaded to struggle to go away. She
dreaded almost too much the icy cold of that other bunk.

"Do you want to go away from me?" asked his strange voice. Oh, if it could only have been a thousand miles away from her! Yet she had willed to have it thus close.

"No," she said.

And she could feel a curious joy and pride surging up again in him: at her expense. Because he had got her. She felt like a victim there. And he was exulting in his power over her, his possession, his pleasure. When dawn came, he was fast asleep. She sat up suddenly.

"I want a fire," she said.

He opened his brown eyes wide, and smiled with a curious tender luxuriousness.

"I want you to make a fire," she said.

He glanced at the chinks of light. His brown face hardened to the day.

"All right," he said. "I'll make it."

She hid her face while he dressed. She could not bear to look at him. He was so suffused with pride and luxury. She hid her face almost in despair. But feeling the cold blast of air as he opened the door, she wriggled down into the warm place where he had been. How soon the warmth ebbed, when he had gone.

He made a fire and went out, returning after a while with water.

"You stay in bed till the sun comes," he said. "It's very cold."

"Hand me my cloak."

She wrapped the cloak fast round her, and sat up among the blankets. The warmth was already spreading from the fire.

"I suppose we will start back as soon as we've had breakfast?"

He was crouching at his camp-stove making scrambled eggs. He looked up suddenly transfixed, and his brown eyes, so soft and luxuriously widened, looked straight at her.

"You want to?" he said.

"We'd better get back as soon as possible," she said, turning aside from his eyes.

"You want to get away from me?" he asked, repeating the question of the night in a sort of dread.

"I want to get away from here," she said decisively. And it was true. She wanted supremely to get away, back to the world of people.

He rose slowly to his feet, holding the aluminium frying-pan.

"Don't you like last night?" he asked.

"Not really," she said. "Why? Do you?"

He put down the frying-pan and stood staring at the wall. She could see she had given him a cruel blow. But she did not relent. She was getting her own back. She wanted to regain possession of all herself, and in some mysterious way, she felt that he possessed some part of her still.

He looked round at her slowly, his face greyish and heavy.

5 "You Americans," he said; "you always want to do a man down." "I am not American," she said, "I am British. And I don't want to do any man down. I only want to go back, now." "And what will you say about me, down there?" "That you were very kind to me, and very good."

10 He crouched down again, and went on turning the eggs. He gave her her plate, and her coffee, and sat down to his own food.

But again he seemed not to be able to swallow. He looked up at her. "You don't like last night?" he asked.

"Not really," she said, though with some difficulty. "I don't care 15 for that kind of thing."

A blank sort of wonder spread over his face, at these words: followed immediately by a black look of anger, and then a stony, sinister despair.

"You don't?" he said, looking her in the eyes.

20 "Not really," she replied, looking back with steady hostility, into his eyes.

Then a dark flame seemed to come from his face.

"I make you," he said, as if to himself.

He rose and reached her clothes, that hung on a peg: the fine linen 25 underwear, the orange breeches, the fleecy jumper, the blue and buff kerchief: then he took up her riding boots and her bead moccasins. Crushing everything in his arms, he opened the door. Sitting up, she saw him stride down to the dark-green pool, in the frozen shadow of that deep cup of a valley. He tossed the clothing and the boots out 30 on the pool. Ice had formed. And on the pure, dark green mirror, in the slaty shadow, the Princess saw her things lying, the white linen, the orange breeches, the black boots, the blue moccasins, a tangled heap of colour. Romero picked up rocks and heaved them out at the ice, till the surface broke and the fluttering clothing disappeared in the 35 rattling water, while the valley echoed and shouted again with the sound.

She sat in despair among the blankets, hugging tight her pale-blue cloak. Romero strode straight back to the cabin.

"Now you stay here with me," he said.

40 She was furious. Her blue eyes met his. They were like two demons

watching one another. In his face, beyond a sort of unrelieved gloom, was a demonish desire for death.

He saw her looking round the cabin, scheming. He saw her eyes on his rifle. He took the gun and went out with it. Returning, he pulled out her saddle, carried it to the tarn,* and threw it in. Then he fetched his own saddle and did the same.

"Now will you go away?" he said, looking at her with a smile.

She debated within herself whether to coax him and wheedle him. But she knew he was already beyond it. She sat among her blankets in a frozen sort of despair, hard as hard ice with anger.

He did the chores, and disappeared with the gun. She got up in her blue pyjamas, huddled in her cloak, and stood in the doorway. The dark-green pool was motionless again, the stony slopes were pallid and frozen. Shadow still lay like an after-death, deep in this valley. Away in the distance she saw the horses feeding. If she could catch one!—The brilliant yellow sun was half way down the mountains. It was nine o'clock.

All day she was alone: and she was frightened. What she was frightened of, she didn't know. Perhaps the crackling in the dark spruce wood. Perhaps just the savage, heartless wildness of the mountains. But all day she sat in the sun in the doorway of the cabin, watching, watching for hope. And all the time, her bowels were cramped with fear.

She saw a dark spot that probably was a bear roving across the pale grassy slope in the far distance, in the sun.

When, in the afternoon, she saw Romero approaching, with silent suddenness, carrying his gun and a dead deer, the cramp in her bowels relaxed, then become colder. She dreaded him with a cold dread.

"There is deer-meat," he said, throwing the dead doe at her feet.

"You don't want to go away from here," he said. "This is a nice place."

She shrank into the cabin.

"Come into the sun," he said, following her. She looked up at him with hostile, frightened eyes.

"Come into the sun," he repeated, taking her gently by the arm, in a powerful grasp.

She knew it was useless to rebel. Quietly he led her out, and seated himself in the doorway, holding her still by the arm.

"In the sun it is warm," he said. "Look, this is a nice place. You

are such a pretty white woman, why do you want to act mean to me?
Isn't this a nice place! Come! Come here! It sure is warm here."

He drew her to him, and in spite of her stony resistance, he took
her cloak from her, holding her in her thin blue pyjamas.

5   "You sure are a pretty little white woman, small and pretty," he
said. "You sure won't act mean to me—you don' want to, I know
you don't."

She, stony and powerless, had to submit to him. The sun shone
on her white, delicate skin.

10   "I sure don't mind hell fire," he said, "after this."

A queer, luxurious good-humour seemed to possess him again. But
though outwardly she was powerless, inwardly she resisted him,
absolutely and stonily.

When later he was leaving her again, she said to him suddenly:

15   "You think you can conquer me this way. But you can't. You can
never conquer me."

He stood arrested, looking back at her, with many emotions
conflicting in his face: wonder, surprise, a touch of horror, and an
unconscious pain that crumpled his face till it was like a mask. Then

20   he went out without saying a word, hung the dead deer on a bough,
and started to flay it. While he was at this butcher's work, the sun sank
and cold night came on again.

"You see," he said to her as he crouched cooking the supper, "I
ain't goin' to let you go. I reckon you called to me in the night, and

25   I've some right. If you want to fix it up right now with me, and say
you want to be with me, we'll fix it up now and go down to the ranch
tomorrow and get married or whatever you want. But you've got to
say you want to be with me. Else I shall stay right here, till something
happens."

30   She waited a while before she answered:

"I don't want to be with anybody against my will. I don't dislike
you: at least, I didn't, till you tried to put your will over mine. I won't
have anybody's will put over me. You can't succeed. Nobody could.
You can never get me under your will.—And you won't have long to

35   try, because soon they will send someone to look for me."

He pondered this last, and she regretted having said it. Then,
sombre, he bent to the cooking again.

He could not conquer her, however much he violated her. Because
her spirit was hard and flawless as a diamond. But he could shatter her.

40   This she knew. Much more, and she would be shattered.

In a sombre, violent excess he tried to expend his desire for her. And she was racked with agony, and felt each time she would die. Because, in some peculiar way, he had got hold of her, some unrealised part of her which she never wished to realise. Racked with a burning, tearing anguish, she felt that the thread of her being would break, and she would die. The burning heat that racked her inwardly.

If only, only she could be alone again, cool and intact. If only she could recover herself again, cool and intact! Would she ever, ever, ever be able to bear herself again.

Even now she did not hate him. It was beyond that. Like some racking, hot doom. Personally he hardly existed.

The next day he would not let her have any fire, because of attracting attention with the smoke. It was a grey day, and she was cold. He stayed around, and heated soup on the petrol stove. She lay motionless in the blankets.

And in the afternoon she pulled the clothes over her head and broke into tears. She had never really cried in her life. He dragged the blankets away and looked to see what was shaking her. She sobbed in helpless hysterics. He covered her over again and went outside, looking at the mountains where clouds were dragging and leaving a little snow. It was a violent, windy, horrible day, the evil of winter rushing down.

She cried for hours. And after this a great silence came between them. They were two people who had died. He did not touch her any more. In the night she lay and shivered like a dying dog. She felt that her very shivering would rupture something in her body, and she would die.

At last she had to speak.

"Could you make a fire? I am so cold," she said, with chattering teeth.

"Want to come over here?" came his voice.

"I would rather you made me a fire," she said, her teeth knocking together and chopping the words in two.

He got up and kindled a fire. At last the warmth spread, and she could sleep.

The next day was still chilly, with some wind. But the sun shone. He went about in silence, with a dead-looking face. It was now so dreary, and so like death, she wished he would do anything rather than continue in this negation. If now he asked her to go down with

him to the world and marry him, she would do it. What did it matter!
Nothing mattered any more.

But he would not ask her. His desire was dead and heavy like ice
within him. He kept watch around the house.

5   On the fourth day as she sat huddled in the doorway in the sun,
hugged in a blanket, she saw two horsemen come over the crest of the
grassy slope, small figures. She gave a cry. He looked up quickly and
saw the figures. The men had dismounted. They were looking for the
trail.

10   "They are looking for me," she said.

"Muy bien!" he answered in Spanish.

He went and fetched his gun, and sat with it across his knees.

"Oh!" she said. "Don't shoot!"

He looked across at her.

15   "Why?" he said. "You like staying with me?"

"No," she said. "But don't shoot."

"I ain't going to Pen.,"* he said.

"You won't have to go to Pen.," she said. "Don't shoot."

"I'm going to shoot," he muttered.

20   And straight away he kneeled and took very careful aim. The
Princess sat on in an agony of helplessness and hopelessness.

The shot rang out. In an instant she saw one of the horses on the
pale grassy slope rear and go rolling down. The man had dropped in
the grass, and was invisible. The second man clambered on his horse,
25   and on that precipitous place went at a gallop in a long swerve towards
the nearest spruce tree cover. Bang! Bang! went Romero's shots. But
each time he missed, and the running horse leaped like a kangaroo
towards cover.

It was hidden. Romero now got behind a rock, watching for the
30   man to show some sign of himself. All was tense silence, in the brilliant
sunshine. The Princess sat on the bunk inside the cabin, crouching
paralysed. For hours, it seemed, Romero knelt behind his rock, in
his black shirt, bare-headed, watching. He had a beautiful alert figure.
The Princess wondered why she did not feel sorry for him. But her
35   spirit was hard and cold, her heart could not melt, though now she
would have given anything if it could have melted. If she could have
called* him to her, with love.

But no, she did not love him. She would never love any man. Never.
It was fixed and sealed in her, almost vindictively.

40   Suddenly she was so startled she almost fell from the bunk. A shot

rang out quite close, from behind the cabin. Romero leaped straight into the air, his arms fell outstretched, turning as he leaped. And even while he was in the air, a second shot rang out, and he fell with a crash, squirming, his hands clutching the earth towards the cabin door.

The Princess sat absolutely motionless, transfixed, staring at the prostrate figure. In a few moments the figure of a man in the Forest Service appeared close to the house: a young man in a broad-brimmed Stetson hat, dark flannel shirt, and riding-boots, carrying a gun. He strode over to the prostrate figure.

"Got you, Romero!" he said aloud. And he turned the dead man over. There was already a little pool of blood where Romero's breast had been.

"Hm!" said the Forest Service man. "Guess I got you nearer than I thought."

And he squatted there staring at the dead man.

The distant calling of his comrade aroused him. He stood up.

"Hallo Bill!" he shouted. "Yep! Got him!—Yep! Done him in, apparently."

The second man rode out of the forest, on a grey horse. He had a ruddy, kind face and round brown eyes dilated with dismay.

"He's not passed out?" he asked anxiously.

"Looks like it," said the first young man cooly.

The second dismounted and bent over the body. Then he stood up again and nodded.

"Yea-a!" he said. "He's done in all right. It's him all right, boy! It's Domingo Romero."

"Yep! I know it!" replied the other.

Then in perplexity he turned and looked into the cabin where the Princess squatted staring with big owl eyes from her red blanket.

"Hello!" he said, coming towards the hut. And he took his hat off. Oh, the sense of ridicule she felt! Though he did not mean any.

But she could not speak, no matter what she felt.

"What'd this man start firing for?" he asked.

She fumbled for words, with numb lips.

"He had gone out of his mind!" she said, with solemn, stammering conviction.

"Good Lord! You mean to say he'd gone out of his mind.—Whew! That's pretty awful. That explains it then. Hm!"

He accepted the explanation without more ado.

With some difficulty they succeeded in getting the Princess down to the ranch. But she too was now a little mad.

"I'm not quite sure where I am," she said to Mrs Wilkieson, as she lay in bed. "Do you mind explaining."

5   Mrs Wilkieson explained, tactfully.

"Oh yes!" said the Princess. "I remember. And I had an accident in the mountains, didn't I? Didn't we meet a man who'd gone mad, and who shot my horse from under me?"

"Yes, you met a man who had gone out of his mind."

10   The real affair was hushed up. The Princess departed east in a fortnight's time, in Miss Cummins' care. Apparently she had recovered herself entirely. She was the Princess, and a virgin intact.

But her bobbed hair was grey at the temples, and her eyes were a little mad. She was slightly crazy.

15   "Since my accident in the mountains, when a man went mad and shot my horse from under me, and my guide had to shoot him dead, I have never felt quite myself."

So she put it.

Later, she married an elderly man, and seemed pleased.

APPENDIX I
THE WILFUL WOMAN

Supplementary note on the text

See note on the texts, p. 2.

The only silent emendations in this unfinished story are the addition of the apostrophe to 'o'clock', and the ampersand is printed as 'and'.

The apparatus records deleted readings of complete words and phrases.

The Wilful Woman

November of the year 1916. A woman travelling from New York to the South west, by one of the tourist trains. On the third day the train lost time more and more. She raged with painful impatience. No good, at every station the train sat longer. They had passed the prairie lands 5 and entered the mountain and desert region. They ought soon to arrive, soon. This was already the desert of grey-white sage and blue mountains. She ought to be there, soon, soon she ought to be there. This journey alone should be over. But the train comfortably stretched its length in the stations, and would never arrive. There was no end. 10 It could not arrive. She could not bear it.

The woman sat in the cubby-hole at the end of the Pullman which is called in America a Drawing-Room. She had the place to herself and her bags. Volts of distracted impatience and heart-brokenness surged out of her, so that the negro did not dare to come in and sweep 15 her floor with his little brush and dust-pan. He left the "Room" unswept for the afternoon.

Frustration, and a painful volcanic pressure of impatience. The train would not arrive, *could* not arrive. Could not arrive. That was it. 20

She was a sturdy woman with a round face, like an obstinate girl of fourteen. Like an obstinate girl of fourteen she sat there devouring her unease, her heavy, muscular fore-arms inert in her lap. So still, yet at such a pressure. So child-like—yet a woman approaching forty.* So naïve-looking, softly full and feminine. And curiously heart-broken 25 at being alone, travelling alone. Of course any man might have rushed to save her, and reap the reward of her soft heavy, grateful magnetism. But wait a bit. Her thick, dark brows like curved horns over the naïve-looking face; and her bright, hazel-grey eyes, clear at the first glance as candour and unquenchable youth, at the second glance made 30 up all of devilish grey and yellow bits, as opals are, and the bright candour of youth resolving into something dangerous as the headlights of a great machine coming full at you in the night. Mr Hercules had better think twice before he rushed to pick up this seductive serpent of loneliness that lay on the western trail. He had picked a snake up 35 long ago,* without hurting himself. But that was before Columbus discovered America.

Why did she feel that the train would never arrive, *could* never arrive, with her in it. Who knows? But that was how she did feel. The train would never arrive. Simple fate. Perhaps she felt that some power of her will would at last neutralise altogether the power of the engines, and there would come an end to motion, so there they would sit, forever, the train and she, at a deadlock on the Santa Fe Line. She had left New York in a sort of frenzy. Since they had passed Kansas City, Gate of the West, the thing had been getting unbearable. Since they had passed La Junta and come to the desert and the Rockies, the fatality had as good as happened. Yet she was only a few hours from her destination. And she would never get there. This train would never bring her there. Her head was one mass of thoughts and frenzied ideas, almost to madness.

Then she sprang out of her Pullman. It was somewhere after Trinidad, she didn't bother where. "Put my bags out," she said to the negro, and he, looking at those serpent-blazing eyes under those eyebrows like thorn-bushes, silently obeyed. Yet with her mouth she smiled a little and was cajoling, and her tip was reckless. Man must needs be mollified. She remembered to be just sufficiently soft and feminine. But she was distracted and heart-broken.

Started her next whirl. She must have an automobile, she *would* have an automobile, to be driven this hundred or hundred and fifty miles that remained. Yes, she would have an automobile. But she had got out at a station where, at least that afternoon, there *was* no automobile. Nevertheless, she would have an automobile. So at last was produced an old worn-out Dodge with no springs left, belonging to a boy of sixteen. Yes, she would have that. The boy had never travelled that trail, didn't know the way. No matter, she would go. She would get to Lamy* in front of that hateful train which she had left. And the boy would get twenty-six dollars. Good enough!

She had never been west before, so she reckoned without her host. She had still to learn what trails round the Rockies and across the desert are like. She imagined roads, or forest tracks. She found what actually is a trail in the south west—a blind squirm up sand-banks, a blind rattle along dry river-beds, a breathless scramble in deep cañons over what look like simple landslides and precipices, the car at an angle of forty-five degrees above a green rocky river, banging itself to bits against boulders, surging through the river then back again through the river and once more swooping through the river with the devil's own scramble up a rocky bank on the other side, and a young boy driving on, driving ahead, without knowing where or what was happening to him, twenty-six dollars at the end. So out on the lurch and bump of the open white-sage desert once more, to follow the trail by scent rather than by sight, cart-ruts this way, tracks that way, please yourself in the god-forsaken landscape, bolting into a slope of piñon 5 and cedar, dark-green bush-scrub, then dropping down to a wire fence and a gate, a sort of ranch, and a lost village of houses like brown mud boxes planked down in the grey wilderness, with a bigger mud box, oblong, which the boy told her was the sort of church place where the Penitentes scourge and torture themselves, windowless so that no-one 10 shall hear their shrieks and groans.

By nightfall she had had a lot of the nonsense bumped and bruised out of her, knocked about as if she were a *penitente* herself. Not that she was a *penitente*: not she. But at least here was a country that hit her with hard knuckles, right through to the bone. It was something 15 of a country.

Luckily she had telegraphed to Mark, who would be waiting for her at Lamy station. Mark was her husband—her third. One dead, one divorced, and Mark* alternately torn to atoms and thrown to the four corners of the universe, then rather sketchily gathered up and put 20 together again by a desirous, if still desperate Isis. She had torn him in two and pitched him piecemeal away into the south-western desert. Now she was after him once more, going to put humpty-dumpty together again with a slam. With a slam that might finally do for him.*

Of course he is an artist, a foreigner, a Russian. Of course she is 25 an American woman, several generations of wealth and tradition in various cities of New York state behind her, several generations of visiting Europe and staying in the Meurice* and seeing Napoleon III or Gambetta* or whoever was figuring on the stage of Paris. She herself had stayed in the old Meurice. She too had had her apartment in a 30 fine old hotel, and if there was no Napoleon III left for her, there had been Ex-Princesses of Saxony, D. Annunzio, Duse, Isadora Duncan or Matisse.*

These American families do actually tend to cumulate and culminate in one daughter. Not that the family had as yet cumulated in Sybil 35 Mond. She had started as Sybil Hamnett, and had been successively Sybil Thomas and Sybil Danks before she married the Jewish artist from somewhere Poland way who was, in her family's eyes, the anti-climax. But she herself admitted no possibility of anti-climax for herself, and kept unpleasant surprises still in store for her family. Her 40 family being her mother and the General, Sybil's second step-father. For she was as well-off for step-fathers as for husbands.

The family had actually culminated in Sybil: all the force of the Hamnett's, on her father's side, and the push of the Wilcox's, on her
5 mother's, focussed into this one highly-explosive daughter. No question of dribbling out. Sybil at forty was heavy with energy like a small bison, and strong and young-looking as if she were thirty, often giving the impression of soft crudeness as if she were sixteen. The old colonial vigour had, we repeat, collected in her as in some final dam,
10 culminated, like the buffalo's force in his forehead. But the old colonial riches had not yet descended upon her. She had her own sufficient income, but the mass of the family wealth rested on her mother, who, aided by the General, exemplified it in the correct and magnificent Italian Mansion on Lake Erie.*

15 The racketty machine in which she rode had of course no headlights, and the November night fell. The boy hadn't thought to put the lamps on. No head-lights! Frustration, always frustration. Sybil annihilated the boy in her soul, and sat still. Or rather, with her body bashed and bruised, her soul sat crying and ominous. There was
20 nothing to be done but to scramble for the nearest station again.

On then, under the many sharp, small stars of the desert. The air was cold in her nostrils, the desert seemed weird and uncanny. But—it was terra nova. It was a new world, the desert at the foot of the mountains, the high desert above the gorges of the cañons, the world
25 of three altitudes. Strange!—doomful!

Yes, destiny had made her get out of the train and into this racketty machine. Destiny even had made the boy bring no head-lights. Her ponderous storm began to evaporate. She looked round the night as they emerged from a dark cañon out onto a high flat bit of vague desert,
30 with mountains guarding the flatness beyond, shadows beyond the shadow. It impressed her, although she *must* get to her journey end, she *must* arrive.—No, it was not like desert. Rather like wilderness, the wilderness of the temptation,* for example. Shadowy scrub of pale grey sage, knee-high, waist-high, on the flat of the table land; and on
35 the slopes of the mountains that rose still further, starting off the flat table, scrub of gnarled pine and cedar, still hardly more than bushes, but like those Japanese dwarf-trees,* full of age, torture, and power. Strange country—weird—frightening too. It would need a battle to gain hold over such a land. It would need a battle. She snuffed the
40 curiously-scented air of the desert.—With her tongue almost jerked

out of her mouth by the jumping of the car, she sat inwardly
motionless, facing destiny again. It was her destiny she should come
to this land. It was her destiny she should see it for the first time thus,
alone, lost, without light. That was destiny, that threw her naked like
the black queen* onto this unknown chess-board. She hugged her furs   5
and her fate round her, in the cold, rare air, and was somewhat
relieved. Her battle! Her hope!

And thus by eight o'clock the frozen, disappointed, but dogged boy
brought her to the railway again, as she bade him. It was impossible
for him to get her to Lamy without lights or anything. He must forfeit   10
some of the twenty-six dollars. He was disappointed, but he admitted
the truth of her contention.

Wagon-Mound,* or some such name. She remembered a sort of
dome of a hill in the night. After which nothing to be done but to go
to the "hotel", to wait three hours for the slow train which followed   15
the one she had abandoned way back at Trinidad.

[End of manuscript]

APPENDIX II

THE FLYING-FISH

The Flying-Fish

I. Departure from Mexico

"Come home else no Day in Daybrook."—This cablegram was the first thing Gethin Day read of the pile of mail which he found at the hotel in the lost town of South Mexico,* when he returned from his trip to the coast. Though the message was not signed, he knew whom it came from and what it meant.

He lay in his bed in the hot October evening, still sick with malaria. In the flush of fever he saw yet the parched, stark mountains of the south, the villages of reed huts lurking among trees, the black-eyed natives with the lethargy, the *ennui*, the pathos, the beauty of an exhausted race; and above all he saw the weird, uncanny flowers, which he had hunted from the high plateaux, through the valleys and down to the steaming crocodile heat of the *tierra caliente*,* towards the sandy, burning, intolerable shores. For he was fascinated by the mysterious green blood that runs in the veins of plants, and the purple and yellow and red blood that colours the faces of flowers. Especially the unknown flora of South Mexico attracted him, and above all he wanted to trace to the living plant the mysterious essences and toxins known with such strange elaboration to the Mayas, the Zapotecas and the Aztecs.*

His head was humming like a mosquito, his legs were paralysed for the moment by the heavy quinine injection the doctor had injected into them, and his soul was as good as dead with the malaria; so he threw all his letters unopened on the floor, hoping never to see them again. He lay with the pale yellow cablegram in his hand:—"Come home else no Day in Daybrook." Through the open doors from the patio of the hotel came the heavy scent of that invisible green night-flower the natives call Reina de noche.* The little Mexican servant-girl strode in barefoot with a cup of tea, her flounced cotton skirt swinging, her long black hair down her back. She asked him in her birdlike Spanish if he wanted nothing more. "*Nada más*," he said. "Nothing more; leave me and shut the door."

He wanted to shut out the scent of that powerful green inconspicuous night-flower he knew so well.

"No Day in Daybrook
For the Vale a bad outlook."

No Day in Daybrook! There had been Days in Daybrook since time began: at least, so he imagined.

Daybrook was a sixteenth-century stone house, among the hills in the middle of England. It stood where Crichdale bends to the south and where Ashleydale joins in.* "Daybrook standeth at the junction of the ways and at the centre of the trefoil. Even it rides within the Vale as an ark between three seas; being indeed the ark of these vales, if not of all England."—So had written Sir Gilbert Day, he who built the present Daybrook in the sixteenth century. Sir Gilbert's *Book of Days*,* so beautifully written out on vellum and illuminated by his own hand, was one of the treasures of the family.

Sir Gilbert had sailed the Spanish seas* in his day, and had come home rich enough to rebuild the old house of Daybrook according to his own fancy. He had made it a beautiful pointed house, rather small, standing upon a knoll above the river Ashe, where the valley narrowed and the woods rose steep behind. "Nay," wrote this quaint Elizabethan, "though I say that Daybrook is the ark of the Vale, I mean not the house itself, but He that Day, that lives in the house in his day. While Day there be in Daybrook, the floods shall not cover the Vale* nor shall they ride over England completely."

Gethin Day was nearing forty, and he had not spent much of his time in Daybrook. He had been a soldier and had wandered in many countries. At home his sister Lydia, twenty years older than himself, had been the Day in Daybrook. Now from her telegram he knew she was either ill or already dead.

She had been rather hard and grey like the rock of Crichdale, but faithful and a pillar of strength. She had let him go his own way, but always when he came home, she would look into his blue eyes with her searching uncanny grey look and ask: "Well, have you come, or are you still wandering?" "Still wandering, I think," he said. "Mind you don't wander into a cage one of these days," she replied; "you would find far more room for yourself in Daybrook than in those foreign parts, if you knew how to come into your own."*

This had always been the burden of her song to him: *if you knew how to come into your own*. And it had always exasperated him with a sense of futility; though whether his own futility or Lydia's, he had never made out.

Lydia was wrapt up in old Sir Gilbert's *Book of Days*; she had written out for her brother a fair copy, neatly bound in green leather, and had given it him without a word when he came of age, merely

looking at him with that uncanny look of her grey eyes, expecting
something of him, which always made him start away from her.
The *Book of Days* was a sort of secret family bible at Daybrook.
It was never shown to strangers, nor ever mentioned outside the
immediate family. Indeed in the family it was never openly alluded
to. Only on solemn occasions, or on rare evenings, at twilight, when
the evening star shone, had the dead father occasionally read aloud to
the two children from the nameless work.

In the copy she had written out for Gethin Lydia had used different
coloured inks in different places. Gethin imagined that her favourite
passages were those in the royal-blue ink, where the page was almost
as blue as the cornflowers that grew tall beside the walks in the garden
at Daybrook.

"Beauteous is the day of the yellow sun which is the common day
of men; but even as the winds roll unceasing above the trees of the
world, so doeth that Greater Day, which is the Uncommon Day, roll
over the unclipt bushes of our little daytime. Even also as the morning
sun shakes his yellow wings on the horizon and rises up, so the great
bird beyond him spreads out his dark blue feathers, and beats his wings
in the tremor of the Greater Day."

Gethin knew a great deal of his *Book of Days* by heart. In a dilettante
fashion, he had always liked rather highflown poetry, but in the last
years, something in the hard, fierce finite sun of Mexico, in the dry
terrible land, and in the black staring eyes of the suspicious natives
had made the ordinary day lose its reality to him. It had cracked like
some great bubble, and to his uneasiness and terror, he had seemed
to see through the fissures the deeper blue of that other Greater Day
where moved the other sun shaking its dark blue wings. Perhaps it was
the malaria; perhaps it was his own inevitable development; perhaps
it was the presence of those handsome, dangerous, wide-eyed men left
over from the ages before the flood in Mexico, which caused his old
connections and his accustomed world to break for him. He was ill,
and he felt as if at the very middle of him, beneath his navel, some
membrane were torn, some membrane which had connected him with
the world and its day. The natives who attended him, quiet, soft, heavy
and rather helpless, seemed, he realised, to be gazing from their wide
black eyes always into that greater day whence they had come and
where they wished to return. Men of a dying race, to whom the busy
sphere of the common day is a cracked and leaking shell.

He wanted to go home. He didn't care now whether England was tight and little and overcrowded and far too full of furniture. He no longer minded the curious quiet atmosphere of Daybrook in which he had felt he would stifle as a young man. He no longer resented the weight of family tradition, nor the peculiar sense of authority which the house seemed to have over him. Now he was sick from the soul outwards, and the common day had cracked for him, and the uncommon day was showing him its immensity, he felt that home was the place. It did not matter that England was small and tight and over-furnished, if the Greater Day were round about. He wanted to go home, away from these big wild countries where men were dying back into the Greater Day, home where he dare face the sun behind the sun, and come into his own in the Greater Day.

But he was as yet too ill to go. He lay in the nausea of the tropics, and let the days pass over him. The door of his room stood open on to the patio where green banana-trees and high strange-sapped flowering shrubs rose from the water-sprinkled earth towards that strange rage of blue which was the sky over the shadow-heavy, perfume-soggy air of the closed-in courtyard. Dark-blue shadows moved from the side of the patio, disappeared, then appeared on the other side. Evening had come, and the barefoot natives in white calico flitted with silent rapidity across, and across, forever going, yet mysteriously going nowhere, threading the timelessness with their transit, like swallows of darkness.

The window of the room, opposite the door, opened on to the tropical parched street. It was a big window, came nearly down to the floor, and was heavily barred with upright and horizontal bars. Past the window went the natives, with the soft, light rustle of their sandals. Big straw hats balanced, dark cheeks, calico shoulders brushed with the silent swiftness of the Indian past the barred window-space. Sometimes children clutched the bars and gazed in, with great shining eyes and straight blue-black hair, to see the Americano lying in the majesty of a white bed. Sometimes a beggar stood there, sticking a skinny hand through the iron grille and whimpering the strange, endless, pullulating whimper of the beggar—por amor de Dios!*—on and on and on, as it seemed for an eternity. But the sick man on the bed endured it with the same endless endurance in resistance, endurance in resistance, which he had learned in the Indian countries. Aztec or Mixtec,* Zapotec or Maya, always the same power of serpent-like torpor of resistance.

The doctor came—an educated Indian: though he could do nothing but inject quinine and give a dose of calomel. But he was lost between the two days, the fatal greater day of the Indians, the fussy, busy lesser day of the white people.

"How is it going to finish?" he said to the sick man, seeking a word. "How is it going to finish with the Indians, with the Mexicans? Now the soldiers are all taking marihuana—hashish!"

"They are all going to die. They are all going to kill themselves— all—all," said the Englishman, in the faint permanent delirium of his malaria. "After all, beautiful it is to be dead, and quite departed."

The doctor looked at him in silence, understanding only too well. "Beautiful it is to be dead!" It is the refrain which hums at the centre of every Indian heart, where the greater day is hemmed in by the lesser. The despair that comes when the lesser day hems in the greater. Yet the doctor looked at the gaunt white man in malice:—"What, would you have us quite gone, you Americans!"

At last Gethin Day crawled out into the plaza. The square was like a great low fountain of green and of dark shade, now it was autumn and the rains were over. Scarlet craters rose the canna flowers, licking great red tongues, and tropical yellow. Scarlet, yellow, green, blue-green, sunshine intense and invisible, deep indigo shade! and small, white-clad natives pass, passing, across the square, through the green lawns, under the indigo shade, and across the hollow sunshine of the road into the arched arcades of the low Spanish buildings, where the shops were. The low, baroque Spanish buildings stood back with a heavy, sick look, as if they too felt the endless malaria in their bowels, the greater day of the stony Indian crushing the more jaunty, lean European day which they represented. The yellow cathedral leaned its squat, earthquake-shaken towers, the bells sounded hollow. Earth-coloured tiny soldiers lay and stood around the entrance to the municipal palace, which was so baroque and Spanish, but which now belonged to the natives. Heavy as a strange bell of shadow-coloured glass, the shadow of the greater day hung over this coloured plaza which the Europeans had created, like an oasis, in the lost depths of Mexico. Gethin Day sat half lying on one of the broken benches, while tropical birds flew and twittered in the great trees, and natives twittered or flitted in silence, and he knew that here, the European day was annulled again. His body was sick with the poison that lurks in all tropical air, his soul was sick with that other day, that rather awful greater day which permeates the little days of the old races. He wanted to get out, to get out of this ghastly tropical void into which he had fallen.

Yet it was the end of November before he could go. Little revolutions* had again broken the thread of railway at the end of which the southern town hung revolving like a spider. It was a narrow-gauge railway, one single narrow little track which ran over the plateau, then
5 slipped down, down the long barranca,* descending five thousand feet down to the valley which was a cleft in the plateau, then up again seven thousand feet, to the higher plateau to the north. How easy to break the thread! One of the innumerable little wooden bridges destroyed, and it was done. The three hundred miles to the north were impassable
10 wilderness, like the hundred-and-fifty miles through the low-lying jungle to the south.

At last however he could crawl away. The train came again. He had cabled to England, and had received the answer that his sister was dead. It seemed so natural, there under the powerful November sun of
15 southern Mexico, in the drugging powerful odours of the night-flowers, that Lydia should be dead. She seemed so much more *real*, shall we say actually vital, in death. Dead, he could think of her as quite near and comforting and real, whereas while she was alive, she was so utterly alien, remote and fussy, ghost-like in her petty Derbyshire day.

20 "For the little day is like a house with the family round the hearth, and the door shut. Yet outside whispers the Greater Day, wall-less, and heartless. And the time will come at last when the walls of the little day shall fall, and what is left of the family of men shall find themselves outdoors in the Greater Day, houseless and abroad, even
25 here between the knees of the Vales, even in Crichdale. It is a doom that will come upon tall men. And then they will breathe deep, and be breathless in the great air, and salt sweat will stand on their brow, thick as buds on sloe-bushes when the sun comes back. And little men will shudder and die out, like clouds of grasshoppers falling in the sea.
30 Then tall men will remain alone in the land, moving deeper in the Greater Day, and moving deeper. Even as the flying-fish, when he leaves the air and recovereth his element in the depth, plunges and invisibly rejoices. So will tall men rejoice, after their flight of fear, through the thin air, pursued by death. For it is on wings of fear, sped
35 from the mouth of death, that the flying-fish riseth twinkling in the air, and rustles in astonishment silvery through the thin small day. But he dives again into the great peace of the deeper day, and under the belly of death, and passes into his own—"

Gethin read again his *Book of Days*, in the twilight of his last
40 evening. Personally, he resented the symbolism and mysticism of his

Elizabethan ancestor. But it was in his veins. And he was going home, back, back to the house with the flying-fish on the roof.* He felt an immense doom over everything, still the same next morning, when, an hour after dawn, the little train ran out from the doomed little town, on to the plateau, where the cactus thrust up its fluted tubes, and where the mountains stood back, blue, cornflower-blue, so dark and pure in form, in the land of the Greater Day, the day of demons. The little train, with two coaches, one full of natives, the other with four or five "white" Mexicans, ran fussily on, in the little day of toys and men's machines. On the roof sat tiny, earthy-looking soldiers, faces burnt black, with cartridge-belts and rifles. They clung on tight, not to be shaken off. And away went this weird toy, this crazy little caravan, over the great lost land of cactuses and mountains standing back, on to the shut-in defile where the long descent began.

At half-past ten, at a station some distance down the barranca, a station connected with old silver mines,* the train stood, and all descended to eat: the eternal turkey with black sauce, potatoes, salad, and apple pie—the American apple pie, which is a sandwich of cooked apple between two layers of pie-crust. And also beer, from Puebla. Two Chinamen administered the dinner, in all the decency, cleanness and well-cookedness of the little day of the white men, which they reproduce so well. There it was, the little day of our civilisation. Outside, the little train waited. The little black-faced soldiers sharpened their knives. The vast, varying declivity of the barranca stood in sun and shadow as on the day of doom, untouched.

On again, winding, descending the huge and savage gully or crack in the plateau-edge, where no men lived. Bushes trailed with elegant pink creeper, such as is seen in hothouses, enormous blue convolvuluses opened out, and in the unseemly tangle of growth, bulbous orchids jutted out from trees, and let hang a trail of white or yellow flower. The strange, entangled squalor of the jungle.

Gethin Day looked down the ravine, where water was running. He saw four small deer lifting their heads from drinking, to look at the train. Los venados!* los venados! he heard the soldiers softly calling. As if knowing they were safe, the deer stood and wondered, away there in the Greater Day, in the manless space, while the train curled round a sharp jutting rock.

They came at last to the bottom, where it was very hot, and a few wild men hung round with the sword-like knives of the sugar-cane. The train seemed to tremble with fear all the time, as if its thread might be cut. So frail, so thin the thread of the lesser day, threading with its business the great reckless heat of the savage land. So frail a thread, so easily snapped! But the train crept on, northwards, upwards.

And as the stupor of
5 heat began to pass, in the later afternoon, the sick man saw among mango trees, beyond the bright green stretches of sugar-cane, white clusters of a village, with the coloured dome of a church all yellow and blue with shiny majolica tiles. Spain putting the bubbles of her little day among the blackish trees of the unconquerable.

10 He came at nightfall to a small square town,* more in touch with civilisation, where the train ended its frightened run. He slept there. And next day he took another scrap of a train across to the edge of the main plateau. The country was wild, but more populous. An occasional big hacienda with sugar-mills stood back among the hills.
15 But it was silent. Spain had spent the energy of her little day here, now the silence, the terror of the Greater Day, mysterious with death, was filling in again.

On the train a native, a big, handsome man, wandered back and forth among the uneasy Mexican travellers with a tray of glasses of ice-cream.
20 He was no doubt of the Tlaxcala tribe.* Gethin Day looked at him and met his glistening dark eyes. "Quiere helados, Señor?"* said the Indian, reaching a glass with his dark, subtle-skinned, workless hand. And in the soft, secret tones of his voice, Gethin Day heard the sound of the Greater Day. "Gracias!"

25 "Patrón!* Patrón!" moaned a woman at the station. "Por amor de Dios, Patrón!" and she held out her hand for a few centavos. And in the moaning croon of her Indian voice the Englishman heard again the fathomless crooning appeal of the Indian women, moaning stranger, more terrible than the ring-dove, with a sadness that had no
30 horizon, and a rocking, moaning appeal that drew out the very marrow of the soul of a man. Over the door of her womb was written not only: Lasciate ogni speranza, voi ch'entrate, but: Perdite ogni pianto, voi ch'uscite.* For the men who had known these women were beyond weeping and beyond even despair, mute in the timeless compulsion
35 of the Greater Day. Big, proud men could sell glasses of ice-cream at twenty-five centavos, and not really know they were doing it. They were elsewhere, beyond despair. Only sometimes the last passion of the death-lust would sweep them, shut up as they were in the white man's lesser day, belonging as they did to the greater day.

40 The little train ran on to the main plateau, and to the junction with

the main-line railway called the Queen's Own, a railway that still belongs to the English, and that joins Mexico City with the Gulf of Mexico.* Here, in the big but forlorn railway restaurant the Englishman ordered the regular meal, that came with American mechanical take-it-or-leave-it flatness. He ate what he could, and went out again. There the vast plains were level and bare, under the blue winter sky, so pure, and not too hot, and in the distance the white cone of the volcano of Orizaba* stood perfect in the middle air.

"There is no help, O man. Fear gives thee wings like a bird, death comes after thee open-mouthed, and thou soarest on the wind like a fly. But thy flight is not far, and thy flying is not long. Thou art a fish of the timeless Ocean, and must needs fall back. Take heed lest thou break thyself in the fall! For death is not in dying, but in the fear. Cease then the struggle of thy flight, and fall back into the deep element where death is and is not, and life is not a fleeing away. It is a beauteous thing to live and to be alive. Live then in the Greater Day, and let the waters carry thee, and the flood bear thee along, and live, only live, no more of this hurrying away.—"

"No more of this hurrying away." Even the Elizabethans had known it, the restlessness, the "hurrying away". Gethin Day knew he had been hurrying away. He had hurried perhaps a little too far, just over the edge. Now, try as he might, he was aware of a gap in his time-space continuum;* he was, in the words of his ancestor, aware of the Greater Day showing through the cracks in the ordinary day. And it was useless trying to fill up the cracks. The little day was destined to crumble away, as far as he was concerned, and he would *have* to inhabit the greater day. The very sight of the volcano cone in mid-air made him know it. His little self was used up, worn out. He felt sick and frail, facing this change of life.

"Be still, then, be still! Wrap thyself in patience, shroud thyself in peace, as the tall volcano clothes himself in snow. Yet he looks down in him, and sees wet sun in him molten and of great force, stirring with the scald sperm of life. Be still, above the sperm of life, which spills alone in its hour. Be still, as an apple on its core, as a nightingale in winter, as a long-waiting mountain upon its fire. Be still, upon thine own sun.

"For thou hast a sun in thee.* Thou hast a sun in thee, and it is not timed. Therefore wait. Wait, and be at peace with thine own sun, which is thy sperm of life. Be at peace with thy sun in thee, as the volcano is, and the dark holly-bush before berry-time, and the long hours of night. Abide by thy sun in thee, even the onion doth so, though you see it not. Yet peel her, and her sun in thine eyes maketh tears. Each thing hath its little sun, even in the wicked house-fly something twinkleth."

5   Standing there on the platform of the station open to the great plains of the plateau, Gethin Day said to himself: My old ancestor is more real to me than the restaurant, and the dinner I have eaten, after all.—The train still did not come. He turned to another page of corn-flower blue writing, hoping to find something amusing.

10   "When earth inert lieth too heavy, then Vesuvius spitteth out fire. And if a nightingale would not sing, his song unsung in him would slay him. For to the nightingale his song is Nemesis, and unsung songs are the Erinyes,* the impure Furies of vengeance. And thy sun in thee is thy all in all, so be patient, and take no care. Take no care, for what

15   thou knowest is ever less than what thou art. The full fire even of thine own sun in thine own body, thou canst never know. So how shouldst thou load care upon thy sun. Take heed, take thought, take pleasure, take pain, take all things as thy sun stirs. Only fasten not thyself in care about anything, for care is impiety, it spits upon the sun."

20   It was the white and still volcano, visionary across the swept plain, that looked back at him as he glanced up from his *Book of Days*. But there the train came, thundering, with all the mock majesty of great equipage, and the Englishman entered the Pullman car, and sat with his book in his pocket.

25   The train, almost with the splendour of the Greater Day, yet ricketty and foolish at last, raced on the level, entered the defile, and crept, cautiously twining round and round, down the cliff-face of the plateau, with the low lands lying thousands of feet below, specked with a village or two like fine specks. Yet the low lands drew up, and the

30   pine trees were gone far above, and at last the thick trees crowded the line, and dark-faced natives ran beside the train selling gardenias, gardenia perfume heavy in all the air. But the train nearly empty.

Vera Cruz at night-fall was a modern stone port, but disheartened and tropical, mostly shut up, abandoned, as if life had quietly left it.

35   Great customs buildings, unworking, acres of pianofortes in packing-cases, all the endless jetsam of the little day of commerce flung up here and waiting, acres of goods unattended to, waiting till the labour of Vera Cruz should cease to be on strike. A town, a port struck numb, the inner sun striking vengefully at the little life of commerce. The

40   day's sun set, there was a heavy orange light over the waters, something

sinister, a gloom, a deep resentment in nature, even in the washing
of the warm sea. In these salt waters natives were still baptised to
Christianity, and the socialists, in mockery perhaps, baptised themselves into the mystery of frustration and revenge. The port was in
the hands of strikers and wild out-of-workers, and was blank. Officials 5
had almost disappeared. Even here, a woman, a "lady" examined the
passports.*

But the ship rode at the end of the jetty: the one lonely passenger
ship. There was one other steamer—from Sweden, a cargo boat. For
the rest, the port was deserted. It was a point where the wild primeval 10
Day of this continent met the busy white-man's day, and the two
annulled one another. The result was a port of nullity, nihilism
concrete and actual, calling itself the city of the True Cross.*

2. The Gulf

In the morning they sailed off, away from the hot shores, from the 15
high land hanging up inwards. And world gives place to world. In an
hour, it was only ship and ocean, the world of land and affairs was
gone.

There were few people on board. In the second-class saloon only
seventeen souls. Gethin Day was travelling second. It was a German 20
boat, he knew it would be clean and comfortable. The second-class
fare was already forty-five pounds. And a man who is not rich, and
who would live his life under as little compulsion as possible, must
calculate keenly with money and its power. For the lesser day of money
and the mealy-mouthed Mammon* is always ready for a victim, and 25
a man who has glimpsed the Greater Day, and the inward sun, will
not fall into the clutches of Mammon's mean day, if he can help it.
Gethin Day had a moderate income, and he looked on this as his
bulwark against Mammon's despicable authority. The thought of
earning a living was repulsive and humiliating to him. 30

In the first-class saloon were only four persons: two Danish
merchants, stout and wealthy, who had been part of a bunch of Danish
business-men invited by the Mexican government to look at the
business resources of the land. They had been fêted and feasted, and
shown what they were meant to see, so now, fuller of business than 35
ever, they were going back to Copenhagen to hatch the eggs they had
conceived. But they had also eaten oysters in Vera Cruz, and the
oysters also were inside them. They fell sick of poison, and lay deathly

ill all the voyage, leaving the only other first-class passengers, an English knight and his son, alone in their glory. Gethin Day was sincerely glad he had escaped the first-class, for the voyage was twenty days.

5   The seventeen souls of the second class were four of them English, two Danish, five Spaniards, five Germans, and a Cuban. They all sat at one long table in the dining-saloon, the Cuban at one end of the table, flanked by four English on his left, facing the five Spaniards across the table. Then came the two Danes, facing one another, and

10   being buffer-state between the rest and the five Germans, who occupied the far end of the table. It was a German boat, so the Germans were very noisy, and the stewards served them first. The Spaniards and the Cuban were mum, the English were stiff, the Danes were uneasy, the Germans were boisterous, and so the first luncheon

15   passed. It was the lesser day of the ship, and small enough. The menu being in correct German and doubtful Spanish, the Englishwoman on Gethin Day's right put up a lorgnette and stared at it. She was unable to stare it out of countenance, so she put it down and ate uninformed as to what she was eating. The Spaniard opposite Gethin Day had come

20   to table without collar or tie, doing the bluff, go-to-hell colonial touch, almost in his shirt-sleeves. He was a man of about thirty-two. He brayed at the steward in strange, harsh Galician Spanish,* the steward grinned somewhat sneeringly and answered in German, having failed to understand and not prepared to exert himself to try. Down the table

25   a blonde horse of a woman was shouting at the top of her voice, in harsh north-German, to a Herr Doktor with turned-up moustaches who presided at the German head of the table. The Spaniards bent forward in a row to look with a sort of silent horror at the yelling woman, then they looked at one another with a faint grimace of

30   mocking repulsion. The Galician banged the table with the empty wine-decanter: wine was "included". The steward, with a sneering little grin at such table-manners, brought a decanter half full. Wine was not *ad lib.*, but *à discrétion*. The Spaniards, having realised this, henceforth snatched it quickly and pretty well emptied the decanter

35   before the English got a shot at it. Which somewhat amused the table-stewards, who wanted to see the two foreign lots fight it out. But Gethin Day solved this problem by holding out his hand to the fat, clean-shaven, Basque, as soon as the decanter reached that gentleman, and saying: "May I serve the lady?"—Whereupon the Basque handed

40   over the decanter, and Gethin helped the two ladies and himself, before

handing back the decanter to the Spaniards.—Man wants but little here below,* but he's damn well got to see he gets it.—All this is part of the little day, which has to be seen to. Whether it is interesting or not depends on one's state of soul.

Bristling with all the bristles of offence and defence which a man has to put up the first days in such a company, Gethin Day would go off down the narrow gangway of the bottom deck, down into the steerage, where the few passengers lay about in shirt and trousers, on to the very front tip of the boat.

She was a long, narrow, old ship, long like a cigar, and not much space in her. Yet she was pleasant, and had a certain grace of her own, was a real ship, not merely a "liner". She seemed to travel swift and clean, piercing away into the Gulf.

Gethin Day would sit for hours at the very tip of the ship, on the bow-sprit, looking out into the whitish sunshine of the hot Gulf of Mexico. Here he was alone, and the world was all strange white sunshine, candid, and water, warm, bright water, perfectly pure beneath him, of an exquisite frail green. It lifted vivid wings from the running tip of the ship, and threw white pinion-spray from its green edges. And always, always, always it was in the two-winged fountain, as the ship came like life between, and always the spray fell swishing, pattering from the green arch of the water-wings. And below, as yet untouched, a moment ahead, always a moment ahead, and perfectly untouched, was the lovely green depth of the water, depth, deep, shallow-pale emerald above and under sapphire-green, dark and pale, blue and shimmer-green, two waters, many waters, one water, perfect in unison, one moment ahead of the ship's bows, so serene, fathomless and pure and free of time. It was very lovely, and on the softly-lifting bow-sprit of the long, swift ship the body was cradled in the sway of timeless life, the soul lay in the jewel-coloured moment, the jewel-pure eternity of this gulf of nowhere.

And always, always, like a dream, the flocks of flying-fish swept into the air, from nowhere, and went brilliantly twinkling in their flight of silvery watery wings rapidly fluttering, away low as swallows over the smooth curved surface of the sea, then gone again, vanished, without splash or evidence, gone. One alone like a little silver twinkle. Gone! The sea was still and silky-surfaced, blue and softly heaving, empty, purity itself, sea, sea, sea.

Then suddenly the faint whispering crackle, and a cloud of silver on webs of pure, fluttering water was soaring low over the surface of

the sea, at an angle from the ship, as if jetted away from the cut-water, soaring in a low arc, fluttering with the wild emphasis of grasshoppers or locusts suddenly burst out of the grass, in a wild rush to make away, make away, and making it, away, away, then suddenly gone, like a lot
5   of lights blown out in one breath. And still the ship did not pause, any more than the moon pauses, neither to look nor catch breath. But the soul pauses and holds its breath, for wonder, wonder, which is the very breath of the soul.

All the long morning he would be there curled in the wonder of this
10 gulf of creation, where the flying-fishes on translucent wings swept in their ecstatic clouds out of the water, in a terror that was brilliant as joy, in a joy brilliant with terror, with wings made of pure water flapping with great speed, and long-shafted bodies of translucent silver like squirts of living water, there in air, brilliant in air, before suddenly
15 they had disappeared, and the blue sea was trembling with a delicate frail surface of green, the still sea lay one moment ahead, untouched, untouched since time began, in its watery loveliness.

Sometimes a ship's officer would come and peer over the edge, and look at him lying there. But nothing was said. People didn't like looking
20 over the edge. It was too beautiful, too pure and lovely, the Greater Day. They shoved their snouts a moment over the rail, then withdrew, faintly abashed, faintly sneering, faintly humiliated. After all, they showed snouts, nothing but snouts, to the unbegotten morning, so they might well be humiliated.

25 Sometimes an island, two islands, three, would show up, dismal and small, with the peculiar American gloom. No land! The soul wanted to see the land. Only the uninterrupted water was purely lovely, pristine.

And the third morning there was a school of porpoises leading the
30 ship. They stayed below surface all the time, so there was no hullabaloo of human staring. Only Gethin Day saw them. And what joy! what joy of life! what marvellous pure joy of being a porpoise within the great sea, of being many porpoises heading and mocking in translucent onrush the menacing, yet futile onrush of a vast ship!

35 It was a spectacle of the purest and most perfected joy in life that Gethin Day ever saw. The porpoises were ten or a dozen, round-bodied torpedo fish, and they stayed there as if they were not moving, always there, with no motion apparent, under the purely pellucid water, yet speeding on at just the speed of the ship, without the faintest show
40 of movement, yet speeding on in the most miraculous precision of

speed. It seemed as if the tail-flukes of the last fish exactly touched the ship's bows, under-water, with the frailest, yet precise and permanent touch. It seemed as if nothing moved, yet fish and ship swept on through the tropical ocean. And the fish moved, they changed places all the time. They moved in a little cloud, and with the most wonderful sport they were above, they were below, they were to the fore, yet all the time the same one speed, the same one speed, and the last fish just touching with his tail-flukes the iron cut-water of the ship. Some would be down in the blue, shadowy, but horizontally motionless in the same speed. Then with a strange revolution, these would be up in pale green water, and others would be down. Even the toucher, who touched the ship, would in a twinkling be changed. And ever, ever the same pure horizontal speed, sometimes a dark back skimming the water's surface light, from beneath, but never the surface broken. And ever the last fish touching the ship, and ever the others speeding in motionless, effortless speed, and intertwining with strange silkiness as they sped, intertwining among one another, fading down to the dark blue shadow, and strangely emerging again among the silent, swift others, in pale green water. All the time, so swift, they seemed to be laughing.

Gethin Day watched spell-bound, minute after minute, an hour, two hours, and still it was the same, the ship speeding, cutting the water, and the strong-bodied fish heading in perfect balance of speed underneath, mingling among themselves in some strange single laughter of multiple consciousness, giving off the joy of life, sheer joy of life, togetherness in pure complete motion, many lusty-bodied fish enjoying one laugh of life, sheer togetherness, perfect as passion. They gave off into the water their marvellous joy of life, such as the man had never met before. And it left him wonderstruck.

.... "But they know joy, they know pure joy!" he said to himself in amazement. "This is the most laughing joy I have ever seen, pure and unmixed. I always thought flowers had brought themselves to the most beautiful perfection in nature. But these fish, these fleshy, warm-bodied fish achieve more than flowers, heading along. This is the purest achievement of joy I have seen in all life: these strong, careless fish. Men have not got in them that secret to be alive together and make one like a single laugh, yet each fish going his own gait. This is sheer joy—and men have lost it, or never accomplished it. The cleverest sportsmen in the world are owls beside these fish. And the togetherness of love is nothing to the spinning unison of dolphins

playing under-sea. It would be wonderful to know joy as these fish
know it. The life of the deep waters is ahead of us, it contains sheer
togetherness and sheer joy. We have never got there—"

There as he leaned over the bow-sprit he was mesmerised by one
5   thing only, by joy, by joy of life, fish speeding in water with playful
joy. No wonder Ocean was still mysterious, when such red hearts beat
in it! No wonder man, with his tragedy, was a pale and sickly thing
in comparison! What civilisation will bring us to such a pitch of swift
laughing togetherness, as these fish have reached?

10   *3. The Atlantic*

The ship came in the night to Cuba, to Havana. When she became
still, Gethin Day looked out of his port-hole and saw little lights on
upreared darkness. Havana!

They went on shore next morning, through the narrow dock-streets
15   near the wharf, to the great boulevard. It was a lovely warm morning,
already early December, and the town was in the streets, going to mass,
or coming out of the big, unpleasant old churches. The Englishman
wandered with the two Danes for an hour or so, in the not-very
exciting city. Many Americans were wandering around, and nearly all
20   wore badges of some sort. The city seemed, on the surface at least,
very American. And underneath it did not seem to have any very deep
character of its own left.

The three men hired a car to drive out and about. The elder of the
Danes, a man of about forty-five, spoke fluent colloquial Spanish,
25   learned on the oil-fields of Tampico.* "Tell me," he said to the
chauffeur, "why do all these *americanos*, these Yankees, wear badges
on themselves?"

He spoke, as foreigners nearly always do speak of the Yankees, in
a tone of half-spiteful jeering.

30   "Ah, Señor," said the driver, with a Cuban grin. "You know they
all come here to drink.* They drink so much that they all get lost at
night, so they all wear a badge: name, name of hotel, place where it
is. Then our policemen find them in the night, turn them over as they
lie on the pavement, read name, name of hotel, and place, and so they
35   are put on a cart and carted to home. Ah, the season is only just
beginning. Wait a week or two, and they will lie in the streets at night
like a battle, and the police doing Red Cross work, carting them to
their hotels. Ah, los americanos! They are so good. You know they

own us now. Yes, they own us. They own Havana. We are a Republic*
owned by the Americans. Muy bien, we give them drink, they give
us money. Bah!"

And he grinned with a kind of acrid indifference. He sneered at the
whole show, but he wasn't going to do anything about it.

The car drove out to the famous beer-gardens, where all drank
beer—then to the inevitable cemetery, which almost rivalled that of
New Orleans*—"Every person buried in this cemetery guarantees to
put up a tomb-monument costing not less than fifty-thousand
dollars."—Then they drove past the new suburb of villas, springing
up neat and tidy, spick and span, same all the world over. Then they
drove out into the country, past the old sugar haciendas and to the
hills.

And to Gethin Day it was all merely depressing and void of real
interest. The Yankees owned it all. It had not much character of its
own. And what character it had was the peculiar, dreary character of
all America wherever it is a little abandoned. The peculiar gloom of
Connecticut or New Jersey, Louisiana or Georgia, a sort of dreariness
in the very bones of the land, that shows through immediately the
human effort sinks. How quickly the gloom and the inner dreariness
of Cuba must have affected the spirit of the Conquistadores, even
Columbus!*

They drove back to town and ate a really good meal, and watched
a stout American couple, apparently man and wife, lunching with a
bottle of champagne, a bottle of hock, and a bottle of burgundy for
the two of them, and apparently drinking them all at once. It made
one's head reel.

The bright, sunny afternoon they spent on the esplanade by the sea.
There the great hotels were still shut. But they had, so to speak, half
an eye open: a tea-room going, for example.

And Day thought again, how tedious the little day can be! How
difficult to spend even one Sunday looking at a city like Havana, even
if one has spent the morning driving into the country. The infinite
tedium of looking at things! the infinite boredom of things anyhow.
Only the rippling, bright, pale-blue sea, and the old fort, gave one the
feeling of life. The rest, the great esplanade, the great boulevard, the
great hotels, all seemed what they were, dead, dried concrete, concrete,
dried deadness.

Everybody was thankful to be back on the ship for dinner, in the
dark loneliness of the wharves. See Naples and die.* Go seeing

any place, and you'll be half dead of exhaustion and tedium by dinner-time.

So! goodbye, Havana! The engines were going before breakfast time. It was a bright blue morning. Wharves and harbour slid past, the high bows moved backwards. Then the ship deliberately turned her back on Cuba and the sombre shore, and began to move north, through the blue day, which passed like a sleep. They were moving now into wide space.*

The next morning they woke to greyness, grey low sky, and hideous low grey water, and a still air. Sandwiched between two greynesses, the long, wicked old ship sped on, as unto death.

"What has happened?" Day asked of one of the officers.

"We have come north, to get into the current running east. We come north about the latitude of New York, then we run due east with the stream."

"What a wicked shame!"

And indeed it was. The sun was gone, the blueness was gone, life was gone. The Atlantic was like a cemetery, an endless, infinite cemetery of greyness, where the bright, lost world of Atlantis* is buried. It was December, grey, dark December on a waste of ugly, dead-grey water, under a dead-grey sky.

And so they ran into a swell, a long swell whose oily, sickly waves seemed hundreds of miles long, and travelling in the same direction as the ship's course. The narrow cigar of a ship heaved up the upslope with a nauseating heave, up, up, up, till she righted for a second sickeningly on the top, then tilted, and her screw raced like a dentist's burr in a hollow tooth. Then down she slid, down the long, shivering downslope, leaving all her guts behind her, and the guts of all the passengers too. In an hour, everybody was deathly white, and sicklily grinning, thinking it a sort of joke that would soon be over. Then everybody disappeared, and the game went on: up, up, up, heavily up, till a pause, Ah!—then burr-rr-rr! as the screw came out of water and shattered every nerve. Then whoo-oosh! the long and awful downrush, leaving the entrails behind.

She was like a plague-ship,* everybody disappeared, stewards and everybody. Gethin Day felt as if he had taken poison: and he slept—slept, slept, slept, and yet was all the time aware of the ghastly motion—up, up, up, heavily up, then Ah! one moment, followed by the shattering burr-rr-rr! and the unspeakable ghastliness of the downhill slither, where death seemed inside the entrails, and water chattered like the after-death. He was aware of the hour-long moaning, moaning of the Spanish doctor's fat, pale Mexican wife, two cabins away. It went on for ever. Everything went on for ever. Everything was like this for ever, for ever. And he slept, slept, slept, for thirty hours, yet knowing it all, registering just the endless repetition of the motion, the ship's loud squeaking and chirruping, and the ceaseless moaning of the woman.

Suddenly at tea-time the second day he felt better. He got up. The ship was empty. A ghastly steward gave him a ghastly cup of tea, then disappeared. He dozed again, but came to dinner.

They were three people at the long table, in the horribly-travelling grey silence: himself, a young Dane, and the elderly, dried English-woman. She talked, talked. The three looked in terror at sauerkraut and smoked loin of pork. But they ate a little. Then they looked out on the utterly repulsive, grey, oily, windless night. Then they went to bed again.

The third evening it began to rain, and the motion was subsiding. They were running out of the swell. But it was an experience to remember.

[End of manuscript]

EXPLANATORY NOTES

EXPLANATORY NOTES

The Overtone

5:5   **a woman,** DHL originally wrote 'a naked woman' and at 13:35 'a man' was originally 'a naked man' (MS pp. 1, 9).

5:14   **the suffrage.** The Representation of the People Act of 1918 gave the vote to women over the age of thirty, but women did not reach equality of suffrage with men until 1928.

5:31   **the State-endowment of mothers.** Welfare payments to mothers as such. The topic had some interest for DHL, who twice mentioned it in *Mr Noon*, chap. VIII (written 1920–1), and much earlier in *The White Peacock*, part III, chap. VI (written 1906–9). State welfare for mothers was demanded by the Women's Suffrage movement and supported by the Fabian Society from the early 1900s; maternity allowances were not introduced until 1945.

6:2   **homespun** Clothes implying 'advanced' intellectual inclinations, stemming from the taste for the hand-made, the authentic and the simple fostered by the Arts and Crafts movement.

6:3   **changed for dinner:** I.e. into correct evening dress: dinner jacket (tuxedo) or long dress.

6:24   **the Soar.** The River Soar runs between Leicester and a few miles south of Nottingham, where it joins the Trent.

7:12   **Paisley** Town in Scotland where cloth in the so-called Paisley pattern (an oriental motif) was woven.

7:28   **He felt** [7:24]...**and nakedness.** This passage originally read: 'Yea, for who can see perfect nakedness?—only those that have known the clean, pure issue from all covering. She was up there, this perfect simple moon, a range beyond him. And it was like a butterfly settling on his glove, that he could see, but not feel. He wanted to unglov[e]' (MS p. 3).

7:35   **watched her** [7:29]...**cherished them,** DHL first wrote: 'wanted to be nearer her. Such a candour, such a perfect nakedness that is at last quite clothed in its own being. Quite clear and perfect in its own being, not full of unrealised darkness. He wanted to go nearer to her. And the moonlight glistened on the finger-tips of his wife as he cherished them,' (MS p. 3).

8:21   **dancing-green,** A piece of level grassy land used for dancing at holiday festivals.

8:27   **the form he had chosen.** Form, the nest or lair in which a hare crouches;

cf. DHL's earlier comparison of the glistening river to 'the starlit rush of a hare' (6:34–7).

9:1 **living [pupil] of an eye,** The conjectural emendation by the typist (adding 'pupil') which was incorporated in both first editions has been followed. DHL has used 'pupil' in the same context at 6:40; 7:18; 8:5; and 15:3–4.

9:27 **You wouldn't have...things off."** These lines were omitted from the first English edition; see the Introduction p. xxiv.

9:38 **the promised land** Canaan, which God promised Abraham that his offspring would possess; cf. Genesis xii. 1–7.

10:3 **They went [9:36]...gradually. For** This passage originally read: 'They had gone down to the bungalow, and gone to bed: and he had loved her. But it had been ⟨simply⟩ almost a ⟨makeshift⟩ formality. And ever since, it had been a sort of makeshift. And gradually, because it was never full of meaning, they had ceased to have one another. And' (MS p. 5). (An earlier deleted reading is given in single pointed brackets.)

10:12 **fencing with the foils.** I.e. unwilling actually to wound.

10:19 **on the Judgment Day.** 2 Peter ii. 9.

10:25 **taking off [10:21]...of herself.** When Moses sees the burning bush on Mount Horeb, God calls out from it: 'Draw not nigh hither: put off thy shoes from off thy feet, for the place whereon thou standest is holy ground' (Exodus iii. 5).

10:27 **Now that [10:8]...the night.** DHL originally wrote:
Now, looking at the night, he felt her denial of him then had been her one sin against him—almost her betrayal of him. And why had she done it? He did not know. It was either perversity, or unwillingness to give herself up, or fear. She had always kept herself. They had never, each of them, given themselves one to the other. That is, they had never loved. Yet they were made to love each other. They should have loved each other. They had failed. It made him writhe off his sofa and go out. He would be alone again with the night. Perhaps she had been afraid to meet him in utter nakedness. She had been afraid lest she should be too impure. Yet she was all purity. But she had been afraid to go into his communion, to partake of this Mystery, which is the core of all religion, which is the ⟨core⟩ heart of all life.—He went quietly out of the room. (MS p. 5)

11:8 **There** The MS originally read 'Yea there', but when DHL deleted 'Yea' he did not capitalise 'there'. The typist did not understand the deletion and typed 'Yea there'.

11:13 **comes with [11:6]...had waited** DHL first wrote: 'takes off the cover, when he lifts the heavy lid of cold away and lets them be born." She had come to him' (MS p. 6).

11:38 **beggar.** DHL wrote 'beggar upwards.' and then deleted the second word, but the typist included it.

12:24 **"Many times...not why.** Cf. Peter's triple denial of Jesus, Mathew xxvi. 33–5, 69–75; Mark xiv. 29–31, 66–72.

13:8 **"Like a garden** [12:7]...**shut chalice."** Cf. The Song of Solomon, especially iv. 10–16.

13:14 **Pan is dead."** See the Introduction pp. xxii–xxiii; cf. 'Pan in America', collected in *Phoenix: The Posthumous Papers of D. H. Lawrence*, ed. Edward D. McDonald (1936), especially pp. 22–3.

14:20 **a sort of fakir pleasure.** A fakir is a Moslem religious mendicant given to self-mortification; hence, a pleasure at denying one's own needs.

14:33 **look under** In the MS these words have been deleted and 'remove' substituted by another hand. This alteration was adopted in the typed carbon copy and the published versions of the story.

14:36 **grown into their limbs, like Hercules' garment."** Out of jealousy, Hercules' wife Deianeira sent him a robe smeared with poisoned blood which clung to his flesh and was so painful that he killed himself.

15:26 **If once...a cross** Cf. Algernon Charles Swinburne (1837–1909), 'Hymn to Proserpine' (1866), lines 23–4: 'Wilt thou yet take all, Galilean? but these thou shalt not take, / The laurel, the palms and the paean, the breasts of the nymphs in the brake.'

15:37 **Dionysos,** The Greek god Dionysus, object of an ecstatic cult, especially among women, who took to the mountains and woods as maenads in fawnskins and masks, dancing and swinging thyrsi and phallic symbols, and singing. They might seize on an animal, even a child, tear it to pieces and devour it raw as a sacramental meal. Dionysus was also identified as Bacchus, god of wine, so satyrs (cf. 14:33), woodland spirits, part-human part-goat, and sileni joined the maenads in their orgies. Maenads represent a liberation from ordinary social life and initiation into the deeper or wilder life epitomised by Pan, and also alluded to in this story via fauns (14:21), Pan's goat-footed attendants, and nymphs (13:17), maidens personifying the spirit of springs, rivers, woods and lonely places. An important background influence is Nietzsche, who emphasised the demonic in Greek religion and culture, and opposed the influence of Dionysus to that of the sun-god Apollo, representing daylight reason.

16:14 **I will set...chase him.** Diana (or Artemis), bathing naked, was surprised by the hunter Actaeon. She turned him into a stag, and his hounds tore him to pieces.

17:16 **"Both moving** [16:38]...**from them.** This final section is written in smaller handwriting and appears to have been added to the story when DHL revised it. See Introduction p. xxiii. DHL originally continued (after 'from them.') with 'They were as' (MS p. 12), but then deleted these three words.

St. Mawr

21:15 *museau,* Muzzle or snout of an animal; used colloquially of the human face (French).

22:37 **the Rotonde** A brasserie-restaurant in the Boulevard Raspail, in Paris, traditionally frequented by artists and writers.

23:6 **charge of grape-shot.** Small cast-iron balls, strongly connected together, used against personnel. The allusion is to the 'whiff of grapeshot' with which Napoleon cleared the streets of Paris in 1795.

23:10   **feel it in the air.** I The omission in the printed text was probably due to the repetition of 'I feel'.

23:21   **Les Halles.** The old central market of Paris.

25:14   *Apache* A red-indian tribe in the southwestern USA; a gangster (French loan-word).

25:30   **the Park** [25:24]…the Row, Rotten Row in Hyde Park was (and is still) used for exercising on horseback.

25:36   **the Bois de Boulogne**…the Pincio: Fashionable parks in Paris and Rome.

26:7   **argus-eyes** Argus or Argos, a monster in Greek mythology, a guardian or sentinel with a third eye in the back of his neck; or four eyes, two before and two behind; or many eyes.

26:21   **Arthur Balfour,** (1848–1930). Prime minister 1902–5; first lord of the admiralty 1915–16; foreign secretary 1916–19; lord president of the council 1919–22 (when he was created an Earl) and 1925–9. He combined his full-time political career with a deep interest in philosophy, writing several books.

27:19   **a mews** A range of stables in a town, originally serving the large houses nearby, often converted into fashionable residences.

27:33   **your Ladyship** Brett sometimes typed 'Your Ladyship' (27:40) and 'my lady' (30:17); DHL corrected some of these to lower-case for the adjective and capitals for the noun (29:19), and his preferred practice has been adopted.

27:34   **Poppy** At the ranch in New Mexico where DHL lived from 1924–5 his sorrel mare was also called Poppy. Cf. DHL's letter to Baroness von Richthofen, 28 June 1924.

28:11   *St. Mawr!*" St Maurus was an obscure Christian saint who in 543 founded the Abbey of St Maur-sur-Loire in France. The French name Maur may have been conflated with the Welsh word Mawr meaning 'big' or 'great'. Cf. Keith Sagar, *D. H. Lawrence: A Calendar of His Works* (1979), p. 139.

28:18   **Isn't that the ticket,** 'Isn't that right, what's wanted' (slang).

30:31   **Christmas walnut.** I.e. something that has been kept too long.

31:2   **red with power.** See Revelation vi. 4 and Frederick Carter's letter of 7 May 1952 to Harry T. Moore in which he described DHL's visit to Pontesbury 3–5 January 1924 to discuss the manuscript of his book, *The Dragon of the Alchemists* (1926): 'From this came the landscape background of *St Mawr* and the red horse itself' Nehls, ii. 515 n. 43. Cf. *Apocalypse and the writings on Revelation*, ed. Mara Kalnins (Cambridge, 1980), pp. 101–4. Carter was the model for Cartwright (see note on 64:30).

32:15   **May we offer the penny?**" From the adage: a penny for your thoughts.

34:18   *suffisance.* Self-sufficiency, self-confidence (French).

34:32 **Mahomet would go *all* the way, to that mountain.** An allusion to the proverb: 'If the mountain will not go to Mahomet, Mahomet must go to the mountain.'

35:17 **Hippolytus,** Virgin-prince, and son of Theseus, falsely accused of raping his step-mother Phaedra: portrayed in Euripides' *Hippolytus* and Racine's *Phèdre* (1677). The name means literally 'killed by horses'. Hippolytus was a keen huntsman and charioteer, and was killed when he attacked a sea-monster which frightened his horses and caused them to bolt, dragging him along the ground.

36:4 **posting.** The English style of riding, with short stirrups and bent legs, rising and falling in the saddle with the horse's movement, in contrast with the American straight-leg style.

37:8 **Medusa** One of the Gorgons, who turned to stone anyone who met her gaze.

38:30 **Queen Alexandra,** (1844–1925). Widow of King Edward VII of England, and mother of George V.

41:39 **Claridge's...the Carlton,** Claridge's Hotel (specialising in royalty) and the Carlton Club are both in fashionable areas of central London.

42:4 **Barmecide food,** Reference to a prince of Baghdad in the *Arabian Nights* who entertained a beggar with a succession of empty dishes pretending that they contained a sumptuous feast.

42:15 **the season** The London season was from May to July when the Court and fashionable society were in town, went to the theatre and opera, gave balls and dinners, etc. Gentry would devote a season to 'bringing out' their débutante daughters.

42:29 **Mrs Witt's "cottage"...big Church.** Cf. Frederick Carter's Georgian rectory in Pontesbury ('Chomesbury') which similarly overlooked the churchyard (Nehls, ii. 314, 316).

42:34 **the Dean or one of the curates** Cf. Frederick Carter's description of the new High Church vicar at Pontesbury, and his curate, to whom DHL took an instant dislike (Nehls, ii. 316–17).

43:31 **a bit of a reverence,** A quick bow or curtsy.

44:12 **"My own country has gone dry,"** Prohibition of the manufacture, transportation and sale of alcoholic beverages in the USA lasted from the Volstead Act of 1919 to the 21st Amendment of 1933.

44:19 **sewing-bee..."social,"...Band of Hope meeting,** A sewing-bee is a meeting of neighbours to unite their labours (sewing, in this case) for the benefit of one of their number. A social is a gathering with music and dancing. The Band of Hope (*c.* 1847) is a young persons' temperance association.

45:12 **weight, even in gold.** The typescript (p. 36) reads 'weight in, ⟨gold⟩ even in gold.' Apparently DHL failed to delete the first 'in' when revising the phrase.

47:34 **in the picture,** Rather self-consciously part of a well-composed scene; cf. 179:10–11.

47:34   **white flannels** Trousers worn in the summer, especially for sport or leisure.

48:32   **Belle-Mère!"** 'Mother-in-law' (French). This and other accents were typed as '-Mère' in TS.

55:35   **"'*Those maids...their generation.*'** Unidentified.

57:7   **the fates.** In classical legend the Fates or Moirai were represented as three old women allotting a new-born child's span of life. One spins the thread of life, another measures its length, and the third cuts it short with her shears.

57:17   **bobbed hair** Cut short, the fashion of 'advanced' young women in the 1920s. Cf. the Princess (165:11–12) and the Hon. Laura Ridley (123:10).

59:29   **our sort of** DHL must have substituted this phrase for 'most' in the Knopf proofs; it is obviously a considered alteration that is intended to defend Lewis from both women's imputations.

60:36   **"Louise," she** [60:5]**...like Lewis."** This passage originally read:
"Well mother, I don't. Men think such a lot of bosh. One gets so frightfully tired of it."
"But Louise, the animals are the same as we are. They have the same emotions and the same desires as we do, in a rough way. Only they can't think. They can't use their *minds*, not having any minds, in the human sense."
"I don't care whether they minds [sic] or not, mother. Look at St. Mawr, how wonderful he is! I'd hate him to have a mind like Dean Vyner. I'm tired of men, mother. I'm simply tired with them."
"Very well! I don't blame you," said Mrs Witt. "But you'd soon be tired of St. Mawr. Think of the limitation. You can't have any kind of finer *intimacy* with a horse." (TS pp. 56–7)

61:7   **dead. Most** [61:1]**...of it."** DHL first wrote (TS p. 57):
ashy, where does it come from, mother? That's the mystery to me."
"From the same place as our life comes from, Louise."

61:29   **once we...know, Louise."** DHL originally wrote (TS p. 58):
worth working for, mother."
"I don't agree, Louise."

62:27   **If only they** [62:19]**...that way."** This originally read (TS p. 59):
Though they are not by any means servile, mother."
"No indeed!" said Mrs Witt.
"Perhaps something in them is just wanting."

62:34   *empressé* Eager, fervent (French).

63:2   **the Devil's Chair.** Frederick Carter recalled a walk he and DHL took from Pontesbury to the brow of Crowsnest Dingle and on to the Devil's Chair which is the largest rock on Stiperstones, the ridgeway running south from Crowsnest (Nehls, ii. 317–18).

64:2   **the bottomless pit.** Revelation xx. 1–3.

64:5   **as if virtue had gone out of him.** Mark v. 25–34.

64:30   **an artist** [64:16]**...frustration.** Cartwright is modelled on Frederick

Carter (1883–1967), painter and etcher. See Nehls, ii. 514–15 n. 43 and the introduction to *Apocalypse*, ed. Kalnins, pp. 3ff.

64:40 **King Edward.** King Edward VII (reigned, 1901–10), well known for his many amours. For deletion of this sentence from 200 copies of the first English edition, see the Introduction p. xxix.

65:12 **Mr Wells' Outline** *The Outline of History* by H. G. Wells was published in 1920.

65:31 **third eye** It is believed that all men possess a third eye, which is the focus of occult power, in the middle of the forehead. The phrase is used in *Apocalypse*, ed. Kalnins, p. 107.

73:1 **Aldecar Chapel** Probably modelled on the chapel of Lordshill, south of Pontesbury. Cf. Nehls, ii. 317.

74:26 **a brick,** A good-hearted person (middle-class slang).

86:8 *Pino real...cedro,* Pino real: regal pine (Spanish); this term can refer to any giant tree, but DHL probably meant the ponderosa pine (*Pinus ponderosa*). Pinavete: fir tree (Spanish); probably the Douglas fir (*Pseudotsuga menziesii*). Piñón: 'nut' pine (*Pinus monophylla*). Cedro: cedar (Spanish); any of several species of juniper (*Juniperacaea*).

87:31 **a bit thick,** Rather excessive (middle-class slang).

88:13 **an order** I.e. an order by a court of law.

89:15 *My head...runneth over* Cf. Psalms xxiii. 5 ['thou anointest my head with oil: my cup runneth over'].

90:22 **a seated pillar of salt,** Like Lot's wife (Genesis xix. 26); cf. 151: 40.

92:25 *Oh Death where is thy sting-a-ling-a-ling?* Cf. 1 Corinthians xv. 55. The main phrase is used in the Church of England service, the Burial of the Dead. Mrs Witt is quoting a parody in a popular song, ending:

> Oh Death, where is thy sting-a-ling-a-ling,
> Oh grave, thy victory?
> The bells of hell go ting-a-ling-a-ling
> For you and not for me.

92:28 *drab slicker,* Fawn-coloured waterproof raincoat.

93:7 **elegies in a country churchyard,** Allusion to *An Elegy written in a Country Churchyard* (1751) by Thomas Gray (1716–71).

93:14 **Kind Words Can Never Die,** First line (and title) of a gospel hymn written by Sister Abby Hutchinson, one of a group of evangelists who toured Unionist camps during the American Civil War.

93:21 **Amazon** Mythical tribe of female warriors, hostile to men.

97:6 **The very apples...inside them.** Reference to the tree of knowledge of good and evil in the Garden of Eden (Genesis ii. 9, 17).

97:35 *Ay, qué gozo!* 'Oh, what a joy!' (Spanish).

101:36   **the Prince of Wales.** Edward (1894–1972), Prince of Wales, became King Edward VIII from January to December 1936, when he abdicated. In March 1922 DHL saw the Prince at Kandy; see letter to Lady Cynthia Asquith, 30 April 1922.

101:39   *Dio benedetto!* 'Blessed God!' (Italian).

102:26   **Cleopatra only...in wine,** Cleopatra (69–30 B.C.) is said by Plutarch to have dissolved a pearl ear-drop in her drink at a banquet in order to impress Mark Antony with her wealth. After Antony's defeat at Actium in 30 B.C. she is supposed to have taken her own life by means of the bite of an asp. Plutarch, 'Life of Antony', *Parallel Lives.*

104:7   **chétif,** Puny (French).

106:39   **puther** Pother, disturbance, commotion (provincial English).

109:11   **make anything...some don't.** DHL first wrote: 'get my bread and butter out of these sort of things. It's nothing but childishness as you say' (TS p. 122).

109:14   **I don't...believe in.** This originally read: 'where you people believe in God, I believe in these sort of things' (TS p. 122).

111:5   **gunpowder. They're...gun, Mam."** This passage first read: 'all sorts of things, like expensive cake. Like you"' (TS p. 125).

111:20   **An anger...set impassive** DHL first wrote: 'A profound, congenital, insurmountable anger' (TS p. 125).

113:19   **Shylock demanding...shekels.** Cf. *The Merchant of Venice* IV. i.

113:29   **Fiorita: or perhaps Florecita.** 'Little flower' (Italian and Spanish respectively).

113:31   *The Collyposy!* An obscure joke; but perhaps the old servant means 'the cauliflower', which looks like a posy or tight bunch of flowers. The logic of the reference would be that just as Rico glamorises the English Flora ('flower') by calling it exotic foreign equivalents like 'Florecita', so William dignifies the humble cauliflower by calling it 'collyposy'. It would be the '*best posy that grow*' because you can eat it. DHL made a similar joke in *Mr Noon*: 'the cauliflower was the abiding blossom...the cauliflower is the flower of human happiness', chap. IX in *Phoenix II: Uncollected, Unpublished and Other Prose Works by D. H. Lawrence*, ed. Warren Roberts and Harry T. Moore (1968).

113:35   *Mademoiselle de Maupin.* Novel (1835) by Théophile Gautier (1811–72) in which the heroine rides about disguised as a man.

114:19   **Flora...the goddess of flowers,** Flora was the Roman deity of fertility and flowers.

114:27   **Priapus** Greek god of fertility and of gardens, normally represented as a grotesque little man with large genitals.

115:1   **like the Yankee at the Court of King Arthur,** Hank Morgan in *A Connecticut Yankee in King Arthur's Court* (1889) by Mark Twain (1835–1910).

115:24   **Father Abraham.** God made Abraham 'a father of many nations' in his covenant with him (Genesis xvii. 1–8); so Phoenix wants to raise a chosen race of horses from St. Mawr.

116:9　**Cassandra preparing...in dying.** Cassandra may have been raped by Ajax, son of Ileus, at the altar of Athena during the sack of Troy, cf. Virgil, *Aeneid* ii. 406. In Euripides' *Iphigenia in Tauris* Iphigenia discovers that as a priestess she is required to sacrifice her own brother, Orestes. Adonis was gored to death by a boar in front of his lover, Aphrodite. On his deathbed King Charles II (1660–85) is said to have apologised for being 'an unconscionable time dying'.

116:20　*Oh my love is like a rred rred rrose!* 'A red red Rose' (1794), line 1, by Robert Burns (1759–96) ['O my Luve's like a red, red rose,'].

117:35　**László...Orpen,** Philip Alexius László (1869–1937) and Sir William Newenham Montague Orpen (1878–1931) were fashionable society portrait painters.

118:5　**pig in clover,** Proverbial phrase for gross self-indulging.

120:20　*Noli me tangere, homine!* Cf. the Vulgate, John xx. 17. Jesus is speaking to Mary Magdalene, while in the text the words are addressed to a man.

120:33　*the Corpus delicti!* The sum or aggregate of the ingredients which make a given fact a breach of a given law.

123:4　**The Honorable Laura Ridley.** Probably modelled on the Hon. Dorothy Eugénie Brett (1883–1977), like the Princess (see note below on 159:2), the Honourable Miss James in 'The Last Laugh', and Carlotta Fell, later Lady Lathkill, in 'Glad Ghosts' (the latter two written January–April 1924 and December 1925, respectively). In all cases the resemblances are superficial.

129:6　**Prohibition!** See note on 44:12.

129:16　**"Plus ça...mieux ici,** 'The more things change, the more they stay the same'...'One is no better here' (French).

129:37　**As they neared Havana [128:17]...the universe.** This journey reverses that which DHL took in November 1923 from Vera Cruz to England, and which he draws on again in 'The Flying-Fish' (see note below on 217:7).

130:31　**a pearl before swine,** See Matthew vii. 6.

131:29　**Zane Grey.** American writer (1875–1939) of best-selling Westerns.

132:25　**Coué** Systematic auto-suggestion, usually of a sanguine kind (from Emile Coué, 1857–1926, French psychologist).

132:39　**"Ça ne change jamais** 'It never changes' (French).

136:8　**cocotte** Loose woman, tart (French).

137:3　**with that furtive...not detected!** DHL originally wrote: 'so unbrokenly, all-of-a-piece stupid' (TS p. 154).

137:12　*Merci, mon cher!* 'No thank you, my dear!' (French).

138:19　**"*Quién sabe!*"** 'Who knows!' (Spanish).

138:38　**the Vestal Virgins...old temples.** Four, later six, virgins from the Roman patrician families served for thirty years of their lives at the Temple of Vesta, the goddess of the blazing hearth. They had to remain virgin and were charged with keeping the goddess's sacred fire always alight in the Temple.

238	*Explanatory notes*

139:6   **mesa** Table-land, plateau, especially in the southwestern USA; from Spanish.

139:31   **Apollo mystery of the inner fire.** Among his other attributes, Apollo was called Phoebus (the bright) as a god of light sometimes identified with the sun As a god of purification, prophecy and oracles he was also the object of mystic cults.

141:33   **to be got** Brett typed 'to the ⟨good⟩ be got'; DHL failed to delete the extraneous 'the'.

142:9   **little tumble-down ranch** [140:35]...**Mexican village.** Cf. DHL's description of Kiowa Ranch to his niece Margaret King, 31 August 1924: 'Forty years ago a man came out looking for gold, and squatted here. There was some gold in the mountains. Then he got poor, and a man called McClure had the place. He had 500 white goats here, raised alfalfa, and let his goats feed wild in the mountains. But the water supply is too bad, and we are too far from anywhere. So he gave up.'

143:8   **padres!** Male animals of the herd, fathers (Spanish).

143:31   **pithed, to use one of Kipling's words.** Cf. Rudyard Kipling's 'With the Night Mail' (1905), collected in *Actions and Reactions* (1909). The pith is the flesh or 'goodness' of a plant or fruit.

144:27   **before the hot-blooded ithyphallic column ever erected itself.** DHL theorises about the phallic pine-tree at Kiowa Ranch at greater length in 'Pan in America', *Phoenix*, pp. 24–6.

145:32   **adobe** Brick of unfired earth dried in the sun (Spanish).

146:15   **like pillars of cloud by day,** Cf. Exodus xiii. 21.

148:20   **columbines...dove** Columbines are also known as 'dove's plant'; 'columbine' means 'dove-like'.

151:7   **Every new stroke...fleece of gold.** In classical myth an unsleeping dragon guarded both the golden apples of the Hesperides and the golden fleece.

151:15   **An Augean stables of metallic filth.** One of the labours of Hercules was to cleanse in one day the dung that had accumulated in the stables of the vast herds of cattle belonging to Augeas, king of Elis.

151:40   **Las Chivas.** 'The Goats' (Spanish).

152:5   **arroyo,** Watercourse, stream (Spanish).

152:34   **cold egg,** Abandoned by the mother-bird, incapable of hatching.

The Princess

159:2   **The Princess.** For DHL's use of Dorothy Brett as a model for the Princess see the Introduction p. xxxi and note on 123:4. Moore first pointed out DHL's use of the fairy tale of the sleeping beauty in this story in *The Intelligent Heart* (1954, rev. edn 1974 as *The Priest of Love*, p. 393). In both Giambattista Basile's and Charles Perrault's versions, when the princess fails to wake up she is raped by a king.

159:9   **Colin Urquhart** [159:4]...**not Stuart.** Colin Urquhart is very loosely modelled on Dorothy Brett's father, Reginald Baliol Brett, the second Viscount Esher (1852–1930), who had an ancestral castle in Scotland. The royal house of Stuart became kings of England with the accession of James VI of Scotland to the English throne as James I in 1603; the connection with the Stuarts ended with the death of Queen Anne in 1714, though the Old and Young Pretenders attempted to return in 1715 and 1745.

159:17   **old Celtic hero...Ossianic past.** Ossian or Oisin, the son of Fingal, was a legendary Gaelic bard and warrior of the third century A.D. In the 1760s James MacPherson published heroic poems which he falsely claimed to have translated from the Gaelic of Ossian.

159:24   **Miss Prescott from New England.** Brett's mother was Belgian. However one of her aunts (Isabella) married a Colonel Arthur Prescott by whom she had three daughters. The name might have been suggested to DHL in this way.

160:31   **contadina...ayah:** Peasant woman...nurse, children's governess (Italian; Indian).

161:31   *noblesse oblige.* In the 'Epilogue', written in September 1924 for the second edition of *Movements in European History* (1925), DHL introduced 'the old motto, *Noblesse Oblige. Noblesse* means, having the gift of power... obliges a man to act with fearlessness and generosity, responsible for his acts to God. A noble is one who may be known before all men' (*Movements*, ed. J. T. Boulton, Oxford, 1971, p. 319).

161:37   **"My little Princess** [161:2]...**you have—"** For the origins of Colin Urquhart's references to fairy royalty in the Tuatha De Danaan (the legendary fairy folk of ancient Ireland), see the Introduction pp. xxx–xxxi.

162:6   **a changeling** A fairy child surreptitiously left in place of a human one by the fairies.

162:8   **Milan point,** Fine, hand-made lace from Milan.

162:36   **the Nibelung poems.** *Das Nibelungenlied* (*The Song of the Nibelungs*) is a medieval German heroic epic poem; it became a source of Wagner's *Ring* cycle.

163:10   **Caliban...the pool of the perfect lotus,** Cf. *The Tempest* IV. i. 181–4. According to Buddhist belief, when the open lotus flower rests on the water (of universal consciousness) facing the sun, it stands for Nirvana, the ultimate repose of the soul.

166:29   **the March of Empire,** Cf. 'Westward the course of empire takes its way' in *On the Prospect of Planting Arts and Learning in America* (1752) by Bishop George Berkeley (1685–1753), stanza 6, line 1.

166:34   **Rancho del Cerro Gordo** 'Big Hill Ranch' (Spanish). This is modelled on Del Monte Ranch, Questa, New Mexico, where the Lawrences lived from December 1922 to March 1923.

167:26   **the Wilkiesons,** For their resemblance to William and Rachel Hawk, who ran a dude ranch at Del Monte Ranch, see the Introduction p. xxxi.

168:6   As if...*raison d'être*, This phrase was omitted from both first editions when either the typist or the typesetter skipped from the first to the second '*raison d'être*'.

168:9   **Penitentes.** Los Hermanos Penitentes or the Penitent Brothers is a religious organisation in New Mexico that traces its origin to the sixteenth-century Spanish conquistadors. They celebrate the Passion of Christ with rituals which include flagellant exercises in their Lenten ceremonies, in order to expiate their sins through physical suffering. See Warren A. Beck, *New Mexico: A History of Four Centuries* (University of Oklahoma Press: Norman, 1962), pp. 218–25.

170:11   **half in love with death.** Cf. John Keats, 'Ode to a Nightingale' (1819): 'for many a time / I have been half in love with easeful Death,' lines 51–2.

172:22   **placer** A deposit of sand or earth in the bed of a stream containing particles of valuable minerals, especially gold; from Spanish. The Taos Mountains have both a Placer Creek (near Black Mountain) and a Placer Fork (near Lobo Peak).

173:6   **Frijoles canyon,"** Northeast of Taos, the Frijoles Canyon runs south of Pueblo Peak to join the Rio Pueblo de Taos. A 'frijol' is any kind of food bean in Spanish.

174:36   **the San Cristobal canyon.** San Cristobal Creek runs from Lobo Peak through the village of San Cristobal into the Rio Grande. For similarities between this journey and the expedition to the Lobo Peak which Brett and Rachel Hawk organised for DHL in 1924, see the Introduction pp. xxxi–xxxii and Brett 149–52.

175:13   **buckskin** A horse of light yellowish dun colour, often with a dark stripe down the back, and a dark mane and tail (chiefly western and southwestern USA).

177:2   **don't take no notice** On this and several other occasions (179:38, 182:7 and 192:24) the MS text has been preferred, as it appears probable that DHL's deliberate use of incorrect English has been 'corrected' by the publisher or printer of the *Calendar*. Cf. 184:4.

178:21   **Rio Grande canyon.** See DHL to John Middleton Murry from Del Monte Ranch, Questa, 30 December 1922: 'It is good fun on this ranch – quite wild – Rocky Mts – desert with Rio Grande canyon away spreading below...' Originating in the San Juan Mountains, the Rio Grande cuts its path south through the New Mexican desert, and serves as the border between Texas and Mexico before flowing into the Gulf of Mexico.

179:1   **like petals...their petals** The typist's eye must have skipped from 'like petals' at the end of one line in MS to 'their petals' at the end of the next, and so this line was omitted from all subsequent texts.

180:14   **stand-back** Fall-back; reserve.

181:1   **Mexicans...drive out the whites.** Not identified. Hispanics struggled in the Southwest to keep their land (guaranteed by treaty with Mexico): in the late nineteenth century they used violence, e.g. burning of property, terrorisation, against white settlers and companies.

184:24   **a round pool...green.** See Introduction p. xxxii.

186:14   **bootleg whiskey** Whisky illicitly distilled and sold during the period of Prohibition; see note on 44:12.

Explanatory notes

241

188:22 **"What? What...the bunk.** Since it is not known whether DHL deleted these lines himself, or whether they were accidentally omitted by the typist or typesetter (they are not likely to have been censored), they have been restored in this edition.

191:5 **tarn,** Small mountain lake, fed from below, having no obvious tributaries.

194:17 **Pen.,"** State Penitentiary (USA slang).

194:37 **rock, watching** [194:29]...**have called** These two omissions are obvious examples of eye-skip, probably by the typist. In the first, one complete line from MS was omitted. At 194:36 the typist probably skipped from the first 'have' to the second, which was immediately beneath on the next line of the MS.

Appendix I: The Wilful Woman

199:24 **a woman approaching forty.** Mrs Mabel Dodge Luhan, née Ganson (1879–1962), was the model for the 'wilful woman'. See Introduction, pp. xix–xxi.

199:36 **Mr Hercules...picked up a snake long ago,** The infant Hercules strangled two serpents which the jealous Hera had sent to kill him in his cot.

200:29 **La Junta** [200:9]...**Trinidad...Lamy** Railway junctions in eastern Colorado, near the southern border of Colorado and near Santa Fe, New Mexico, respectively. Lamy was the nearest station to Taos.

201:19 **One dead...Mark** Cf. Introduction p. xvii.

201:24 **alternately torn** [201:19]...**do for him.** The third husband is first compared to Osiris of the torn limbs (whose fragments Isis searched for the world over, though she finally failed to retrieve his phallus). He is then down-graded to Humpty-Dumpty of the nursery rhyme whom 'All the king's horses and all the king's men / Couldn't put...together again.'

201:28 **the Meurice** Hotel Meurice, in the rue de Rivoli, Paris, and once known as 'the hotel of kings'.

201:29 **Napoleon III or Gambetta** Charles Louis Napoleon Bonaparte (1808–73), the third son of Louis Bonaparte, brother of Napoleon I, and of Hortense de Beauharnis; emperor of the French 1852–70. Léon Gambetta (1838–82), French republican statesman who came to prominence at the fall of Napoleon III.

201:33 **Ex-Princesses of Saxony,... or Matisse.** In 1902 crown-princess Louise of Saxony absconded with her children's French tutor to Paris, causing a scandal. Gabriele d'Annunzio (1863–1938) was an Italian novelist, poet and dramatist, and a flamboyant public figure. Eleanora Duse (1859–1924) was a leading Italian actress whose romantic liaison with d'Annunzio led to her frequent performances of his dramatic poems in Paris and elsewhere. Isadora Duncan (1878–1927), the American dancer, also with a stormy emotional life, made her reputation in Europe, especially France, where she died. Henri Matisse (1869–1954), the French artist, spent much of his life in Paris.

202:14 **Italian Mansion on Lake Erie.** Mabel Luhan was born in the Ganson mansion at Buffalo on Lake Erie.

202:33   **the wilderness of the temptation,** Allusion to Christ's temptation by Satan in the wilderness (Matthew iv. 1–11).

202:37   **Japanese dwarf-trees,** Bonsais; Japanese potted trees cultivated in miniature form.

203:5   **like the black queen** Probably a misremembered reference to the White Queen, in Lewis Carroll's *Through the Looking Glass* (1872), whom Alice picks up from the hearth and deposits on the chess-table in the opening chapter.

203:13   **Wagon-Mound,** Railway station in New Mexico between Lamy and Trinidad.

Appendix II: The Flying-Fish

207:5   **the lost town of South Mexico,** DHL stayed in Oaxaca, Mexico in November 1924 and February 1925. Oaxaca provides the model for the opening setting of this fragment. Cf. DHL's letter to Martin Secker of 9 December 1924: 'The little town of Oaxaca is lonely, away in the south and miles from anywhere except the Indian villages of the hills.' The mountains to the south are the Sierra Madre del Sur.

207:14   *tierra caliente,* 'Hot land or region' (Spanish). Here the specific reference is to the coastal lowlands of the Isthmus of Tehuantepec.

207:20   **the Mayas, the Zapotecas and the Aztecs.** The Mayan civilisation enjoyed two periods of prosperity in pre-Columbian Mexico, the Old Empire (A.D. 500–900) and the New Empire (ninth–eleventh centuries). After the break-up of the New Empire into nomadic tribes, the Mixtecs and Zapotecs settled in the mountains round Oaxaca. The Aztecs founded Mexico City in 1325 and increased their hold over much of the country during the next two centuries until Cortés defeated them in the 1520s.

207:28   **Reina de noche.** A common name for more than one plant which blooms at night and exudes a heavy fragrance. Although DHL here and in *The Plumed Serpent* gives the name as 'Buena de Noche', he must be mistaken; cf. also 'They call them Noche Buenas, flowers of Christmas Eve' in 'Market Day' (*Mornings in Mexico*, 1927). 'Flor de Nochebuena' is the name for the poinsetta.

208:5   **Daybrook...Ashleydale joins in.** DHL has situated his imaginary Elizabethan manor in Derbyshire. Crich lies between Eastwood and Matlock. There is an Ashleyhay to the south-west. DHL doubtless borrowed the name 'Daybrook' from a village now a northern suburb of Nottingham.

208:10   *Book of Days,* Apart from the pun, DHL seems to be modelling Sir Gilbert's *Book of Days* on a late medieval Book of Hours (i.e. the seven canonical 'hours' of prayer), an illuminated book of devotions for private use.

208:12   **sailed the Spanish seas** In the sixteenth century the Carribean Sea was known as the Spanish Main. Under Elizabeth I many English buccaneers made their fortunes by plundering Spanish bullion ships or making raids on the coastal towns of New Spain, as Mexico was then called.

208:19   **the floods shall not cover the Vale** Cf. Genesis vi–ix.

208:33   **to come into your own.** " I.e. to enter into your inheritance (both property or title and, in this context, self-possession).

210:34   **por amor de Dios!** 'For the love of God' (Spanish).

210:38   **Mixtec,** See note on 207:20.

212:2   **Little revolutions** Adolfo de la Huerta (1881–1955), after participating in a successful revolution, served as provisional president May–December 1920 until Obregón was elected; he then became Minister of Finance. In 1923 de la Huerta rebelled against the government in opposition to the official presidential candidate, and, though he won the support of a large part of the army, he was eventually defeated and driven into exile in the spring of 1924; at least 7000 people died, and the Obregón regime was seriously shaken. DHL's 'little revolutions' probably refers to the dozens of local, particularist uprisings which were the manifestations of the national revolution. The country remained unsettled until the new president took office in 1925. Cf. DHL's letter to Murry, 15 November 1924: 'The country is always unsettled.' See also Brett 175 and Nehls, ii. 315.

212:5   **barranca,** Gorge or ravine (Spanish).

213:2   **the flying-fish on the roof.** See the Introduction p. xxxiv. In the plot summary for 'The Weather-Vane' DHL writes: 'weather-vane is a fish...When woman's thoughts turn on herself Fish turns his belly up.' Finally she tries 'to reverse the vane again: lightning kills her'. Tedlock, *Lawrence MSS* 57.

213:16   **a station connected with old silver mines,** Possibly Ejutla.

213:34   **Los venados!** 'The deer!' (Spanish).

214:10   **a small square town,** Tehuacán; cf. letter to Luis Quintanilla, ?11 November 1924 in which DHL describes the route from Mexico City to Oaxaca via Esperanza and Tehuacán.

214:20   **the Tlaxcala tribe.** The Tlaxcaltec Indians settled in Tlaxcala, east of Mexico City. They held out against the Aztecs and sided with Cortes in his advance on Mexico City. Tlaxcala is the smallest state in modern Mexico.

214:21   **"Quiere helados, Señor?"** 'Would you like ice-cream, Sir?' (Spanish).

214:25   **"Gracias!...Patrón!** 'No, thank you!...Master, Patron' (Spanish).

214:33   **Lasciate ogni...voi ch'uscite.** Abandon all hope, you who enter...Lose all tears, you who depart (Italian). The first is the inscription over the gate of Hell in Dante's *Inferno* iii. 9.

215:3   **to the junction with the main-line...Gulf of Mexico.** The junction is Esperanza; cf. Brett 166. In 1888 the Interoceanic Railway Company was formed in London to amalgamate existing narrow-gauge lines into a single system linking Vera Cruz with Mexico City and eventually with Acapulco. It never completed the westerly link, but its line to Vera Cruz offered easier gradients and a safer ride than its rival, the Mexican Railway Company.

215:8   **the volcano of Orizaba** At 18,850 feet Mexico's highest volcano, the Pico de Orizaba has long been extinct and snow-covered. DHL stayed in the town of Orizaba on 20 April 1923; cf. Nehls, ii. 223–6.

215:23   **time-space continuum**; In 1916 Einstein extended his Special Theory of Relativity to replace the Euclidian concept of space as independent from time by a four-dimensional space–time continuum. (Albert Einstein, *The Meaning of Relativity*, 5th ed., 1955, based on lectures Einstein delivered in 1921.)

215:37   **thou hast a sun in thee.** Cf. Mrs Renshaw's musings about her husband's failure to come to her with his deeper sunshine in 'The Overtone' above 11:4–26.

216:13   **Nemesis…Erinyes,** Divine retribution for human presumption…the gods' emissaries sent in pursuit of offenders (the Furies); in Greek myth.

217:7   **Vera Cruz [216:33]…passports.** Cf. DHL's plan to sail from Vera Cruz in November 1923 'if that infernal port is open' (letter to Frieda Lawrence, 10 November 1923). According to Frederick Carter 'the rebellion in Mexico settled things, for he [DHL] took ship at Vera Cruz and came back when the town was threatened by hostile forces' (Nehls, ii. 313).

217:13   **True Cross.** I.e. Vera Cruz (Spanish).

217:25   **mealy-mouthed Mammon** Hypocritical god of wealth.

218:22   **Galician Spanish,** Galicia is an isolated province in the north-west of Spain. Galicians speak a half-Spanish half-Portuguese dialect.

219:2   **Man wants but little here below,** Cf. *Edwina and Angelina, or the Hermit* (1766) by Oliver Goldsmith (1730–74) ['Man wants but little here below, / Nor wants that little long'] (lines 31–2).

222:25   **the oil-fields of Tampico.** Located on the Gulf of Mexico, Tampico's oil-fields were discovered and developed between 1901 and 1921, mainly with the help of foreign capital and expertise.

222:31   **they all come here to drink.** See note on 44:12.

223:1   **We are a Republic** After the defeat of Spanish forces in 1898, the first Republican government of Cuba under Tomás Estrada Palma was established on 20 May 1902.

223:8   **cemetery…New Orleans** Colón Cemetery in Havana and the St Louis Cemetery Number One in the Vieux Carré quarter of New Orleans are famous for their opulent tombs.

223:22   **the Conquistadores, even Columbus!** The original Spanish conquerors of the New World, starting with Columbus's discovery of America in 1492.

223:40   **See Naples and die.** Italian proverb of obscure origin ('Vedi Napoli, e poi muori'), implying that nothing more beautiful remains to be seen on earth.

224:8   **space.** The first edition has a gap after this paragraph not present in TS (or TCC).

224:19   **Atlantis** In Plato's dialogues, *Timaeus* and *Critias*, he recounts the Athenian conquest of Atlantis, a continent west of the Pillars of Hercules, which subsequently sank below the Atlantic Ocean.

224:35   **a plague-ship,** Ship hulks moored offshore were used for quarantine purposes by the British up to the nineteenth century to isolate victims of infectious diseases.

TEXTUAL APPARATUS

TEXTUAL APPARATUS

The following source-symbols are used to distinguish states of the text:

MS	= Autograph manuscript
TS	= Ribbon copy typescript
TCC	= Carbon copy typescript
Per	= First periodical publication
E1	= First English edition
E2	= First English edition, second-state
A1	= First American edition

The text adopted for this edition appears within the square bracket. When the text of this edition differs from the base-text described in note on the texts it is followed by a symbol denoting its source.

Variant readings to the text adopted for this edition follow the square bracket in chronological sequence and are identified by a source-symbol. The specific orders of precedence for each text are:

The Overtone
E1 follows *TCC*, and *A1* follows *E1*, unless otherwise indicated.

St. Mawr
E1 follows *TS*, and *A1* follows *E1*, unless otherwise indicated.

The Princess
Per follows *MS*, and *E1* follows *Per*, unless otherwise indicated.

The Wilful Woman
The final *MS* reading is given to the left of the square bracket. Following the bracket is an earlier *MS* reading or an *E1* reading. If the earlier *MS* reading is the variant reading, it is given without a source-symbol; it is identified with one or two sets of pointed brackets (see below) if there is more than one deleted reading or if there is an *E1* variant.

The Flying-Fish
TCC follows *TS*, and *A1* follows *TCC*, unless otherwise indicated.

The following symbols are used editorially:

Ed.	= Editor
Om.	= Omitted
P	= Paragraph
~	= Repeated word in recording an accidental variant
/	= Line break resulting in punctuation, hyphenation or spelling error

= Internal division
⟨ ⟩ = First deletion (in 'The Wilful Woman' only)
⟪ ⟫ = Second deletion (in 'The Wilful Woman' only)

The Overtone

5:4	door,] ~ *A1*	10:5	joints—] ~. *TCC*
5:5	naked] ~, *A1*	10:10	places,] ~ *E1*
5:5	hair,] ~ *E1*	10:11	did] and did *TCC*
5:6	grey,] ~ *E1*	10:22	had refused,] refused, *TCC*
5:8	still was] was still *TCC*		refused him, *E1*
5:11	fifty one] fifty-one *E1*	10:25	afraid for] afraid of *TCC*
5:11	fifty two] fifty-two *E1*	10:32	dark-purple] dark purple *A1*
5:13	leaves. *P* She] ~. She *TCC*	10:33	rose leaves] rose-leaves *TCC*
5:29	him] ~ : *A1*	10:38	rose leaves] rose-leaves *E1*
5:30	ever—] ~. *TCC*	11:4	quietly,] ~ *TCC*
6:5	a lover] her lover *TCC*	11:4	saying:] saying, saying: *TCC*
6:6	hostess] ~, *E1*	11:8	There *Ed.*] there *MS* Yea there
6:8	long,] ~ *TCC*		*TCC* Yea, there *E1 see note*
6:9	fifty two] fifty-two *E1*	11:8	suns:] ~ ; *TCC*
6:13	hostess,] ~ *A1*	11:9	sky,] ~ *TCC*
6:13	host,] ~ *TCC*	11:29	censers *E1*] censors *MS*
6:26	little,] ~ *TCC*	11:31	much,] much, that *E1*
6:29	drunk *MS, A1*] drank *TCC*	11:33	her: *MS, A1*] ~ *TCC*
6:32	moon,] ~ *TCC*	11:34	cruellest *E1*] cruelest *MS*
6:34	rustling!] ~, *TCC* ~. *E1*	11:36	her to a] her a *TCC*
7:1	mystery,] ~ *A1*	11:38	beggar.] beggar upwards. *TCC*
7:13	filtered] foltered *TCC* faltered		*see notes*
	E1	11:40	lips,] ~ *TCC*
7:16	wedding-ring] wedding ring	12:3	said,] ~ *E1*
	TCC	12:6	room:] ~. *TCC*
7:29	cried it] cried *TCC* cried, *A1*	12:13	said] ~, *TCC*
7:33	water] ~, *A1*	12:21	said] ~, *TCC*
7:35	fingertips] finger-tips *A1*	12:21	striking'] ~,' *TCC*
8:1	dumbly,] ~ *A1*	12:22	answered] ~, *TCC*
8:3	at] to *TCC*	12:25	garden,] ~ *TCC*
8:5	a pupil] the pupils *TCC*	12:25	but] and *TCC*
8:27	down] *Om. TCC*	12:25	grass] the grass *TCC*
8:27	form] place *E1 see note*	12:27	said] ~, *TCC*
9:1	[pupil] *Ed.*] *Om. MS* (? pupil)	12:31	no-one] no one *E1*
	TCC pupil *E1 see note*	12:33	is over] was over *TCC*
9:23	Yes—] ~, *E1*	12:36	everlasting. Yea] everlasting Yea
9:23	said, "yes] ~ "Yes *TCC* ~.		*TCC* everlasting sea *E1*
	"Yes *E1*	12:38	but am] but I am *TCC*
9:24	it. You…off." *P* "Not] it. Not	12:40	formless,] ~ *E1*
	E1 see note on 9:27	12:40	beauty. *P* "Yea] ~. Yea *E1*
9:30	bungalow—why] bungalow.	13:5	was never] never was *TCC*
	Why *TCC*	13:8	dark, shut] dark *TCC*
10:1	lied] ~, *E1*	13:9	her hostess] the hostess *TCC*
10:4	said: *P* "I] ~: "I *E1*	13:12	herself.] ~ ? *E1*

13:15 said 'Pan] ~, ' ~ *TCC* ~, " ~
       E1
13:15 dead'] ~,' *TCC* ~," *E1*
13:16 Dane's *TCC*] Danes *MS*
13:17 and] ~, *A1*
13:22 it] ~, *E1*
13:32 do? *TCC*] ~. *MS*
13:33 her] *Om. TCC*
13:33 wrap] ~, *E1*
13:35 man] ~, *E1*
13:37 improper, *TCC*] ~ *MS*
13:39 near—] ~...*A1*
14:5   amiably *TCC*] aimiably *MS*
14:9   saying] ~, *A1*
14:13 farm-lands] farmlands *A1*
14:17 saying] ~, *A1*
14:18 he] He *E1*
14:27 died,] ~? *TCC*
14:32 wife. *P* "But] ~. "But *TCC*
14:33 look under] remove *TCC see note*
14:36 Hercules' *MS, A1*] Hercules's
       E1
14:40 lonely] lovely *A1*
15:4   skipping—] ~...*A1*
15:9   Oh] ~, *E1*
15:13 Yes] ~, *E1*
15:16 been—] ~ *E1*
15:18 singsong] sing-song *E1*
15:20 satyrs—ah] ~ ~, *E1* ~, ~, *A1*
15:21 cross] Cross *E1*
15:22 honorably] honourably *TCC*
15:24 his] His *E1*
15:26 he] He *E1*
15:26 cross] Cross *E1*
15:28 he] He *E1*
15:29 his] His *E1*
15:29 he] He *E1*
15:31 it. *P* "I *Ed.*] ~. *P* I *MS* ~. I
       TCC
15:37 Dionysos] Dionysus *E1*
15:40 him] ~, *TCC*
16:9   crucifix.] ~? *E1*
16:12 'Touch *TCC*] " ~ *MS*
16:12 fairly,' *TCC*] ~," *MS*
16:14 perchance] ~, *A1*
16:17 say: *P* 'Touch *Ed.*] ~: *P*
       "Touch *MS* ~ : 'Touch *TCC*
16:18 fairly.' *E1*] ~." *MS* ~'. *TCC*

16:39 christian] Christian *E1*
16:39 robe-less] robeless *E1*
16:40 a Pan's] Pan's *TCC, E1*
17:4   Nor] Now *TCC*
17:6   christian,] Christian; *E1*
17:8   black bird] black-bird *TCC*

St. Mawr

21:2   long,] ~ *A1*
21:5   sure] ~, *A1*
21:11 Oh] ~, *A1*
21:34 round] around *A1*
22:4   be, and] ~ ~, *E1* ~, ~, *A1*
22:26 there,] ~ *E1*
22:29 and] ~, *A1*
22:32 correspondence,] ~ *E1*
22:38 New Orleans *A1*] New-Orleans
       TS, E1
22:38 conceit] ~, *A1*
23:10 feel it in the air. I] *Om. E1*
       see note
23:13 No] ~, *E1*
23:25 America,] ~. *A1*
23:28 portrait painter] portrait-painter
       A1
23:31 down,] ~ *E1*
24:17 watching] ~, *A1*
24:17 were] ~, *A1*
24:20 ménage] *ménage A1*
24:35 war,] ~ *E1*
24:35 in the *E1*] in *TS* with the *A1*
24:38 débâcle] debacle *A1*
24:39 débris] debris *A1*
25:1   half-breed *E1*] halfbreed *TS*
25:4   curiously-set] curiously set *A1*
25:12 high-schools] high schools *E1*
25:36 Pincio:] ~; *E1*
26:2   Park.—] ~. *E1*
26:15 car] ~, *A1*
26:18 *life!*—] ~! *E1*
26:20 Lincoln] ~, *A1*
26:20 aristocratic *E1*] Aristocratic *TS*
26:30 on] in *A1*
26:33 *Witt* etc:] ~, etc. *E1*
27:6   life-long] lifelong *A1*
27:8   fashionable, and] ~ ~, *A1*
27:8   time] ~, *A1*
27:9   and] ~, *A1*

27:17	hm?,] ~ ?, *E1* ~ ? *A1*		33:23	morning] ~ , *E1*
27:26	engagements] ~ , *A1*		33:28	pale grey] pale-grey *A1*
27:29	horsey] horsy *A1*		33:29	wild cat] wildcat *A1*
27:30	well] ~ , *A1*		34:10	pale grey] pale-grey *A1*
27:33	Ladyship *A1*] ladyship *TS see note*		34:22	this,] ~ *A1*
			34:22	recognised *E1*] recognized *TS*, *A1*
27:39	country? *TS, A1*] ~ . *E1*			
27:40	your *E1*] Your *TS*		34:23	recognised *E1*] recognized *TS*, *A1*
28:2	cleanshaven] clean-shaven *A1*			
28:20	twist—] ~ . *A1*		34:25	half way] half-way *E1*
28:22	him. *E1*] ~ ? *TS*		34:30	half way] half-way *E1*
28:26	Park—] ~ ? *E1*		34:30	hmm *TS, A1*] hm *E1*
28:29	Park—] ~ . *E1*		34:31	way,] ~ *E1*
28:34	her that *E1*] her *TS*		35:9	that? *TS, A1*] ~ , *E1*
29:2	it.—] ~ . *E1*		35:12	judgement] judgment *E1*
29:8	horse, *TS, A1*] ~ *E1*		35:24	half way] half-way *E1*
29:14	horse,] ~ *E1*		35:25	half way] half-way *E1*
29:15	lightning conductor] lightning-conductor *A1*		35:31	half-Indian *TS, A1*] half Indian *E1*
29:18	Griffith *E1*] Griffiths *TS*		35:39	tribe;] ~ : *A1*
29:19	They] they *E1*		36:11	eyes, *TS, A1*] ~ *E1*
29:21	—Well] ~ *E1* ~ , *A1*		36:11	pupil *TS, A1*] ~ , *E1*
29:25	ride.—] ~ . *E1*		36:12	focussed] focused *A1*
29:31	Dean *Ed.*] Deane *TS*		36:17	pre-historic] prehistoric *A1*
29:32	oak bough *E1*] oak bow *TS* oak-bough *A1*		36:24	horsey] horsy *A1*
			36:30	instant,] ~ *E1*
29:32	Autumn] autumn *A1*		36:31	curious] ~ , *A1*
29:34	fatally.—] ~ . *E1*		36:39	per-cent] per cent. *E1* per cent *A1*
29:40	horse, *TS, A1*] ~ *E1*			
30:1	hand,] ~ *E1*		37:4	Why] ~ , *E1*
30:17	Well] ~ , *E1*		37:5	Yes] ~ , *E1*
30:17	Lady *E1*] lady *TS*		37:14	latent,] ~ *A1*
30:17	last. "There] ~ , "there *E1*		37:23	vantage ground] vantage-ground *A1*
31:29	big] ~ , *E1*			
31:31	fear. As] ~ , as *E1*		37:25	You] You have *E1*
31:31	uneasy.—] ~ . *E1*		37:30	green,] ~ ; *E1*
31:31	He too] ~ , ~ , *E1*		37:32	Lewis,] ~ *A1*
31:32	forever] for ever *A1*		38:18	Never!—Since] ~ , since *A1*
31:37	life,] ~ *E1*		38:18	Victoria. But,] ~ ! ~ —*A1*
32:4	everything.—] ~ . *E1*		38:19	know] ~ ?—*A1*
32:23	granted.] ~ ! *A1*		38:30	Park,] ~ *E1*
32:38	Yes] ~ , *A1*		38:35	Mayfair;] ~ , *A1*
33:1	composition *TS, A1*] Composition *E1*		39:1	think] ~ , *E1*
			39:13	rear,] ~ *E1*
33:6	loosely-built] loosely built *A1*		39:40	will,] ~ *E1*
33:12	unheedingly] ~ , *A1*		39:40	or *E1*] of *TS*
33:15	Mawr] ~ , *A1*		40:6	barbarically *A1*] barbaricly *TS*
33:18	But] ~ , *A1*		40:33	on top] on the top *A1*

40:35	someday] some day *E1*		46:16	quietly,] ~ *E1*
40:36	timepieces,] ~ *A1*		46:31	master] Master *A1*
40:40	Sevres] Sèvres *A1*		46:35	fresh,] ~ *A1*
41:6	main-spring] mainspring *A1*		46:39	Common] common *A1*
41:26	another,] ~ *E1*		47:3	that] ~, *A1*
41:32	side-stepping] sidestepping *A1*		47:3	Oh] ~, *A1*
41:33	lets-be-happy] let's-be-happy *A1*		47:5	you] *you A1*
			47:12	still *E1*] silent *TS*
42:1	weekend] week-end *E1*		47:13	round, and] ~ ~, *A1*
42:1	Enderley's:—] Enderleys: *E1*		47:16	maple tree] maple-tree *A1*
42:15	over,] ~ *A1*		47:19	out] ~, *E1*
42:28	churchyard *A1*] Churchyard *TS*		47:36	Oh!"—] ~!" *A1*
42:29	looming,] ~ *E1*		47:39	tears.—] ~. *E1*
42:29	Church] church *A1*		47:39	results!—] ~! *E1*
42:31	grave-stones] gravestones *A1*		48:3	Government Official] government official *E1*
43:1	Church] church *A1*			
43:16	Church] church *A1*		48:16	terrible:] ~ ; *A1*
43:18	laborers] labourers *E1*		48:20	women *E1*] woman *TS*
43:19	very few] ~ ~, *E1*		48:23	Come] ~, *A1*
43:19	cottagers *E1*] cottages *TS*, *A1*		48:24	understand.—] ~. *E1*
43:20	ill-living] ill living *A1*		48:32	Belle-Mère *A1*] Belle-Mére *E1 see note*
43:21	in-bred] inbred *A1*			
43:22	Quarry] quarry *A1*		48:33	Belle-Mère *A1*] Belle-Mére *E1*
43:26	Yes] ~, *E1*		48:33	"If I'm...colts?" *E1*] ' ~ ~...~ ?' *TS*
43:32	Street] street *A1*			
43:33	laborers] labourers *E1*		48:34	She] she *A1*
43:35	terrible.] ~, *E1*		48:40	Lou———] ~ —— *E1*
44:1	that"] ~," *E1*		49:8	Elena] Flena *E1*
44:2	*Moon and Stars.*] 'Moon and Stars'. *E1* 'Moon and Stars.' *A1*		49:9	riding-breeches *A1*] riding breeches *TS*
44:4	*Moon and Stars,*] "Moon and Stars," *E1*		49:10	crape] crêpe *A1*
44:6	laborers] labourers *E1*		49:11	riding-boots *A1*] riding boots *TS*
44:11	laborers] labourers *E1*		49:26	sidewalk *E1*] side walk *TS*
44:21	episcopalian] Episcopalian *E1*		49:33	high-road *Ed.*] high road *TS*
44:31	other *E1*] others *TS*		49:39	Marvellous] ~, *A1*
44:35	pre-supposes] presupposes *A1*		49:40	creature.] ~! *A1*
44:36	pre-supposes] presupposes *A1*		50:2	To ride] ~ ~, *E1*
44:37	pre-supposes] presupposes *A1*		50:10	conqueror,] ~ *E1*
45:12	weight, *A1*] weight in, *TS* weight *E1 see note*		50:16	flushed-like!] flushed like, *E1*
			50:22	post office *TS*, *A1*] post-office *E1*
45:18	Something] ~, *A1*		50:24	day.] ~ ? *A1*
45:18	all] ~, *A1*		50:30	church-yard] churchyard *A1*
45:19	to *E1*] like *TS*		50:32	life,] ~ *E1*
45:30	Manbys: *E1*] ~ ; *TS*		50:35	courtyard] court-yard *A1*
45:34	bathing party] bathing-party *A1*		50:36	maple tree] maple-tree *A1*
46:3	don'] don't *E1*		50:37	fruit trees] fruit-trees *A1*
46:10	somebody!—] ~! *E1*			

50:37 currant bushes] currant-bushes *A1*

50:39 sweet williams] sweet-williams *A1*

51:2 amused,] ~ *E1*

51:7 in *E1*] on *TS*

51:7 onion bed] onion-bed *A1*

51:10 path,] ~ *E1*

51:10 apple trees] apple-trees *A1*

51:19 intensely-living] intensely living *A1*

51:26 And] ~, *A1*

51:35 pale grey *Ed.*] pale-grey *TS*

52:1 wrong?—"] ~ ?" — *E1*

52:4 don't!"] ~ " *E1* ~ " — *A1*

52:11 him—?—] ~ ?— *E1*

52:13 thick-set] thick set *E1* thickset *A1*

52:19 morning] ~, *A1*

52:20 morning] ~, *A1*

52:20 Carrington—] ~.— *E1*

52:24 Henry *E1*] Richard *TS*

52:25 right———] ~ — *E1* ~ — *A1*

52:29 Henry *E1*] Richard *TS*

52:31 Carrington.—] ~. *E1*

52:34 course!—] ~! *E1*

52:36 biscuit—] ~, *E1*

52:37 Lady.—] ~. *E1*

52:40 whisky *E1*] whiskey *TS*

53:3 trees:] ~. *A1*

53:20 you] ~, *A1*

53:21 whisky *E1*] whiskey *TS*

53:24 mad,] ~ *E1*

53:24 kind."—] ~." *E1*

53:28 but] ~, *A1*

53:31 underneath,] ~ *E1*

53:33 And] ~, *A1*

53:34 circumstance] ~, *A1*

54:8 mind,] ~ *E1*

54:11 angry?— *TS*, *A1*] ~? *E1*

54:13 No] ~, *E1*

54:18 know"—] ~—" *E1* ~—" *A1*

54:19 naive] naïve *E1*

54:39 to *E1*] *Om. TS*

55:4 realise.—] ~. *E1* realize.— *A1*

55:16 fox gloves *Ed.*] foxgloves *TS*

55:21 yew-trees,] ~ *A1*

55:25 Mother] mother *E1*

55:33 *Those maids thank God / ...their generation.'*—No *Ed.*] *Those... generation.*—No *TS Those maids, thank God, / ...generation.' P* No *E1* Those maids, thank God, / Are 'neath the sod, / And all their generation.' "No, *A1*

55:35 but,] ~ *A1*

55:39 her.— *TS*, *A1*] ~. *E1*

56:10 truth.— *TS*, *A1*] ~. *E1*

56:11 Shrewsbury.— *TS*, *A1*] ~. *E1*

56:13 No] ~, *E1*

56:25 dust-sheet *E1*] dust sheet *TS*

56:26 Witt, *E1*] ~ *TS*

56:33 yew hedge] yew-hedge *A1*

56:38 But] ~, *E1*

57:7 fates *TS*, *A1*] Fates *E1*

57:8 by-gone] bygone *A1*

57:11 by-gone] bygone *A1*

57:12 eighteenth-century *TS*, *A1*] 18th century *E1*

57:13 eighteenth-century] 18th century *E1* eighteenth century *A1*

57:24 Now] ~, *E1*

57:24 interfere.— *TS*, *A1*] ~. *E1*

57:40 handywork] handiwork *A1*

58:12 said;] ~, *A1*

58:12 surprised.—] ~. *E1*

58:20 pale grey *Ed.*] pale-grey *TS*

58:22 Now] ~, *E1*

58:22 besides—] ~, *E1*

58:24 chair—] ~, *A1*

58:26 cold] ~, *E1*

58:29 Yes] ~, *E1*

58:34 extraordinary,] ~ *E1*

58:35 Paris,] ~ *A1*

58:35 hotel,] ~ *E1*

58:40 said,] ~ : *A1*

59:4 strange,] ~ *A1*

59:5 hair.] ~ ; *E1* ~, *A1*

59:8 curious,] ~ *E1*

59:11 boys,] ~ *A1*

59:17 forty-one *E1*] forty one *TS*

59:23 hair.— *TS*, *A1*] ~. *E1*

59:28 No] ~, *E1*

59:28 our sort of *A1*] most *TS see note on* 59:29

59:34   Why] ∼, *E1*
60:1   me,] ∼ *E1*
60:5   said. "You] ∼, "you *E1*
60:10   Men] men *E1*
60:16   do, *TS*, *A1*] ∼ *E1*
60:25   Yes] ∼, *E1*
60:27   belief,] ∼ *E1*
60:29   Yes] ∼, *E1*
60:35   under.—] ∼. *E1*
61:1   them,] ∼ *A1*
61:8   No] ∼, *E1*
61:12   not?] ∼. *A1*
61:17   cave man] cave-man *A1*
61:17   think] ∼, *A1*
61:19   men,] ∼ *E1*
61:28   crochetting] crocheting *A1*
61:37   cave man] cave-man *A1*
61:40   cave man] cave-man *A1*
62:6   one,] ∼ *A1*
62:7   Ah] ∼, *A1*
62:8   criticizing *TS*, *A1*] criticising *E1*
62:15   dead,] ∼ *E1*
62:17   Lewis,] ∼! *E1*
62:18   servants!] ∼. *E1*
62:20   then *TS*] their *E1*
62:20   then] their *E1*
62:29   Lou,] ∼ *E1*
62:30   understood,] ∼ *E1*
62:39   do!] ∼? *A1*
63:2   fun! *E1*] ∼? *TS*
63:3   returned,] ∼ *E1*
63:4   newcomers] new-comers *A1*
63:7   why] ∼, *A1*
63:11   overcrowded."—] ∼." *E1*
63:12   Witt. "The] ∼, "the *E1*
63:14   Why] ∼, *A1*
63:14   don't we] ∼ ∼, *E1*
63:22   grounds, *TS*, *A1*] ∼ *E1*
63:26   Carrington—!] ∼!— *E1*
63:31   Oh] ∼, *A1*
63:36   Oh] ∼, *E1*
64:7   Forever] For ever *E1*
64:14   teatime:] tea-time, *E1*
64:24   laborer] labourer *E1*
64:29   goat's *Ed*] goats, *TS* goat's; *E1*
64:40   Even our late King Edward.]
        Om. E2 see note
65:1   me,] ∼ *E1*
65:3   Cartwright.—] ∼. *E1*

65:3   She too] ∼, ∼, *E1*
65:6   Oh] ∼, *A1*
65:8   great god] Great God *A1*
65:16   Cartwright] ∼, *E1*
65:17   God *TS*, *A1*] god *E1*
65:18   God *TS*, *A1*] god *E1*
65:29   great] Great *E1*
65:29   great] Great *A1*
65:29   Pan,] ∼. *E1*
65:32   hidden: you *E1*] ∼: You *TS*
65:38   Cartwright] ∼, *E1*
66:1   wonderful,] ∼ *E1*
66:3   drawing-room,] ∼ *E1*
66:5   like?] ∼. *A1*
66:13   said, *TS*, *A1*] ∼ *E1*
66:16   question,] ∼ *E1*
66:23   But] ∼, *E1*
66:27   No] ∼, *E1*
66:28   pan-cake] pancake *A1*
66:31   Oh] ∼, *A1*
66:31   pancake!— *TS*, *A1*] ∼! *E1*
66:35   did?] ∼. *A1*
66:36   no] ∼, *E1*
66:38   Listen] ∼, *E1*
66:38   Louise.— *TS*, *A1*] ∼. *E1*
66:40   why?— *TS*, *A1*] ∼? *E1*
67:1   know?— *TS*, *A1*] ∼? *E1*
67:5   Pan.— *TS*, *A1*] ∼. *E1*
67:9   tea-spoonful...tea-spoonful]
        teaspoonful...teaspoonful *A1*
67:10   baking powder] baking-powder
        A1
67:10   extraordinary,] ∼; *E1* ∼ *A1*
67:12   all.] ∼? *A1*
67:14   know—] ∼. *E1* ∼—— *A1*
67:23   no-one] no one *E1*
68:7   half-past] half past *A1*
68:7   seven,] ∼ *E1*
68:10   quietly,] ∼ *E1*
68:16   horse,] ∼ *E1*
68:28   No-one] No one *E1*
68:33   moment,] ∼ *E1*
68:37   ap—ricot] ap-ricot *A1*
68:38   him,] ∼ *E1*
69:3   fore-feet *Ed*.] fore feet *TS*
        forefeet *A1*
69:10   Say] ∼, *E1*
69:12   Then] ∼, *A1*
69:15   saddle,] ∼ *E1*

69:21	man,] ~ *EI*
69:22	regiment,] ~ *EI*
69:31	pardon] ~, *EI*
69:34	*Mam!*] ~ *EI* ~ *! AI*
70:9	countryside,] ~ *EI* country-side *AI*
70:11	fox gloves] foxgloves *EI*
70:11	Ahead,] ~ *EI*
70:12	Mawr,] ~ *EI*
70:19	trail,] ~ *EI*
70:21	hare-bells *Ed.*] harebells *TS*
70:24	hollow] ~, *EI*
70:30	No] ~, *EI*
70:34	No] ~, *EI*
70:37	myself.] ~, *EI*
70:40	No] ~, *EI*
71:5	she] She *AI*
71:7	Yes] ~, *EI*
71:9	No] ~, *EI*
71:11	Yes] ~, *EI*
71:13	Yes] ~, *EI*
71:16	*home!*] ~ *! EI* ~. *AI*
71:21	go *AI*] went *TS* want *EI*
71:24	No] ~, *EI*
71:26	No] ~, *EI*
71:33	Yes] ~, *EI*
71:35	Yes] ~, *EI*
72:2	pale grey] pale-grey *AI*
72:7	No] ~, *EI*
72:9	No] ~, *EI*
72:11	No] ~, *EI*
72:19	child.] ~? *EI*
73:5	sky-line *TS, AI*] skyline *EI*
73:5	rocks:] ~; *AI*
73:5	right,] ~ *EI*
73:9	No] ~, *EI*
73:14	right.—"] ~." *EI* ~."— *AI*
74:1	Oh] ~, *AI*
74:6	Why] ~, *EI*
74:7	rosebud,] ~? *AI*
74:14	No] ~, *EI*
74:22	days *EI*] day *TS*
74:28	was,] ~ *EI*
74:33	this,] ~ *EI*
75:3	exist?] ~. *AI*
75:8	England;] ~: *AI*
75:9	that,] ~ *EI*
75:13	chilled,] ~ *AI*
75:15	hare-bells] harebells *AI*
75:26	No] ~, *AI*
75:33	grooves] groves *AI*
76:7	forward *EI*] forw[a]rds *TS*
76:9	backwards,] ~ *EI*
76:25	backwards *EI*] backward *TS*
76:28	fore-feet *Ed.*] forefeet *TS*
76:31	fore-feet] forefeet *AI*
76:38	Oh] ~, *EI*
76:39	dismounted—] ~.— *EI*
76:40	spell-bound] spellbound *EI*
77:9	ghost-like] ghostlike *AI*
77:16	pleading] ~, *EI*
78:2	morning!] ~. *EI*
78:27	No-one *Ed.*] No one *TS*, *EI*
78:35	pale gold] pale-gold *AI*
79:26	hemorrhage] hæmorrhage *AI*
80:8	existences] existence *AI*
80:15	and] ~, *EI*
81:8	him *EI*] himself *TS*
81:11	Manbys' *AI*] Manby's *TS*
81:12	game-keepers] game-/ keepers *EI* gamekeepers *AI*
81:15	true,] ~ *EI*
81:18	he mean!] ~ ~? *AI*
81:28	house,] ~ *EI*
81:29	Because] ~, *AI*
81:30	so] *Om. AI*
82:12	Ah] ~, *EI*
82:23	a new *EI*] an new *TS*
82:27	michaelmas *Ed.*] Michaelmas *TS*
83:6	said,] ~. *EI*
83:11	roused] aroused *AI*
83:16	uneasy,] ~ *EI*
83:17	something, *EI*] ~ *TS*
83:38	matters,] ~ *AI*
84:3	*laisser-faire*] *laissez-faire EI*
85:12	him.— *TS, AI*] ~. *EI*
85:20	abyss *EI*] abysses *TS*
85:24	Three-quarters] Three quarters *EI*
85:29	been west] ~ West *AI*
85:30	go west] ~ West *AI*
86:6	mountains,—Trees] ~—trees *EI*
86:7	Pine] pine *EI*
86:7	*Pino real Ed.*] *Pino-real TS* *Pino—real AI*

86:7 pinavete Ed.] pinovetes TS
86:8 piñón Ed.] piñon TS
86:34 watches.— TS, A1] ~. E1
87:5 husband? E1] ~. TS
87:11 Oh] ~, E1
87:12 dreadful,] ~ A1
87:20 neigh!] ~. E1
87:28 Ah] ~, A1
87:32 horse.—] ~. E1
87:39 course— E1] ~.— TS
87:39 definitions—! Ed.] ~—! TS
  ~!— E1
88:3 But] ~, A1
88:11 Ah] ~, E1
88:11 breezily. "You] ~, "you E1
88:16 fine looking] fine-looking A1
88:18 Yes indeed!] ~, ~, E1
88:19 tea,] ~? A1
88:22 human-beings] human beings A1
88:23 dressing room] dressing-room E1
88:27 out. "Don't] ~, "don't A1
88:36 drawing-room, E1] ~ TS
89:1 eighteenth-century E1] eighteenth century TS
89:4 No] ~, E1
89:6 ceremoniously-effusive] ceremoniously effusive A1
89:14 cup!] ~? A1
89:15 over—] ~.— E1
89:20 bull-dog] bulldog A1
89:29 colourless E1] colorless TS
89:32 like a E1] like TS
89:33 full stop Ed.] fullstop TS full-stop E1
89:34 naively] naïvely E1
89:38 loop-hole] loophole A1
89:40 belle mère Ed.] belle mére E1 belle-mère A1 see note on 48:32
89:40 it,] ~; E1
90:4 Now] ~, A1
90:7 earnestly,] ~ E1
90:10 himself.] ~, E1
90:12 Why] ~, E1
90:15 Why] ~, E1
90:25 No] ~, E1
90:27 horse.] ~, E1
90:31 you E1] You TS

90:32 youth— Ed.] ~— TS ~. E1
  ~! A1
90:34 He's E1] He is TS, A1
91:3 stallion E1] Stallion TS
91:6 Vyner—" She] ~ " —she E1
91:7 belle-mère's Ed.] belle-mére's E1
  belle-mères A1 see note on 48:32
91:14 clinging] ~, E1
91:15 female:] ~. A1
91:21 Then] ~, A1
91:26 Goodbye] Good-bye, A1
91:27 Sunday.] ~? A1
91:28 goodbye] good-bye, A1
91:30 anything] any thing A1
91:31 Mother] mother E1
91:36 her an odd E1] her her odd TS
91:39 serenely E1] severely TS
92:11 flowers.— TS, A1] ~. E1
92:24 say] ~: A1
92:24 Death] ~, A1
93:14 sting-aling-aling]sting-a-ling-a-ling E1
93:22 there,] ~ A1
93:33 Lou] ~, E1
93:34 a while] awhile A1
94:2 amiable E1] aimiable TS
94:7 weak,] ~ A1
94:8 away, TS, A1] ~ E1
94:9 life,] ~ A1
94:11 coach house] coach-house E1
94:13 doorstep] door-step A1
94:15 Outside] ~, A1
94:18 Phoenix. Ed.] ~, TS Phœnix. E1
94:22 dogcart.— TS, A1] ~. E1
95:24 me,] ~ E1
95:30 extraordinary,] ~ E1
95:37 think.] ~? E1
95:39 Moon and Stars] 'Moon and Stars' E1
95:40 him,] ~ E1
95:40 him,] ~ A1
96:6 Lou.— TS, A1] ~. E1
96:7 practical] practicable A1
96:23 world,] ~ E1
96:28 up] ~, E1
96:39 Yes] ~, E1
97:7 untameable] untamable A1
97:24 quotation-mark's] quotation-marks A1

97:34 Ah] ~, *Eɪ*
98:7   Witt. "What *Eɪ*] ~, "What *TS*
98:13 thinking,] ~ *Aɪ*
98:26 And] ~, *Aɪ*
98:26 Witt. "My] ~, "my *Eɪ*
98:33 then.— *TS, Aɪ*] ~. *Eɪ*
98:36 afternoon.] ~, *Eɪ*
99:6   waterproof *Eɪ*] water-proof *TS*
99:14 splashed up] splashed-up *Aɪ*
99:21 *Dearest Loulina*...[99:29] *dear!
       R.*] [*Aɪ* prints in roman]
99:22 *years.*] years? *Aɪ*
99:28 *tomorrow*]   *to-morrow,*   *Eɪ*
       to-morrow, *Aɪ*
99:29 *A rivederci Ed.*] *A rivederti TS*
       Arrivederci *Eɪ* Arivederti *Aɪ*
99:36 No] no, *Eɪ*
100:4 fox gloves] foxgloves *Eɪ*
100:6 she *Eɪ*] She *TS*
100:23 heavily,] ~ *Eɪ*
101:4 she always *Eɪ*] she had always
       TS
101:17 admired: *TS, Aɪ*] ~— *Eɪ*
101:18 man: *TS, Aɪ*] ~— *Eɪ*
101:23 strong] ~, *Eɪ*
101:26 Gods *TS, Aɪ*] gods *Eɪ*
101:37 world,] ~ *Eɪ*
102:6 Caesar] Cæsar *Eɪ*
102:8 Antony *Eɪ*] Anthony *TS*
102:9 Caesar] Cæsar *Eɪ*
102:11 Antony *Eɪ*] Anthony *TS*
102:13 Oh] oh *Eɪ* O *Aɪ*
102:15 *him*] *Him Eɪ*
102:16 was] ~, *Aɪ*
102:18 consolation.] ~! *Aɪ*
102:22 hourglass] hour-glass *Eɪ*
102:27 ever] every *Aɪ*
102:28 Caesar] Cæsar *Eɪ*
102:28 Antony *Eɪ*] Anthony *TS*
102:30 Ah] ~, *Aɪ*
103:11 No] ~, *Eɪ*
103:14 aunt *Eɪ*] Aunt *TS*
103:16 Well] ~, *Aɪ*
103:18 church.—] ~. *Aɪ*
103:24 No] ~, *Eɪ*
103:38 to] ~, *Eɪ*
104:7 chétif *Eɪ*] *chétif Aɪ see note on*
       48:32

104:8   horsey] horsy *Aɪ*
104:9   Yes] ~, *Aɪ*
104:9   No] ~, *Aɪ*
105:3   Well] ~, *Aɪ*
105:9   you to *Eɪ*] you got to *TS*
105:21 No] ~, *Eɪ*
105:22 No] ~, *Aɪ*
105:24 Yes] ~, *Eɪ*
105:26 Yes] ~, *Eɪ*
105:29 look *Eɪ*] sort *TS*
105:30 emotions. *P* He] ~. He *Eɪ*
105:31 cold, *TS, Aɪ*] ~ *Eɪ*
106:28 teatime *Ed.*] tea-time *TS*
107:21 alongside *TS, Aɪ*] along side *Eɪ*
107:21 wood's-edge] wood's edge *Aɪ*
107:22 artificially-lit] artificially lit *Aɪ*
107:37 night time] night-/time *Aɪ*
107:39 that *Eɪ*] *Om. TS*
108:7   ate *Eɪ*] eat *TS*
108:11 them,] ~ *Aɪ*
108:21 say,] ~ *Aɪ*
108:22 kindle fire] kindle *Aɪ*
108:22 make] made *Eɪ*
108:29 Then] ~, *Aɪ*
108:38 stupefied *Eɪ*] stupified *TS*
109:1   naïveté] ~, *Eɪ*
109:14 believe *Eɪ*] believes *TS*
109:14 We] ~, *Aɪ*
109:27 other *Eɪ*] others *TS*
109:37 Yes] ~, *Eɪ*
109:39 by. Or] ~, or *Aɪ*
110:3   rubbish heap] rubbish-heap *Aɪ*
110:7   No] ~, *Eɪ*
110:8   night-time.—] night-time. *Eɪ*
110:9   Heaven] heaven *Aɪ*
110:9   heathen] ~, *Aɪ*
110:11 at school *Eɪ*] at School *TS*
110:17 trades-union *Aɪ*] trade's union
        TS trades' union *Eɪ*
110:37 Why] ~, *Eɪ*
111:8   Yes] ~, *Aɪ*
111:8   No] ~, *Aɪ*
111:11 No] ~, *Eɪ*
111:22 No] ~, *Eɪ*
111:25 No] ~, *Eɪ*
111:25 it," *Eɪ*] ~ " *TS*
111:29 that,] ~ *Aɪ*
111:30 fondle,] ~ *Eɪ*

111:30 repellant] repellent *A1*
111:30 repellant] repellent *A1*
111:38 But!—] ~— *A1*
111:38 stammered.] ~, *A1*
112:23 slave,] ~ *A1*
113:15 Marshal] Marshall *A1*
113:17 victim;] ~ : *A1*
113:22 household,] ~ *A1*
113:23 is,] ~ *A1*
113:30 *posey*] *posy A1*
113:31 *The E1*] The *TS*
113:32 feel.] ~ ? *A1*
113:35 à la *Ed.*] á la *E1* á la *A1* see note on 48:32
113:36 half way] half-way *A1*
113:39 better:] ~, *E1*
114:7 him.—Me *Ed.*] ~.—ME *TS* ~. Me *E1*
114:12 *befall E1*] *befal TS*
114:17 *Oh*] ~, *A1*
114:18 *Wasn't E1*] *wasn't TS*
114:19 *Why*] ~, *A1*
114:19 *flowers, TS, A1*] ~ *E1*
114:26 Weingartner:] ~, *E1*
114:27 least,] ~ *A1*
114:29 stage] ~, *A1*
114:29 he said] ~ ~ : *A1*
114:30 *Oh*] ~, *E1*
114:34 life-like] lifelike *A1*
115:1 bye-lanes] by-/lanes *A1*
115:11 bedclothes] bed-clothes *A1*
115:11 mine,] ~ *A1*
115:15 were *E1*] was *TS*
115:18 cardboard, *E1*] card-board, *TS*
115:21 water-cresses] watercresses *E1*
115:25 again?] ~. *A1*
115:27 Anything,] ~ *E1*
115:28 Au revoir] *Au revoir A1*
115:30 Mother—] ~ : *E1*
115:36 here,] ~ *A1*
116:4 the *Times TS, A1*] The Times *E1*
116:8 Iphigenia *A1*] Iphegenia *TS*
116:13 *Oh*] ~, *A1*
116:13 *Oh*] ~, *A1*
116:20 *Oh*] ~, *A1*
116:20 *a rred*] ~ ~, *E1*
116:23 ante-chamber] antechamber *A1*
116:30 bright] ~, *E1*

116:38 *better,*] ~ *A1*
117:3 libido] *libido A1*
117:8 *Mother*] mother *E1*
117:10 *t-he-e-re-e*] *t—he—e—re—e E1*
117:10 Mother] mother *E1*
117:13 *But*] ~, *A1*
117:16 *can*] Om. *E1*
117:20 *Mother*] mother *E1*
117:21 Orleans— *E1*] ~—, *TS*
117:22 *west*] West *A1*
117:23 *But*] ~, *A1*
117:27 Mother] mother *E1*
117:34 László *Ed.*] Laslow *TS, A1* Laszlo *E1*
117:35 Mother] mother *E1*
118:4 have *E1*] had *TS*
118:6 life,] ~ ; *E1*
118:9 'mix' *E1*] " ~ " *TS*
118:14 no-one] no one *E1*
118:16 *ill,*] ~ *A1*
118:17 *But*] ~, *A1*
118:25 *South-West*] South-west *A1*
118:31 *Cabin*] *cabin E1*
118:34 *No*] ~, *A1*
118:35 He *TS, A1*] He *E1*
119:9 abiding place] abiding-place *A1*
119:14 better] had better *E1*
119:18 obedient *E1*] Obedient *TS*
119:26 life,] ~ *E1*
119:30 down, *TS, A1*] ~ *E1*
120:3 good] ~, *A1*
120:14 that sort *E1*] sort sort *TS*
120:18 not bear *E1*] not bear not *TS*
120:19 ah] ~, *A1*
120:20 *homine*] homo *A1 see note*
120:27 Ah] ~, *A1*
120:30 west] West *A1*
120:33 *Corpus*] corpus *A1*
120:38 seemed,] ~ *E1*
121:2 ghostly. *TS, A1*] ghostly. *E1*
121:12 *August*] ~, *A1*
121:17 hat! *TS, A1*] ~. *E1*
121:33 way, *TS, A1*] ~ *E1*
121:39 pale grey] pale-grey *A1*
122:8 anymore] any more *E1*
122:14 should *TS, A1*] Om. *E1*
122:17 tone] ~, *E1*

122:19	eyes:] ~— A1
122:25	in A1] by TS
122:28	thing] ~, A1
122:36	Yes] ~, A1
123:1	then, TS, A1] ~ E1
123:3	Honorable] Honourable E1
123:4	to] of A1
123:6	go] ~, A1
123:11	newcomer] new-comer A1
123:21	Mother] mother E1
123:28	premonition,] ~ E1
123:31	full grown man] full-grown man, A1
123:32	Yes] ~, A1
123:35	Corner E1] corner TS, A1
123:39	back," E1] ~" TS
124:5	few, very E1] ~ ~ TS
124:13	People] people E1
124:17	No] ~, E1
124:18	she] She E1
124:24	No] ~, E1
125:9	stable? E1] ~. TS
125:30	travel,] ~ A1
125:38	hiss,] ~. E1
125:39	beautiful.] ~! A1
125:40	gimlet-sharp] gimlet, sharp E1
126:13	*really, TS, A1]* ~ E1
126:23	weary,] ~ A1
126:35	No] ~, E1
127:2	little,] ~ E1
127:2	countryside] country-side A1
127:18	shadowily] shadowly E1
127:23	she,] ~ A1
127:25	soon,] ~ A1
127:28	rocks] rock A1
127:29	Paris,] ~ A1
127:32	No no, one must not] No, no one must E1 No, one must not A1
128:2	Captain] captain A1
128:9	south *Ed.*] South TS
128:11	south! *Ed.*] South! TS
128:11	south,] South, E1
128:13	seeping] sweeping E1
128:13	blanketing A1] blanketting TS
128:16	north] North E1
128:24	But] ~, A1
129:2	port—] ~.— E1
129:8	débâcle] debacle A1

129:15	Plus…chose] *Plus ça change, plus c'est la même chose* A1
129:16	On…ici] *On n'est pas mieux ici* A1
129:19	Why] ~, E1
129:20	dollar E1] dollars TS
129:23	Pittsburgh A1] Pittsburg TS
129:27	Gulf E1] gulf TS
129:31	cork-screwing] ~, E1 corkscrewing, A1
129:34	flying-fishes A1] flying fishes TS
130:4	used-up] used up A1
130:20	stoicism] ~, A1
130:29	Mawr E1] Mawr himself TS
130:33	chiefly,] ~ A1
131:10	a cinematograph E1] the cinematograph TS
131:13	all.— TS, A1] ~. E1
131:16	least, this] ~ ~ A1
131:20	long-legged E1] longlegged TS
131:26	Cowboys E1] Cow-boys TS
131:28	East E1] east TS
131:29	of E1] on TS
132:6	oh] O A1
132:24	eh?] ~, A1
132:32	north] North E1
132:36	*Welcome*] ~, A1
132:36	*Tourist*] ~, A1
132:36	high-road] high road A1
132:38	Plus ça change] *Plus ça change* A1
132:39	Ça ne change jamais] *Ça ne change jamais* A1
133:5	a while] awhile A1
133:7	very E1] every TS
133:9	And] ~, A1
133:12	mayonnaise] salad-bowl A1
133:13	down] ~, A1
133:27	Come] ~, E1
133:31	Gonzalez *Ed.*] Gonzalez TS Gonzales A1
133:34	Oh] ~, A1
134:7	South-West *Ed.*] south-west TS South-west A1
134:8	summer:] ~; E1
134:16	splashing E1] plashing TS
134:16	rain] ~, A1

134:16 succeed *A1*] succeeds *TS*
134:20 moment,] ∼ *E1*
134:36 self-satisfied] ∼, *E1*
134:37 but,] ∼ *A1*
135:27 *her*,] ∼ *A1*
135:39 mousey] mousy *A1*
136:8 cocotte] *cocotte A1*
136:15 moving-pictures *Ed.*] moving pictures *TS*
136:17 Phœnix's *Ed.*] Phœnix' *TS* Phœnix's *E1*
136:21 very very] ∼, ∼ *E1*
136:21 car: *TS, A1*] ∼— *E1*
136:24 behind-hand] behind-/ hand *E1* behindhand *A1*
136:24 movements: *TS, A1*] ∼— *E1*
136:35 moving-pictures] moving pictures *A1*
137:2 rat-holes] rat holes *E1* rat-/ holes *A1*
137:4 No] ∼, *E1*
137:18 one half] one-half *A1*
137:28 *need*] need *E1*
138:1 me!] ∼, *E1*
138:6 up,] ∼? *E1*
138:13 said,] ∼; *A1*
138:19 *Quién Ed.*] *Quien TS*
138:27 Phœnix's *Ed.*] Phœnix' *TS* Phœnix's *E1*
138:29 no no] ∼, ∼ *E1*
138:31 No] ∼, *E1*
138:33 repellant *Ed.*] repellent *TS*
139:3 childish] ∼, *A1*
139:4 Phœnix's *Ed.*] Phœnix' *TS* Phœnix's *E1*
139:5 piñón trees *Ed.*] piñon trees *TS* piñon-trees *A1*
139:12 No] ∼, *E1*
139:19 penetrate] ∼, *A1*
139:23 she *E1*] She *TS*
139:26 No] ∼, *E1*
139:29 virgin] ∼, *E1*
139:33 broken veils, *E1*] ∼ ∼ *TS*
139:38 young,] ∼ *A1*
139:40 East *E1*] east *TS*
140:13 dried up] dried-up *A1*
140:14 Phoenix. *Ed.*] Phoenix, *TS* Phœnix. *E1*

140:16 pine-trees *TS, A1*] pine trees *E1*
140:20 michaelmas] Michaelmas *A1*
140:23 place,] ∼ *E1*
140:27 and] ∼, *A1*
140:29 flank: and] ∼: ∼, *A1*
140:31 untameable] untamable *A1*
140:32 and] ∼, *A1*
140:35 hundred-and-sixty] hundred and sixty *A1*
140:38 East *E1*] east *TS*
141:16 for being] ∼, ∼ *A1*
141:33 to be got *E1*] to the be got *TS* see note
141:37 And] ∼, *A1*
141:38 goat's *TS, A1*] goats' *E1*
142:14 five-hundred] five hundred *E1*
142:17 two-thousand] two thousand *E1*
142:21 goats] ∼, *E1*
142:26 dark green] dark-green *A1*
142:26 pine-trees *E1*] pine trees *TS*
142:35 years,] ∼ *E1*
142:39 goats-milk] goats'-milk *E1*
142:40 cheese making] cheese-making *A1*
143:1 And] ∼, *A1*
143:2 And] ∼, *A1*
143:4 mountain-side *A1*] mountain side *TS*
143:7 angora] Angora *E1*
143:26 ears,] ∼ *E1*
143:28 the place *E1*] place *TS*
143:30 South-West *Ed.*] south-west *TS* South-west *A1*
144:6 pine-trees *E1*] pine trees *TS*
144:19 downslope] down-slope *A1*
144:24 flakey-ribbed] flaky-ribbed *A1*
144:33 pine-tree *E1*] pine tree *TS*
144:34 pine-trees *E1*] pine trees *TS*
144:39 orange red] orange-red *A1*
145:21 tense] ∼, *E1*
145:28 sometimes,] ∼ *A1*
145:34 cotton-wood tree] cotton-wood-tree *A1*
146:9 cotton-wood trees] cottonwood-trees *A1*
146:11 Ah:] ∼! *E1*
147:24 drug like *TS, A1*] drug-like *E1*
148:4 pine-tree *E1*] pine tree *TS*

148:9 also,] ~ *A1*
148:20 uniform: *TS, A1*] ~— *E1*
148:22 blue-bell] bluebell *A1*
148:22 snap-dragon] snapdragon *A1*
148:26 smoke colour] smoke-colour *A1*
148:37 michaelmas] Michaelmas *A1*
149:3 seen,] ~ *A1*
149:8 sweet-briar roses] sweet brier-roses *A1*
149:8 dark blue hare-bells] dark-blue harebells *A1*
149:15 squaw-berry bushes] squawberry-bushes *A1*
149:31 water-less] waterless *E1*
149:33 out-post] outpost *A1*
150:9 Oh] ~, *E1*
150:19 caldron] cauldron *E1*
150:21 forever] for ever *A1*
150:24 go *E1*] *Om. TS*
150:24 ranch,] ~ *A1*
151:10 half-sordid] half sordid *A1*
152:8 daffodil yellow] daffodil-yellow *A1*
152:13 michaelmas] Michaelmas *A1*
152:16 ricketty] rickety *A1*
152:20 hands,] ~ *E1*
152:24 And] ~, *A1*
152:24 pleasant] ~, *E1*
152:29 cotton-wood tree *Ed.*] cottonwood tree *TS* cottonwood-tree *A1*
152:30 Well Louise, *Ed.*] ~ ~ *TS* ~, ~, *E1*
152:30 said.] ~, *A1*
152:32 But] ~, *E1*
152:33 But] ~, *A1*
152:39 beau-ti-ful] beau—ti—ful *E1*
153:4 Anyhow] ~, *E1*
153:22 No] ~, *E1*
153:24 back-yard] back yard *A1*
153:27 out.] ~? *E1*
153:29 I!] ~? *A1*
153:31 drily] dryly *A1*
153:35 half-naked] half naked *A1*
153:37 Oh] ~, *E1* oh, *A1*
154:3 Well] ~, *E1*
154:3 pause.] ~, *E1*
154:6 broken!] ~? *A1*

154:18 more!] ~? *E1*
154:21 honied] honeyed *A1*
154:23 it— *Ed.*] ~ ÷ *TS* ~. *E1*
154:31 them] ~, *A1*
154:36 am....] ~ ... *E1*
154:37 not—?] ~?— *E1* ~? *A1*
154:38 know?—" *E1*] know it—?" *TS*
155:1 men.] ~, *E1*
155:8 No] ~, *E1*
155:11 *know*, is] ~ ~, *E1* ~ ~ *A1*
155:29 back-yard] back yard *A1*
155:39 name!] ~. *E1*

The Princess

159:9 was not *Per*] wasn't *MS*
159:19 means, who] ~, ~, *Per* ~ ~ *E1*
159:19 ago *MS, E1*] ~, *Per*
159:20 definitely *Per*] even definitely *MS*
159:23 forty:] ~, *Per*
159:24 Miss Prescott] ~ ~, *Per*
159:27 his very vagueness, *Per*] very vagueness *MS*
159:32 ghostlily] ghostly *E1*
159:34 Not all there,] " ~ ~ ~," *Per*
159:36 him *Per*] him any *MS*
160:3 bit *Per*] *Om. MS*
160:7 tiny] ~, *Per*
160:8 thing:] ~ *Per*
160:9 always:] ~ *Per*
160:11 took *Per*] took on *MS*
160:11 childlike] ~, *Per*
160:13 old,] ~ *Per*
160:16 income, *MS, E1*] ~ *Per*
160:19 of *Per*] in *MS*
160:24 all:] ~— *Per*
160:28 father:] ~, *Per*
160:31 a contadina: *Ed.*] an Italian: *MS* *a contadina*; *Per* a contadina; *E1*
160:31 an ayah:] *an ayah*; *Per* an ayah; *E1*
160:34 went,] ~ *Per*
160:38 wide *Per*] the wide *MS*
160:39 grown-up:] grown up; *Per*
160:39 she *Per*] and she *MS*
161:3 say and do *Per*] do or say *MS*
161:5 another] ~, *Per*

161:6 little *Per*] *Om. MS*
161:9 everybody,] ~ *Per*
161:15 woman:] ~ ; *Per*
161:17 primitive *Per*] tall *MS*
161:17 fairies] ~ , *Per*
161:18 care—.—] ~ . *Per*
161:18 But] ~ , *Per*
161:19 splendid *Per*] fine *MS*
161:19 demonish fairies *Ed.*] green
     fairies *MS* demonish fairies, *Per*
161:20 little *Per*] *Om. MS*
161:21 the old...my Princess. *Per*]
     demons: the last, my Precious.
     MS
161:28 princess] Princess *Per*
161:28 I am...blood. And *Per*] I a
     prince, and you a princess, and
     MS
161:32 forget,] ~ *Per*
161:32 princesses] Princesses *Per*
161:33 are:] ~ , *Per*
161:37 have—"] ~ —." *Per*
161:38 early:] ~ — *Per*
161:39 father:] ~ ; *Per*
162:2 crystal *Per*] a crystal *MS*
162:4 old-fashioned:] ~ ; *Per*
162:7 usually *Per*] nearly always *MS*
162:11 doors, *Per*] ~ ; *MS*
162:13 no-one] no-/ one *Per* no one *E1*
162:17 her:] ~ , *Per*
162:19 time,] ~ *Per*
162:19 knowing,] ~ *Per*
162:21 relations *Per*] relatives *MS*
162:22 spellbound:] ~ ; *Per*
162:28 crochetty] crochety *Per*
162:30 world,] ~ — *Per*
162:32 later,] ~ *Per*
162:33 The others *Per*] But the others
     MS
162:36 *uncanny Per*] *canny MS*
163:2 a curious] curious *Per*
163:5 grotesque] ~ , *Per*
163:7 frail] ~ , *Per*
163:8 were a *Per*] were only a *MS*
163:10 would *Per*] this would *MS*
163:11 Mediterranean,] ~ *Per*
163:11 *mâle*] *male E1*
163:13 fashion,] ~ — *Per*

163:14 him,] ~ *Per*
163:18 people:] ~ , *Per*
163:22 north] North *Per*
163:23 she] and *Per*
163:23 never *Per*] never never *MS*
163:24 her,] ~ *Per*
163:25 early,] ~ *Per*
163:28 flower,] ~ *Per*
163:29 cabman *Per*] cab-man *MS*
163:36 conditions!] ~ ? *Per*
163:39 little *Per*] *Om. MS*
163:39 Now] No, *Per*
164:9 Lakes,] ~ *E1*
164:9 South West] South-West *Per*
164:11 Lakes] lakes *Per*
164:11 redwood] red-wood *Per*
164:14 Princess *Per*] princess *MS*
164:15 undaunted:] ~ ; *Per*
164:16 tired,] ~ *Per*
164:17 astride *Per*] astride on *MS*
164:20 rôle] role *E1*
164:21 her,] ~ *Per*
164:27 elfin *Per*] elvin *MS*
164:33 more!] ~ ? *Per*
164:34 passed,] ~ *Per*
164:35 thirty-three *Per*] thirty three
     MS
164:38 It *Per*] This *MS*
164:38 task *Per*] ~ : *MS*
164:39 He spent *Per*] She ~ *MS*
164:39 of life *Per*] of his life *MS*
165:1 her,] ~ ; *Per*
165:3 sensitive *Per*] subtle *MS*
165:4 man. So *Per*] man, and *MS*
165:7 man] ~ , *Per*
165:8 at all *Per*] really *MS*
165:8 violence,] ~ *Per*
165:9 died: and] ~ . And *Per*
165:14 manner,] ~ *Per*
165:14 bearing,] ~ *Per*
165:15 shadowy *Per*] cold *MS*
165:16 Princess' *Ed.*] princess' *MS*
     Princess's *Per*
165:17 Princess *Per*] princess *MS*
165:24 Quoi faire?] *Quoi faire? Per*
165:26 for *Per*] of *MS*
165:28 Cummins,] ~ *Per*
165:29 for *Per*] of *MS*

165:31 vessel,] ~ *Per*
165:32 Quoi faire?] *Quoi faire? Per*
165:33 nothingness] ~, *Per*
165:39 time,] ~ *Per*
166:2 No!] ~. *Per*
166:2 was still *Per*] still was *MS*
166:2 attracted towards men *Per*] attracted, *MS*
166:3 But *Per*] Only, *MS*
166:5 marriage] *marriage Per*
166:5 man,] ~ *Per*
166:13 from Philadelphia, of scholastic stock, *Per*] well bred *MS*
166:13 intelligent,] ~ *Per*
166:14 four *Per*] and four *MS*
166:15 her "lady." *Per*] Miss Urquhart. *MS*
166:16 Princess, who...timeless. *Per*] Princess. *MS*
166:17 Princess'] Princess's *Per*
166:19 reverence, almost of awe. *Per*] of reverence. *MS*
166:20 virginal:] ~, *Per*
166:24 whisper:] ~; *Per*
166:27 turned *Per*] to turn *MS*
166:32 South West] South-West *Per*
166:35 drift back *Per*] drift *MS*
166:37 pueblo *MS, E1*] *pueblo Per*
166:38 rich:] ~; *Per*
167:3 "marriage."] *marriage. Per*
167:7 and many *Per*] but many *MS*
167:11 a good *Per*] a full, good *MS*
167:12 or *Per*] of *MS*
167:13 "marriage"] *marriage Per*
167:15 just *Per*] just about *MS*
167:19 two *MS, E1*] two *Per*
167:22 Princess'] Princess's *Per*
167:25 Romero:] ~— *Per*
167:27 away:] ~, *Per*
167:28 Romeros] Romero *Per*
167:29 man *Per*] men *MS*
167:30 sheep] ~, *Per*
167:36 fellow] ~, *Per*
167:37 sullenly *Per*] sullen *MS*
167:37 behind,] ~ *Per*
167:38 body] ~, *Per*
168:4 energies *Per*] energy *MS*
168:5 *raison d'être.* As...*raison*

d'être,] *raison d'être, Per* see note on 168:6
168:7 meaning *Per*] existence *MS*
168:7 die,] ~ *Per*
168:8 eyes,] ~ *Per*
168:17 on *Per*] over *MS*
168:18 was *almost Per*] was *MS*
168:19 dark] ~, *Per*
168:20 Indian looking] Indian-looking *Per*
168:21 of self-confidence, of] or self-confidence, or *E1*
168:25 bearing,] ~ *Per*
168:30 cook] ~, *Per*
168:32 forthcoming: *Ed.*] forth-coming: *MS* forthcoming, *Per*
168:37 eye:] ~, *Per* ~; *E1*
169:8 cottonwood *Ed.*] cotton-wood *MS*
169:8 and *Per*] *Om. MS*
169:8 canyon *Per*] canyon was *MS*
169:9 cottonwoods *Ed.*] cotton-woods *MS*
169:10 soft] ~, *Per*
169:11 neatly cut] neatly-cut *Per*
169:11 riding-breeches] riding breeches *Per*
169:12 straggling *Per*] bushing *MS*
169:13 A changeling *Per*] An elf, a changeling *MS*
169:15 fisherwoman] fisherman *Per*
169:17 riding-boots] riding boots *Per*
169:18 him,] ~; *Per*
169:23 Then] ~, *Per*
169:25 withdrew *Per*] with-drew *MS*
169:25 silence] ~, *Per*
169:33 before,] ~ *E1*
169:38 vague *Per*] delicate *MS*
169:39 Spanish,] ~; *Per*
170:2 appearance,] ~; *Per*
170:3 shaved,] ~; *Per*
170:8 suède] *suède Per*
170:19 every *Per*] nearly every *MS*
170:25 curious,] ~ *Per*
170:27 on] of *Per*
170:30 thrilling *Per*] lovely *MS*
170:34 her, she...Princess self. *Per*] her. *MS*

170:35 vivid *Per*] proud *MS*
170:37 woman,] ∼ *Per*
170:39 the *idée E1*] her *idée MS*
171:4 dæmons *E1*] demons *MS*
171:5 selves, *Per*] ∼ *MS*
171:8 could] would *Per*
171:13 yet,] ∼ *Per*
171:13 cottonwoods] cotton-woods *Per*
171:13 valleys] valley *Per*
171:22 squirrels] ∼, *Per*
171:26 Yes!] ∼, *Per*
171:30 Why] ∼, *Per*
171:32 tracks,] ∼ *Per*
171:33 a deer *Per*] deer *MS*
171:35 Well] ∼, *Per*
171:37 with a *Per*] with *MS*
171:40 You would] ∼ will *Per*
172:4 belong] belongs *Per*
172:4 what] that *Per*
172:6 night, *Per*] night, or two nights, *MS*
172:9 Well] ∼, *Per*
172:14 run] runs *Per*
172:16 there—"] ∼ "— *Per*
172:18 West *Per*] west *MS*
172:19 rock—"—] ∼ "— *Per*
172:22 father, he] father he *Per* father *E1*
172:22 placer claim *MS, E1*] place, claim *Per*
172:26 in *Per*] *Om. MS*
172:27 leaves; *Per*] ∼, *MS*
172:28 darker; *Per*] ∼, *MS*
172:37 go:] ∼; *Per*
172:37 least,] ∼ *Per*
173:8 strenuous] ∼, *Per*
173:8 cold] ∼, *Per*
173:12 me,] ∼ *Per*
173:15 not!] ∼. *Per*
173:15 trip." *Per*] ∼, and cold—" *MS*
173:22 on *Per*] *Om. MS*
173:33 bringing in *Per*] bringing *MS*
173:37 dumb, *Per*] ∼ *MS*
174:2 He's so trustworthy. *Per*] *Om. MS*
174:6 pueblo *MS, E1*] *pueblo Per*
174:10 colour,] ∼ *Per*
174:10 South West *Ed.*] South-West *MS*

174:13 Side-slopes] Sideslopes *Per*
174:28 wanted. For] ∼. *P* For *Per*
174:33 greasewood *Per*] grease-wood *MS*
174:38 rocky,] ∼; *Per*
174:39 in,] ∼; *Per*
174:40 in,] ∼ *Per*
175:3 gold] ∼, *Per*
175:4 chill] still *Per*
175:5 waters,] ∼ *E1*
175:6 old-man's-beard] old man's beard *E1*
175:6 here and there a *Per*] an occasional *MS*
175:7 débris *MS, E1*] debris *Per*
175:8 Princess' *Ed.*] Princes's *MS* Princess's *Per*
175:8 heart,] ∼ *Per*
175:10 across-stream] across stream *Per*
175:11 of *MS, E1*] on *Per*
175:13 Princess'] Princess's *Per*
175:13 Cummins'] Cummins's *Per*
175:14 round *Per*] around *MS*
175:20 yellow] ∼, *Per*
175:20 spruce firs, *Per*] spruce, *MS*
175:21 blue lying high and *Per*] blue, floating high and sailing *MS*
175:28 stepping *Per*] stepped *MS*
175:29 floundering *Per*] floundered *MS*
175:31 footing:] ∼; *Per*
175:32 great,] ∼ *Per*
175:33 round] ∼, *Per*
175:37 *almost*] almost *Per*
176:3 Oh my Goodness] ∼, ∼ goodness *Per*
176:4 horse,] ∼ *Per*
176:4 *awful!*] ∼? *Per* ∼? *E1*
176:14 What, *Per*] ∼ *MS*
176:30 stiff—] ∼. *Per*
176:31 What! Ride *Per*] ∼ ride *MS*
176:31 mountains!] ∼? *Per*
176:33 Let me walk. *Per*] *Om. MS*
176:34 Cummins] ∼, *Per*
176:34 right—?] ∼? *Per*
176:40 sat *Per*] sat down *MS*
177:1 Why] ∼, *Per*
177:2 you don't] you *Per* see note
177:24 ridden,] ∼ *Per*

177:27 well] ~, *Per*
177:30 after—"] ~." *Per*
177:33 Romero,] ~— *Per*
177:35 cried *Per*] said *MS*
177:35 *want*] want *Per*
177:37 looked] looked at *E1*
178:6 Cummins,] ~ *Per*
178:7 inclinations *Per*] inclination *MS*
178:13 pure] ~, *Per*
178:13 yellow, leaves] ~ ~, *Per*
178:14 petals, while *Per*] ~. While *MS*
178:15 yellow; fleecy *Per*] ~. Fleecy *MS*
178:15 fox-skin] foxskin *Per*
178:18 dark hue *Per*] dark *MS*
178:21 canyon] Canyon *Per*
178:25 her,] ~ *Per*
178:25 This *Per*] That *MS*
178:27 to look *Per*] and looks *MS*
178:29 her,] ~ ; *Per*
178:32 great *Per*] great grey *MS*
178:32 stark] ~, *Per*
178:33 black, bristling *Per*] black bristling of the *MS*
178:39 delicate *MS*, *E1*] ~, *Per*
178:40 like petals...their petals] *Om. Per see note on* 179:1
179:8 sorrel] ~, *Per*
179:12 saddle-pouches *Ed.*] saddle pouches *MS*
179:17 fairyland] fairy-land *Per*
179:22 ghostlike] ghost-like *Per*
179:38 Ah] ~, *Per*
179:38 You with him? *Per*] You come with him! *MS*
179:38 Where] Where are *Per see note on* 177:2
179:40 to Pueblo *Per*] to the pueblo *MS*
180:2 little,] ~ *Per*
180:5 No, we] ~. We *Per*
180:6 suspicious-looking] suspicious looking *Per*
180:7 saddles:] ~— *Per*
180:10 he *Per*] Joe *MS*
180:11 laugh. P Under] ~. Under *Per*
180:13 Princess *Per*] princess *MS*
180:15 it *Per*] bacon *MS*
180:18 blue and brown] blue-and-brown *Per*

180:35 time,] ~ *Per*
180:39 spruce trees *Ed.*] spruce-trees *MS*
180:40 grey,] ~ *Per*
181:4 Service *Per*] Service men *MS*
181:4 stark corpse slope, *Per*] corpse slope, stark *MS*
181:5 spruce] ~, *Per*
181:10 hastening *Per*] hastening and halting to breathe, hastening *MS*
181:12 rowing *Per*] halting to breathe, rowing *MS*
181:15 them,] ~ ; *E1*
181:18 rush *Per*] sort of rush *MS*
181:19 forest,] ~ *Per*
181:25 near by *MS*, *E1*] nearby *Per*
181:27 hog-backed *Per*] hog-back *MS*
181:28 other,] ~ *Per*
181:32 repellent *Per*] repellant *MS*
181:33 gigantic] ~, *Per*
181:35 intestinal *Per*] massive, gruesome intestinal *MS*
181:37 riding *Per*] riding slowly *MS*
181:38 her,] ~ *Per*
181:39 hand:] ~. *Per*
181:40 said. P It] ~. It *Per*
182:1 scratched out] scratched-out *Per*
182:7 come] comes *Per see note on* 177:2
182:7 government] Government *Per*
182:8 see,] ~ *Per*
182:10 was *Per*] *Om. MS*
182:11 as *Per*] *Om. MS*
182:13 *see*] see *Per*
182:14 in *Per*] on *MS*
182:24 vastly,] ~ *Per*
182:27 was *Per*] *Om. MS*
182:31 They *Per*] Then they *MS*
182:32 trail:] ~ ; *Per*
182:34 trees *Per*] tree *MS*
182:39 descend:] ~ ; *Per*
183:1 downward *Per*] downwards *MS*
183:2 heavens:] ~— *Per*
183:12 toboggan,] ~ *Per*
183:14 her:] ~ ; *Per*
183:15 cheeks,] ~ *Per*
183:25 forefeet,] ~ *Per*
183:25 descent *Per*] jerky descent *MS*

183:29 legs *Per*] orange legs *MS*
183:30 bound round *Per*] ducked *MS*
183:32 Princess,] ~ *Per*
183:34 wonder *Per*]a sort of wonder *MS*
183:35 drugging] dragging *Per*
183:37 zigzagging *Per*] zigzagging rapidly *MS*
183:38 bright coloured] bright-coloured *Per*
183:39 four-foot-sliding] four-footed, sliding *Per*
184:1 near, *Per*] up, *MS*
184:3 kerchief *Per*] silk kerchief *MS*
184:4 make *Per*] made *MS see note on* 177:2
184:7 But] ~, *Per*
184:12 grove *Per*] groove *MS*
184:20 a semblance *Per*] the semblance *MS*
184:24 it. *P* Indeed *MS*, *E1*] ~./Indeed *Per*
184:26 herself; *Per*] ~, *MS*
184:30 log-lengths,] ~ *Per*
184:30 on,] ~ *Per*
184:30 fire-place,] fireplace; *Per*
184:38 stone] stove *Per*
184:39 mechanically] ~, *Per*
184:40 blaze] ~, *Per*
185:2 delapidated] dilapidated *Per*
185:5 delapidated] dilapidated *Per*
185:8 whiskey] whisky *Per*
185:10 comprehending,] ~; *Per*
185:12 whiskey] whisky *Per*
185:16 above,] ~ *Per*
185:18 aspens] aspen *Per*
185:23 camp-stove *Per*] camp stove *MS*
185:23 axe:] ~, *Per*
185:23 camp *Per*] camping *MS*
185:33 profound *Per*] the *MS*
185:35 gazed] ~, *Per*
186:4 escaping:] ~; *Per*
186:5 bob tail] bob-tail *Per*
186:7 repulsiveness *Per*] the repulsiveness *MS*
186:9 dark inside *Per*] growing dark *MS*
186:14 whiskey] whisky *Per*
186:14 in the *Per*] in *MS*
186:22 unwrapped *Per*] unroped *MS*

186:28 heating:] ~; *Per*
186:31 movement] ~, *Per*
186:36 chicken,] ~ *Per*
186:36 butter,] ~ *Per*
187:1 move,] ~ *Per*
187:11 into *Per*] to look at *MS*
187:14 below,] ~ *Per*
187:14 pit *Per*] den *MS*
187:20 ricketty, half opened] rickety, half-opened *Per*
187:28 the *Per*] her *MS*
187:37 cold. Perhaps] ~; perhaps *Per*
187:40 fire:] ~, *Per*
188:1 thick,] ~ *Per*
188:3 "What...want?"—] ~...~? *Per*
188:5 cold,] ~; *Per*
188:7 taken away from herself *Per*] cherished *MS*
188:8 anything] ~, *Per*
188:9 no-one] no one *Per*
188:9 power over...to her *Per*] powers or rights over her *MS*
188:10 her:] ~ *Per*
188:10 no-one] no one *Per*
188:11 power *Per*] powers *MS*
188:11 no-one] no one *Per*
188:14 to beat.] ~ ~? *Per*
188:16 strangely. "It] ~, "It *Per* ~, "it *E1*
188:16 cold!] ~. *Per*
188:20 "What? What...the bunk.] *Om. Per see note on* 188:22
188:23 warm.] ~? *Per*
188:31 *willed Per*] willed *MS*
188:33 mauled] and mauled *E1*
188:36 when *Per*] that *MS*
189:4 up again *Per*] *Om. MS*
189:14 said. *MS*, *E1*] ~, *Per*
189:19 gone.] ~! *Per*
189:25 breakfast?" *Per*] breakfast," she said. *MS*
189:27 suddenly] ~, *Per*
189:30 said, turning...his eyes. *Per*] said. *MS*
189:39 frying-pan *Per*] frying pan *MS*
190:2 way,] ~ *Per*
190:5 said; "you] ~, "You *Per* ~, "you *E1*

190:6 said,] ∼. *Per*
190:16 face, *MS, E1*] ∼ *Per*
190:16 words:] ∼, *Per*
190:20 hostility,] ∼ *Per*
190:25 blue and buff] blue-and-bluff *Per*
190:26 kerchief:] ∼; *Per*
190:28 pool,] ∼ *Per*
190:31 slaty *Per*] slatey *MS*
191:1 unrelieved gloom *Per*] weariness *MS*
191:2 desire for death *Per*] recklessness *MS*
191:6 saddle] ∼, *Per*
191:9 he was already *Per*] already he was *MS*
191:13 stony slopes *Per*] stones *MS*
191:14 lay] ∼, *Per*
191:14 Away] Always *Per*
191:16 mountains] mountain *Per*
191:18 alone:] ∼, *Per*
191:19 of,] ∼ *Per*
191:19 didn't *Per*] did not *MS*
191:22 time,] ∼ *Per*
191:24 bear *Per*] bear go *MS* bear, *E1*
191:25 in the far *Per*] of far *MS*
191:30 feet. *Per*] feet. *P* Then he came to her with a still little smile on his face. *MS*
191:36 into *Per*] in *MS*
192:2 a nice *Per*] nice *MS*
192:2 place!] ∼? *Per*
192:2 Come!] ∼? *E1*
192:2 sure is] is sure *Per*
192:6 don'] don't *Per see note on 177:2*
192:7 you don't. *Per*] that. *MS*
192:8 shone *Per*] shone hot *MS*
192:10 said, "after] ∼. "After *E1*
192:11 him again. *Per*] him. *MS*
192:18 face:] ∼— *Per*
192:23 crouched] ∼, *Per*
192:24 goin'] going *Per see note on 177:2*
192:25 right now *Per*] *Om. MS*
192:26 up now *Per*] up right now *MS*
192:28 me. *Per*] me, and stop with me. *MS*

192:28 stay *Per*] keep you *MS*
192:32 you:] ∼; *Per*
192:32 mine *Per*] me *MS*
192:35 they will *Per*] they'll *MS*
192:37 the cooking *Per*] his cooking *MS*
193:3 had *Per*] had really *MS*
193:8 intact.] ∼! *Per*
193:10 again.] ∼? *Per*
193:11 Even now *Per*] Even *MS*
193:20 went *Per*] went and stood *MS*
193:21 mountains] ∼, *Per*
193:22 violent,] ∼ *Per*
193:25 were *Per*] were like *MS*
193:25 had *Per*] have *MS*
193:33 me *Per*] *Om. MS*
193:39 dreary,] ∼ *Per*
193:39 death,] ∼ *Per*
194:1 matter!] ∼? *Per*
194:7 slope,] ∼— *Per*
194:11 bien!] ∼, *Per*
194:17 Pen.] Pen *Per*
194:18 Pen.] Pen *Per*
194:18 shoot.] ∼! *Per*
194:20 straight away] straightaway *Per*
194:23 man *Per*] rider *MS*
194:26 spruce tree] spruce-tree *Per*
194:29 watching...All was] *Om. Per see note on 194:37*
194:31 crouching] ∼, *Per*
194:32 his] this *Per*
194:33 beautiful] ∼, *Per*
194:35 melt, though] ∼. Though *Per*
194:36 have given...she could] *Om. Per see note on 194:37*
194:38 Never.] ∼! *Per*
195:1 close,] ∼ *Per*
195:2 arms fell *Per*] arms *MS*
195:8 house:] ∼; *Per*
195:8 in a *Per*] in *MS*
195:14 Hm] H'm *Per*
195:16 there] ∼, *Per*
195:18 Hallo] Hullo, *Per*
195:18 him! *Per*] 'im! *MS*
195:20 forest,] ∼ *Per*
195:21 face] ∼, *Per*
195:21 eyes] ∼, *Per*
195:23 man] ∼, *Per*
195:25 again] ∼, *Per*

195:28 Yep! I know it! *Per*] Go on, boy!
You don't say! *MS*
195:29 in *Per*] in his *MS*
195:29 cabin] ∼, *Per*
195:30 squatted] ∼, *Per*
195:31 And he...mean any. *Per*] *Om.*
MS
195:33 speak, no...she felt. *Per*]
answer. *MS*
195:36 out of his mind *Per*] mad
MS
195:36 stammering *Per*] crazy *MS*
195:38 mean to say *Per*] mean *MS*
195:38 mind.—] ∼? *Per*
195:39 awful.] ∼! *Per*
195:39 Hm] H'm *Per*
195:40 He accepted...more ado. *Per*]
Om. MS
196:2 she too] ∼, ∼, *Per*
196:2 now] not *Per*
196:4 explaining.] ∼? *Per*
196:5 explained,] ∼ *Per*
196:6 Oh] ∼, *Per*
196:11 Cummins' *Per*] Cummins *MS*
Cummin's *E1*
196:19 an elderly *Per*] a middle-aged
MS

Appendix I: The Wilful Woman

199:2 November] Early winter
199:3 west] West *E1*
199:3 one of the] a
199:4 lost] began losing
199:5 the prairie] the flat prairie
199:14 distracted impatience and heart-
brokenness] ⟨impatient rage⟩
distracted ⟨⟨overwhelming⟩⟩...
heart-brokenness
199:16 dust-pan.] ⟨shovel⟩ dustpan.
E1
199:16 "Room"] ' ∼ ' *E1*
199:18 Frustration,] ⟨Rage⟩ Frustration *E1*
199:18 painful] silent
199:18 pressure] ⟨fury⟩ storm
199:19 Could not arrive.] *Om. E1*
199:21 sturdy] ⟨woman of thirty
seven⟩ rather short

199:21 like an obstinate girl of] somewhat childish face
199:23 unease,] frenzy,
199:24 a woman] she was
199:28 curved horns] a thundercloud
199:29 bright,] clear,
199:30 as] like
199:31 grey and yellow bits,] grains &
flakes,
199:34 seductive] final
199:35 loneliness that lay on the
western] caress ⟨life and show his
prowess⟩
199:36 without] but
200:4 neutralise] neutralize *E1*
200:8 getting unbearable.] coming on.
200:12 ideas,] ∼ *E1*
200:14 somewhere after] at
200:15 she didn't bother where.] or
somewhere there.
200:15 "Put my bags out,"] ' ∼ ∼ ∼
∼,' *E1*
200:17 thorn-bushes] thorn bushes *E1*
200:18 her tip] his tip *E1*
200:20 But] And
200:21 whirl.] campaign.
200:21 she *would*] she must
200:25 would] *would E1*
200:26 produced an...of sixteen.]
found a springless crude affair
and a boy of sixteen to drive it.
200:30 Good enough!] All right.
200:32 round] though the cañons of
200:33 tracks.] trails.
200:40 and a young...knowing where]
⟨⟨and ⟨for driver⟩ a frightened
boy who had no idea where he
was⟩⟩ and a...where, *E1*
201:5 slope] thicket
201:8 planked] plonked *E1*
201:10 no-one] no one *E1*
201:13 *penitente* herself] penitente ∼
E1
201:17 Luckily] ∼, *E1*
201:20 sketchily] recklessly
201:21 desperate] dangerous
201:23 once more,] again,
201:25 he is] he was

201:26 an American] a pure
201:32 Ex-Princesses of Saxony,] ⟨Joubert or⟩ ex-Princesses of Saxony, *E1*
201:32 D. Annunzio] d'Annunzio *E1*
201:32 Duse, Isadora...Matisse.] or ⟨George Moore⟩ Wilfred Scawen Blunt.
201:37 Jewish] Polish
201:38 way] ~, *E1*
202:1 Sybil's] her
202:4 Hamnett's] Hamnetts *E1*
202:4 push] energy
202:4 Wilcox's] Wilcoxes *E1*
202:5 focussed] focused *E1*
202:7 small bison,] ⟨thunder-cloud,⟩ small buff[alo]
202:7 often giving] and could give
202:10 culminated,] *Om. E1*
202:11 descended upon] cumulated around
202:13 exemplified it...Lake Erie.] justified it all
202:15 racketty] rackety *E1*
202:17 head-lights] headlights *E1*
202:19 bashed] lashed *E1*
202:21 of] over
202:23 terra nova.] ⟨her country.⟩ terra nuova
202:26 racketty] rackety *E1*
202:27 head-lights] headlights *E1*
202:28 storm] rage
202:29 vague] night
202:31 shadow. It] shadows. *P* It *E1*
202:32 arrive.—] ~. *E1*
202:36 still hardly more than] only
202:37 torture,] ~ *E1*
202:40 air] breeze
202:40 desert.—] ~. *E1*
203:6 somewhat relieved.] soothed.
203:8 disappointed,] scared,
203:8 dogged] dauntless
203:9 as she...her contention.] and after waiting an hour at the station, with her bags, she picked up the slow train that followed the express she had so tempestuously abandoned, and

was landed at the destination ⟨Lamy⟩ at three in the morning
203:15 "hotel"] ' ~ ' *E1*

Appendix II: The Flying-Fish

207:1 **Flying-Fish** *Ed.*] FLYING FISH. *TS* FLYING FISH *A1*
207:2 *Departure from Mexico.*] DE-PARTURE FROM MEXICO *A1*
207:3 home *TS, A1*] ~, *TCC*
207:11 *ennui*] ennui *A1*
207:13 valleys] ~, *A1*
207:14 *tierra A1*] *lierra TS*
207:19 toxins *A1*] toxines *TS*
207:20 Zapotecas] ~, *A1*
207:25 hand:—] ~ : *A1*
207:25 home *A1*] ~, *TS*
207:28 Reina de noche *Ed.*] Buena de Noche *TS* Buena de Noche *TCC see note*
207:31 *más A1*] *mas TS*
207:35 "No] ~ *A1*
207:35 Daybrook] ~ ; *A1*
207:36 outlook."] ~. *A1*
208:16 steep *A1*] step *TS*
208:24 telegram] cablegram *A1*
208:32 those] these *A1*
209:7 dead father] father, now dead, *A1*
209:9 Gethin] ~, *A1*
209:16 doeth] doth *A1*
209:22 poetry, *A1*] ~ *TS*
209:23 fierce] ~, *A1*
209:24 natives] ~, *A1*
209:32 connections] connexions *A1*
209:35 heavy] ~, *A1*
210:1 overcrowded] over-crowded *A1*
210:15 banana-trees] banana trees *A1*
210:20 and the *A1*] And ~ *TS*
210:21 forever] for ever *A1*
210:34 por amor de Dios! *Ed.*] por l'amor de Dios! *TS por l'amor de Dios! TCC "por amor de Dios!" A1*
210:37 resistance, which] ~ ~ *A1*
211:6 marihuana] *marihuana TCC*
211:15 Americans!] ~ ? *A1*

211:16 last] ~, *A1*
211:28 towers,] ~ ; *A1*
212:5 barranca] *barranca* TCC
212:8 One *A1*] one *TS*
212:10 hundred-and-fifty] hundred and fifty *A1*
212:31 flying-fish] flying fish *A1*
212:35 flying-fish] flying fish *A1*
212:38 own—] ~. *A1*
213:2 flying-fish] flying fish *A1*
213:13 cactuses] cacti *A1*
213:15 barranca] *barranca* TCC
213:24 barranca] *barranca* TCC
213:34 Los...venados!] *Los venados! los venados!* TCC "*Los venados! los venados!*" *A1*
214:14 hacienda] *hacienda A1*
214:20 Tlaxcala *Ed.*] Tlascala *TS*
214:21 Quiere...Señor?] *Quiere helados, Señor? A1*
214:24 "Gracias!"] "*Gracias!*" *A1*
214:25 "Patrón! Patrón!" *Ed.*] Padròn! Padròn! *TS* "*Patrón! Padrón!*" *A1*
214:25 "Por amor...Patrón!" *Ed.*] "Por l'amor de Dios, Padròn!" *TS* "*Por amor de Dios, Padrón!*" *A1*
214:32 Lasciate...ch'entrate,] "~...~," *TCC* "*Lasciate...ch'entrate,*" *A1*
214:32 Perdite...pianto...ch'uscite. *Ed.*] ~...piànto...~. *TS* "~ ...piànto...~." *TCC* "*Perdite...pianto...ch'uscite.*" *A1*
215:20 away".] ~." *A1*
215:23 continuum] *continuum A1*
216:9 corn-flower blue] cornflower-blue *A1*
216:13 Erinyes *A1*] Erinnyes *TS*
216:17 sun.] ~? *A1*
216:21 *Book of Days* TCC] Book of Days *TS*
216:26 ricketty] rickety *A1*

216:33 Vera Cruz] Veracruz *A1*
216:38 Vera Cruz] Veracruz *A1*
217:11 Day] day *A1*
217:11 white-man's] white man's *A1*
217:14 *The Gulf*] **THE GULF** *A1*
217:33 business-men] business men *A1*
217:37 Vera Cruz] Veracruz *A1*
218:3 first-class] first class *A1*
218:6 five Spaniards *A1*] four Spaniards *TS*
218:13 the Cuban *A1*] Mexicans *TS*
218:24 understand] ~, *A1*
218:26 north-German] North-German *A1*
218:31 included".] ~." *A1*
218:34 decanter *A1*] decanters *TS*
219:12 liner".] ~." *A1*
219:15 bow-sprit] bowsprit *A1*
219:29 bow-sprit *Ed.*] bowsprit *TS*
219:32 flying-fish] flying fish *A1*
219:34 away] ~, *A1*
220:10 flying-fishes] flying fishes *A1*
221:30 ...."But] " ~ *A1*
222:3 there—] ~." *A1*
222:4 bow-sprit] bowsprit *A1*
222:10 *The Atlantic*] **THE ATLANTIC** *A1*
222:18 not-very] not very *A1*
222:21 underneath] ~, *A1*
222:38 los americanos] *los americanos* TCC
223:2 Muy bien] *Muy bien* TCC
223:8 Orleans—] ~. *A1*
223:11 spick and span TCC] sprick ~ ~ *TS* spick-and-span *A1*
223:12 haciendas] *haciendas A1*
223:25 burgundy] Burgundy *A1*
224:2 dinner-time] dinner time *A1*
224:8 space.] ~. # *A1 see note*
224:32 Ah] ah *A1*
224:38 Ah] ah *A1*
225:11 horribly-travelling] horribly travelling *A1*
225:13 sauerkraut] *Sauerkraut A1*

Of the compound words which are hyphenated at the end of a line in this edition,
only the following hyphenated forms should be retained in quotations:

33:6	loosely-built	134:24	eagle-shadows
35:35	high-boned	140:35	hundred-and-sixty
37:16	handsome-moving	143:17	onward-pushing
42:39	passing-bell	149:33	long-snouted
48:15	over-controlled	150:17	onward-struggle
48:16	dark-coloured	150:34	stream-irrigated
50:16	flushed-like	161:12	chatter-chatter
56:28	piquant-looking	162:8	finely-worked
82:4	self-assertion	162:39	railway-porters
85:25	Spanish-American	174:15	blue-black
89:1	eighteenth-century	180:18	dark-headed
91:4	son-in-law	211:19	blue-green
97:24	fox-hunting	211:28	Earth-coloured
131:32	self-conscious	216:35	packing-cases